Cultural Adaptation of CBT for Serious Mental Illness

This book pulls together all the current data on the effectiveness of culturally sensitive CBT in this area, as well as providing clinicians with a manual to learn and practice culturally informed CBT. I can confidently recommend it as helpful for anyone working with severely mentally ill clients.

Aaron T. Beck, MD, University Professor Emeritus of
Psychiatry, University of Pennsylvania

This volume offers a practical guide to culturally adapting CBT for severe mental health conditions. The authors are gifted clinicians and investigators that present a sophisticated overview of key conceptual and pragmatic issues in working with diverse communities. The book proposes novel concepts and applications of a well-established evidenced-based treatment in which language, culture, race, and ethnicity are integral to the conceptualization and process of therapy. This book is a remarkable contribution to the growing literature on cultural adaptations and as such it represents a major contribution to multicultural psychology and mental health. This is essential reading for clinicians and scholars interested in working with the diverse majority-world communities.

Guillermo Bernal, PhD, Director, Institute for Psychological Research,
University of Puerto Rico, Rio Piedras, Puerto Rico

There was a time when psychological therapies were not thought to be appropriate for all patients, especially those of low socio-economic or poor educational status, and ethnic minorities, refugees, migrants or people from low and middle-income countries. Clinicians did not have the tools to adapt their skills. No more! Combining psychoanalytic, cognitive behavioural and general therapeutics theory with evidence on the cultural adaptation of psychological therapies, this impressive, accessible and timely volume offers hope to patients of diverse cultural heritage, beliefs, and practices.

Kamaldeep Bhui, Professor of Cultural Psychiatry & Epidemiology,
Queen Mary University of London

In a globalized world we need methods to adapt interventions so they are equally effective for different groups. One size fits all and culture and color blind approaches hardwire inequity. Many have undertaken cultural adaptations but to have some of the major voices in CBT produce guidance on cultural adaptation produces a priceless treasure. Whether you are developing services in a low income country or for marginalised groups in a high income country this book will help you produce the most effective CBT for the people you serve.

Kwame McKenzie, MD, FRCPsych (UK), Medical Director CAMH,
Professor of Psychiatry, University of Toronto

With its clear, thoughtful prose and its diverse, vivid case examples, this guide will help CBT practitioners sensitively handle the challenges of working with individuals and families from a wide variety of cultural, religious, and spiritual backgrounds. By using these approaches, unique and thorny challenges to the cross cultural application of CBT can be creatively and collaboratively addressed and resolved.

Ron Unger LCSW, CBT for Psychosis Therapist and
Adjunct Professor at Portland State University

Culturally informed mental health care is rapidly moving from an attitudinal orientation to an evidence-based approach. This textbook makes an important contribution towards understanding the conceptual basis and evidence behind cultural adaptation of cognitive behavioral therapy, but also provides clinical and contextual guidance in application for diverse populations and serious psychiatric disorders. A must-read for the clinician who wishes to serve the majority of patients we will be serving as cultural plurality is achieved in the US and globally.

Andres J Pumariega, MD, Professor and Chair, Department of Psychiatry,
Cooper Medical School of Rowan University and Cooper Health System;
Cochair, Diversity and Culture Committee; and first author of the Practice
Parameter for Cultural Competence, American Academy of
Child and Adolescent Psychiatry

Cultural Adaptation of CBT for Serious Mental Illness

A Guide for Training and Practice

Shanaya Rathod
David Kingdon
Narsimha Pinninti
Douglas Turkington
Peter Phiri

WILEY Blackwell

This edition first published 2015
© 2015 John Wiley & Sons, Ltd.

Registered Office
John Wiley & Sons, Ltd, The Atrium, Southern Gate, Chichester, West Sussex,
PO19 8SQ, UK

Editorial Offices
350 Main Street, Malden, MA 02148-5020, USA
9600 Garsington Road, Oxford, OX4 2DQ, UK
The Atrium, Southern Gate, Chichester, West Sussex, PO19 8SQ, UK

For details of our global editorial offices, for customer services, and for information about how to apply for permission to reuse the copyright material in this book please see our website at www.wiley.com/wiley-blackwell.

The right of Shanaya Rathod, David Kingdon, Narsimha Pinninti, Douglas Turkington and Peter Phiri to be identified as the authors of this work has been asserted in accordance with the UK Copyright, Designs and Patents Act 1988.

Library of Congress Cataloging-in-Publication Data

Rathod, Shanaya, author.
   Cultural adaptation of CBT for serious mental illness : a guide for training and practice / Shanaya Rathod, David Kingdon, Narsimha Pinninti, Douglas Turkington, Peter Phiri.
      p. ; cm.
   Includes bibliographical references and index.
   ISBN 978-1-118-97620-3 (hardback : alk. paper) – ISBN 978-1-118-97619-7 (paperback : alk. paper)
   I. Kingdon, David G., author. II. Pinninti, Narsimha, author. III. Turkington, Douglas, author.
   IV. Phiri, Peter, author. V. Title.
   [DNLM: 1. Cognitive Therapy–methods. 2. Cultural Diversity. 3. Mental Disorders–therapy.
   WM 425.5.C6]
   RC489.C63
   616.89′1425–dc23
                                                                     2015000040

A catalogue record for this book is available from the British Library.

Cover image: Illustration © Paul Oakley

Set in 10/12.5pt Sabon by SPi Publisher Services, Pondicherry, India

Printed in Singapore by C.O.S. Printers Pte Ltd

1 2015

Contents

Appendix

About the Authors

The authors are recognized authorities in CBT for mental illness and have written a number of well-received books on these topics. In this new volume, they combine their expertise to produce a compelling learning program for clinicians who want to gain CBT skills for working with patients from different cultures.

Shanaya Rathod, DM, MRCPsych
Dr Rathod is a Consultant Psychiatrist, Clinical Services Director and Director of Research at the Southern Health NHS Foundation Trust in the UK. She has been a Fellow of the National institute for Health and Care Excellence, UK. She has a particular interest in the cultural and religious aspects of psychopathology of mental illness and has received grants from the Department of Health Delivering Race Equality Group (UK) to explore this area further and develop culturally sensitive cognitive behaviour therapy for psychosis. She has authored a number of papers in peer reviewed journals, book chapters and books. She has been invited to present nationally and internationally.

David Kingdon, MD, FRCPsych
Prof Kingdon is Professor of Mental Health Care Delivery at the University of Southampton, UK and honorary Consultant Psychiatrist at the Southern Health NHS Foundation Trust. He has chaired the Expert Working Group leading to the Council of Europe's Recommendation 2004 (10) on Psychiatry and Human Rights (1996–2003) and has advised on many national policy initiatives. His research interests are in cognitive behaviour therapy (CBT) of severe mental illness and mental health service development on which he has published over 100 papers, chapters and books. He is visiting Professor at State University of New York and Anding Hospital, Beijing and has given many invited workshops and lectures internationally.

Narsimha R. Pinninti, MBBS, DPM, MD (Psy)
Dr Pinninti is Professor of Psychiatry at Rowan University school of Osteopathic Medicine in New Jersey and also Chief Medical Officer, at Twin Oaks Community

mental health services Inc in Cherry Hill, NJ. Dr Pinninti is a clinician, administrator, teacher and researcher who works at the interface of research and clinical practice. His main interest is in adapting cognitive behaviour therapy and other psychosocial interventions in real world clinical situations and systems of care. He is the treating psychiatrist for Camden County Assertive community treatment team, oversees psychiatric services for Twin Oaks Community health services, and course director for CBT training for psychiatric residents at Rowan School of Osteopathic Medicine. He has been invited to present in a number of national workshops and published over 40 articles in peer reviewed journals.

Douglas Turkington, DM, MRCPsych

Prof Turkington is Professor of Psychosocial Psychiatry, Newcastle University, UK. He has project managed a number of high impact randomized controlled trials in CBT of schizophrenia in the UK and done research on this topic in Texas, Beijing, Valencia and Illinois. His work has strongly influenced the NICE guidelines in the UK. He has lectured widely throughout China, Europe and North America, including Rome, Turkey, Spain, Ontario, Ohio, Sacramento and York. He is founding fellow of the Faculty of Cognitive Therapy in Philadelphia and has written more than 100 articles on the subject of CBT in schizophrenia. He has also with Professor David Kingdon co-authored or edited eight highly influential books on CBT for schizophrenia.

Peter Phiri, RMN, DipCBT, BSc, PhD

Dr Phiri is a Senior Researcher and a Cognitive Behaviour Therapy Specialist (accredited with the British Association of Behavioural and Cognitive Psychotherapies: BABCP) at Southern Health NHS Foundation Trust in the UK. His interest is in cultural adaptations of CBT with diverse groups. He is also an Honorary Lecturer and Academic Supervisor in CBT Diploma and IAPT programmes at the University of Southampton and a Visiting Lecturer at Bath University. He has published a number of papers in this field and has presented in workshops and conferences both nationally and internationally.

Preface

Globalisation has given us the opportunity to celebrate diversity. Diversity encompasses all the potential differences in the way we view ourselves, others, and the world. These differences are so commonly encountered that we on occasion fail to understand their power and impact. We must therefore try and embrace such differences and adapt any approach at treatment to make it more relevant.

Relevance is an important concept in any subject, but widely overlooked in the clinical field. We adapt most things in our day to day lives – from food to language – and yet fail to understand the importance of adapting treatments for our clients. When working with patients, the emotional experience is as important as clinical outcomes, if not more. It is only through a patient based conscience that we are able to apply any form of relevant treatment that is beneficial.

Cognitive behaviour therapy (CBT) is now recognised as a key evidence-based therapy that is widely used across the globe for various illnesses. However the concepts and constructs used in therapy have been criticised as being West centric and not in tune with varied cultural beliefs. As a result, people from diverse cultural backgrounds are reluctant to work with therapists, who in turn often do not have the confidence to work with people from diverse cultures. With such realisations, the concept of cultural relevance is one that has become significantly more important in recent years. Generalised approaches have been used but sometimes only serve to isolate factions. With careful modification, we can tune our methodology to fit a variety of cultural backgrounds, allowing the practice to fit the patient and not the other way around. Cultural adaptation of CBT is therefore a step further towards the personalization of therapy.

Our intention in writing this book is to enable clinicians to use techniques that will be beneficial in engaging patients from culturally diverse communities and enhance their confidence and competence regarding their interactions to improve outcomes. The goal is to develop a comprehensive guide to adaptations in technique that allows a clinician to adjust their stance to different cultural groups. The adaptation discussed in this book maintains fidelity to the core elements of CBT, thereby ensuring that the basic principles of therapy remain the same. Adaptations are applied to the delivery of therapy and use of culture as a strength to enhance recovery.

It is important to clarify that, this book is not a manual, nor can it provide a template for treatment for any specific cultural group. A 'how to' guide of CBT for any specific culture is just not possible as there are so many diverse cultures and even within cultures there are subcultures. But above all, each individual has their own unique culture. The book is envisioned as a single source for clinicians interested in culturally adapted CBT for mental disorders, and is intended to be an essential resource for education and clinical practice. Current available manuals are very limited in their description of cultural adaptations of therapy. The book is a combination of theory and cases used as examples.

We begin this book with an explanation of the impact of globalisation and introduce the concept of differences in outcomes for various cultural groups.

This concept flows through the different chapters. Chapter 2 discusses the basic model of CBT and then emphasises the opportunities and challenges in adaptation of CBT. This chapter also introduces the model that we have used for adaptation of CBT and Chapter 3 continues to elaborate on the model. Chapters 4 through 7 have been organized around the chronology of therapy from engagement and assessment through case formulation, treatment planning and beginning therapy. Finally, Chapters 8, 9, and 10 each directly focus on specific kinds of severe mental illness. Chapter 11 discusses relapse prevention and 12 is about services and implications for policy development where differences in the systems of care in United States compared to United Kingdom and the interactions between the systems of care and culture have been explored. The reader may find that some concepts are repeated in different sections or chapters but that is inevitable as some cultural concepts have an impact on different aspects of therapy.

Our intention in moving from a generalised approach to more specific illnesses in Chapters 8–10 is to enable all clinicians to benefit from the work as the concepts can be used in therapy but also help in interactions of clinicians and medical outpatient clinics. Adaptation relevant to the influence of culture has been developed through case examples. The book has used case examples to demonstrate application of theory and intervention to the range of cases likely to be encountered by those working with these groups of patients.

Adaptation of key therapies has been discussed for many years. Through our work over the years, we have finally, managed to take a large step forward towards such an adaptation. We hope that patients and clinicians across the globe will benefit from reading this book, and by adapting their stance in therapy. We wish you all the best.

Shanaya Rathod
David Kingdon
Narsimha Pinninti
Douglas Turkington
Peter Phiri

It is however interesting to note that cognitive behavioural techniques in psychosis were first used in 1952 by Beck in a patient who was paranoid about the Federal Bureau of Investigation (FBI). The patient was encouraged to trace the antecedents of the delusion, and behavioural techniques such as reality testing were used. The patient was eventually able to recognize that all his alleged persecutors were normal people going about their daily business. Subsequently, Hole, Rush, and Beck (1979) described eight patients with chronic delusions, half of whom appeared to improve when cognitive and behavioural techniques were used.

Over time, evidence has developed from case studies, randomized controlled trials, and meta-analyses confirming the effectiveness of cognitive behavioural therapy (CBT) in depression, schizophrenia, anxiety, post-traumatic stress disorder (PTSD), and borderline personality disorder. Among the different disorders, there is different degree of evidence base to support effectiveness of CBT. A review of meta-analyses of CBT by Butler, Chapman, Forman, and Beck (2006) identified 16 quantitative reviews that included 332 clinical trials covering 16 different disorders or populations. They reported effect sizes that contrast outcomes for CBT with outcomes for various control groups for each disorder. Large effect sizes were found for CBT for unipolar depression, generalized anxiety disorder (GAD), panic disorder with or without agoraphobia, social phobia, PTSD, and childhood depressive and anxiety disorders. They also reported that effect sizes for CBT of marital distress, anger, childhood somatic disorders, and chronic pain were in the moderate range and concluded that while CBT was somewhat superior to antidepressants in the treatment of adult depression, it was equally effective as behavioural therapy in the treatment of adult depression and obsessive–compulsive disorder. Hofmann, Asnaani, Vonk, Sawyer, and Fang (2012) identified 269 meta-analytic studies and reviewed a representative sample of 106 meta-analyses examining CBT for the following problems: substance use disorder, schizophrenia and other psychotic disorders, depression and dysthymia, bipolar disorder, anxiety disorders, somatoform disorders, eating disorders, insomnia, personality disorders, anger and aggression, criminal behaviours, general stress, distress due to general medical conditions, chronic pain and fatigue, and distress related to pregnancy complications and female hormonal conditions. They concluded that the strongest support exists for CBT of anxiety disorders, somatoform disorders, bulimia, anger control problems, and general stress. They also reported that no meta-analytic studies of CBT had been reported on specific subgroups, such as ethnic minorities and low-income samples.

Studies on CBT for schizophrenia started gathering momentum in the 1990s, and more than 35 randomized controlled trials and meta-analyses have now been published reporting the efficacy of CBT. Over the last decade, the effect size reported by several reviewers suggested that cognitive therapy is an effective treatment of patients with schizophrenia (Rathod et al., 2010). A meta-analysis of 34 studies in schizophrenia (Wykes, Steel, Everitt, & Tarrier, 2008) demonstrated improvement in positive symptoms, negative symptoms, mood, and social anxiety with effect size in moderate range. In another meta-analysis, Dutch researchers analysed 48 outcome trials comparing psychological interventions for psychosis and concluded that CBT was significantly more efficacious than other interventions pooled in reducing positive symptoms and significantly more efficacious when compared directly with befriending for overall symptoms and supportive counselling for positive symptoms (Turner, Gaag, Karyotaki, & Cuijpers, 2014). Morrison et al. (2014) demonstrated that cognitive therapy significantly reduced psychiatric symptoms as a safe and acceptable alternative for people with schizophrenia spectrum disorders who had chosen not to take antipsychotic drugs. CBT is also shown to reduce the risk of relapse by more than 50% when followed over a 24-month period in individuals with psychosis (Hutton & Taylor, 2013).

In bipolar disorder, CBT has been shown to reduce the risk of relapse (Lam et al., 2003), but there have also been negative findings. Scott (2006) reported after an 18-month study of 256 subjects that there was no difference in relapse with CBT at the end of 18 months.

CBT complements and builds on the psychopharmacological management of severe mental illnesses. For many mild to moderate mental illnesses like depression and anxiety, it may even be as good as or superior to medication management (DeRubeis, Gelfand, Tang, & Simons, 1999; Friedman, Wright, Jarrett, & Thase, 2006; Hollon et al., 2005). The guidelines for use of CBT in severe mental illness reflect the current evidence base for different severe enduring mental illnesses. CBT is regarded as an essential component of treatment for a variety of psychiatric disorders in the United Kingdom and Europe (e.g. National Institute of Health and Care Excellence [NICE]) and clinical treatment guidelines in the United States (e.g. American Psychiatric Association Steering Committee on Practice Guidelines, APA (2006)). In the United States, Schizophrenia Patient Outcomes Research Team (PORT) recommends CBT for all individuals who have persistent symptoms despite adequate pharmacotherapy (Dixon et al., 2010). However, the recommendations for other conditions such as bipolar disorder are less clear. In addition to the differences based on individual diagnoses, there are some cross-continental differences in the recommendations. The NICE recommends that CBT should be offered to all individuals with schizophrenia and not necessarily limited to those with persistent symptoms (NICE, 2014) as in the PORT guidelines.

The Cognitive Model: Key Principles

The original cognitive approach to psychopathology was based on an information-processing model that proposed that processing of external events or internal stimuli is biased and leads to characteristic psychopathology (Beck, 2005). The cognitive model of psychopathology was initially constructed to explain the psychological processes in depression. Clark, Beck, and Alford (1999) defined the role of automatic thoughts and schemas in mental illness and the role of CBT in modifying these. Therapy draws on the person's beliefs and experiences through a discussion of thoughts, feelings, and behaviour to understand and develop a formulation and treatment plan. Beck (1976) developed a formulation to illustrate the interplay of the various factors as follows.

Early experiences shape and influence the formation of core beliefs and assumptions. Core beliefs are defined as fundamental, inflexible, absolute, and generalized beliefs that people hold about themselves, others, the world, and/or the future (Dobson, 2012). A critical incident can activate dysfunctional assumptions and trigger negative automatic thoughts. Dysfunctional assumptions are often rigid, narrow, and controlling unconscious conditional thoughts that may be culturally defined. These feed into negative automatic thoughts that are negative thoughts and images that pop into our minds and can be associated with intense emotions (Sweet, 2010). Thinking biases are formed that are interpretations of an event in a way that is consistent with underlying dysfunctional schemas (Beck et al., 1979). Examples of thinking biases include all-or-nothing thinking, mental filters that focus only on the negatives, overgeneralization, and catastrophization, personalization, and jumping to conclusions. Thoughts then have an impact on mood and behaviour and may present as symptoms of emotional disorder. Therapy focuses on thoughts and their interpretations and aims to reappraise them with a view to modifying them, thereby decreasing vulnerability to emotional distress (Figure 2.1).

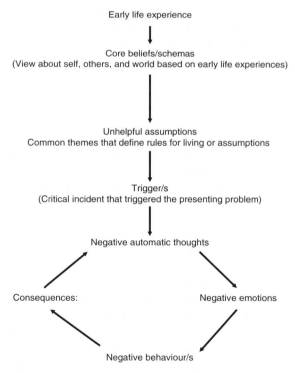

Figure 2.1 Longitudinal formulation. From Wills (2012). Reproduced with permission from Sage.

Culture and Cognitive Model

An individual's culture has an influence on early experiences, core beliefs, assumptions, and hence psychopathology. Early experiences are determined by parenting styles and the environment in which people grow like home, school, neighbourhood, friends, etc. Parenting styles are often influenced by culture. Culture influences family values which has implications on early development, achievement in schools, and how individuals learn to view themselves in the context of the family and wider community. Positive or negative experiences like migration, bullying, or discrimination in early years have a further impact on development. The early experiences and cultural and religious values adopted in childhood shape an individual's belief systems and assumptions.

How a person interprets psychological distress is based on a variety of factors including his or her culture, education, social class, and religion. These interpretations arise from beliefs about illness and health, treatment options, and systems of care. Clients' belief systems determine their and their families' perspectives about their distress, influence the different culturally influenced pathways they take to find help, and affect their decisions to engage with the services.

An individual's cultural background can be a source of support or a source of distress depending on individual circumstances. Behaviours in response to situations and thoughts are also determined by culture, and therefore, every aspect of the cognitive model can be influenced by culture. All these aspects will be discussed in detail in later chapters (Figure 2.2).

Basic Principles of Therapy

Assessment

Therapy begins with assessment. The focus is on creating a therapeutic relationship that is perceived as safe, equitable, and non-stigmatizing by the clients. Therapist style that emphasizes collaboration, warmth, and mutual respect is considered critical and is likely to facilitate such a relationship. Towards that end, assessment is designed to focus on engagement and relationship building along with information gathering. The cumulative role of traumas in contributing to the development and maintenance of psychotic and other symptoms is recognized (Beard et al., 2013), and a trauma-sensitive approach is taken to engage clients. Assessment builds and shifts focus, exploring sensitive areas as the person is able to handle them and moves the discussion to neutral and non-threatening topics when the person is distressed. Assessment is also seen as an ongoing process that is not completed until the end of therapy and the client is out of the door (Kingdon & Turkington, 2005). Part of the assessment process is affording therapeutic benefit early on in a variety of ways such as providing a normalizing rationale for symptoms, instilling hope, or helping problem-solve a pressing issue. A positive experience by the client enhances and deepens the engagement and allows deeper exploration of the problem.

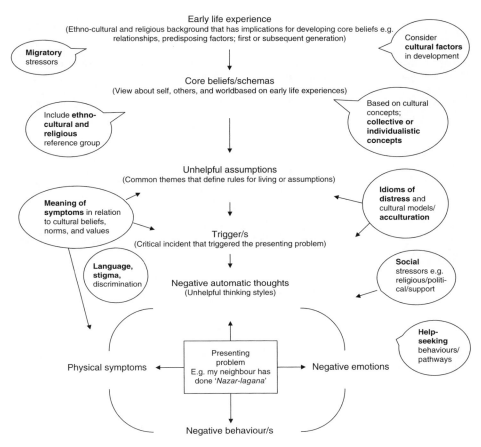

Figure 2.2 Adapted longitudinal formulation. From Wills (2012). Reproduced with permission from Sage.

Formulation

Information on current beliefs and how they were arrived at is assembled into a formulation which draws together predisposing, precipitating, perpetuating, and protective factors with current and underlying concerns with the interactions between thoughts, feelings, and behaviours as illustrated in Figure 2.3.

Treatment strategy

A treatment plan is agreed based on the formulation with key objectives for therapy. A number of techniques are used to work on the objectives. A rationale based on a stress–vulnerability model is explored with normalizing of symptoms – where appropriate – as forming part of the continuum between normal and distressing or disturbing experiences. The stress–vulnerability

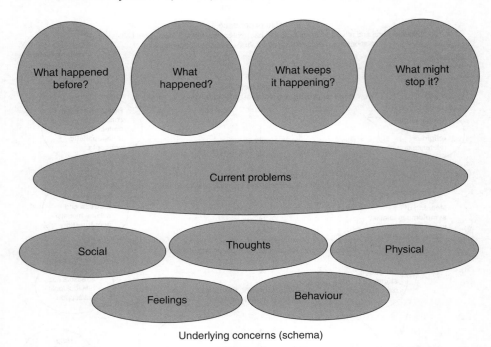

Figure 2.3   Underlying concerns. From Kingdon and Turkington (2005). Reproduced with permission from Guilford Press.

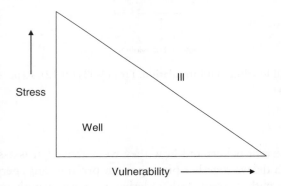

Figure 2.4   Stress–vulnerability model. From Zubin and Spring (1997). Reproduced with permission from APA.

model described by Zubin and Spring (1997) and further elaborated by Nuechterlein and Dawson (1984) emphasizes the interaction between life events, circumstances, and individual genetic, physiological, psychological, and social predispositions which lead to variation in vulnerability. This rationale is used to normalize symptoms using the CBT model described earlier (Figure 2.4).

Normalizing rationale (process by which thoughts, feelings, behaviours, and experiences are compared with similar thoughts, feelings, and experiences of other individual who are not diagnosed as mentally ill) (Kingdon & Turkington, 2005) is frequently used early on during the assessment and engagement process and subsequently as appropriate. Normalizing along with psychoeducation places the client's experiences in context of human reactions to difficult situations, reduces the stigma and catastrophic fears, enhances self-esteem, and strengthens adaptive coping skills. It thus helps to re-evaluate a previous conclusion or form a new idea.

Methods to draw up and debate or explore key beliefs are applied such as Socratic questioning and guided discovery (Kingdon & Turkington, 2005; Wright et al., 2009). Cognitive therapists aim to ask questions out of genuine curiosity in order to help clients to explore and review their thoughts. This is referred to as Socratic questioning or guided discovery. Good questions are more open ended than closed, more general to begin with than specific, and probe-type questions. Socratic questioning has four stages of guided discovery – a series of questions to uncover relevant information, accurate listening and reflection by the therapist, summarizing, and asking synthesizing and analytical questions (Padesky, 1993). The aim is to encourage the individual to view their thoughts as hypotheses or guesses which are open to debate (Figure 2.5).

Other cognitive techniques include imagery, role play, rehearsal exercises, and homework assignments to modify core beliefs. Behavioural interventions include activity monitoring and rescheduling, graded task assignment, relaxation, distraction techniques, surveys, manipulation of safety behaviours, and hierarchical exposures. These are also aimed at modifying the beliefs (Wright et al., 2009). Preventative strategies are aimed at preparing for the future.

In psychotic illnesses, specific work with hallucinations, delusions, and negative symptoms can assist in reattribution of the experiences and beliefs to the self rather than to others or external sources. Delusions are approached as beliefs that can be subject to evidence. The process of gathering and evaluating the evidence for delusions is therapeutic and leads to a loosening or even change in delusional beliefs. Hallucinations are conceptualized as automatic thoughts that client perceives as originating externally and maintained by safety behaviours and dysfunctional beliefs about the power of the voices. Therapeutic work involves reattribution, debating the content that includes the similarity between the content of voices and self-beliefs, evaluating the beliefs about voices, and developing coping strategies to deal with distress. Coping strategies can include distraction, focusing, or metacognitive methods like acceptance, assertiveness, etc. (Wright et al., 2009). Learning new ways of coping with persistent hallucinations and strong beliefs allows behavioural change including socialization to occur. This in turn can help break the cycle of isolation and distress which frequently fuels the dysfunctional beliefs.

Negative symptoms are conceptualized in terms of their positive value to the individual, for example, reduction of anxiety or protection against increase in voices or paranoia, and then alternative ways for the individual to control and

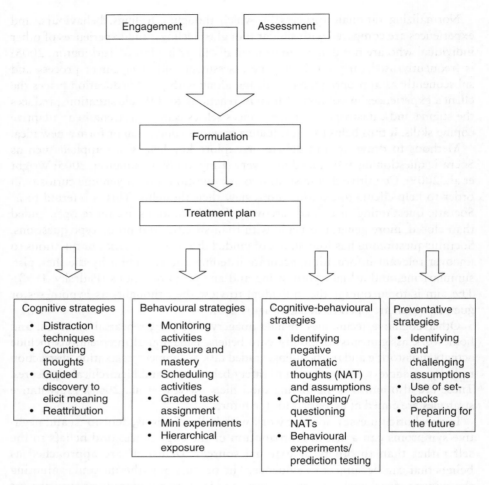

Figure 2.5   Elements of treatment.

manage these symptoms are found. A normalizing rationale is used to explain the genesis of negative symptoms, and it can mitigate the demoralization that contributes to the negative symptoms. Normalizing rationale along with psychoeducation gives a framework for the families to be more empathic to their loved ones and helps reduce the high expressed emotion in families. This may involve initially improving understanding of the positive symptoms, for example, paranoia, voices, and anxiety, better, and then through long-term goal setting (instilling hope) and short-term graded collaborative task assignment, begin a process of behavioural activation (Kingdon & Turkington, 2005). Self-defeating beliefs are shown to be involved in the genesis and maintenance of negative symptoms, and working on core negative beliefs has been shown to help negative symptoms in schizophrenia (Beck, Grant, Huh, Perivoliotis, & Chang, 2013).

CBT for severe mental illnesses (schizophrenia, bipolar disorder, severe depression, etc.) will be discussed in detail throughout this book, exploring cultural context and adaptations.

Why Do We Need to Culturally Adapt Cognitive Therapy?

Before we discuss CBT specifically, let's discuss culture and its relationship to evidence-based treatments. We will then debate why we need to culturally adapt CBT.

Influence of culture on evidence-based treatment

It is well acknowledged that empirically supported psychological treatments (ESTs) need to be disseminated to practice-focused clinics, practitioner training settings, and service-providing organizations (Sobell, 1996). However, establishing efficacy is only a first step in the introduction of a therapy into practice. The next three steps are establishing effectiveness in real-world clinical populations that are different – more generalizable – from research samples, followed ideally by demonstration of cost-effectiveness and finally feasibility and overall clinical utility (Chambless & Hollon, 1998). The extent to which these steps are fully explored has varied considerably over the years. In most psychotherapy trials, minority groups or groups outside the developed world are under-represented; hence, the generalization of findings to other ethnicities and cultural groups may not be valid or appropriate.

The subject of culture and ethnicity in ESTs is not always discussed objectively and scientifically, as it can evoke deep feelings resulting in polarization. Generally, discussions of culture focus on non-dominant groups – 'otherness' – emphasizing their deficits rather than their adaptive strengths and how they are different from the dominant societal definitions of 'normality' (McGoldrick, Giordano, & Garcia-Preto, 2005). The alternate, clinically meaningful, and more accurate perspective views culture and ethnicity as pertaining to everyone and influencing everyone's values, beliefs, and behaviours. Each individual has a unique culture, which is an amalgam of multiple cultures with usually one predominating. In addition, cultural practices and norms are not 'set in stone' but constantly evolving based on an individual's experiences and that of their cultural group. There is, however, an underlying sense of belonging that tethers humans to a cultural group. People's perception of their culture is affected by their relationship to the groups they come from and their relationships to the dominant or majority group (McGoldrick et al., 2005). A small number of groups exist based on, often abhorrent, premises involving excluding rather than including others, due to a perceived moral superiority like 'white supremacy' groups or from misperceived 'elite' social status such as various secret societies. They increase the sense of alienation and invalidation of other especially less dominant cultural groups.

There has been a lot of speculation about why clients from non-majority cultures do not access evidence-based therapies like CBT or whether they would respond favourably to them. Some arguments include historical assumptions and explanations that, at least implicitly, psychotherapy is only appropriate where a level of societal development has occurred. The initial growth of psychotherapy in Europe was misattributed to suggestions that this was because 'European culture is civilised' (Lewis, 1965; Thomas & Sillen, 1972) and implicitly therapies can only benefit those societies which can utilize them – 'civilized people.' Stereotyping of minority cultural clients, especially the African Caribbean group, as 'not psychologically minded' (Sabshin, Diesenhaus, & Wilkerson, 1970) has also impeded dissemination. There have been assumptions about difficulty in engaging clients from culturally diverse backgrounds adequately (Rosenthal & Frank, 1958) reflected in perceptions and attitudes of professionals (Byford, Barber, Fiander, Marshall, & Green, 2001). Communication barriers can result in clients being misunderstood and thus inaccurately diagnosed (Fernando, 1998). Inappropriate diagnoses may mean poor access to evidence-based therapies which in turn disengages and disadvantages clients as discussed in Chapter 1.

Client-related factors and their views about a treatment can also adversely influence access and outcomes for cultural minorities. Mistrust of the health-care system is common in some minorities and is a reason they may not engage with services or terminate prematurely. For example, Latino clients may be more likely than white clients to feel that a provider has judged them unfairly (Schwarzbaum, 2004). Psychological therapies like CBT, as currently delivered, have been criticized as being West-centric and grounded in an 'ineffably Western version of a person' (Summerfield & Veale, 2008). This thinking is further demonstrated in a study from India, where 82% of students felt that principles underlying cognitive therapy conflicted with their values and beliefs (Scorzelli & Scorzelli, 1994). Of these, 46% reported that therapy conflicted with their cultural or family values, and 40% described conflict with their religious beliefs. The main reasons for this incompatibility were described to be beliefs that 'our destiny is fixed and based on our previous good or bad deeds, people do not have free will and are controlled by a high power, that the individual must abide by the rules and the values of their family or community to have a meaningful and conflict free life and females will always need support from a stronger individual.' An example of the conflict described in the study can be found in our day-to-day practice where we work with many individuals from Western cultures, where independence from the family and individualism are valued. In many Eastern or collectivist cultures (as they are sometimes referred to), the predominant emphasis is on being part of a group, especially the family (Hays & Iwamasa, 2006; Mason & Sawyer, 2002; Tseng, Chang, & Nishjzono, 2005). If a therapist who values individual needs and independence were treating a client from a collectivist culture (who values communal needs), the client might not engage or respond effectively if the therapist assumes their own values are shared by the client. The reason may be that the treatment solutions offered are inevitably weighted towards individualistic

Table 2.1   Differences between traditional and nontraditional societies regarding personal and professional relationships and their relevance to medical treatment.

Traditional societies	Western societies
Family and group oriented	Individual oriented
Extended family	Nuclear family
Status determined by age and position in the family	Status achieved by own effort
Relationship between kin obligatory	Relationships an individual choice
Arranged marriages with an element of choice	Choice of marital partner, determined by interpersonal relationship
Family decision making	Individual autonomy
External locus of control	Internal locus of control
Physicians' decisions respected and considered holy	Doubt in doctor–patient relationships, malpractice suits not uncommon
Deference to God's will	Self-determination
Pride in family care of mentally ill	Community care of mentally ill
Pride in family tie	Pride in self

Source: From Okasha and Okasha (2000). Reproduced with permission from Sage.

assumptions which may run counter to the expectations of the client's native culture and lead to distrust and possibly disengagement. Another scenario may occur when the client has acculturated to the host culture, and their family has not. The client may then embrace the therapist's ideas in therapy but find it difficult to practice them at home, rendering the intervention ineffective. There are many other core values that are fundamentally different in Western and traditional cultures as described in Table 2.1. We will discuss them and how they impact on therapy with examples in further chapters.

The effectiveness of a number of evidence-based treatments in different clinical groups, across the diversity of minority cultural groups, has yet to be established. But does this mean we should not use them with these populations? Evidence needs to be weighed as to whether results can be generalizable. All studies involve restricted groups including those prepared to consent to come into a study in the first place and those meeting strict inclusion and exclusion criteria, and practitioners have to judge whether their balance of evidence is such that an evidence-based practice is appropriate to their individual client – and whether they themselves have the expertise to provide it. Treatments that have been shown in research trials to be efficacious with majority culture clients could be expected to be effective and generalizable across groups in the absence of evidence to the contrary or reasons to believe that they are not appropriate. However, we do suggest that for most treatments, modifications are needed to make them more likely to be effective for individuals from cultural minority groups (Voss & Sarah, 2008) and, of course, that appropriate research continues to be done to establish that they are indeed effective in these circumstances. But it is usually not possible to wait for definitive research to arrive in the meantime. Modification though is reasonable through individualization of practice and understanding and adaptation to cultural context – as we will justify further.

The evidence for psychotherapies in diverse cultural groups

Work on psychotherapies in a range of disorders has concluded that the outcome of psychotherapy for minority ethnic groups is not as good as for white people (Bhugra, 1997). Few evaluations of the effectiveness of psychotherapy have included adequate numbers of non-Western ethnic groups (Alvidrez, Azocar, & Miranda, 1996), and few studies report on adaptations of proven interventions for use by culturally distinct populations. For example, Hispanics and Asians are highly under-represented in research samples (Hussain-Gambles et al., 2004; Miranda et al., 2005; Wells, Klap, Koike, & Sherbourne, 2001), as requirements of English literacy systematically exclude individuals who do not speak English. Even when language is not an issue, clinical trials on psychotherapy interventions generally enrol few minority clients, and analysis of trial results is usually not done separately based on ethnic group (Carroll et al., 2009). There are therefore few studies of effectiveness of evidence-based interventions in minority groups.

We demonstrated for the first time in psychosis that although there was clear efficacy for CBT for schizophrenia within a large study sample, outcomes for minority ethnic groups were not as good as for the white population (Rathod, Kingdon, Smith, & Turkington, 2005). In this multicentred, randomized controlled trial, 422 participants with a diagnosis of schizophrenia were allocated to either an intervention group or treatment as usual (TAU). The intervention consisted of six sessions of individual insight-focused CBT with the participants and three sessions of psychoeducation with their families. These treatments were delivered by nurses who were trained and supervised in a manualized approach. Among other findings, the CBT group demonstrated significantly greater improvement in insight at the end of therapy and at 1-year follow-up. However, there was a significantly smaller change in insight as well as an increased dropout rate in African Caribbean and Black African participants. The study re-emphasized previous findings of difficulties in engaging clients of African Caribbean origin and their poor response to psychological therapies as currently delivered. These findings were not dissimilar to studies in the United States that documented similar results of higher attrition rates with minority clients who were treated with CBT for depression (Organista, Muñoz, & González, 1994).

Under-representation of all minorities in research samples is a significant concern that prompted the National Institutes of Health (NIH) to issue a policy in 1994 mandating that ethnic minorities be included in all NIH-funded research. This policy was updated in 2001 (NIH, 2001). One recent randomized trial to evaluate the efficacy of cognitive therapy for low-functioning clients with schizophrenia conducted by Grant, Huh, Perivoliotis, Stolar, and Beck (2012) found that CBT was superior to TAU, with clinically significant mean improvements in global functioning. Of particular interest in this trial was the ethnic diversity of the sample, of whom 68% were from minority groups (African American, 31 [65%]; Asian American, 1 [3%]; biracial, 1 [3%]). Attrition rates were found to be low. This study paves the way for more trials with participants from ethnic minority groups.

Despite the potential for cultural mismatch to render treatments ineffective, clinicians and researchers are disseminating CBT globally, across widely diverse cultures (Casas, 1988; Chen et al., 2007; Naeem, Waheed, Gobbi, Ayub, & Kingdon, 2010; Williams, Hean, & Beverly, 2006). Sometimes, local adaptations are made based on local cultural knowledge. However, while CBT remains the most widely recommended psychological therapy for most mental health problems, explanations used in CBT continue to be based on Western concepts and illness models. CBT involves exploration and attempts to modify core beliefs and schemas. Such core beliefs, underlying assumptions and even the content of automatic thoughts, vary with culture (Padesky & Greenberger, 1995). Little attention has, as yet, been given to modifying the therapeutic framework and practice of CBT (Williams et al., 2006) to incorporate an understanding of diverse ethnic, cultural, and religious contexts (Rathod, Naeem, Phiri, & Kingdon, 2008).

There is a risk that continuing to practice CBT in minority groups without adaptation may lead to disengagement of clients from therapy (Rathod et al., 2005) as they perceive that they or their culture are not understood. It has the potential to impair the therapeutic alliance which is the central foundation on which any therapeutic intervention depends, leading to poor outcomes and the therapist feeling and, indeed, proving relatively incompetent. Without sensitivity to cultural norms and culturally specific explanations of phenomena, using generic or traditional CBT could create obstacles in the cognitive and behaviour change process, especially if the therapist's explanations for change conflict with the client's cultural models.

Reasons why CBT is an appropriate therapy for adaptation

CBT could and probably should be the psychotherapeutic model of first choice across cultures for people with mental health concerns if appropriately adapted (Hays, 2014; Rathod, Phiri, Kingdon, & Gobbi, 2010) although there are some arguments that other modalities such as interpersonal therapy may be equally valid. However, the evidence or the effectiveness of the latter in conditions other than depression is considerably less, and there is very little in more severe conditions. As described previously, CBT has an extensive evidence base, and its interactional, personalized, and pragmatic approach provides a conceptual framework using reasoning approaches consistent with Eastern and other philosophies (Rathod & Kingdon, 2009). The cognitive model and the influence of culture as discussed earlier in the chapter lend itself to adaptation. Many people from minority cultural backgrounds do not trust the health-care system and, particularly, mental health services (Schwarzbaum, 2004; Thornicroft, Davies, & Leese, 1999), but the strong focus on collaboration and engagement that are key principles in CBT can help to counter this mistrust.

CBT has the potential, with adaptation, to achieve multiple objectives within multicultural health care – it allows for the incorporation of tradition and languages and uses personal, cultural, and collective resources to increase self-awareness in healing. CBT can also serve to modify health-related behaviours, improve self-management, and instill hope and resilience. All of these culminate in a service that embraces recovery, and the strengths of an individual's culture can add to this potential. Bennett-Levy et al. (2014) reported that the qualities of CBT that were perceived to be effective were its adaptability, pragmatic here-and-now approach, capacity for low-intensity interventions, safe containing structure, promotion of self-agency, and valuable techniques. The authors suggested that the prime requirement for adaptations to CBT were that they would need to fit different social and cultural contexts.

Specific components of CBT may be particularly straightforward to culturally adapt. As in majority cultures, many clients from minority cultures, for example, Hispanic people, are monolingual with Spanish as clients' only language of communication, and even where they are bilingual, the preferred language of communication for a sizable proportion remains to be Spanish. The behavioural components of therapy as structured approaches with simple instructions and negotiation have been found to be amenable to reliable conduction in a client's second language or through an interpreter (Ghassemzadeh, 2007; Hays, 1995).

Such behavioural activation approaches are a key component of CBT in achieving change, and these have also been used successfully in developing societies where dissemination of psychological interventions for treating depression has involved training generic health workers in these relatively straightforward techniques (Rahman, Malik, Sikander, Roberts, & Creed, 2008). In this instance, this training was to female workers who provided perinatal care to women in local communities, and the outcomes were demonstrable.

Evidence of effectiveness of cultural adaptations to psychotherapy

Various researchers have suggested cultural modifications to therapy, including ethnic match of the therapist and client (Sue, Fujino, Hu, & Takeuchi, 1991), multicultural training for therapists (Hays, 1995), conducting therapy in an important cultural setting (e.g. church or synagogue), conducting therapy in the client's native language, and addressing the issue of cultural differences at the outset of therapy (Sue & Sue, 2003). Of these, only ethnic match, multicultural training, and modifications of therapy have been investigated in research studies, with mixed results (Voss & Sarah, 2008). Racial matching has the clear advantages of the therapist possessing knowledge of the client's culture. However, while the therapist may belong to the same racial group as the client, their core values and beliefs may or may not be the same. They may, for example, come from very different economic or educational groups. As we discussed earlier, every individual, even within the same cultural group has their own value system influenced by group beliefs. There may also be differences in subcultures within the same culture. Therefore, there may be an assumption of knowledge and similarities through racially matching a therapist to a client. Racial matching does have the major disadvantage, if imposed rigidly, of potentially limiting access to the full range of skilled therapists or choice of gender or simply being able to select an individual with whom you can get on – whatever their race and culture.

There are a few meta-analyses of interventions in which attempts have been made to culturally adapt them and inevitably some such attempts have been more complete and thorough than others. These mainly show better effect for the adapted interventions than comparison groups. Griner and Smith (2006) examined a total of 76 studies. They reported efficacy of the adapted intervention with a moderate effect size ($d = 0.45$, $SE = 0.04$, $p < 0.0001$; confidence interval of $d = 0.36$–0.53). Smith, Domenech Rodríguez, and Bernal (2010) describe a meta-analysis of 65 experimental and quasi-experimental studies involving 8,620 participants that demonstrated an effect size, $d = 0.46$, indicating that treatments specifically adapted for clients of different groups were moderately more effective with that clientele than traditional treatments. According to the authors, the most effective treatments tended to be those with a greater number of cultural adaptations. Mental health services targeted to a specific cultural group were several times more effective than those provided to clients from a variety of cultural backgrounds.

In contrast, Huey and Polo's (2008) meta-analysis was inconclusive. The authors argued that there was no evidence to suggest that culturally adapted interventions were effective, and therefore, findings from these studies should be interpreted with caution. As with all meta-analyses, methodological rigor was and should be taken into consideration.

The Griner and Smith (2006) and Huey and Polo (2008) meta-analyses assessed different targeted populations and age groups. Huey and Polo's work was solely on youth and adolescents, whereas Griner and Smith pooled studies from the adult population. The adolescent age group is usually more acculturated compared to adults, because of schooling considerations and therefore contact and education in the host countries' norms and values. Hence, they may not show increased efficacy from culturally adapted interventions.

A number of small studies conducted in various countries demonstrate better outcomes with cultural adaptations of evidence-based therapies. Successful cultural adaptation has been demonstrated in an innovative study conducted in Australia with aboriginal people suffering from chronic mental illness (Nagel, Robinson, Condon, & Trauer, 2009). The treatment development invited both aboriginal mental health workers and recovered clients as key informants to understand indigenous views of mental illness. Group and individual in-depth interviews were conducted as well as field observations completed. The themes that emerged were the importance of the family, strength derived from cultural traditions, and the value of storytelling to share information. These themes were used to inform the process and content of the assessment, treatment, and ancillary materials. The resulting culturally adapted psychotherapy was subsequently compared with TAU. In all, 49 clients were randomly assigned, and outcomes were evaluated at baseline, 6-, 12-, and 18-month follow-ups. The culturally adapted therapy produced better outcomes in well-being, health, and substance dependence with changes maintained over time. Conducted in a remote indigenous area of Australia with a historically underserved population, this study is an excellent example of collaboratively adapting evidence-based intervention and improving outcomes.

There is some evidence from small pilot studies suggesting locally adapted CBT with minority populations has been successful in other places (Carter, Sbrocco, Gore, Marin, & Lewis, 2003; Hinton et al., 2004, 2005; Kubany, Hill, & Owens, 2003; Patel et al., 2007; Rahman et al., 2008; Rojas et al., 2007). Kubany et al. (2003) studied a sample of 37 ethnically diverse women who were abused and suffered from PTSD. At 3-month follow-up, all 16 women who completed therapy were free of PTSD. The study did not mention any cultural adaptations to therapy. Carter et al. (2003) studied the efficacy of culturally modified CBT in a group of 32 African American (AA) women as a treatment for panic disorder with agoraphobia. The CBT group also had a significant reduction in anxiety symptoms, fear of anxiety symptoms, cognitive concerns, and severity of avoidance, with large effect sizes (d) for all outcome variables; in the range of 0.85–0.97.

Hinton et al. (2004) examined the effectiveness of a culturally modified CBT in 12 Vietnamese refugees diagnosed with PTSD and panic attacks. CBT significantly reduced symptoms of PTSD, anxiety, depression, and severity of panic attacks. In a second study, Hinton et al. (2005) examined the effectiveness of a culturally modified version of CBT for the treatment of co-morbid PTSD and GAD in 40 Cambodian refugees. The CBT group had significantly lower scores than the wait-list group on all measures with large between-the-group effect sizes (d), range 2.17–3.78.

Rojas et al. (2007) compared the effectiveness of a multicomponent intervention with TAU to treat postnatal depression in low-income mothers in primary care clinics in Santiago, Chile. They reported that low-income mothers with postnatal depression could be effectively helped, even in low-income settings, through multicomponent interventions. Rahman et al. (2008), as mentioned previously, conducted a cluster-randomized trial of a CBT-based intervention provided by trained community health workers in Pakistan and reported that it can effectively treat perinatal depression and improve infant outcomes.

Munoz and colleagues have conducted a number of studies on cultural adaptation of CBT for treatment and prevention of adult depression in ethnic minority participants in the United States (e.g. Kohn, Oden, Munoz, Robinson, & Leavitt, 2002; Miranda et al., 2003; Muñoz & Mendelson, 2005). Kohn et al. (2002) compared standard group CBT with adapted CBT for African American women presenting with major depression and reported promising results for adapted CBT. In Pakistan, Naeem, Irfan, Zaidi, Kingdon, and Ayub (2008) have adapted CBT for depression with positive results. Group CBT for seasonal affective disorder (SAD) has been acceptable and found to bring about a similar degree of symptom reduction among Japanese clients as among Western clients (Chen et al., 2007). Cognitive behavioural approaches have also received support for use in therapy with Hispanic groups (Casas, 1988; Runz & Casas, 1981).

We developed a culturally adapted CBT for psychosis for ethnic minority clients by exploration and incorporation of clients, laypersons, and health professionals' views and opinions (Rathod, Phiri, Kingdon, & Gobbi, 2010). The key finding of this qualitative study was that CBT would be acceptable to participants if culturally adapted. We tested the therapy through a feasibility study. This was a randomized controlled trial that was conducted in two centres in the United Kingdom ($n = 35$) in participants with a diagnosis of schizophrenia, schizoaffective, or delusional disorder. Assessments were conducted at three time points – baseline, post-therapy, and at 6-month follow-up – using the Comprehensive Psychopathological Rating Scale (CPRS) and Insight Scale. Outcomes on specific subscales of CPRS were also evaluated. Participants in the treatment arm completed the Patient Experience Questionnaire (PEQ) to measure satisfaction with the adapted CBT intervention. Administration of outcome measures was conducted by assessors blind to randomization and treatment allocation. In total, (n) 33 participants were randomly allocated to intervention arm ($n = 16$) and TAU arm ($n = 17$) after (n) 2 participants were excluded following randomization. Participants in the intervention arm were offered 16 sessions of culturally adapted CBT with trained therapists, and the TAU arm continued with their standard treatment. Post-treatment, the intervention group showed statistically significant reductions in symptomatology on overall CPRS scores, insights, and subscales – the Montgomery–Asberg Depression Rating Scale, the Brief Anxiety Scale, and the Brief Assessment of Negative Symptoms Scale – compared to TAU. Overall satisfaction was found to be correlated with the number of sessions attended ($r = 0.563$; $p = 0.03$). The intervention was effective and achieved statistically significant results, and satisfaction with the adapted treatment was high (Rathod et al., 2013).

Although limited, available evidence points towards the clear rationale and need for adaptation of CBT to a client's culture for acceptability and effectiveness. In fact, some experts (Bernal & Domenech Rodríguez, 2012) go further to challenge an underlying assumption upon which much of the debate over cultural adaptations is based: that culture and psychotherapy ever have or ever could exist in isolation.

Challenges to Cultural Adaptation

Despite the need for cultural adaptation of evidence-based interventions such as CBT, it is important to acknowledge and consider the challenges to adapting CBT to different cultures.

Tendency to overgeneralize

Cultural orientation influences psychopathology, attributions to illness, and help-seeking behaviours and pathways and determines barriers to engaging with therapy. There can be resistance to exploring psychopathology that is rooted in the cultural system, despite adaptations. Adaptation requires conceptualization of a particular culture in the design of the adapted therapy with acknowledgement of cultural relevance (Castro, Barrera, & Holleran Steiker, 2010; Frankish, Lovatto, & Poureslami, 2007) and the ability to generalize between subgroups and to achieve targeted outcomes. There is a need to acknowledge the fact that even within cultures, subcultures vary and, within the same culture, different individuals may have diverse sets of beliefs and values. Culture is not a homogenous entity and individual values and beliefs within it could be understood best as being on a spectrum. For example, among four very similar rural East African societies, attributions to mental illness differ considerably. In one community, 60% of people interviewed believed that psychosis was caused by witchcraft, compared with only 1% in another. While in one none believed that psychosis was an illness, in another, two-thirds said it was an illness caused by a worm in the front of the brain accompanied by stress. Interestingly, those communities that believed illness is caused by witchcraft also believed it was curable and pursued a policy of treatment and care, while those who believed in an underlying organic cause tended to beat clients and leave them to starve (Edgerton, 1966). The issue is further compounded by the impact of the process of acculturation or level of adjustment to the host culture, discussed in detail later in the book. Adapting an intervention carries an inherent challenge and risk of presuming global understanding from knowledge of the culture or subculture, when the intervention should allow latitude and flexibility for an assessment of every individual's personal values that are significant to them him or her.

Stereotyping

The danger with trying to be more culturally competent is that stereotyping of ethnic minorities and cultural groups can occur, and also, the use of general strategies rather than individualized approaches may increase when treating diverse clientele from similar communities (Sue et al., 1998). Therapists' understanding through reflection about their own beliefs and assumptions can help them avoid falling into this trap of stereotyping cultural differences (Chao, Okazaki, & Hong, 2011). Any adaptation of therapy needs to allow therapists to develop the skill of 'dynamic sizing' – knowing when to generalize and when to flexibly individualize treatments on the basis of the client's individual characteristics. The chapters on therapy will discuss and provide examples on how to do this.

It has been predicted that problems can be expected to emerge when culture is mistakenly equated with ethnicity and/or when using ethnicity or nationality as proxy variables for culture (Castro, Barrera, & Martinez, 2004) which is why we have defined these terms in Chapter 1 as interchanging them can cause confusion.

Fidelity and effectiveness

There is an ongoing debate on the process of cultural adaptation of evidence-based treatments and the extent to which modification is necessary. We face the dilemma of fidelity and the question as to whether adaptation compromises the effectiveness of an intervention (Castro et al., 2004). One school of thought argues that adaptations of an evidenced-based intervention should strive to remain, as closely as possible, aligned to the original intervention (Chambless & Ollendick, 2001) but allow limited flexibility to incorporate cultural values and adaptations. The concept of the universality of emotional expression – that there are more similarities than differences in human behaviours (Bentall, Corcoran, Howard, Blackwood, & Kinderman, 2001; Kaney & Bentall, 1989) – supports this approach. In our adaptation of CBT, we have followed this school of thought as distinct signs and symptoms of mental health problems – psychopathology – are generally recognized across cultures. Sometimes, these signs and symptoms are identified by different names, and there are a small number of exceptional culture-bound syndromes. There is often recognition of psychopathology, although attributions to mental illness and help-seeking behaviour pathways may vary among cultures. For example, despite beliefs in witchcraft and voodoos, traditional Yoruba healers in Nigeria distinguish a wide variety of psychological abnormalities which bear close parallels to Western systems of classification. Among the psychoses they identify are chronic hallucinatory psychosis (*were*), acute psychotic episodes (*asinwin*), chronic withdrawn psychosis (*dindinrin*), regressed psychosis (*danidani*), psychosis with good preservation of personality (*were alaso*), congenital psychosis (*were dile*), and psychosis with childbirth (*abisinwin*), old age (*were agba*), and epilepsy (*ipa were*) (Prince, 1964).

Our work on adaptation, described in this book, ensures fidelity to the basic concepts of CBT while allowing for modifications to make it culturally appropriate. The core elements of CBT are such that they can be retained with adaptation. It is also important to note that there are various aspects to adaptation – like in the pre-engagement and engagement stages that help prior to starting actual therapy. We will discuss this later and in subsequent chapters. Any such modifications need to be fully justified by reference to research where it exists, including both qualitative and quantitative work and carefully assessed expert opinion, especially from within the communities represented, where it does not.

There is another school that argues that rather than adapt existing interventions, new interventions should be developed for specific cultural groups (Voss & Sarah, 2008). The dilemma for practicing clinicians working cross-culturally is that accepting this school of thought would mean developing and learning from a manual for every cultural and subcultural group for each disorder. There is cause for concern already over the proliferation of disorder-specific treatment manuals available. Clinicians may become lost in the vast bibliography of treatment manuals and services, unable to sustain the cost of the training and resources needed. Therefore, in practice, even if desirable, it may not be feasible to develop a different CBT for every cultural group and subgroup within them.

Models of Cultural Adaptation

Western therapists practicing in multicultural settings have frequently described the need for better knowledge and models to work with different cultural populations, and over the years, a number of such models of cultural adaptation of

Table 2.2   Culturally sensitive elements and the dimensions of treatment for clinical research interventions with Hispanics.

Intervention	Culturally sensitive elements
Language	Culturally appropriate; culturally syntonic language
Persons	Role of ethnic/racial similarities and differences between client and therapist in shaping therapy relationship
Metaphors	Symbols and concepts shared with the population; 'dichos,' that is, sayings or slogans, in treatment
Content	Cultural knowledge: values, costumes, and traditions; uniqueness of groups (social, economic, historical, political)
Concepts	Treatment concepts consonant with culture and context: dependence versus interdependence versus independence; emic (within culture, particular) over etic (outside culture, universal)
Goals	Transmission of positive and adaptive cultural values; support adaptive values consensually derived from the culture of origin
Methods	Development and/or cultural adaptation of treatment methods. For example, 'modelling' to include culturally consonant traditions (e.g. cuento therapy – therapy based on folk tales), 'cultural reframing' of drug abuse as intergenerational cultural conflicts, use of language (formal and informal), cultural hypothesis testing, use of genograms, 'cultural migration dialogue'
Context	Consideration of changing contexts in assessment during treatment or intervention: acculturative stress, phase of migration, developmental stage, social supports and relationship to country of origin, economic and social context of intervention

Source: From Bernal et al. (1995). Reproduced with permission from Springer.

various therapies have emerged. In this section, we will describe those of most relevance. We believe that there has been a process of evolution in thinking as the models have developed and that understanding some of their key elements is helpful to therapists. The discussion provides an overview and guide to the level and type of flexibility required to work with an adapted therapy. We will then describe the model that we have followed in our own work and subsequently this book and explain the rationale for selecting it.

Bernal, Bonilla, and Bellido (1995) published the first adaptation framework based on the ecological validity model for cultural adaptation in Latino clients, which contains eight elements: language, persons, metaphors, content, concepts, goals, methods, and context (Table 2.2).

Leong and Lee (2006) developed an integrative and multidimensional model of cross-cultural psychotherapy and subsequently modified it to the cultural accommodation model, an enhanced theoretical guide based on slow accommodation to effective cross-cultural clinical practice and research. Domenech Rodríguez and Weiling (2004) used Bernal's ecological validity model to describe three general phases and ten specific target areas of adaptation and research. During the initial phase, the change agent (researcher) and a community opinion leader collaborate to find a balance between community needs and scientific integrity. In phase 2, evaluation measures are selected and adapted in a process parallel to the adaptation of the intervention. The final phase consists of integrating the observations and data gathered in phase 2 into a new packaged intervention. Each phase consists of an ongoing process of evaluation, revision, and reinvention of the therapeutic process.

Tseng (1999) differentiated therapies around the world into three types: culture-embedded therapies (e.g. recognized as religious ceremonies or healing exercises related to supernatural or natural powers – folk psychotherapy), culture-influenced therapies (e.g. mesmerism, rest therapy, and Morita and Naikan therapies that make use of the cultural fabric of any society, with its associated beliefs and aspirations and ways of seeing the world), and culture-related therapies (e.g. CBT, family therapy, group therapy) which have been developed in specific cultures taking on the characteristic approaches inherent in them and therefore requiring adaptation if they are to be used in other settings.

Two dimensions of cultural adaptation have been described: surface structure adaptations and deep structure adaptations (Resnicow, Soler, Braithwait, Ahluwalia, & Butler, 2000). Surface structure adaptations involve changes in original materials or activities of the intervention that address the observable and superficial aspects of a particular cultural group, such as language, foods, clothing, etc. Deep structure adaptations involve changes based on deeper cultural, social, historical, environmental, and psychological factors that influence the health behaviours of members of a specific cultural group.

Hwang, Wood, Lin, and Cheung (2006), on the basis of Bernal et al.'s (1995) work with Chinese clients in the United States, proposed a more detailed framework which consists of six therapeutic domains and 25 therapeutic principles. The therapeutic domains include the following: (a) dynamic issues and cultural complexities; (b) orienting clients to psychotherapy and increasing mental health awareness; (c) understanding cultural beliefs about mental illness, its causes, and what constitutes appropriate treatment; (d) improving the client–therapist relationship; (e) understanding cultural differences in the expression and communication of distress; and (f) addressing cultural issues specific to the population.

The models described earlier have similarities between them in the dimensions they consider for adaptation, for example, language, context, concepts, and content. Most of them are developments from, and therefore adaptations of, the original Bernal's model. They differ in the level of detail given and the different cultural groups for which they were described. Although the models are useful in working with Asian and Hispanic groups, they may have limitations in relation to other cultures. Hays and Iwamasa's (2006) framework addressed this by adopting a broader consideration of factors pertinent to adaptation across a range of cultures.

Various cognitive therapists from the United States have described their experience of working with American Indians, Alaska native people, Latinos and Latinas,

African Americans, Asian Americans, people of Arab heritage, and Orthodox Jews (Hays & Iwamasa, 2006). Hays and Iwamasa (2006) have offered a framework for therapists using CBT with their minority ethnic clients, which forms the acronym ADDRESSING and consists of the following areas of importance:

(A)   Age and generational influences
(D)   Developmental
(D)   Acquired disabilities
(R)   Religion and spiritual orientation
(E)   Ethnicity
(S)   Socio-economic status
(S)   Sexual orientation
(I)   Indigenous heritage
(N)   National origin
(G)   Gender

An important distinction has also been drawn between two broad aspects of psychological interventions, namely, engagement and outcome (Lau, 2006). We have also recognized the importance of cultural adaptation to techniques used in engagement and in determining outcomes from our findings of the insight study into schizophrenia (described earlier; Rathod et al., 2005). Lau's focal argument was that cultural adaptations of evidence-based treatments should be 'selective to specific areas and directed by research findings.' Based on Lau's recommendations, Barrera and Castro (2006) described a sequence for developing adaptations that consist of systematic phases: (a) information gathering about the form and content required, examined across three domains – (1) group characteristics, (2) program delivery staff, and (3) administrative/community factors; (b) preliminary adaptation design through qualitative research to gather opinions from potential participants and community experts on draft materials and descriptions of intervention activities; (c) preliminary adaptation tests through pilot studies with small groups to identify and discuss (1) sources of program non-fit, (2) implementation difficulties, or (3) difficulties with program content or activities (satisfaction with treatment elements and suggestions for improvements are assessed); and (d) adaptation refinement through case studies or pilot studies. Interestingly, Barrera and Castro's (2006) heuristic framework incorporated and modified much of Lau's concepts but with a specific emphasis on developing mechanisms that would allow for both measuring and evaluating of impact of cultural adaptations using specific outcome measures. This framework is unique and identifies another underdeveloped area in considering evidence-based treatments adapted for cultural groups. There are other models and frameworks of cultural adaptation of evidence-based treatments that derived from qualitative and quantitative methodology such as the Strengthening Families Program (Kumpfer, Pinyuchon, Melo, & Whiteside, 2008) and HIV/AIDS prevention programme (McKleroy et al., 2006; Wingood & DiClemente, 2008).

Cultural Adaptation Framework

Our journey of cultural adaptation of CBT began with the insight study that we have described. The study showed compelling need for further exploration of this concept due to the significant findings in the African Caribbean and Black African participant groups (Rathod et al., 2005). Our work has developed over the years and has been informed by research using qualitative (Rathod, Phiri, Kingdon, & Gobbi, 2010) and quantitative (Rathod et al., 2013) methodology. We have incorporated existing evidence and experience of patients, clinicians, and lay members from minority cultural communities.

In examining different models of adaptation, the work that has seemed most comprehensive and relevant to the task of culturally adapting CBT for severe mental illness in our work has been that proposed by Tseng et al. (2005). When Beck developed CBT, he identified principles that distinguish this intervention from other talking therapies. We assumed that while adaptation of the therapy is important, fidelity to the basic principles is also important and adaptation of the model should allow adequate flexibility for cultural beliefs while preserving validity to the original treatment. Use of the Tseng et al. framework also allows the various dimensions described by Bernal, namely, language, persons, metaphors, content, concepts, goals, methods, and context, to be considered when adapting the therapy. Hence, the Tseng model was suitable as it is adaptable and explores the philosophical orientation, practical considerations, and theoretical considerations before technical adjustments of the therapy.

Tseng et al. (2005) described the following framework that includes four levels of adjustment to culture competent psychotherapy as:

1. Philosophical re-orientation or re-examination and orientation of the fundamental view of life which affects the direction and goal of therapy, for example, acceptance or conquering and normality and maturity. From a philosophical perspective, culture determines an individual's basic view of and attitude towards human beings, society, and the meaning of life and thus will have an obvious impact on the client in his or her search for improvement. When differences in cultural background exist between the client and therapist, there may also be differences in general philosophy and values, and therapists need to understand the issues. An individual's philosophical orientation can be understood by their:
    a) Level of acculturation and its influence on world view
    b) Beliefs and attributions to illness – supernatural/natural/medical–psychological, assessment of pathology, meaning of interpretations, and other communications
    c) Help-seeking behaviours
    d) Cultural orientation towards psychotherapy – the understanding and expectation of therapy, shaped by views, beliefs, and experiences which therefore impact on help-seeking behaviours, knowledge, and barriers regarding accessing therapy

2. Practical considerations of societal factors that impact on the performance of therapy, for example, economic conditions, immigration policies, health systems, and reputation of local units, funding arrangements, level of stigma associated with mental illness, racism, etc. that impact on the client's experiences and often determine their trust or lack of it in the system of care.

3. Technical adjustments of methods and skill in providing psychotherapy, including the mode and manner of therapy and various clinical issues within the therapy for clients of various backgrounds. This incorporates an understanding of:
   a) Setting and environment of therapy.
   b) Therapeutic relationship – society defines the therapist client relationship and differs from a culture that stresses authority or democracy.
   c) Choice of therapy – this can differ among cultures as Western therapy values the rational, cognitive approach to understanding the nature and cause of problems and how to deal with them. Eastern therapies stress the importance of actual experience without cognitive understanding.
   d) Family structures and goals.
   e) Role of religion.

4. Theoretical modifications of concepts need to be made for a best fit for the individual and their cultural strength:
   a) Body and mind – the explanations around the relationship between physical symptoms and mental illness often reflecting the holistic view of health can vary. Understanding the clients view can be helpful in explanations in therapy.
   b) Self and ego boundaries – in Eastern cultures boundaries of self can merge with society and interactions with the family and wider culture. For instance, the boundary between self and others is less distinctly defined and more permeable within societies that encourage and foster interdependent relationships with family and others.
   c) Individuality and collectiveness – this has been described earlier in the context of cultural differences in individual and collective goals.
   d) Personality development – the theory of personality development needs cross-cultural modifications to psychosocial development. This includes concepts like prolonged dependence in children from some Eastern cultures. Although the concept of personality development is universal, the pace of development and the major themes emphasized at each stage are subject to societal influence (e.g. the stage for autonomy is much delayed, and the theme of independence is less emphasized in many cultures).
   e) Parent–child complex – different cultures have different types of parent–child complexities and different solutions.
   f) Defence mechanism and coping – differences through suppression and repression among cultures of certain defence mechanisms impact on outcomes of therapy.

The Cognitive Model and Our Adaptation Framework

We have discussed the cognitive model earlier in this chapter. The cognitive model emphasizes the role of early experiences in development of core beliefs and assumptions. Early and subsequent experiences influence an individual's fundamental view of life or determine their philosophical orientation. Practical considerations of societal factors have a role in influencing early experiences and maintaining or acting as supportive factors for an individual. Theoretical modifications of concepts of therapy take into account core belief systems developed in relation to the practical considerations and philosophical orientation. Based on this understanding for every individual, technical adjustments to CBT are made, thereby personalizing the adaptation to every patient.

The adaptation framework will be explored and explained in detail in the book, using the cognitive model in relation to the process of therapy: assessment, formulation, and treatment planning. We begin by describing a broad application of the framework with examples in Chapters 3 and 4 before we discuss the adaptation to specific CBT techniques in subsequent chapters.

Conclusion

Despite the challenges presented in adaptation and the paucity of evidence-based trials, a wealth of literature is developing that supports the validity of culturally adapting CBT. A good understanding of the ethical considerations and systemic issues would further help to develop culturally adapted CBT. While the collaborative nature of CBT maximizes the possibility of responsive adaptation of the intervention to the individual, it does seem that an understanding of cultural background, norms, traditions, and beliefs enhances the therapist's ability to engage and empathize with a client and adapt interventions to him or her as an individual. Applying this understanding and making skilful adaptations are likely to result in diminishing the current disparities in outcomes for minority cultural groups.

References

Alvidrez, J., Azocar, F., & Miranda, J. (1996). Demystifying the concept of ethnicity for psychotherapy researchers. *Journal of Consulting and Clinical Psychology, 64,* 903–908.

American Psychological Association. (2006). Evidence-based practice in psychology: APA presidential task force on evidence-based practice. *American Psychologist, 61,* 271–285.

Barrera, M., & Castro, F. G. (2006). A heuristic framework for the cultural adaptation of interventions. *Clinical Psychology: Science and Practice, 13*(4), 311–316.

Beard, S., Gayer-Anderson, C., Borges, S., Dewey, M. E., Fisher, H. L., & Morgan, C. (2013). Life events and psychosis. *Schizophrenia Bulletin, 39,* 740–747.

Beck, A. (1976). *Cognitive therapy and the emotional disorders.* New York, NY: Penguin Books.

Beck, A. (2005). The current state of cognitive therapy: A 40-year retrospective. *Archives of General Psychiatry, 62*(9), 953–959.

Beck, A., Grant, P., Huh, G., Perivoliotis, D., & Chang, N. (2013). Dysfunctional attitudes and expectations in deficit syndrome schizophrenia. *Schizophrenia Bulletin.* doi:10.1093/schbul/sbr040

Beck, A., Rush, A., Shaw, B., et al. (1979) *Cognitive therapy of depression.* New York, NY: Guilford Press.

Bennett-Levy, J., Wilson, S., Nelson, J., Stirling, J., Ryan, K., Rotumah, D., ... Beale, D. (2014). Can CBT be effective for aboriginal Australians? Perspectives of aboriginal practitioners trained in CBT. *Australian Psychologist, 49,* 1–7.

Bentall, R., Corcoran, R., Howard, R., Blackwood, N., & Kinderman, P. (2001). Persecutory delusions: A review and theoretical integration. *Clinical Psychology Review, 21,* 1143–1192.

Bernal, G., Bonilla, J., & Bellido, C. (1995). Ecological validity and cultural sensitivity for outcome research: Issues for the cultural adaptation and development of psychosocial treatments with Hispanics. *Journal of Abnormal Child Psychology, 23,* 67–82.

Bernal, G., & Domenech Rodríguez, M. M. (Eds.). (2012). *Cultural adaptations: Tools for evidence-based practice with diverse populations* (p. 307). Washington, DC: American Psychological Association.

Bhugra, D. (1997). Setting up psychiatric services: Cross-cultural issues in planning and delivery. *International Journal of Social Psychiatry, 43*(1), 16–28.

Blackburn, I. M., Twaddle, V., & Associates. (1996). *Cognitive therapy in action.* London, UK: Souvenir Press (E & A) Ltd.

Butler, A. C., Chapman, J. E., Forman, E. M., & Beck, A. T. (2006). The empirical status of cognitive-behavioral therapy: A review of meta-analyses. *Clinical Psychology Review, 26*(1), 17–31.

Byford, S., Barber, A., Fiander, M., Marshall, S., & Green, J. (2001). Factors that influence the cost of caring for patients with severe psychotic illness – Report from the UK 700 trial. *British Journal of Psychiatry, 178,* 441–447.

Carroll, K. M., Martino, S., Ball, S. A., Nich, C., Frankforter, T., Anez-Nava, L., ... Farentinos, C. (2009). A multisite randomized effectiveness trial of motivational enhancement therapy for Spanish-speaking substance users. *Journal of Consulting and Clinical Psychology, 77,* 993–999.

Carter, M. M., Sbrocco, T., Gore, K. L., Marin, N. W., & Lewis, E. L. (2003). Cognitive–behavioral group therapy versus a wait-list control in the treatment of African American women with panic disorder. *Cognitive Therapy and Research, 27,* 505–518.

Casas, J. M. (1988). Cognitive behavioral approaches: A minority perspective. *Counseling Psychologist, 16,* 106–110.

Castro, F., Barrera, M., Jr., & Holleran Steiker, L. K. (2010). Challenges in the design of culturally adapted evidence-based interventions. *Annual Review of Clinical Psychology, 6,* 213–239.

Castro, F., Barrera, M., Jr., & Martinez, R. (2004). The cultural adaptation of prevention interventions: Resolving tensions between fidelity and fit. *Prevention Science, 5,* 41–45.

Chambless, D. L., & Hollon, S. D. (1998). Defining empirically supported therapies. *Journal of Consulting and Clinical Psychology, 66*(1), 7–18.

Chambless, D. L., & Ollendick, T. H. (2001). Empirically supported psychological interventions: Controversies and evidence. *Annual Review of Psychology, 52*, 685–716.

Chao, M., Okazaki, S., & Hong, Y. (2011). The quest for multicultural competence: Challenges and lessons learned from clinical and organizational research. *Social and Personality Psychology Compass, 5*(5), 263–274.

Chen, J., Nakano, Y., Letzugu, T., Ogawa, S., Funayama, T., Watanabe, N., ... Furukawa, T. A. (2007). Group cognitive behaviour therapy for Japanese patients with social anxiety disorder: Preliminary outcomes and their predictors. *BMC Psychiatry, 7*, 69.

Clark, D. A., Beck, A. T., & Alford, B. A. (1999). *Scientific foundations of cognitive theory and therapy of depression.* New York, NY: John Wiley & Sons, Inc..

DeRubeis, R. J., Gelfand, L. A., Tang, T. Z., & Simons, A. A. (1999). Medications versus cognitive behaviour therapy for severely depressed outpatients: Mega-analysis of four randomized comparisons. *American Journal of Psychiatry, 156*(7), 1007–1013.

Dixon, L. B., Dickerson, F., Bellack, A. S., Bennett, M., Dickinson, D., Goldberg, R. W., Lehman, A., Tenhula, W. N., Calmes, C., Pasillas, R. M., Peer, J., & Kreyenbuhl, J.; Schizophrenia Patient Outcomes Research Team (PORT). (2010). The 2009 PORT psychosocial treatment recommendations and summary statements. *Schizophrenia Bulletin, 36*(1), 48–70.

Dobson, K. S. (2012). *Cognitive therapy.* Washington, DC: APA Books.

Domenech Rodríguez, M. M., & Weiling, E. (2004). Developing culturally appropriate, evidence-based treatments for interventions with ethnic minority populations. In M. Rastogin & E. Weiling (Eds.), *Voices of color: First person accounts of ethnic minority therapists* (pp. 313–333). Thousand Oaks, CA: Sage in Bernal, G., Jimenez-Chafey, M. I., & Domenech Rodríguez, M. M. (2009). Cultural adaptation of treatments: A resource for considering culture in evidence-based practice. *Professional Psychology: Research and Practice, 40*(4), 361–368. doi:10.1037/a0016401

Edgerton, R. (1966). Conceptions of psychosis in four East African societies. *American Anthropologist, 68*, 408–425.

Fernando, S. (1998). *Race and culture in psychiatry.* London, UK: Billing & Sons Ltd.

Frankish, C. J., Lovatto, C. Y., & Poureslami, I. (2007). Models, theories, and principles of health promotion. In M. V. Kline & R. M. Huff (Eds.), *Health promotion in multicultural populations: A handbook for practitioners and students* (2nd ed., pp. 57–101). Los Angeles, CA: Sage.

Friedman, E., Wright, J., Jarrett, R., & Thase, M. (2006). Combining cognitive therapy and medication for mood disorders. *Psychiatric Annals, 36*, 320–328.

Ghassemzadeh, H. (2007). The practice of cognitive-behaviour therapy in Roozbeh Hospital: Some cultural and clinical implications of psychological treatment in Iran. *American Journal of Psychotherapy, 61*(1), 53–69.

Grant, P. M., Huh, G. A., Perivoliotis, D., Stolar, N. M., & Beck, A. T. (2012). Randomised trial to evaluate the efficacy of cognitive therapy for low-functioning patients with schizophrenia. *Archives of General Psychiatry, 69*(2), 121–127.

Griner, D., & Smith, T. B. (2006). Culturally adapted mental health intervention: A meta-analytic review. *Psychotherapy: Theory, Research, Practice, Training, 43*(4), 531–548.

Hays, A. (1995). Multicultural applications of cognitive behaviour therapy. *Professional Psychology, 26*, 309–315.

Hays, P. (2014). An international perspective on the adaptation of CBT across cultures. *Australian Psychologist, 49*, 17–18.

Hays, P. A., & Iwamasa, G. Y. (2006). *Culturally responsive cognitive-behavioral therapy.* Washington, DC: American Psychological Association.

Hinton, D. E., Chhean, D., Pich, V., Safren, S. A., Hofmann, S. G., & Pollack, M. H. (2005). A randomized controlled trial of cognitive behavior therapy for Cambodian refugees with treatment-resistant PTSD and panic attacks: A cross-over design. *Journal of Traumatic Stress, 18,* 617–629.

Hinton, D. E., Pham, T., Tran, M., Safren, S. A., Otto, M. W., & Pollack, M. H. (2004). CBT for Vietnamese refugees with treatment-resistant PTSD and panic attacks: A pilot study. *Journal of Traumatic Stress, 17,* 429–433.

Hofmann, S., Asnaani, A., Vonk, I., Sawyer, A., & Fang, A. (2012). The efficacy of cognitive behavioral therapy: A review of meta-analyses. *Cognitive Therapy Research, 36*(5), 427–440.

Hole, R. W., Rush, A. J., & Beck, A. T. (1979). A cognitive investigation of schizophrenic delusions. *Psychiatry, 42,* 312–319.

Hollon, S., Jarrett, R., Nierenberg, A., Thase, M., Trivedi, M., & Rush, A. (2005). Psychotherapy and medication in the treatment of adult and geriatric depression: Which monotherapy or combined treatment? *Journal of Clinical Psychiatry, 66,* 455–468.

Huey, S., & Polo, A. (2008). Evidence-based psychosocial treatments for ethnic minority youth. *Journal of Clinical Child and Adolescent Psychology, 37* (1), 262–301.

Hussain-Gambles, M., Leese, B., Atkin, K., Brown, J., Mason, S., & Tovey, P. (2004). Involving South Asian patients in clinical trials. *Health Technology Assessment, 8*(42), 1–109.

Hutton, P., & Taylor, P. J. (2014) Cognitive behavioural therapy for psychosis prevention: A systematic review and meta-analysis. Psychological Medicine vol 44, pp 449–468.

Hwang, W., Wood, J. J., Lin, K., & Cheung, F. (2006). Cognitive behavioural therapy with Chinese Americans. Research, theory and clinical practice. *Cognitive and Behavioural Practice, 13,* 293–303.

Kaney S., & Bentall, P. (1989). Persecutory delusions and attributional style. *British Journal of Medical Psychology, 62,* 191–198.

Kingdon, D., & Turkington, D. (2005). *Cognitive therapy of schizophrenia.* New York, NY: Guilford Press.

Kohn, P., Oden, T., Munoz, F., Robinson, A., & Leavitt, D. (2002). Adapted cognitive behavioural group therapy for depressed low-income African American women. *Community Mental Health Journal, 38,* 497–504.

Kubany, E. S., Hill, E. E., & Owens, J. A. (2003). Cognitive trauma therapy for battered women with PTSD: Preliminary findings. *Journal of Traumatic Stress, 16,* 81–91.

Kumpfer, L., Pinyuchon, M., Melo, T., & Whiteside, O. (2008). Cultural adaptation process for international dissemination of the strengthening families program. *Evaluation & the Health Professions, 31,* 226–239.

Lam, D. H., Watkins, E. R., Hayward, P., Bright, J., Wright, K., Kerr, N., ... Sham, P. (2003). A randomized controlled study of cognitive therapy for relapse prevention for bipolar affective disorder: Outcome of the first year. *Archives of General Psychiatry, 60,* 145–152.

Lau, A. S. (2006). Making the case for selective and directed cultural adaptations of evidence-based treatments: Examples from parent training. *Clinical Psychology: Science and Practice, 13,* 295–310.

Leong, T., & Lee, H. (2006). A cultural accommodation model for cross cultural psychotherapy: Illustrated with the case of Asian American. *Psychotherapy, 43*(4), 410–423.

Lewis, A. (1965). Chairmans opening remarks, In A. V. S. De Rueck & R. Porter (Eds.), *Transcultural psychiatry* (pp. 1–3). London, UK: Churchill. From Fernando, S. (1991). *Mental health, race and culture*. Palgrave Macmillan. New York, NY: St. Martins.

Mason, B., & Sawyer, A. (2002). Introduction. In *Exploring the unsaid: Creativity, risks and dilemmas in working cross-culturally*. London, UK: Karnac.

McGoldrick, M., Giordano, J., & Garcia-Preto, N. (2005). *Ethnicity and family therapy*. New York, NY: Guilford Press.

McKleroy, S., Galbraith, S., Cummings, B., Jones, P., Harshbarger, C., Collins, C., ... ADAPT Team (2006). Adapting evidence-based behavioral interventions for new settings and target populations. *AIDS Education and Prevention, 18*(Suppl. A), 59–73.

Miranda, J., Bernal, G., Lau, A., Kohn, L., Hwang, W. C., & LaFromboise, T. (2005). State of the science on psychosocial interventions for ethnic minorities. *Annual Review of Clinical Psychology, 1*, 113–142.

Miranda, J., Chung, J. Y., Green, B. L., Krupnick, J., Siddique, J., Revicki, D. A., & Belin, T. (2003). Treating depression in predominantly low-income young minority women: A randomized controlled trial. *JAMA, 290*, 57–65.

Morrison, A., Turkington, D., Pyle, M., Spencer, H., Brabban, A., Dunn, G., ... Hutton, P. (2014). Cognitive therapy for people with schizophrenia spectrum disorders not taking antipsychotic drugs: A single-blind randomised controlled trial. *The Lancet, 383*(9926), 1395–1403. doi:10.1016/S0140-6736(13)62246-1

Muñoz, F., & Mendelson, T. (2005). Toward evidence-based interventions for diverse populations: The San Francisco General Hospital prevention and treatment manuals. *Journal of Consulting and Clinical Psychology, 73*(5), 790–799.

Naeem, F., Irfan, M., Zaidi, Q., Kingdon, D., & Ayub, M. (2008). Angry wives, abusive husbands: Relationship between domestic violence and psychosocial variables. *Women Health Issues, 18*(6), 453–462.

Naeem, F., Waheed, W., Gobbi, M., Ayub, M., & Kingdon, D. (2010). Preliminary evaluation of culturally sensitive CBT for depression in Pakistan: Findings from developing culturally sensitive CBT Project (DCCP). *Behavioural and Cognitive Psychotherapy, 39*(2), 165–173.

Nagel, T., Robinson, G., Condon, J., & Trauer, T. (2009). Approach to treatment of mental illness and substance dependence in remote indigenous communities: Results of a mixed methods study. *The Australian Journal of Rural Health, 17*(4), 174–182.

National Institutes of Health (NIH). (2001). *NIH policy and guidelines on the inclusion of women and minorities as subjects in clinical research*. Bethesda, MD: Author.

National Institute of Health and Care Excellence (2014, February). Psychosis and schizophrenia in adults: Treatment and management. Clinical guidelines, CG178. London, NICE.

Nuechterlein, K., & Dawson, M. E. (1984). A heuristic vulnerability-stress model of schizophrenia. *Schizophrenia Bulletin, 10*, 300–312.

Okasha, A., & Okasha, T. (2000). Notes on mental disorders in pharaonic Egypt. *History of Psychiatry, 11*, 413–424.

Organista, K. C., Muñoz, R. F., & González, G. (1994). Cognitive–behavioural therapy for depression in low-income and minority medical outpatients: Description of a program and exploratory analyses. *Cognitive Therapy and Research, 18*, 241–259.

Padesky, C. (1993, September). *Changing minds or guiding discovery*. European Congress of Behavioural & Cognitive Therapies, London, UK.

Padesky, C., & Greenberger, D. (1995). *Clinician's guide to mind over mood*. New York, NY: Guilford Press.

Patel, V., Araya, R., Chatterjee, S., Chisholm, D., Cohen, A., De Silva, M., … van Ommeren, M. (2007). Treatment and prevention of mental disorders in low-income and middle-income countries. *The Lancet, 370*, 991–1005.

Prince, R. (1964). Indigenous Yoruba psychiatry. In A. Kiev (ed.), *Magic, faith and healing.* New York, NY: Free Press.

Rahman, A., Malik, A., Sikander, S., Roberts, C., & Creed, F. (2008). Cognitive behaviour therapy based intervention by community health workers for mothers with depression and their infants in rural Pakistan: A cluster-randomised controlled trial. *The Lancet, 372*, 902–909.

Rathod, S., & Kingdon, D. (2009). Cognitive behaviour therapy across cultures. *Psychiatry, 8*(9), 370–371.

Rathod, S., Kingdon, D., Smith, P., & Turkington, D. (2005). Insight into schizophrenia: The effects of cognitive behavioral therapy on the components of insight and association with sociodemographics – data on a previously published randomised controlled trial. *Schizophrenia Research, 74*, 211–219.

Rathod, S., Naeem, F., Phiri, P., & Kingdon, D., (2008). Expansion of psychological therapies. *The British Journal of Psychiatry, 193*, 256.

Rathod S., Phiri, P., Harris, S., Underwood, C., Thagadur, M., Padmanabi, U., & Kingdon, D. (2013). Cognitive behaviour therapy for psychosis can be adapted for minority ethnic groups: A randomised controlled trial. *Schizophrenia Research, 143*(2–3), 319–326.

Rathod, S., Phiri, P., & Kingdon, D. (2010). Cognitive behaviour therapy for schizophrenia. *Psychiatric Clinics of North America, 33*(3), 527–536.

Rathod, S., Phiri, P., Kingdon, D., & Gobbi, M. (2010). Developing culturally sensitive cognitive behaviour therapy for psychosis for ethnic minority patients by exploration and incorporation of service users' and health professionals' views and opinions. *Behavioural and Cognitive Psychotherapy, 38*, 511–533.

Resnicow, K., Soler, R., Braithwait, L., Ahluwalia, S., & Butler, J. (2000). Cultural sensitivity in substance abuse prevention. *Journal of Community Psychology, 28*, 271–290.

Rojas, G., Fritsch, R., Solis, J., Jadresic, E., Castillo, C., González, M., … Araya, R. (2007). Treatment of postnatal depression in low-income mothers in primary-care clinics in Santiago, Chile: A randomised controlled trial. *The Lancet, 370*, 1629–1637.

Rosenthal, D., & Frank, J. (1958). The fate of psychiatric clinic outpatients assigned to psychotherapy. *Journal of Nervous and Mental disease, 127*, 330–343. From S. Fernando, (1991). *Mental health, race and culture.* Mind Publication, Macmillan Press.

Runz, A., & Casas, J. M. (1981). Culturally relevant and behavioristic counseling for Chicano college students. In P. Pedersen, J. Draguns, W. J. Longer, & J. Trimble (Eds.), *Counseling across cultures* (Rev. ed., p. 181e202). Honolulu, HI: East West Center.

Sabshin, M., Diesenhaus, H., & Wilkerson, R. (1970). Dimensions of institutional racism in psychiatry. *American Journal of Psychiatry, 127*, 787–793.

Schwarzbaum, S. E. (2004). Low-income Latinos and dropout: Strategies to prevent dropout. *Journal of Multicultural Counselling and Development, 32*, 296–306.

Scorzelli, J., & Scorzelli, M. R. (1994). Cultural sensitivity and cognitive therapy in India. *The Counselling Psychologist, 22*, 603–610.

Scott, J. (2006). Psychotherapy for bipolar disorders: Efficacy and effectiveness. *Journal of Psychopharmacology, 20*, 46–50.

Smith, T., Domenech Rodríguez, M. M., & Bernal, G. (2011). Culture. Journal of Clinical Psychology, 67, 166–175. doi: 10.1002/jclp.20757

Sobell, L. C. (1996). Bridging the gap between scientists and practitioners: The challenge before us. *Behavior Therapy, 27*, 297–320.

Sue, D. W., Carter, R. T., Casas, J. M., Fouad, N. A., Ivey, A. E., Jensen, M., … Vasquez-Nuttall, E. (1998). *Multicultural counselling competencies: Individual and organizational development.* Thousand Oaks, CA: Sage.

Sue, D. W., & Sue, D. (2003). *Counselling the culturally diverse: Theory and practice* (4th ed.). New York, NY: John Wiley & Sons, Inc..

Sue, S., Fujino, D. C., Hu, L., & Takeuchi, D. T. (1991). Community mental health services for ethnic minority groups: A test of the cultural responsiveness hypothesis. *Journal of Consulting and Clinical Psychology, 59*, 533–540.

Summerfield, D., & Veale, D. (2008). Proposals for massive expansion of psychological therapies would be counterproductive across society. *The British Journal of Psychiatry, 192*, 326–330.

Sweet, C. (2010). *Change your life with CBT.* Harlow, UK: Prentice Hall Life.

Thomas, A., & Sillen, S. (1972). *Racism and psychiatry.* New York, NY: Brunner/Mazel. From Fernando, S. (1991). *Mental health, race and culture.* Mind Publication, Macmillan Press.

Thornicroft, G., Davies, S., & Leese, M. (1999). Health service research and forensic psychiatry: A Black and White case. *International Review of Psychiatry, 11*(2/3), 250–257.

Tseng, W. S. (1999). Culture and psychotherapy: Review and practical guidelines. *Transcultural Psychiatry, 36*, 131–179.

Tseng, W.-S., Chang, S. C., & Nishjzono, M. (2005). *Asian culture and psychotherapy: Implications for East and West.* Honolulu, HI: University of Hawaii Press.

Turner, D., Gaag, M., Karyotaki, E., & Cuijpers, P. (2014). Psychological interventions for psychosis: A meta-analysis of comparative outcome studies. *American Journal of Psychiatry, 171*(5), 523–538. doi:10.1176/appi.ajp.2013.13081159

Voss, H. l., & Sarah, C. (2008). Effectiveness of cognitive–behavioral therapy with adult ethnic minority clients: A review. *Professional Psychology: Research and Practice, 39*(2), 160–168.

Wells, K., Klap, R., Koike, A., & Sherbourne, C. (2001). Ethnic disparities in unmet need for alcoholism, drug abuse, and mental health care. *American Journal of Psychiatry, 158*(12), 2027–2032.

Williams, W., Hean, K., & Beverly, H. (2006). Cultural considerations in using cognitive behaviour therapy with Chinese people: A case study of an elderly Chinese woman with generalized anxiety disorder. *New Zealand Journal of Psychology, 35*(3), 153–162.

Wills, F. (2012). Assessment and formulation in CBT. In W. Dryden & R. Branch (Eds.), *The CBT handbook.* London, UK: Sage.

Wingood, M., & DiClemente, J. (2008). The ADAPT-ITT Model: A novel method of adapting evidence-based HIV interventions. *Journal of Acquired Immune Deficiency Syndromes, 47*(Suppl. 1), S40–S46.

Wright, J. H., Turkington, D., Kingdon, D., & Basco, M. (2009). *Cognitive behaviour therapy for severe mental illness: An illustrated guide.* Washington, DC: American Psychiatric Publishing Inc.

Wykes, T., Steel, C., Everitt, B., & Tarrier, N. (2008). Cognitive behaviour therapy for schizophrenia: Effect sizes, clinical models, and methodological rigor. *Schizophrenia Bulletin, 34*(3), 523–537.

Zubin, J., & Spring, B. (1997). Vulnerability: A new view on schizophrenia. *Journal of Abnormal Psychology, 86*, 103–126.

3

Philosophical Orientation and Ethical and Service Considerations

We have described the model of adaptation of therapy that we have used and why we have chosen it for our work. Now, we expand on two of the four components of this developing model that were originally set out by Tseng, Chang, and Nishjzono (2005) – philosophical orientation and practical considerations. We will consider these concepts' broad applications and illustrate adaptations with examples. Again, you may want to directly get onto the clinical chapters of this book, but understanding the concepts presented here will serve to broaden your view and knowledge – as the therapist or clinician – of the different factors that come into play when interacting with clients from diverse cultural groups. The knowledge can then improve the quality of interaction with clients and their clinical outcomes. The other two components, that is, theoretical modification and technical adjustment, are discussed in detail in later chapters. You may find an element of repetition as we discuss the adaptation, but this is only because some themes remain common across the framework.

Philosophical Orientation: Differences in World View

The fundamental view of life differs between different cultures to a lesser or greater degree and affects everything from the perceptions of illness, relationships with professionals, and health services and treatment to styles and goals of therapy. Such views are both formed and influenced by the cultural influences on the individual. Similarly, whether a therapy such as CBT is suitable and acceptable once adapted is also heavily influenced by an individual's culture. We have already

Cultural Adaptation of CBT for Serious Mental Illness: A Guide for Training and Practice,
First Edition. Shanaya Rathod, David Kingdon, Narsimha Pinninti, Douglas Turkington, and Peter Phiri.
© 2015 John Wiley & Sons, Ltd. Published 2015 by John Wiley & Sons, Ltd.

noted when discussing the cognitive model how an individual's early experiences including culture influence their philosophical orientation and thus core beliefs and assumptions. In addition, one's philosophical orientation can influence maintaining factors of an individual's assumptions and negative automatic thoughts and behaviours. Hence, therapists can benefit from having an understanding of differences and similarities in world view across different cultural groups and how the dynamic nature of culture can impact on an individual's thoughts and behaviours. We will discuss the impact of philosophical orientation of clients in relation to:

1. Level of acculturation
2. Beliefs and attributions to illness
3. Help-seeking behaviours and pathways into care
4. Cultural orientation towards psychotherapy

Acculturation

In the case of populations and individuals who have migrated to a new environment, understanding of their native cultural beliefs is a good beginning but is usually not adequate. This is because immigrants undergo a process of adaptation called 'acculturation.' A merging of the original cultural values and attitudes occurs during the period of prolonged contact with the host culture after immigration. Due to this interaction, there is an inevitable modification of the individuals' attitudes and behaviours. This culture-shifting process is not an abrupt event, and the time period is variable for each individual. There tends to be a gradual blending of the two cultures (Garcia & Zea, 1997), that is, the culture of the host country and that of their original native country, and sometimes, this continues over several generations.

The process of acculturation can be understood as occurring in four ways: integration, assimilation, separation, and marginalization. These describe different attitudes of individuals towards acculturation and influence behaviours of individuals when interacting with others (Berry, 2005):

Integration occurs when an immigrant identifies and involves themselves with both cultures.
Assimilation refers to the situation where an immigrant chooses to identify solely with the new culture.
Separation is the process where an immigrant prefers to be involved with the traditional native culture.
Marginalization is characterized by lack of involvement and rejection of both cultures.

It is common for an individual to adopt a mixture of different attitudes in different phases of life, through the influences of positive and negative life experiences/

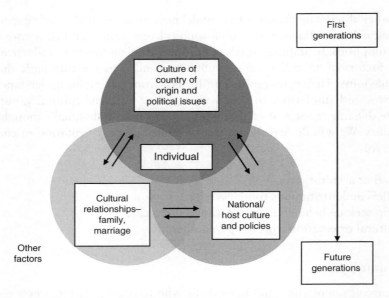

Figure 3.1   Oscillation of an individual's cultural values. Adapted from Rathod and Kingdon (2009). © 2009 Elsevier Ltd 'Printed with permission.'

stressors and through the influence of environmental factors. In addition, the same individual may choose assimilation in one role such as at work but a different role such as separation in social circumstances. Different generations of immigrants may differ in their choices regarding acculturation. Older generations may be more likely to choose separation, while younger generations are more likely to become integrated or assimilated. Different choices can cause intergenerational conflicts around the issue of perceived cultural betrayal (Felix-Ortiz, Fernandez, & Newcomb, 1998) and influence the choice of treatments. Cultural betrayal becomes an issue where an individual – often a parent when the conflict is intergenerational – feels that the other is betraying their cultural values. While the process of acculturation usually helps immigrants to cope and adjust, it may not always have a positive impact, for example, increasing levels of acculturation among Latinos have been associated with higher rates of depression, drug use, adolescent pregnancy, and mortality (Clark & Hofsess, 1998).

Many integrated bicultural individuals learn the essential components of the majority (host) culture in order to adapt successfully, but they may also need to hold on to their culture of origin in order to maintain contact with that community and can use its traditions and practices as a coping resource. Therefore, the culture of origin is often maintained but in such a way that it coexists with influences from the host culture (Felix-Ortiz et al., 1998; Gurnaccia & Roaiouaz, 1996; Melville, 1983). Figure 3.1 explains how for many individuals two or three cultural contexts can coexist, namely, the culture of their country of origin, a local host country-based community culture, and the wider host country-based societal culture. Different attitudes, practices, and attributions may come into play at different times. An individual's values can oscillate between the cultures depending on circumstances, conflict, or dissonance at relational interfaces – between them. Generally with successive generations, the individual's values tend to adapt to their country of residence. Family practices, for example, arranged marriage in some South Asian second-/third-generation Muslim men and women with partners from their country of origin, may reinforce deep-rooted value systems from the original culture and continue to have an impact on new generations.

Many external factors impact on the process of acculturation. Some of these include public health and national immigration policies that impact on cultural integration and the extent of people's acculturation. Other factors include economic factors, support systems in the host country, and reasons for immigration, for example, voluntary or involuntary.

In the example below, we describe Ramani from Sri Lanka who was able to adjust to the effects of migration from her country of origin under normal circumstances but presented with 'separation' when under stress.

Case example

Ramani, a 47-year-old female immigrant from Sri Lanka, lived in Toronto, Canada, with her husband, two daughters, and son. The family had emigrated from Sri Lanka 8 years ago, but her husband had struggled to support the family financially over the last couple of years due to the wider economic conditions. Ramani had adjusted extremely well since her move and managed her home within available resources. She had made friends in the neighbourhood and attended English language classes.

The financial pressures on the family had however increased in those 2 years, and her daughters had become of marriageable age which would require money. Ramani had started presenting to the physician regularly with somatic symptoms like headaches, episodic dizziness, and breathlessness. However, all physical investigations were normal. It was difficult to reassure her, and over time, she lost motivation and started spending most of her time in bed. At her last appointment with her physician, she told him that she wanted 'Sanni Yakuma' (a Sinhalese exorcism ritual) as she believed that demons were affecting her and making her unwell. The physician recommended a psychiatric evaluation.

While Ramani had become depressed, her beliefs regarding demons were reaffirmed. These beliefs were embedded in a traditional Sri Lankan belief that the Sanni Yakuma ritual summons the demons and banishes them back to their world. According to this belief, 18 demons originated during the time of Buddha, who tamed them.

Case discussion

Ramani's attitude towards her symptoms demonstrates the oscillation in the acculturation process. Normally, she had been well adjusted in the host environment and was integrating; but when stressed, she demonstrated 'separation,' a return to resorting to traditional help. Attitudes towards illness and help-seeking pathways are influenced by the level of acculturation that oscillates in relation to circumstances.

In well-integrated individuals, illness can swing beliefs towards cultural influences that hold traditional beliefs especially where cultures are strongly bonded. The oscillation of beliefs can happen even in those individuals who normally do not practise traditional religious and cultural rituals. Due to cultural and family influence, it can become acceptable to seek help from elders, priests, or traditional healers rather than mainstream health services. Help givers are generally figures of authority and have paternalistic attitudes. It is seen among some Indian immigrants (South Asian background from India) that they typically turn to families for help in case of problems. They visit temples and religious leaders as a first step (Avasthi, 2011).

The example of Shobha below illustrates how parents can be a source of tremendous support for some families. The extent of the support varies in cultures and can range from taking care of the house and children to sometimes raising the grandchildren and on occasion making treatment decisions.

Case example

Shobha, a 28-year-old Hindu woman from the south of India, presented to an outpatient clinic with a history of new-onset psychosis, 4 months after arriving in the United States. Originally in India, she belonged to an extended family who lived closely together, worked, and contributed to household chores. She had an arranged marriage. Within 3 months of her marriage, she migrated to the United States. In the United States, she had no job. She was alone at home, while her husband worked. In the United States, she found her home as 'empty,' a stark contrast from her previous home in India which had housed three generations of family. Alongside all this was the unfamiliarity of her environment causing her distress.

Slowly, she became withdrawn from interacting with both strangers and family members and in time also stopped talking to her husband.

Her husband reported that she had resorted to various odd gestures during conversations and on occasion smiled and laughed when others were not around. Her self-care had deteriorated and she had not been sleeping or eating properly. At the psychiatrist's recommendation, the couple agreed to try low-dose antipsychotic medication, but, by the next visit, they informed the clinician that they had stopped treatment. Shobha's parents had arrived from India to support her, and they had convinced her not to take medication. Within 4 weeks, they left for India with Shobha, and 6 months later, her husband called to inform the clinician that his wife was stable off medication and doing well with her family in India. She had plans to return in the future with her mother who was going to stay with them.

Case discussion

In Shobha's case, she had not had enough time to integrate after immigration. There were a number of stressors in her life that included immigration, loss of family support, and the absence of a job. Onset of symptoms (or relapse) led her parents to make a trip to the United States to be with her. Their visit led Shobha to disengage from mainstream mental health treatment and stop taking medication. On the other hand, the family support mitigated the psychosocial stressors to a significant extent so that she was able to stabilize and the couple felt supported. We often work with clients who present in this way. The issue is not about what '*she should have done*' but how the level of acculturation has impacted on her behaviour.

Exercise: Consider the level of acculturation of a client you are working with and how this impacts on their presentation and engagement. How does this analysis inform your formulation?

Health beliefs and attributions to mental illness

Culture and the level of acculturation influence health beliefs and attributions to mental illness in people. Personal and cultural background influences insight into psychiatric illness, and societal views of mental illness and disability are equally important (Blackwell, 1976). For any type of illness, be it physical or emotional, there are likely to be an immediate cause and a more distant one (Mayr, 1961). Science is more focused on immediate or proximal causes, while culture and religion attempt to explain the future or the distal causes. In mental illness and indeed sometimes in physical illness, people can simultaneously hold apparently conflicting beliefs about what caused their illness. However, when we look closely, some of them may hold differing views of immediate and distal causes. For example, failure in an exam may be considered an immediate or proximate cause of depression, but a sin in prior life and consequent retribution may be considered to be the distant cause of failure. As a result, an individual may take medication for depression and could also seek help from a priest to pray and expiate sins from prior life. Indeed, many patients will comply with treatment while not regarding themselves as ill (McEvoy, Aland, Wilson, Guy, & Hawkins, 1981; McPherson, Double, Harrison, & Rowlands, 1993). An understanding of how an individual views illness therefore helps in effective engagement and recommending treatment options in a way that they are more likely to be accepted.

Traditions and cultural beliefs influence presentations of illnesses which can determine pathways into care. It is common in many Chinese, Japanese, Malayan, Tahitian, and other cultural groups to somatize their symptoms to different body parts, for example, abdomen, liver, intestines, or heart. The reason for this is that somatic symptoms are explained through a perceived imbalance in body functions and are considered less stigmatizing than psychiatric symptoms. Secondly, the dichotomization of the body and mind is a characteristic of Western culture, and many people from Eastern cultures are used to manifesting and communicating their problems through their bodies even though the problems are psychological (Tseng et al., 2005). Furthermore, Chinese and other minority groups who somatize are likely to see a primary care physician for their symptoms as opposed to approaching psychological or mental health services. Somatization may also be viewed and understood as an expression of distress in cultures where the norm is stress conformity and verbal expressiveness is discouraged (Lee, 1997).

A number of culture-bound syndromes provide further examples of the prominence of somatic attribution. Taijin kyofusho presents with intense fear that one's body, its parts, or its functions displease, embarrass, or are offensive to other people in appearance, odour, or facial expressions. These symptoms are essentially manifestations of social anxiety. In Koreans, hwa-byung presents as a broad range of physical symptoms like lasting anger, disappointments, sadness, miseries, grudges, and unfulfilled dreams and expectations that are associated with multiple causes. In West Africans, brain fag manifests as difficulties in concentrating, remembering, and thinking, and the person complains of 'fatigued' brain with pain or pressure in the head and neck with blurred vision and burning sensations.

Case example

Lin, a 26-year-old woman of Chinese origin, migrated to the United States following her marriage. Within 3 months of her arrival, she had multiple presentations to hospital with somatic symptoms, predominantly tiredness, headaches, back and chest pain with sleeplessness, and hopelessness. Despite a number of investigations, no physical cause was found. She herself attributed her symptoms to energy imbalances or 'hot intestine.' Despite a number of attempts being made, she was unwilling to accept assessment by psychiatric services. Eventually, her husband convinced her to see a 'specialist' to rule out 'neurasthenia.' She agreed to this as this is a diagnosis widely offered by traditional herbalists in China.

Case discussion

One of the strong threads running through Chinese culture is a holistic view of health and illness, as demonstrated in traditional Chinese medical practice. This view focuses primarily on the body's functions rather than its anatomy: the balance and imbalance of functions determining health and illness. For many clients of Chinese heritage, mental illnesses are associated with shame and stigma, whereas physical illness or complaints are more socially acceptable. Thus, depression and other mental illnesses often manifest themselves in somatic symptoms rather than in mood, lethargy, or other emotional or psychological symptoms as described earlier. Kleinman (1982) reported that psychological symptoms of depression were attributed to neurasthenia (meaning weakening of nerves) and higher rates of somatization have been reported among patients with emotional disorders in Chinese society (Kleinman, 1977). The Chinese Classification of Mental Disorders-2R, which is largely based on ICD-10, excludes almost all the somatoform disorders, so that particular prominence can be given to the category of neurasthenia, which is one of the most frequent diagnoses in Chinese psychiatry (Gelder, Harrison, & Cowen, 2006), thereby demonstrating the local adaptation of the classification system to incorporate cultural attributions to illness.

A qualitative study on attributions to psychosis (McCabe & Priebe, 2004) concluded that biological explanations were much more frequently cited by Caucasians than African Caribbean and West Africans. Al-Krenawi, Graham, and Kandah (2000) reported that Israeli subjects in their study gave more diverse

Table 3.1   Attributions of mental illness by ethnicity.

Theme: Causation	African Caribbean	Bangladeshi	Pakistani
Previous wrongdoing	+++++	+++++	+++++
Supernatural beliefs	+++++	+++++	+++++
Social factors	++++	++++	++++
Biological	+++	+++	+++
Being arrested	+++		
Drug induced	+++		

From Rathod et al. (2010). Reproduced with permission from Cambridge University Press.

explanations of mental health aetiologies including citing physical, family, divorce, and economic causes including unemployment, whereas Jordanians tended to emphasize divine and spiritual sources. The differences in attributions to mental illness and their consequences could explain why patients from some cultures would not want to accept the concept of mental illness and would rather seek help from traditional healers. Our group (Rathod, Phiri, Kingdon, & Gobbi, 2010) gathered data that was shared and triangulated between clients, lay participants from minority communities, therapists, and mental health practitioners. The following explanations and table 3.1 show the emergent themes in order of strength of belief relating to the participant's explanatory models and attributions to mental illness, in particular psychosis. This data was confined to two ethnic minority groups, namely, South Asian Muslims and African Caribbean/black African participants from the study (Table 3.1).

In the following section, we will discuss and explain the relevance of the different attributions and how an understanding of the differences can improve the therapist's ability to adapt their stance in therapy.

Previous wrongdoing, superstition, and supernatural causes

Belief in superstitions is universal, and many cultures share beliefs in supernatural causes of mental illness. Cultural beliefs in the supernatural can be common and range from widely practised customs which have no impact on health and well-being to those that influence attributions of illness and thereby influence individuals in following appropriate help-seeking pathways. A widely practised superstitious custom by Caucasians involves the expression 'touch wood' followed by the behaviour of touching an object or item made of wood. The 'evil eye' appears in translations of the Old Testament and is a widely prevalent belief among Mediterranean cultures. The casting of an evil eye is called 'nazar lagna' by South Asian Muslims, 'malocchio' in Italy, 'obeah' by the Afro-Caribbean, 'mati' in Greece, 'ojear' in South America, 'mau olhado' in Portugal, 'Eye of Horus' in Egypt, and 'mal de ojo' in Spain as examples. In some cultures, spells and curses are associated with special community days, like emancipation from slavery in the Caribbean. In Seenigama Devale, a shrine in Sri Lanka, Devol is the local God who is believed to have magical powers and is capable of placing curses on adversaries. People all over the country are drawn to the temple where they grind chillies on a special stone as the curse is made.

Cultures have practices to mitigate the effects of their attributions. For example, in cultures that attribute illness to harm from the evil eye or envy of others, a number of protective measures are used like talismans are worn by some in Muslim cultures; blue turquoise beads in necklaces by Assyrians; spitting on the ground in Ethiopia and over the shoulder in China; an amulet bracelet in Mexico and Central America; eye charms in Greece; horn-shaped charms in Italy; hamsa in Jews; lemon and chillies in some Hindu cultures; and masks at the entrance of houses in Sri Lanka and in some traditional Chinese homes.

Illness can be attributed to previous wrongdoing, the evil eye, or 'Jinn(s)' and ghosts which in some South Asian Muslim communities are defined as 'evil spirits, demons, magic curses or spells' cast by someone who is 'jealous' of them. Similarly, beliefs in the spirits of ancestors and ghosts are found in some South Asian Hindu communities. Some cultures in Mexico, for example, Sal si Puedes, believe in witches, evil spirits, and other supernatural forces. Similarly, usog is believed to be a psychological disorder attributed to a greeting by a stranger who casts an evil eye in the Philippines. Among the Sakalava of northwest Madagascar, spirit possession and madness occupy opposing poles on a spectrum of experiences, ranging from a good, powerful, and inescapable state to a destructive, dangerous, and frightening illness (Sharp, 1994). In Latin America, particularly Brazil, the spiritist theory plays an important role in explaining the aetiology of mental disorders. The spiritist theory supports the survival of the spirit after death with an exchange of knowledge between the incarnate and disincarnate spirits. The spiritist aetiologic model for mental disorders therefore includes the negative influences of disincarnate spirits (termed 'obsession') or trauma experienced in previous lives (Moreira-Almeida & Neto, 2005). The theory is embraced by the general public and health-care professionals alike although belief in the spiritist theory does not discard organic causes of mental disorders.

Therefore, although superstition and belief in supernatural are universal, the context and mitigating rituals may vary among cultures and subcultures. Not only do these beliefs and customs influence assumptions and automatic thoughts (using the cognitive model), the cultural mitigating factors can influence behaviours of individuals. The knowledge of universality of superstitions and supernatural attributions of illness can help in engaging clients and can be used by therapists when using normalization techniques.

Exercise: Reflect on your own superstitious beliefs, their underlying meanings, and how they influence your behaviours.

Case example

Matheus, a 26-year-old immigrant to the United Kingdom from Brazil, first came to the attention of the psychiatric services when his work colleagues contacted his general practitioner and expressed concern about some of the content of his conversations. He worked as an information analyst in a big company. Lately, he had become increasingly stressed at work due to workload pressures and the threat of further redundancies in the company. He had been spending longer hours at work to complete his tasks, and some of his colleagues had noticed that he had become 'obsessional' about getting things right. On further exploration, he revealed that he had not been sleeping at night and explained that 'the persecution exerted by discarnate spirits upon the incarnate spirits' was the cause for his distress. He spoke about the 'spirit transmitting harmful messages to his body.' He asked to consult a spirit protector via a medium.

Matheus accepted a small dose of medication and started attending therapy sessions. The therapy sessions did not proceed as planned, and Matheus stopped attending. However, his mental state improved with the medication, and he returned back to work. At a later date, his psychiatrist explored the reason for his disengagement from therapy. He explained that the therapist spent majority of his time trying to work with him on his beliefs and could not understand that it was common in his culture to attend a spiritist centre for treatment, often in addition to seeking help from a doctor.

Case discussion

Superstitions and belief in supernatural causes of illness are important to understand as they have a bearing on engagement and help-seeking pathways. A therapist who can understand these attributions based on differences in world view can explain the universality of the beliefs in different cultures, thereby making the client feel heard and accepted. As discussed earlier, it can also help when using normalization techniques. In the example of Matheus, the therapist would have benefitted from recognizing and accepting the culturally determined attributions to illness and therefore help-seeking pathways.

Case example

Neeta, a 22-year-old Hindu girl in the United Kingdom, suffered with delusions of persecution and auditory hallucinations of her deceased grandmother's voice and would communicate with the voice. Neeta could not be there for her grandmother's funeral and had strong feelings of guilt associated with that. Neeta interpreted this voice as coming from her grandmother's spirit. This young girl was advised by a member of her community that *'your grandma's spirit is not comfortable because she loved you and she has come to haunt you in England. So you need to go to India and visit her grave to put her spirit to rest – then you will be fine.'* In her psychiatric consultation, she sought permission to go to India. She was very ambivalent about her treatment and had not been compliant with her medication for some time. The clinician was able to negotiate an escorted trip to India with family on the basis that Neeta was fully compliant with treatment for 6 months. Her mental state improved, and although she did visit India after 6 months, she was not suffering with delusions of persecution anymore. On return from India, she started therapy, and the therapist was able to explore her beliefs about spirits and ghosts. Initially, she was guarded about her views, but when the therapist normalized her belief and explained that it was common in a number of cultures like Chinese and some African Caribbean cultures to believe in spirits of ancestors, she felt comfortable and started talking about her beliefs. She completed therapy successfully.

Case discussion

In this example, we see attributions of some symptoms of illness (voices) to the spirit of grandmother, while the persecutory delusions were more accepted as illness for which Neeta was willing to consider medication. The attributions of symptoms to spirits caused her to be ambivalent about medication. The therapist with his understanding of the culture was able to normalize her belief, engage his client in therapy, and successfully complete therapy.

Case example

Aida, a 26-year-old woman of Nigerian descent, was raised by her grandmother in Nigeria until age 16 when she migrated to the United Kingdom to live with her aunt. From a very young age, she aspired to be a singer and practised at the church choir regularly. According to tradition, when baptized at 14 years of age, she was meant to start serving the Lord, but instead she had been going to parties with friends and enjoying herself. She started smoking cannabis from age 15 onwards. At age 25, she had been in an abusive relationship for 2 years. When this relationship ended, she started hearing the voices of her ancestors, as she described them, telling her '*you will serve the Lord.*' She started reading the Bible, was fasting for long periods of time, and was ministering to the Bible on the bus.

Her treating psychiatric team appreciated the importance to her of her religious beliefs and agreed that many people pray and get comfort from their religious practice. She explained that she was not religious but her ancestors sent messages from a tree near her residence and she understood it as '*read the word*' when the branches tilted in a certain direction. She therefore stayed on the bus, reading the Bible until she received another message to stop, often after several hours of being on the bus. She explained that she needed permission to eat and therefore fasted for long periods, sometimes needing hospital admission.

Aida agreed that her quality of life could be better but refused to believe that she was mentally unwell or needed treatment. At best, she was willing to attend a session with a 'Yoruba healer.' Her reasoning was that she was being punished or was under a voodoo spell.

Case discussion

We have discussed earlier, it is common in some African cultures to believe in ghosts of ancestors residing in trees and protecting or punishing as appropriate. Traditional faith healers are preferred over psychiatric services. Aida's symptoms and help-seeking behaviours were influenced by her cultural beliefs and tradition. This knowledge is helpful when engaging clients and working on compliance with medication in her case. We have discussed her formulation in the appendix 2.

Social factors
Attribution of illness to social factors is a consistent theme across many cultural groups, although the strength of the belief varies. Social inequalities, stigma, and family stresses are often significant contributory factors in the manifestation of psychological symptoms and pathways into care that are chosen. Individuals living in poverty or socially deprived environments are vulnerable. Social isolation can be an important contributing factor that may be brought about by migration

from country of origin or through internal movement within a country. Stressors related to immigration or movement can be described on the usual timeline of immigration (see Appendix 1) and include:

1. Pre-immigration stressors
2. Stressors associated with process of immigration
3. Post-immigration stressors

The pre-immigration stressors can include exposure to different types of trauma (war, torture, natural disasters, terrorism, etc.), often threat to life and liberty. The process of immigration itself can be very traumatic for many people including the stress of getting documentation to legally arrive in a country, enormous expense, and sometimes having to come in illegally.

The post-immigration stressors include loss of family and support networks, loss of status, living in run-down and often crime-infested areas, discrimination, and racism (Pumariega, 2003). Perceived discrimination post-immigration has been associated with psychosis (Veling et al., 2007). A common Jamaican belief is that individuals who migrate to the United Kingdom would acquire a mental illness. The attribution is understandable against the backdrop of social difficulties and isolation often faced by some immigrant populations especially from lower socio-economic groups. This leads to stress, which is often a precipitating and maintaining factor in mental illness. The following case examples illustrate the impact of immigration.

Case example

A judge in a country in the Middle East decided to immigrate to the United States following the murder of his two children by the military of the country. Once in the United States, he was granted asylum but did not have any marketable skill set and ended up working in restaurant as a waiter. He had not only lost his children but also his position, his standard of living, and the extended family network and support system in country of origin and had become a 'nobody' leading to subsequent depressive symptoms.

Case example

Matwa, a 24-year-old immigrant from Kenya, came to the United States to do a master's degree in computer science. He was offered a teaching assistantship to partially support his tuition. After the first semester, a budget cut coupled with poor grading of his performance led to his tuition support being withdrawn. Matwa had to deal with a number of stressors since immigrating to the United States including losing all the family support he had in Kenya, had to adapt to a new system of education, and had to cook and fend for himself for the first time in his life. He was the only one from the African diaspora in his class and could not completely trust anyone. The financial difficulty was the final straw, and he became acutely psychotic. He presented with persecutory beliefs that two professors in the faculty along with the dean conspired to prevent him from graduating. He acted on his beliefs and confronted a professor and verbally threatened him. This led to him being suspended, and his delusions were further reinforced.

Case discussion

Immigration, either voluntary or involuntary, is associated with significant stressors. In the first example, the judge had difficulty in adjusting to a different lifestyle which was not what he was used to. In the instance of Matwa, he had to deal with a number of post-immigration stressors that made him vulnerable to psychosis. His difficulty in trusting people translated into persecutory delusions involving two of his professors and the dean.

In some cultures, stigma is more pronounced than in others and may even have tacit state support. Although stigma against mental illness is a universal phenomenon, it can differentially influence health beliefs and attributions to illness. In the past, and in some cultures even in the present day, it often seems that mentally ill people have taken the place of lepers as targets of public disgust and rejection (Lewis, 1934). People are more likely to deny mental illness if they come from a social group in which it is highly stigmatized. For this reason, sometimes even within similar cultures, concepts of mental illness may vary. For example, among four very similar rural East African societies, the concept of mental illness differs considerably. In one community, 60% of people interviewed believed that psychosis was caused by witchcraft compared with only 1% in another. While, in some, none believed that psychosis was an illness, in another, two-thirds said it was an illness caused by a worm in the front of the brain accompanied by stress. Interestingly, those communities which believed that illness is caused by witchcraft also believed it was curable and pursued a policy of treatment and care, while those who believed in an underlying organic cause tended to leave the patient to starve and beat them (Edgerton, 1966). For similar reasons, diagnosis among the Ganda in East Africa is negotiable – mentally ill or eccentric. Mentally ill would mean a divine punishment as one of their proverb suggests 'a Lubaale punishes with reason.'

The level of stigma can vary depending on gender due to consequences of mental illness on prospect for marriage. For instance, in many South Asian Muslim communities, mental illness among women is far more stigmatizing than in men. If daughters develop a mental illness, parents worry about their marriage; if they are married, there is a worry that their husbands will divorce them. Their plight is then compounded as future prospects can seem dim. The term 'pagal' – meaning 'mad' – is often used in a derogatory sense in these cases.

Attributions to mental illness may vary even among cultures where the perceived stigma is reducing and evidence-based treatments are sought. Perceptions of patients in psychiatric hospitals and non-patients seem to differ in Germany and the United States (Townsend, 1975). The German view of mental illness is that mental illness is inherited, enduring, and difficult to cure and not influenced by personal effort. Americans saw it as transient and a result of difficult circumstances. The German patients were more likely than those in the American group to deny being mentally ill and were less optimistic about the prognosis. In another study, lay beliefs about schizophrenia were studied by population survey in Germany (Angermeyer & Matschinger, 1994). In the order of frequency, psychosocial stresses, biological factors like brain disease, intrapsychic factors like lack of will power and too much ambition, influence of socialization like broken homes, and, finally, state of society and supernatural powers were the attributions made. There was no observed association with age, sex, or level of education. There was also a major preference of the public for psychotherapy as opposed to treatment with psychotropic drugs. Hispanic patients attributed the causes of depression to social pressures and life circumstances rather than to internal mechanisms related to biological, genetic, or chemical factors (Cabassa, Lester, & Zayas, 2007).

An understanding of social circumstances and attributions of illness to social factors can be helpful to the therapist in understanding the precipitating and maintaining factors and underlying concerns for the client. The therapist can use this understanding with the client in developing the formulation and discussion of coping strategies, confidence building, and techniques like reality testing, seeking alternative explanations, and challenging negative automatic thoughts.

Biological explanations

Attribution of illness to biological factors and the impact of genetics are recognized in all cultures, although the strength of this attribution varies and often may be an explanation in addition to others. We have discussed this in our example of Matheus who attributed his illness on the spiritist theory but also accepted biological explanations.

Below is an explanation from a participant (in our qualitative study) regarding his own understanding and attribution to his illness:

> I am trying to explain to you that I am not mentally unwell – I was unbalanced – break it down: disease means dis – ease, your body is at dis – ease you are not at ease you have to balance your mind.

Biological differences between races, such as the levels of various enzymes that metabolize medication differently, have been documented, but discussion in an objective manner can be difficult as it ties into the concerns that some races are discriminated against. Therapists would benefit from an awareness of differences where they occur in the biological make-up of certain races that either predisposes them for more side effects or on the contrary affords them protection against certain illnesses and offer a better response to certain medications. For example, Asian Americans have been shown to respond to lower levels of Naltrexone (Ray, Bujarski, Chin, & Miotto, 2010). If physicians are not aware of these differences, they can end up prescribing inappropriate doses of medication that would cause side effects and lead to premature treatment termination.

Being arrested and drug induced

These were two attributions that emerged from our study (Rathod et al., 2010) and were specific to the African Caribbean and black African groups. The participants echoed a belief that mental illness could be caused by a series of events that caused misunderstandings with the police which then resulted in an arrest. One of the explanations was use of body language which was misinterpreted as aggressive and use of language like Patois (Patwa or Patwah or Jamaican Creole) which was misinterpreted by police and professionals as thought disorder. Below are quotes from participants that illustrate misunderstandings through use of Patois and the accompanying physical expressions, particularly when someone is angry or emotional:

> I have heard of cases where people haven't been suffering from mental illness…They don't have a mental illness at all. But the police have arrested them and they have been loud and moody. They were waving their hands, shouting and began to speak in the Patois. Because when somebody gets angry their normal slow way of speaking English that is heard and understood goes out of the window. Especially when they feel that they are being wronged.

The participant then describes how the person's body language and mannerisms change as they shout and the consequences of this change:

> What are you arresting me for, what you want with me? The police officer doesn't understand your language because this person was speaking English before. But now it sounds like it is not English. Because it is Patois {respondent is waving hands in the air} or it is a mixture of French-or…something else…they are misunderstood. They are shouting. They are yelling. They are waving their hands about, they get arrested. And before you can say two words somebody has pumped them with some sort of drug… Because they didn't have an illness, certainly now they have got one.

A different participant discusses not only the effect of use of Patois but also the reaction caused by an injection:

> I am talking about somebody who has been diagnosed as being a psychotic...because he has been arrested by the police – he struggled. And he has just gone. And his brain has gone and he is just bubbling out. And he is talking in Patois and nobody understands him and he has gone and he is really mad now. He is given an injection. Then his body is having a chemical reaction to the injection. And really and truly that is, that person is psychotic. So how do you then find the cause there? What do you say? Do you then say the police caused it?

While the attribution is to the event, that is, the arrest and the emotions associated with it, there are many possible explanations of it. For example, it is possible that the person had been stressed and had early signs of illness that were not recognized and the incident with the police highlighted the symptoms. It is also possible that the stressful event with the police acted as a trigger for symptoms. We also discuss this later in help-seeking pathways into care.

The attribution to drugs was again a theme that echoed within the African Caribbean group in our study (Rathod et al., 2010). There was an acknowledgement of common use in certain villages in their host countries and the possibility of indirect inhalation of cannabis by minors, suggesting likelihood of vulnerability to future use and subsequent links with drug-induced psychosis later in life. Below are some quotes from participants that demonstrate the point:

> ...and therefore people will never understand that a six year old child will have drug induced psychosis. It is drug induced because it is a ritual for the father to sit in a little circle at home and smoke and blow (cannabis) in the child's face and the child is inhaling it.

> ...with drug induced psychosis...people tend to think it is always voluntary. ...You have the Rastafarians, because the Rastafarians thinks that using the ganja, marijuana...makes you intelligent and brilliant. You have the father he has his chilon pipe in the house and he smokes it ever so often and the child inhales it. So it is both from inhalation and the fact that the child has a little cold on his chest, they don't give the child cough medicine. Instead, they give the child the ganja to drink. So from a very tiny age the child has been exposed both to inhalation and for medicinal purposes. And it blows out of proportion from there...

> **Exercise:** Think of a client you are working with and identify their attributions to their symptoms. How does this impact on their engagement in therapy? Now that you understand the impact of attributions better, how would you change your stance?

Given the various attributions to mental illness in different cultures, there is a need for greater sensitivity in approaching and managing cultural issues in therapy. The view is supported by the strategy known as 'black psychology' devised by black professionals in the United States (Fernando, 1991). Black psychology is defined by Baldwin (1986) as the uncovering, articulation, operationalization, and application of the principles of the African reality structure relative to psychological phenomena (Belgrave & Allison, 2006). Americans have also pioneered the notion of the 'cultural broker.' The cultural broker is a member of the minority group who works with mental health professionals and who is able to assist in interpreting attributions and mediate between lay groups and biomedical practitioners particularly in the area of family therapy. If psychotherapy is a new experience for a particular group, the practice offered is based on appropriate existing models like clergy and traditional healer (Littlewood & Lipsedge, 1978). The brokering system of intervention is aimed at achieving better engagement of clients from minority groups. Some specific centres have been developed to engage clients from minority cultures such as the Nafsiyat Intercultural Centre in London where African Caribbean clients showed good participation rates (Acharya, Moorhouse, Kareem, & Littlewood, 1989).

However, a few scattered centres are not sufficient to combat the widespread disparities in access to care for minority cultures. The best way to address these inequalities is by a robust public health policy requiring cultural sensitivity training and adaptation of services to meet the needs of the diverse communities they service. Despite a number of initiatives to combat inequalities in access to care for minority cultures, there remains a fundamental gap between desirable practice and reality which can be tackled only by robust public health policy and training around cultural adaptation of services that suit the needs of clients.

Help-seeking behaviours and pathways into care

Differing attributions to mental illness and degrees of acculturation define differences in help-seeking behaviours and pathways among different cultural groups and individuals. A negative experience of the health service in any area of medicine would lead to reluctance to have further contact unless in an emergency (Lloyd & St Louis, 1996). Due to different choices in help-seeking pathways, clients may present to services at different stages of illness, often in crisis, through the criminal justice system or to the general hospital rather than the normal routes of help-seeking pathways. Delays in accessing services impact the prognosis and future engagement of clients. The case examples discussed later demonstrate this point.

Some individuals from cultural minorities may choose to seek help from traditional healers either in isolation or in addition to conventional services. We have discussed this earlier as well in the context of spiritist centres. Traditional healers are often believed to have the power to 'get rid of' evil spirits, sometimes by the use of sacrifice or other means. For example, there are rituals in the Caribbean associated with feeding (appeasing) the ancestral spirits in order to drive them away. In Sri Lankan villages, the healer performs a mask dance to scare spirits away. Similar beliefs are held by Malay cultures whose members visit their traditional healers or bomohs. In rural Mexico, the folk healer (curandero) sweeps a raw egg over the body of the victim which is then broken into a glass or bowl of water.

The desire to resort to cultural healers rather than conventional treatments is understandable. From a client's perspective, who is in distress, the cultural healer understands their problem and attributes it to an external agent, thereby validating that their experiences are not their fault and have a 'cure.' The cure is a ritual that is visible to all. The cultural healer commands the respect of the community, and therefore, there is less shame in visiting them. A therapist who understands the differences in world view and can use this knowledge with their clients in therapy would have a similar impact in engagement. Once a community recognizes that therapies provided by conventional services in their areas are in tune with their beliefs, they find them more accepting and are more ready to use them where traditional approaches are not fully effective.

There are a number of moderators that influence choices of access to services (Table 3.2).

Table 3.2 Moderators influencing help-seeking behaviours.

Influences on help-seeking behaviours
Cultural views of mental illness
Level of acculturation – first or second generation
Denial/stigma/shame
Level of education and awareness
Experience of health services
Symptom severity/extent of illness
Level of family influence including return to host country for marriage/treatment
Experience of racism, isolation, and social adversities
Community pressure/grapevine
Level of influence of faith healers/bush doctors/exorcists
Level of religiosity
Language/terminology
Fear of being hospitalized

We have drawn the following illustrations and examples from experiences of clients, and they demonstrate the influence of moderators in choice of help-seeking pathways, thereby impacting on treatment choices.

Case example

The first case example is of an African Caribbean client who lived in the United Kingdom. In the United Kingdom, mental health services include acute services (inpatient and community crisis teams that also provide home treatment) and community mental health teams (CMHT) including assertive outreach teams (AOT) and early intervention in psychosis (EIP) teams. The normal route of referral to specialist mental health services is through the general practitioner (GP or 'family doctor'). Within the African Caribbean/black African and Caribbean communities, people sometimes report a common cultural practice to seek help initially from faith healers.

In Figure 3.2, the dotted line route is the conventional pathway into care for a patient with psychosis in the United Kingdom. The route following the solid arrows demonstrates the one that may be used by some African Caribbean clients through faith healers and/or incidents which lead to the police being called. Arrest by the police may then lead to assessment by mental health services but in circumstances where there have been delay and heightened stress and aggravation has occurred.

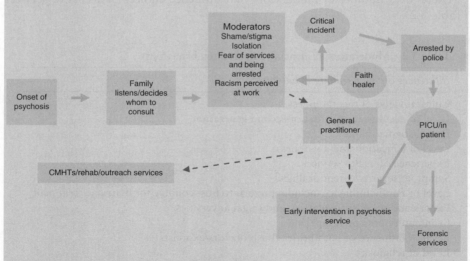

Figure 3.2   Case example – African Caribbean help-seeking behaviour pathway.

Case discussion

In the above example, the client described several factors contributing to the psychotic episode. These included social factors such as change of environment, social class, isolation, and stresses like experience of discrimination at work. This client had a supportive family who suggested contacting the GP for help but also took the client to the faith healer. The client did not contact their GP and noted the moderators as influential in his decision making. The critical incident involved conflict with a neighbour and police were involved. He was subsequently arrested and detained under the Mental Health Act (1983). He was admitted to a psychiatric intensive care unit (PICU). During recovery, he was transferred to an open ward and later discharged to EIP team. Ideally, he should have been referred by his GP to the EIP service for early care and treatment which may have avoided the detention and a subsequent traumatic experience for the client.

African American life experience in the United States is characterized by an acute awareness of the history of slavery and at the same time current experiences for many of racism, discrimination, bias, and negative stereotyping in the media (Coltrane & Messineo, 2000). There is a natural distrust and a reluctance to engage with the system that has historically discriminated against them. Most African Americans can recite both historical facts about racism and recount personal or family experiences of discrimination that are too real and too difficult to forget (http://www.ncbi.nlm.nih.gov/pmc/articles/PMC1497554/). The unemployment rates in African Americans are twice those of their white counterparts and the rate of poverty is significantly higher. A combination of all the above factors leads to distrust of the states, governments, and political system generally. This will include the health-care system which can be difficult to access and limited in response for both physical and especially mental health care. A reduced sense of optimism about the future becomes associated with demoralization, negative beliefs about the self, and an external locus of control (Hines, 1998). Hence, African Americans are more likely to access services when they are in crisis or enter health care through the criminal justice system and are less likely to stay engaged and prematurely terminate treatment.

Case example

The next example is of a South Asian Muslim client. Mental illness can often be dealt with by the family or within the extended family in many cultures where families are tightly knit. This is frequently much more available than in white communities. Recommendations of remedies or advice of elder's or imams may be preferred over conventional services or treatments. This includes belief in 'talisman' or arm lockets with Koran verses inscribed on them. The general practitioner and health-care sources can often be the second choice for help. Sometimes, a return to the country of origin of the family may be the chosen option and even arranged marriage in the belief that the responsibility and possible support of having a partner may change the situation. This may be successful but is obviously fraught with problems for the client and their prospective partner and their family. They may have limited understanding and possible misconceptions about the nature of the issues and potential stressors involved. Stigmatized and unnecessarily negative views of mental health issues can complicate this further both for the partner and also their extended family and community (Figure 3.3).

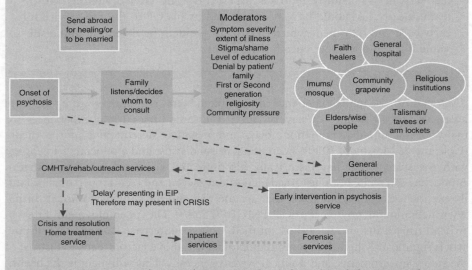

Figure 3.3   Case example – South Asian Muslim help-seeking behaviour pathways.

Case discussion

In this example, the client developed symptoms of psychosis in the form of delusions of the soma (body). He lived with his extended family where the elders in the family made decisions on who to consult. A number of moderators as described in the diagram (Figure 3.2) came into play, and the client sought help from a number of sources including faith healers, imams, and the general hospital. He resorted to treatments like wearing the 'taweez,' and he also brought a wife from his parents' native country to the United Kingdom. The marriage did not help, and one day, he presented to crisis services after an aggressive episode in the emergency department of the general hospital. As illustrated by the case example, where statutory mainstream services are avoided, clients may present in crisis and at a later stage. The literature also documents alternative help-seeking behaviours as a common reason why some patients from different cultural groups present in an emergency (Keating, Robertson, McCulloch, & Francis, 2002). This example emphasizes the role of the family in many cultural groups. Engagement of family members may be equally important in order to engage the client and influence help-seeking behaviours.

Help-seeking routes are very variable, and a further case example depicts the help-seeking pathway that a Hispanic client took.

Case example

Elsie is a Hispanic woman living in the United States with three children. The stress of immigration coupled with a difficult marriage led to her experiencing a psychotic breakdown. Her husband separated from her due to the shame of her developing a mental illness. Her mother took her with the grandchildren into her house. Both Elsie and her mother attributed her earlier breakdown to stress of the marriage and motherhood and did not believe that this was presenting as a mental illness that could benefit from help. As a result, Elsie did not see a primary care physician for her emotional problems and was not taking any kind of medication. Elsie took an overdose of medication in response to command auditory hallucinations, was taken to an emergency department, and was briefly hospitalized in a mental health unit on an involuntary status. When she was discharged from the hospital, she was referred to an outpatient clinic for medication monitoring and case management services, while her son with behavioural issues was referred to therapy. Her case manager was Hispanic, and Elsie and her mother were comfortable engaging with her. Elsie's son was also referred to a therapist for his own mental health problems, and she encouraged Elsie to obtain CBT through a research study. Elsie and her mother took the case manager with them to the intake assessment and felt comfortable enough to raise their concerns and ask for further help. Subsequently, they decided that Elsie should enrol in the study to obtain CBT (Figure 3.4).

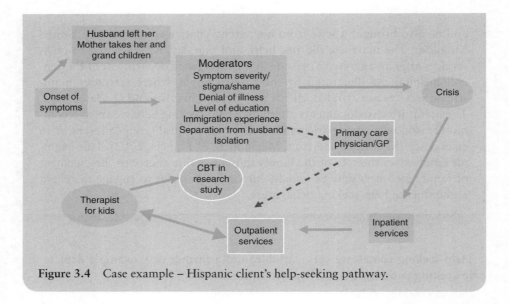

Figure 3.4   Case example – Hispanic client's help-seeking pathway.

Case discussion

In this particular instance, Elsie took a circuitous pathway to mental health care due to a variety of factors. After her first breakdown, her husband divorced her due to the stigma of dealing with a 'mentally ill' wife. Stigma also contributed to the denial of mental illness by both Elsie and her mother. As a result, Elsie did not get any treatment, for example, appropriate medication, relapsed, and ended up in hospital following an overdose of painkillers. However, meeting with a Hispanic case manager gave Elsie and her mother an adequate level of comfort to keep outpatient appointments and subsequently be enrolled in therapy. Therapists who recognize these cultural issues are able to understand and empathize with the complex pathways that Hispanic clients can take, however frustrating it may be to see clients later in their course of illness and having suffered unnecessary distress. Demonstrating such understanding is an important way of gaining the trust of the clients – while other solutions are found to address the broad cultural issues that exist.

Exercise: Work with your client in understanding their help-seeking pathways. How is this influenced by their level of acculturation and attributions to illness? How is their family involved? How does this inform your formulation and treatment plan?

Barriers to accessing CBT

Cultural beliefs not only influence an individual's opinions about health services in general but also impact on decisions regarding specific treatment choices. Perceptions of both referrers and therapists about clients and their cultural background are equally important moderators in access to therapies like CBT. In Chapter 2, we have discussed reasons why, historically, psychological therapies had not been easily available to clients from minority ethnic backgrounds. In this section, we will discuss this further in the context of specific barriers to accessing CBT.

Opinions regarding treatment and CBT

Cultural thinking can determine an individual's preference for different treatment options. Compared to many whites, Hispanic and African Americans are more likely to view antidepressant medication as addictive and less likely to find medications acceptable (Cooper et al., 2003). Hispanics in particular have been found to prefer counselling over medication to treat depression. Side effects are often identified as a contributory factor to non-concordance with treatment. High doses of medication make it difficult for some patients to engage in therapy. However, there are some groups who may prefer medication, for example, South Asian Muslim, and some white clients may prefer pills. Preference for injections, seen as potentially most potent, has also been expressed compared to talking therapies. The colour of the medication as pills or in the injection or intravenous drip can matter to some as well. A participant in our study (Rathod et al., 2010) who originated from Pakistan explained the concept of the *"drip hanging and the person lying down is like strength is being transferred to a person."* The concept of 'cure' as opposed to 'coping' may be a stronger expectation in some cultures, for example, South Asian Muslim, than others although present to some degree in all individuals. The client may expect 'full and instant cure' to a problem and will go to great lengths to find someone to 'cure them.' The expectation is explained by their attributions of illness to external factors that one does not have to change anything about themselves, and so this reduces tendency to self-blame and is considered less stigmatizing. Clients seek to get rid of a problem rather than learning alternative ways of coping or tolerating distress. As explained earlier, it is therefore easier and emotionally more comfortable to have a ritual performed rather than seek therapy.

Knowledge of cultural expectations can be used productively by a therapist in exploring the cognitive errors, for example, dichotomous reasoning, involved and equating rituals used to manage mental health issues to agree homework and behavioural tasks in CBT. Small achievements through task-oriented therapy may change the client's mindset about therapy and its benefits. Similarly, a change in perceptions in the wider community and policymakers regarding the acceptability of adapted CBT through 'word of mouth' and from respected community members who would have successfully completed therapy and recommended it can impact on wider opinions.

Access and referrer's perceptions
Sometimes, there is less awareness of the availability and value of CBT as a treatment option in severe mental illness (SMI) among health professionals. In the United States and many international health systems, there remains a dominant emphasis on biological treatments, unfortunately, often to the exclusion of psychological treatments. These are often seen as non-evidence based despite the published evidence and inclusion in practice guidelines (e.g. those of the American Psychiatric Association and PORT). There are also more subtle and less overt beliefs that psychological treatments are inherently and conceptually inappropriate for brain diseases such as the more SMI. This, of course, presupposes that there are physical problems in the brain which are central to their causation but also that the only way to treat them is by biological methods in physical interventions such as medication. This is a logical fallacy as even where brain dysfunction is clearly central to an illness, for example, in 'stroke' (cerebrovascular accidents), there is nevertheless a role for interventions which assist in coping, for example, physiotherapy, occupational therapy, and even psychotherapy to help with the depression that often understandably results. Similarly with severe mental health problems, psychological approaches can assist the individual in coping and managing the experiences that interfere with the person's functioning and cause them distress.

CBT for mental illness is not generally available in abundance in the United States or elsewhere (Weiden et al., 2006) with the exception of the United Kingdom where it is increasingly being provided through the National Health Service (Department of Health, 2004). We have discussed how CBT could be acceptable to potential clients with adequate information and cultural sensitivity (Rathod et al., 2010), but this is also the case for referrers who need to be confident of the value of CBT in cultural minority patients. There is a need for the treatment to be recognized as credible within referrers and policymakers equally. Perception of the referrer is one of the barriers to accessing therapy. If a referrer does not understand what CBT is or believe it to be an effective intervention for different cultural clients, it is unlikely that they would consider or refer their clients for CBT. However, if adapted CBT was available and they had seen success in some of their clients, their views would be influenced positively.

Therapist's experience with clients from different cultural groups
Often, therapists have limited experience of working with clients from different cultural backgrounds. This is more of an issue in areas of Westernized countries that have fewer minority residents. We have already discussed variability in settlement of immigrant populations in Chapter 1. In those areas where there is relative aggregation of specific minority cultural groups, often therapists feel more confident in their skills of working with clients from minority cultures as their experience grows. In these areas, therapists can modify aspects of therapy delivery to suit the local needs, and on many occasions, they themselves may be of the same cultural background as the client. A lack of confidence and limited experience may translate into not accepting clients from minority cultures into therapy. We have already discussed in Chapter 2 that it could not be possible for a therapist

to understand the culture of every individual but an overall understanding of how culture may impact on client's views, illness presentation, and perceptions can help the therapist in developing the confidence to start working with clients from minority cultures. The client is an expert in their own culture, and a collaborative effort utilizing that knowledge results in better engagement and potential outcome. It is usually appropriate for the therapist to start therapy by acknowledging to the client that '*While I am the expert in delivering the therapy, you are an expert in your own culture. I understand and respect the impact of cultural beliefs and hope that we can work together so that I can learn some things about your culture from you.*' This approach is described in case examples in further chapters – being able to draw examples from a wider collective knowledge base as they accumulate on how this can work in practice may help engagement and improve the confidence of the client and therapist in each other.

Language can be a limiting factor, and the role of interpreters in therapy has been debated (Rathod & Naeem, 2012). There is evidence that where lack of a common language is a barrier, when interpreters are used well and appropriately in therapy, the benefits include greater understanding, better engagement, and more accurate empathy and cooperation between client and therapist (Faust & Drickey, 1986; Tribe, 1999). We believe that on balance, meaningful CBT can be delivered through interpreters due to the pragmatic and flexible nature of the therapy but that is not to diminish the difficulties that can be involved and the extra time and patience of all concerned that may be needed.

Interpreters should be selected with care, and supervision by a clinician who is used to working with interpreters is important. Consistency, continuity, and preparation are key to successful working. Therapists need to be aware that despite these considerations, clients from some communities, for example, South Asian Muslim clients, can fear breaches of confidentiality where interpreters are from their community. A discussion of these fears and the necessary parameters for interpreters can be helpful at the outset to build the confidence of the client. Where a family member is prepared to take upon themselves the role of interpretation, complex issues can arise although it should not be assumed that these cannot be overcome especially where no alternative is possible or the client themselves wants the family member to interpret for them as they may be able to do this effectively and provide support. This can include being a 'chaperone' where gender issues arise.

There can nevertheless be conflicts of interest or simply difficulties in disclosure in cases where a family member is involved. An example is when they are younger members of the family who have the necessary language skills, which can prevent disclosure of more intimate details by the client or anything that can be perceived as stigmatizing or representing failure. In extreme circumstances, the family member like a spouse may have been a contributing factor to the service user's distress. Awareness and discussion of these challenges can help the therapist in working their way forwards but can be very difficult if options are limited. It can sometimes be possible to find a member of hospital staff who is able to assist so that the issues regarding interpretation and use of a family member or professional interpreter can be explored even if the person cannot act as interpreter themselves for the duration of the therapy sessions.

Case example

Irena, a 22-year-old Polish girl, immigrated to the United Kingdom after separation from her husband who had been physically abusive towards her in Poland. Her sister resided in the United Kingdom with her husband and two children and offered to support Irena. Irena's sister lived in a two-bedroom apartment, so the living quarters were very cramped, and Irena had to sleep on the couch each night. She thus had very little space and privacy in the house. She had developed symptoms of a post-traumatic stress disorder (PTSD) following the previous abusive experiences and used to wake up screaming in the night. The overall situation for Irena following her distressing experience, symptoms of PTSD, migration, and living circumstances led her to becoming moderately depressed with suicidal thoughts. She was referred to psychiatric services.

At the first assessment, her sister helped in translating for the assessor as Irena did not have fluent English. However, following the assessment, it was clear that Irena had been guarded about the amount of information that she had shared. The assessor discussed this issue openly with Irena and her sister, and it was agreed that an independent interpreter might be more beneficial. This was arranged, but during the first consultation with the interpreter, a prior discussion of the parameters involving confidentiality and disclosure had not occurred. The assessor felt that during the session, the interpreter was having conversations with Irena which were not fully translated. Following the session, the assessor discussed their concerns with the interpreter. The interpreter acknowledged that she felt obliged to offer solutions to some of Irena's problems and decided that translating them may not be relevant as they were culturally derived. The assessor discussed the roles and responsibilities expected of the interpreter and at the next session also discussed these again with Irena. Once the parameters of the roles were reiterated, therapy could be started and continued successfully with the interpreter also assisting in providing information and explanation of issues that were culturally significant.

Case discussion

The above example highlights potential pitfalls in working with interpreters when language is a barrier and how the therapist can work through the barriers and with them. The important thing is to be aware of the challenges and openly discuss them with client to find ways forwards.

Table 3.3 Cultural barriers to accessing therapy.

Mistrust of services or practitioners
Worries about confidentiality breaches
Poor information on psychological therapies/accessibility/doubt on effectiveness
Language and terminology leading to being misunderstood
Fear of being stigmatized
Previous experiences of services
Stereotyping by therapists
Lack of understanding of cultural norms and values by therapist
Cultural incompetence or Eurocentric approach
Faith/spirituality and religion
Individualism versus collectivism issues
Gender issues
Racism/colonial history
Interpretation problems
Financial implications
Practical issues, for example, environment of therapy or transport

Cultural barriers to accessing therapy

We have discussed these barriers in detail in this chapter in the different sections. Some of the barriers affect accessing and accepting CBT and are important to understand for the therapist so that they can be discussed to improve engagement. Table 3.3 further summarizes cultural barriers to accessing therapy.

One of the solutions that has been suggested in literature to overcome the cultural barriers is cultural matching of the therapists which was also alluded to in Chapter 2 in a different context. This is not necessarily an ideal or even appropriate solution in all instances due to pragmatic and clinical concerns. At a pragmatic level, it would be nearly impossible to be able to find adequate numbers of trained therapists to culturally match with clients. The American Psychological Association has, for example, only 3% African American psychologists, while African Americans constitute 12% of the population. The clinical concerns are that while some clients identify with their therapists from similar background, others can feel uncomfortable when working with therapists from the same background due to personal issues or, it has been suggested, from issues of over-identification with them. In these situations, the dilemma for the therapist can be that they get easily caught up in the client's negative experiences and perceptions of the world and can end up focusing on a biased formulation even without knowing that this is occurring. Over-identification can occur in situations where there are unresolved or simply complex issues affecting the therapist (Cowdrill & Keeling, 2007). For example, unresolved personal issues and experiences of racism can impact on therapy leading to a therapist jumping to conclusions and making these a focus of therapy when they might not be the key issue for the client. It is helpful for therapists to be cognizant of these issues so that assumptions and overgeneralizations are not made – as can occur with any personal issue for any therapist.

Table 3.4 Key points in understanding philosophical orientation.

Understand the level of acculturation of the client
Explore culturally determined attributions to illness
Identify preferred help-seeking behaviours
Uncover barriers to engaging with CBT

Another reason for client's preference not to be seen in therapy by a practitioner from their ethnic background, as described for interpreters, is due to worries about confidentiality in their community. The underlying worries are due to stigma and shame of mental illness and its impact on, for example, marital prospects and family honour. This is despite them valuing a therapist who can understand their cultural background, norms, and values and respect their religious beliefs. It has been described as a particular issue with some communities where general constraints on confidentiality are different and loyalty to the family or community is seen as overwhelmingly important. It can also be a particular issue where the local community is small, for example, American Arab or some black African groups.

We therefore restate that where the therapist happens to be of the same background as the client in minority cultures, they need to be aware of these issues but where they are not from the same background, they need to have the confidence and humility to work through the cultural issues collaboratively.

Similarly, gender issues have a cultural context and are an influencing factor. For example, in some cultural groups, a young female client may not be allowed to see a male therapist, again due to perceived adverse effects on prospects of marriage and honour. A lack of understanding of these issues could be misconstrued as an inability to engage people from minority cultures, whereas acknowledging the issues allows flexibility in approach, thereby improving access (Table 3.4).

Practical Considerations

Politics, religion, and health systems in any country have an intricate and complex relationship. They impact on access, therapeutic intervention, and the adaptation of services to people from different backgrounds. Economic conditions, immigration and related policies, health systems, funding arrangements and the reputation of local units, and level of stigma and racism, for example, have a bearing on treatments offered and access to care. It is hypothesized that political, social, and ideological pressures current in society also impinge on the diagnostic process in Western psychiatry and criteria for outcomes (Fernando, 1998).

Cultural evolution of communities is influenced by migration across countries and within countries (as discussed in Chapter 1). Culture is influenced by the global context, the macro environment of the nation, the community, and the individual's micro environment. For example, in China, historically, Confucianism has had an influence in society through its meaning to the 'family' (filial piety). However, the concept of collectivism replaced the central role of families from 1949 to 1979, and since 1979, changes in market economy and the one-child policy have led to further cultural changes. The market economy has led to domestic and international immigration, students abroad, expansion of international business, and intercultural marriage due to love marriages as opposed to arranged marriage and predominance of nuclear families. The one-child policy has led to the 4-2-1 syndrome (Wang, Leichtman, & White, 1998) leading to focus on growth of one child. This in turn impacts on the personality development of the child and their level of dependence on the family and independence. An understanding of the societal context impacting on an individual's development, early experiences, and formation of core beliefs is important for therapists.

Practical facilities influence engagement and outcomes from therapy. Providing therapy in wide rural areas or where transport links are difficult or resources concentrated in one central, usually urban base, is a difficult practical issue common in developing countries. It might be difficult, indeed impossible, for some clients to return to a health facility for therapy on a weekly or even monthly basis. With an increase in focus of care in the community and centralizing resources in developed countries, the same issues regarding travel and convenience may apply. For clients living in the periphery, one option is to increase the length of sessions (or do two in one day) and widen the gap between the sessions to fortnightly or even monthly. Alternative strategies, for example, intense therapy as inpatients or providing with self-help material, can be tried when client cannot even do that. The very widespread availability of mobile or landline phones even in relatively low-income countries may provide opportunities to communicate for brief top-up sessions and even more extended work where the client is able to concentrate sufficiently well over the telephone. Such work is possible, but the lack of awareness of each other's non-verbal communication does usually interfere with effective engagement and understanding. There are also the disadvantages of not being able to demonstrate concepts and exercises by using diagrams of links between key issues with emotions, thoughts, and behaviours, and certainly, more complex formulations cannot be drawn up although sometimes there are other routes, for example, Internet or post, that can be used. Phones can also be used to enlist support of family members or local health workers who with supervision may be able to assist.

Racism and its effects

Understanding and acknowledging the impact of racism and addressing it appropriately in a skilful way are important. If not dealt with sensitively, clients will often feel dissatisfied and may disengage from therapy. Sometimes, therapists find talking about racism in therapy anxiety provoking, and some avoid it for fear of infringing 'politically correct' boundaries. They fear that they might say something that could be misinterpreted as insensitive or indeed 'racist.' Therapists are often not well prepared, that is, are not trained to address racial issues in therapy. For this reason, some clients may identify better with a therapist of the same culture or background – or simply who come from a minority ethnic community themselves – to discuss race issues as they feel they would be better understood. Moreover, they feel that a therapist from their background can relate better to their experiences. On the other hand, there are disadvantages as discussed, and overall, it is important for any therapist to be able to develop the trust and confidence of the client so that they can speak about their experiences. Validation that racial discrimination may be occurring and may be a key stressor in their lives, past and present, is important to gain the trust of the client. But there is a fine balance between validation of a perception and feeding into a misunderstanding, for example, unduly negative and depressive beliefs that they can never achieve their goals as a result of racist attitudes or even psychotic symptoms where, for example, the client has delusions of racial persecution. Case formulations which can be evaluated as therapy progresses should be considered to clarify, explore, and understand patients' experiences of racism. In doing this, the right balance can be achieved and conclusions reached so that the client feels believed, can problem-solve relevant issues, and does not disengage.

Case example

Emelia, 35 years of age, mother of two young children, had separated from her husband after 14 years of marriage. She came from a black African background and had immigrated into the United Kingdom following her marriage to her husband. Following separation, she rented a flat, and her children's school had to be changed as they moved with her. She also changed her job due to her move. It had been a stressful time for her and her children but she had managed to cope.

Over the next couple of years, she had difficulties at work and felt that her voice was not heard. She had started perceiving discrimination due to her cultural background. Her mood started to deteriorate and she began isolating herself. As her symptoms worsened, she was signed off 'sick' from work. She had stopped talking to her neighbours as she felt they may be racist towards her too. The teachers at her children's school noticed a change in their performance. They asked to meet Emelia to discuss this with her. At the meeting, Emelia broke down and shouted at the teachers that they had been *racist towards my children* and hence wanted to complain about them.

Emelia was eventually referred to and attended psychiatric services. She was started on medication and also offered CBT. Through the sessions, it transpired that Emelia had experienced some discrimination at work. However, as her mental health deteriorated, she had generalized these experiences to the wider environment and people with whom she had contact. As her mental state improved, she was able to discuss the issues that initially caused concern with her line manager at work. The therapist, who had been working with her collaboratively, had very skilfully helped her to tease out the real from perceived experiences and supported her in having the necessary discussions at work to deal with the original issues.

Case discussion

The complexities described above could have been very challenging for the therapist as it would have been easy to either assume that Emelia was voicing her experiences due to illness and was therefore wrong, even deluded, thereby disbelieving her, or, alternatively, assume that she had been a victim of discrimination on every front. Exploration and clarification of the actual experiences and then assumptions made engaged Emelia in therapy and led to the issues being worked through and a positive outcome.

Political Considerations

In the United States over the course of the last half century, care of severely mentally ill people has moved from the state institutions to the community setting through the establishment of community mental health centres (CMHCs) in a process of deinstitutionalization. This process has three components: discharging people from hospitals, diverting people away from hospitals, and providing care in community settings. Deinstitutionalization addressed one issue of reducing the length of stay, and the trend is not dissimilar to other developed countries like the United Kingdom.

There are four significant problems in providing care for the severely mentally ill in the community:

1. Severely limited funding leading to poor staffing and mental health service resources
2. The mental health system remaining focused on biological treatments to the detriment of necessary psychosocial treatments
3. The complex, fragmented system of care that is difficult for people to negotiate
4. The system not being consumer and family friendly with a focus on symptom remission as opposed to the goal of recovery

The community services have been severely underfunded leading to some unanticipated consequences of deinstitutionalization for the SMI including homelessness, criminalization and alternate institutionalization in the prisons, and overcrowding of the emergency departments due to lack of adequate psychiatric beds (Lamb & Bachrach, 2001; Lamb & Weinberger, 2005). Except for the Assertive Community Treatment model that is very limited in availability, care of SMI is limited in time and scope, is not integrated, and lacks the continuity necessary for long-term functional recovery. Assertive Community Treatment, in contrast to other services, provides a comprehensive continuum of community services round the clock for an indefinite period of time by a dedicated interdisciplinary team that works with patients in their natural environments (Rosen, Mueser, & Teesson, 2007). Personal accounts of individuals who have recovered from schizophrenia attest that people who are treated in the mental health system have to recover from the mental illness that impairs their functioning and the mental health system that is very impersonal and focused on symptom remission and diminishes the individual as a person (Fisher, 2006). The use of culturally adapted CBT in these settings is clearly indicated in enhancing the care provided and focus on recovery.

There has been a change in perspective in psychiatry in the 1970s from a humanistic and interpersonal one to technical and scientific one, thereby undercutting the importance of psychosocial interventions (Burti & Mosher, 2003). The advent of new psychiatric medications and enormous amounts spent by pharmaceutical industry to market psychotropic drugs led to the focus being on access to these medications and a 'crowding out' of any psychosocial interventions in the United States specially. In addition, the liaison between academic institutions and the pharmaceutical industry led to an increased focus on biological treatments and further neglect of psychosocial interventions. Even when studies show the equivalence or superiority of psychosocial interventions, marketing strength favours medications (Clark & Samnaliev, 2005).

Hence, it is not a surprise that effective psychosocial interventions are shown to be highly underutilized in the treatment of illnesses such as schizophrenia (Lehman & Steinwachs, 2003). Current treatment guidelines from different countries for schizophrenia recommend that CBT be offered and be available for any individual with first episode psychosis and persistent symptoms despite adequate pharmacotherapy (Dixon et al., 2009; NICE, 2014). However, CBT for SMI is provided by trained staff that is not available in CMHCs, and hence, CBT is not available in most routine clinical care settings (Pinninti, Fisher, Thompson, & Steer, 2010). It is a challenge for both the CMHCs that deliver the mental health services and the states that fund them to find more cost-effective ways of providing psychosocial interventions such as culturally sensitive CBT for most individual with SMI.

While the US mental health system has been described as a maintenance, symptom reduction system that diminishes the individual, forward trends offer the opportunity to transform the current system of care into consumer- and family-driven one with a recovery and wellness-oriented approach (Fisher, 2006).

In the United Kingdom, mental health services saw major development during the period of financial growth after the millennium, through political initiatives based on the National Service Framework for Mental Health (2001). This funded new teams in all areas of England with parallel developments elsewhere in the United Kingdom: early intervention in psychosis (EIP) services, assertive outreach team (AOT), and crisis resolution/home treatment teams (CRHTs) in order to improve access and quality of care in community settings. CRHTs demonstrated an impact on achieving care in the community rather than in a hospital setting which was in line with the overall intention to move care into the community. The duration of untreated psychosis (DUP) has been shown to be reduced by cost-effective measures which include early intervention teams and mental health promotion campaigns.

Austerity measures have more recently required services to streamline, integrate, and align in order to improve cost-efficiency. Cost more directly now affects prioritization of what can be provided. There is a drive for commissioning of services to relate to appropriate care, reducing variability, eliminating waste, and decommissioning interventions of limited clinical value. Economic and political changes therefore have an impact on setting expectations with regard to access to services and expectations of quality within society.

However, evidence-based treatments as described in national clinical guidelines especially those provided by the National Institute for Health and Care Excellence for treatment of schizophrenia, bipolar disorder, and common mental disorders are being promoted, and this particularly applies to treatments which are not being made available. The UK Department of Health's Improving Access to Psychological Therapies programme has now expanded to include SMI. Demonstration sites have been established and competency frameworks drawn up (www.ucl.ac.uk/CORE/) to assist in providing effective training and subsequently services to people with severe problems. The application of these techniques to people from the diverse multicultural communities that comprise the United Kingdom has been given priority although such exhortation is not immediately leading to rapid expansion in availability.

CBT availability for people with severe problems in Australasia and Europe has developed at varying rates but remains very restricted indeed, outside of these areas. Australia has invested considerable resources and research into EIP over the past couple of decades although, as everywhere else, resources have been restricted. Scandinavia has a strong tradition of using psychosocial approaches to psychosis in particular and has embraced CBT to a considerable degree although it is difficult to determine exactly how available it is. Traditions and psychological therapies in France are understood to remain quite psychodynamic with a small number of CBT practitioners who are active. Germany has tended towards approaches based on cognitive remediation although a number of CBT studies are emerging. Southern Europe has its own austerity issues to contend with, and so availability of CBT remains restricted despite work by a number of outstanding individual practitioners.

Practical aspects of specific working within these services to overcome the difficulties described are discussed in detail later in the book.

Conclusion

Differences in world view influence presentation of mental illness and the pathways to care that individuals from different cultural backgrounds take. Therapists and other providers working with mentally ill patients need to be aware of these influences and appreciate the practical considerations of providing services so that they can mitigate the barriers in improving access and achieving positive clinical outcomes.

References

Acharya, S., Moorhouse, S., Kareem, J., & Littlewood, R. (1989). Nafsiyat: A psychotherapy center for ethnic minorities. *Psychiatric Bulletin, 13*, 358–360.

Al-Krenawi, A., Graham, J. R., & Kandah, J. (2000). Gendered utilization differences of mental health services in Jordan. *Community Mental Health Journal, 36*(5), 501–511.

Angermeyer, M., & Matschinger, H. (1994). Lay beliefs about schizophrenic disorder: The result of a population survey in Germany. *Acta Psychiatrica Scandinavica, 89*(Suppl. 382), 39–45.

Avasthi, A. (2011). Indianizing psychiatry – Is there a case enough? *Indian Journal of Psychiatry, 53*(2), 111–120.

Baldwin, J. (1986, March). African (Black) psychology issues and synthesis. *Journal of Black Studies, 16*(3), 235–249.

Belgrave, F. Z., & Allison, K. W. (2006). *African American Psychology: From Africa to America*. Thousand Oaks, CA: Sage Publications.

Berry, J. (2005). Acculturation: Living successfully in two cultures. *International Journal of Intercultural Relations, 29*(2005), 697–712.

Blackwell, B. (1976). Treatment adherence. *British Journal of Psychiatry, 129*, 513–531.

Burti, L., & Mosher, L. R. (2003). Attitudes, values and beliefs of mental health workers. *Epidemiologia e Psichiatria Sociale, 12*(4), 227–231.

Cabassa, L., Lester, R., & Zayas, L. (2007). "It's like being in a labyrinth:" Hispanic immigrants' perceptions of depression and attitudes toward treatments. *Journal of Immigrant and Minority Health, 9*(1), 1–16.

Clark, L., & Hofsess, L. (1998). Acculturation. In S. Loue (Ed.), *Handbook of immigrant health* (pp. 37–59). New York, NY: Plenum Press.

Clark, R. E., & Samnaliev, M. (2005). Psychosocial treatment in the 21st century. *International Journal of Law and Psychiatry, 28*, 532–544.

Coltrane, S., & Messineo, M. (2000). The perpetuation of subtle prejudice: Race and gender imagery in 1990s television advertising. *Sex Roles, 42*(5/6), 363–389.

Cooper, L., Gonzales, J., Gallo, J., Rost, K., Meredith, L., Rubenstein, L., … Ford, D. (2003). The acceptability of treatment for depression among African-American, Hispanic and White primary care patients. *Medical Care, 41*(4), 479–489.

Cowdrill, V., & Keeling, C. (2007). *Race and culture issues in cognitive behaviour therapy. Lecture to Diploma in CBT for severe mental health problems*. Southampton, UK: University of Southampton.

Department of health (1983). Reference guide to the Mental Health Act 1983. TSO (The Stationery Office), London.

Department of Health (1999a) *National Service Framework for Mental Health*: modern standards and service models. London: HMSO.

Department of Health. (2004). *Organising and delivering psychological therapies*. London, UK: Author.

Dixon, L. B., Dickerson, F., Bellack, A. S., Bennett, M., Dickinson, D., Goldberg, R. W., Lehman, A., Tenhula, W. N., Calmes, C., Pasillas, R. M., Peer, J., & Kreyenbuhl, J.;

Schizophrenia Patient Outcomes Research Team (PORT) (2009). The 2009 schizophrenia PORT psychosocial treatment recommendations and summary statements. *Schizophrenia Bulletin, 36*(1) 48–70.

Edgerton, R. B. (1966). Conceptions of psychosis in four east African societies. *American Anthropologist, 68*(2), 408–425.

Faust, S., & Drickey, R. (1986). Working with interpreters. *The Journal of Family Practice, 22,* 131–138.

Felix-Ortiz, M., Newcomb, M.D., Meyers, H., (1994). A multidimensional measure of cultural identity for Latino and Latina adolescents. *Hisp. J. Behav. Sci.* 16, 99–115.

Felix-Ortiz, M., Fernandez, A., & Newcomb, M. D. (1998). The role of intergenerational discrepancy of cultural orientation in drug use among Latina adolescents. *Substance Use & Misuse, 33*(4), 967–994.

Fernando, S. (1991). *Mental health, race and culture.* London, UK: Macmillan/Mind.

Fernando, S. (1998). *Race and culture in psychiatry.* London, UK: Billing and Sons Ltd. In Rathod, S., Kingdon, D., Smith, P., & Turkington, D. (2005). Insight into schizophrenia: The effects of cognitive behavioural therapy on the components of insight and association with sociodemographics-data on a previously published randomised controlled trial. *Schizophrenia Research, 74,* 211–219.

Fisher, D. M. (2006). *Recovery from schizophrenia: From seclusion to empowerment.* Retrieved from http://www.medscape.com/viewarticle/523539 (accessed on September 17, 2014).

Garcia, G., & Zea, C. (Eds.). (1997). *Psychological interventions and research with Latino populations.* Boston, MA: Allyn & Bacon.

Gelder, M., Harrison, P., & Cowen, P. (2006). Classification and diagnosis. In *Shorter Oxford textbook of psychiatry* (5th ed., pp. 21–34). Oxford, UK: Oxford University Press.

Gurnaccia, P., & Roaiouaz, O. (1996). Concepts of culture and their role in the development of culturally competent mental health services. *Hispanic Journal of Behavioral Sciences, 18,* 419–443.

Hines, P. M. (1998). Climbing up the rough side of the mountain: Hope, culture and therapy. In M. McGoldrick (Ed.), *Re-visioning family therapy: Race, culture, class and gender* (pp. 78–90). New York, NY: Guilford Press.

Keating, F., Robertson, D., McCulloch, A., & Francis, E. (2002). *Breaking the circles of fear: A review of the relationship between mental health services and African and Caribbean communities.* London, UK: The Sainsbury Centre for Mental Health.

Kleinman, A. (1977). Depression, somatization and the new cross-cultural psychiatry. *Social Science & Medicine, 11*(1), 3–10.

Kleinman, A. (1982). Neurasthenia and depression: A study of somatization and culture in China. *Culture, Medicine and Psychiatry, 6,* 117–190.

Lamb, H. R., & Bachrach, L. L. (2001). Some perspectives on deinstitutionalization. *Psychiatric Services, 52*(8), 1039–1045.

Lamb, H. R., & Weinberger, L. E. (2005). The shift of psychiatric inpatient care from hospitals to jails and prisons. *The Journal of the American Academy of Psychiatry and the Law, 33*(4), 529–534.

Lee E. (Ed.). (1997). *Working with Asian Americans: A guide for clinicians.* New York, NY: Guilford Press.

Lehman, A. F., & Steinwachs, D. M. (2003). Evidence-based psychosocial treatment practices in schizophrenia: Lessons from the client outcomes research team (PORT) project. *The Journal of the American Academy of Psychoanalysis and Dynamic Psychiatry, 31*(1), 141–154.

Lewis, A. (1934). The psychopathology of insight. *British Journal of Medical Psychology, 14*, 332–348.

Littlewood, R., & Lipsedge, M. (1978). Migration, ethnicity and diagnosis. *Psychiatrica Clinica, 11*, 15–22.

Lloyd, K., & St Louis, L. (1996). Common mental disorders among Africans and Caribbeans. In D. Bhugra & V. Bhal (Eds.), *Ethnicity: An agenda for mental health*. London, UK: Gaskell.

Mayr, E. (1961). Cause and effect in biology. *Science, 134*, 1501.

McCabe, R., & Priebe, S. (2004). Explanatory models of illness in schizophrenia: Comparison of four ethnic groups. *British Journal of Psychiatry., 185*, 25–30.

McEvoy, J., Aland, J., Wilson, W., Guy, W., & Hawkins, L. (1981). Measuring chronic schizophrenic patients attitudes towards their illness and treatment. *Hospital and Community Psychiatry, 32*(12), 586–588.

McPherson, R., Double, D., Harrison, D., & Rowlands, R. (1993). Long term psychiatric patients' understanding of neuroleptic medication. *Hospital and Community Psychiatry, 44*, 71–73.

Melville, B. (1983). Ethnicity: An analysis of its dynamism and variability focusing on the Mexican/Anglo/Mexican American interface. *American Ethnologist, 10*, 272–289.

Moreira-Almeida, A., & Neto, F. (2005). Spiritist views of mental disorders in Brazil. *Transcultural Psychiatry, 42*(4), 570–595.

National Institute of Health and Care Excellence (2014, February). Psychosis and schizophrenia in adults: Treatment and management. Clinical guidelines, CG178. London, NICE.

Pinninti, N. R., Fisher J., Thompson, K., & Steer, R. (2010). Feasibility and usefulness of training assertive community treatment team in cognitive behavioral therapy. *Community Mental Health Journal, 46*, 337–341.

Pumariega, A. J. (2003). Cultural competence in systems of care for children's mental health. In A. J. Pumariega & N. C. Winters (Eds.), *Handbook of community systems of care: The new child & adolescent community psychiatry* (pp. 82–106). San Francisco, CA: Jossey Bass Publishers.

Rathod, S., & Kingdon, D. (2009). Cognitive behaviour therapy across cultures. *Psychiatry, 8*, 370–371.

Rathod, S., & Naeem, F. (2012). Can you do meaningful cognitive–behavioural therapy with an interpreter? In K. Bhui (Ed.), *Elements of culture and mental health: Critical questions for clinicians*. London, UK: Royal College of Psychiatrists.

Rathod, S., Phiri, P., Kingdon, D., & Gobbi, M. (2010). Developing culturally sensitive cognitive behaviour therapy for psychosis for ethnic minority patients by exploration and incorporation of service users' and health professionals' views and opinions. *Journal of Behavioural and Cognitive Psychotherapies, 38*, 511–533.

Ray, L. A., Bujarski, S., Chin, P. F., & Miotto, K. (2010). Pharmacogenetics of naltrexone in Asian Americans: A randomized placebo-controlled laboratory study. *Neuropsychopharmacology, 37*(2), 445–455.

Rosen, A., Mueser, K. T., & Teesson, M. (2007). Assertive community treatment: Issues from scientific and clinical literature with implications for practice. *Journal of Rehabilitation Research and Development, 44*(6), 813–826.

Sharp, A. (1994). Exorcists, psychiatrists, and the problems of possession in northwest Madagascar. *Social Science & Medicine, 38*(4), 525–542.

Townsend, J. (1975). Cultural conceptions and mental illness: A controlled comparison of Germany and America. *Journal of Nervous and Mental Disease, 160*, 409–421.

Tribe, R. (1999). Therapeutic work with refugees living in exile: Observations on clinical practice. *Counselling Psychology Quarterly, 12*(3), 233–243.

Tseng, W.-S., Chang, S. C., & Nishjzono, M. (2005). *Asian culture and psychotherapy: Implications for East and West.* Honolulu, HI: University of Hawaii Press.

Veling, W., Selten, J. P., Susser, E., Laan, W., Mackenbach, J. P., & Hoek, H. W. (2007). Discrimination and the incidence of psychotic disorders among ethnic minorities in the Netherlands. *International Journal of Epidemiology, 36*, 761–768.

Wang, Q., Leichtman, M., & White, S. (1998). Chinese adults: The impact of growing up an only child. *Cognition, 69*(1), 73–103.

Weiden, P., Burkholder, P., Kingdon, D., Landa, Y., Temple, S., Pinninti, N. (2006). CBT for Schizophrenia. Can we do it here? Challenges of implementing CBT for treatment of schizophrenia in United States. Paper presented at the 159th annual meeting of the American Psychiatric Association, Toronto, Canada, May 20–25.

4

The Therapeutic Relationship and Technical Adjustments

Key issues regarding the general world view – philosophical orientation – and practical considerations in the treatment of different cultural groups have now been established. Now, we get on to the key part of this book – how to actually use a culturally adapted framework to enhance therapy. This involves making modifications and technical adjustments to the process of engagement covered in this chapter and therapy discussed in subsequent chapters. We will provide case examples from different cultural groups that illustrate the modifications based on broader considerations of cultural issues as well as the specific technical adjustments a therapist has to make to adapt the therapy to the individual client in question.

Every clinician, in drawing on their personal experiences of both positive and negative relationships with their clients, can intuitively recognize the importance of a sound therapeutic relationship in determining client outcomes. Here, we will focus on the role of the therapeutic relationship during the various phases of cognitive behavioural therapy (CBT) in individuals from different minority cultures and address some of the issues that can arise. We will briefly review the literature looking at evidence for the importance of therapeutic relationship in different psychiatric illnesses with a particular focus on severe mental illness (SMI) and minority cultures. This will allow us to understand the difference in world view about SMI, their treatments in different cultures, and some of the technical adjustments that clinicians have to make in their interventions to build and maintain strong therapeutic relationship.

The changing health-care landscape in general and mental health care in particular are shifting the locus of care from the clinic to a community model of

Cultural Adaptation of CBT for Serious Mental Illness: A Guide for Training and Practice,
First Edition. Shanaya Rathod, David Kingdon, Narsimha Pinninti, Douglas Turkington, and Peter Phiri.
© 2015 John Wiley & Sons, Ltd. Published 2015 by John Wiley & Sons, Ltd.

treating individuals in their natural settings as we have discussed in the previous chapter. We discuss the interventions that are effective for different cultures in their natural settings with clinical examples. In addition, we will describe CBT techniques that can also be used by other staff like case management workers that do not have therapy training as such, but may find it helpful in engaging with clients to address their social service and case management needs. There are a number of case examples scattered throughout the chapter with a detailed description of one case example of a South Asian Muslim woman highlighting the cultural factors that played a major part in her engagement and therapy.

Importance of the Therapeutic Alliance

The therapeutic relationship or alliance is generally accepted to be one of the critical factors, if not the critical factor in determining the outcome of psychotherapy (Warwar & Greenberg, 2000). Although it can be argued that there is a great deal that can be done to enhance it and produce gains over and above it, a good therapeutic alliance with a skilful, trusting, accepting, and respectful therapist is still considered the foundation for optimal psychotherapeutic intervention (Beutler, Forrester, & Hannah Stein, 2000). A consistent but moderate correlation between therapeutic alliance and psychotherapy outcome was found in a review of 79 studies (Martin, Garske, & Davis, 2000). Similarly, a moderate degree of correlation between therapeutic alliance and outcome emerged in an analysis of over 200 research reports, covering more than 14,000 treatment sessions (Horvath, Del Re, Fluckiger, & Symonds, 2011). In evaluating the impact of therapeutic alliance for CBT specifically, relationship factors do seem to have a consistent though moderate impact on outcome (Keijsers, Schaap, & Hoogduin, 2000). The other factors that impact on outcome are therapist skill set as perceived by clients and the client's openness to accept psychological treatment. Some degree of variation in the relationship of therapeutic alliance to outcomes in different studies can be attributed to the concept and measurement of alliance. However, therapeutic alliance is not a unitary construct, and the various components of the therapeutic alliance that have been measured in studies include collaboration, affective bonding, agreement, trust, and empathy (Pinto et al., 2012).

While most of the studies of the alliance have looked at individuals with anxiety and depression, the importance of therapeutic alliance has also been shown in SMI. Therapist alliance formed in early stages of therapy is shown to be positively correlated with the outcome in CBT for individuals with schizophrenia and SMI in an inpatient setting (Svensson & Hansson, 1999). Evans-Jones, Peters, and Barker (2009) studied the various factors associated with the therapeutic relationship in CBT for psychosis (CBTp) and broke them into client-, therapy-, and therapist-related factors. Interestingly, they found that none of the client factors (including severity of psychosis) were related to therapeutic relationship but a number of therapist and therapy factors were linked, such as clients' ratings of therapist empathy, expertness, attractiveness, and trustworthiness. In addition, a number of sessions of CBTp interventions and the presentation of a formulation showed trend towards significance. Therapists were able to develop a good therapeutic relationship with clients suffering any degree of psychosis, and thus, the severity of psychosis should not be a reason for therapists to exclude clients from consideration of CBTp. This is contrary to the prevailing thinking in some quarters that it is difficult to develop and maintain therapeutic relationship with more severely psychotic individuals. On a different note, we can examine therapeutic alliance from the perspective of high-functioning individuals in recovery, who attest to the importance of a long-term, positive, and mutually respectful relationship with professionals in promoting recovery from SMI. Some even view a long-term therapeutic relationship as a critical piece in completing the recovery 'puzzle' (Cunningham, 2002).

Technical Adjustments in Enhancing the Therapeutic Alliance

The therapeutic alliance is therefore of critical importance in all psychotherapy relationships including those with cultural minorities with SMI. It spans all the following four broad phases involved in using CBT:

1. Engagement and assessment
2. Individualized collaborative case formulation
3. Effective sequential interventions based on the case formulation
4. Relapse prevention and termination

However, the degree of focus of the therapist varies depending on the stage of therapy. At present, there are gaps in our knowledge and understanding of the development and maintenance of therapeutic relationship in various cultural minority groups. In the following sections, we will move from a general discussion to describe issues related to the alliance in a number of selected cultural groups. This cannot be comprehensive but will give some idea of how the therapeutic alliance may be influenced in these and other groups.

When considering the various cultural groups and the importance of the therapeutic alliance, we have to be very cautious in trying to generalize from various studies described to all ethnicities. Hispanic groups can be highly under-represented in the majority of clinical and research samples (Miranda et al., 2005) as many studies exclude individuals who do not speak English. Exclusion of ethnic minorities is not confined to one ethnic group as similar descriptions of exclusion from clinical studies have been reported in African American clients (Adebimpe, 1994) as well as South Asian clients (Hussain-Gambles et al., 2004). Exclusion of minorities could be due to multiple factors including ethnicity and cultural stereotypes, language barrier, and the possible need for greater resources to include them in clinical trials (Hussain-Gambles, Atkin, & Leese, 2006). In the few clinical trials where the focus has been on minority groups, therapeutic alliance has been shown to be very important for better client outcomes. The therapeutic alliance accounted for 45% of the variance in psychotherapy outcome in one study of Hispanics from Puerto Rico (Bernal, Bonilla, Padilla-Cotto, & Perez-Prado, 1998).

Hispanic groups

Therapist interactions from the very first contact may be important in building a strong alliance. In one particular study, ratings of the therapeutic alliance after the first session were shown to be reliable predictors of premature termination in Hispanic clients (Anez, Paris, Bedregal, Davidson, & Grilo, 2005). The personal style of the therapist can play a role in the development of therapeutic alliance. Some suggest (Taylor, Beatriz-Gambourg, Rivera, & Laureano, 2006) a more personal and friendly style – which conveys warmth and trust – in the first session as helpful in fostering therapeutic alliance. This echoes the construct of 'personalismo' which signifies projecting a personal rather than 'institutional' or relatively cold and severe professional demeanour – valuing interpersonal harmony and relating to others on a personal level (Anez et al., 2005). On the other hand, concerns have been expressed in an allied context – working with people with drug and alcohol problems – that informal discussions ('small talk') in the first few sessions may have adverse consequences on Hispanic clients' motivation for change and substance abuse treatment outcomes (Bamatter et al., 2010). The authors suggested that maintaining a more formal relationship in early treatment sessions may work best with some Hispanic clients. Different results in different studies indicate the heterogeneity of Hispanic clients, and we continue to reiterate that therapists should be very cautious not to stereotype the entire cultural groups – there is at least as great variation within as between different cultural groups. A very good analogy to focus our attention on the differences between individuals of the same cultural group has been given (Nezu, 2010): 'Not all apples look or taste the same. This simple (and rather obvious) statement should also be applied to people of similar cultures.' The best way to understand a particular client is to ask them about their background and what the symptoms mean to them, get regular feedback on how sessions are progressing, and be aware of the verbal and non-verbal communication and the strength of the relationship at any given point in time.

Black African, African American, and African Caribbean ethnic groups

There are significant differences between black African, African American, and African Caribbean groups in their histories that account for some differences in how they may respond to therapy. The latter will often be only second or third generation in the United Kingdom or United States, whereas African Americans will have had centuries of history with the consequences thereof. Black African people may have just come to the United States or United Kingdom and have different economic or educational experiences.

African American clients often develop better therapeutic alliances with therapists of their own background and often state a preference for this. A study of reactions of African American clients towards therapy by African American and European therapists showed that clients assigned to African American therapists rated the therapeutic alliance stronger. They were perceived to have better understanding and acceptance of therapeutic interventions and reported greater benefit of therapy. The discussion of the topic of culture in the sessions by members of either therapist group did not seem to determine the quality of relationship. Therapists' initiation of, or non-initiation of, discussions about race had no effect on ratings of therapy (Thompson & Alexander, 2006).

Another important factor that impacts on the therapeutic alliance includes therapeutic self-disclosure by the therapist, which we have discussed in detail later in the chapter. Engagement with clients from African American as well as other minority cultural groups and their families is facilitated by communicating respect and genuineness in words and actions. Respect can be communicated in a variety of ways such as relating in a direct but supportive manner, asking them as to how they would like to be addressed, addressing people by their titles when they have one, and discussing the strengths of the individual and their culture (McGoldrick, Giordano, & Garcia-Preto, 2005).

Asian American and British South East Asian groups

Asian Americans have been shown to prefer directive, solution-oriented counselling (Li & BSK, 2004), and Asian Americans who work with more directive therapists report a stronger working alliance (Kim, Li, & Liang, 2002). The therapeutic relationship of this type is described as a 'vertical' relationship. Cultural concepts such as the vertical therapeutic relationship and a focus on degree of acculturation have been used to modify standard CBT for phobias and tested in Asian American ethnic groups as part of pilot studies. The adapted CBT has been found to be more effective than standard treatment in Asian Americans with low levels of acculturation (Pan, Huey, & Hernandez, 2011). According to Park, Chesla, Rehm, and Chun (2011), in Asian Americans, a positive therapeutic alliance could be maintained by cultural brokering (helping clients and families negotiate cultural norms), supporting families in making transitions, and utilizing cultural knowledge to provide appropriate care. Our understanding of the therapeutic alliance and therapy process in Asian Americans is still evolving, and further research is needed to inform us and bridge the gaps that exist (Sue, Yan Cheng, Saad, & Chu, 2012).

In our work in the United Kingdom, we found that Southeast Asian clients also seemed to be more likely to seek direct advice from the therapist, replicating the 'vertical' relationship described in the United States. We also found that self-disclosure was not expected as part of the engagement process in contrast to the African Caribbean group (Rathod, Kingdon, Phiri, & Gobbi, 2010a).

Technical Adjustments: Pre-engagement

Traditionally, engagement begins when the client meets with the therapist. This scenario assumes that clients recognize that the problems are bothering them, consider the mainstream mental health services as the right places to get help, and reach the mental health services where their problems can be assessed and dealt with. However, cultural minority clients face various barriers to accessing mental health care including their attributions of illness, limited English proficiency, remote geographic settings, stigma, fragmented services, cost, co-morbidity of mental illness and chronic diseases, cultural understanding of health-care services, and incarceration (Primm et al., 2010). Availability of childcare and transport can be further barriers. A number of these have been discussed in the previous chapter. There are steps services and therapists can take even before the engagement stage to anticipate and address some of the barriers.

Exercise: Think of two clients from minority cultural background that you have seen in the past 6 months and make a list of the various barriers that you experienced in engaging these two clients. Also think about the interventions that you and your treatment team made to deal with these barriers. With your current knowledge and understanding, what would you do differently for those clients?

The term pre-engagement is used to denote the various steps that are often needed to link clients to therapy providers. Pre-engagement can involve efforts at the level of the individual, the family, or the entire community and include educational, interventional, and advocacy activities.

Many cultural minority clients trust and rely on their family members, elders in the community, or priests more than traditional services and health-care professionals, and the help-seeking pathways they take reflect the relative lack of trust in health-care systems as we have discussed in detail in Chapter 3. For many clients from Hispanic cultural group, family loyalty, reciprocity, and solidarity (familismo) are very important, and surveys show that in the Eastern United States, about 75% of Hispanic patients with persistent mental disorders lived with the primary caregiver's family compared with 33% of the Euro-American patients (Parra & Guarnaccia, 1998). Similarly, for many African Americans, the extended family is an important source of strength and support and can include blood kin such as cousins and 'fictive kin' such as members of a church family or play mama (Boyd-Franklin, 2003). The extended family plays a variety of roles such as mediators in problems, providing temporary shelter in times of hardship and emotional support.

In addition, ministers have been key players in providing mental health care for African Americans who encounter life problems and challenges, including SMI

(Mattis et al., 2007). Some surveys show that 21% of respondents with a serious personal problem reported seeking help from a minister, while only 9.4% went to a psychiatrist and 8.7% went to other mental health provider (Chatters et al., 2011). Asian Americans have very low rate of utilization of mental health services, and a number of factors that account for this reduced utilization have been described in the literature. Age, sex, and education predicted higher odds of mental health service use among Latinos, none of which were significant among Asians. Needs factors were strongly associated with higher odds of mental health service use (Cho, Kim, & Velez-Ortiz, 2014). Asian American's family cultural conflict, but not family cohesion, was associated with service use (Chang, Natsuaki, & Chen, 2013). Targeted efforts based on the understanding of the factors that promote and hinder mental health service use in Asian Americans are needed to bridge the gaps between mental health needs and available effective treatments to promote better service acceptance (Ihara, Chae, Cummings, & Lee, 2014).

Pre-engagement efforts have to take into account the strengths and cultural attitudes of particular cultural groups and devise interventions to optimize dissemination of information about mental illness and the available resources and address the barriers to engagement in available services. The message to educate and encourage people taking adaptive pathways to mental health care in cultural minorities is likely to be more accepted if it is provided by respected and acculturated members of the community including celebrities or peers from the same background who have experienced mental illness. Voluntary sector, advocacy organizations, and media are powerful enablers in community engagement exercises. There are initiatives in the United Kingdom that use celebrities like Stephen Fry, and this has had an impact on reducing stigma and people's perception of illness. For some Hispanic ethnic groups, innovative strategies have been tried to educate the community about mental illness and available treatments including use of popular cultural items from film and video clips and well-known popular song lyrics to arouse and maintain interest while illustrating symptoms of psychosis and recommending use of mental health services. Outreach efforts using mass media have been found helpful in increasing awareness and help seeking in elderly Hispanic clients (Szapocznik, Lasaga, Perry, & Solomon, 1979).

In the United States, the National Alliance on Mental illness (NAMI) is the largest advocacy organization for the mentally ill with a multicultural action centre that works to ensure access to culturally competent services for all Americans with mental illnesses, support individuals with diverse backgrounds, and provide resources for cultural minorities (http://www.nami.org/). The NAMI Family-to-Family Education Program provides free education for individuals with SMI and their caregivers utilizing ethnically matched experienced family members and consumers as teachers (www.NAMI.org).

The various efforts at the level of the community have to be complemented with targeted efforts directed at individuals and their family members to engage them in therapy. The degree of family involvement in lives of individuals with mental illness can vary between different cultural groups and also within the same cultural group.

Generally, in the collectivist cultures such as eastern Asian cultures and in Hispanic cultures, families are very involved and can be part of the decision-making process. Sometimes, the family members who provide shelter and logistical and emotional support have to be convinced about the mental health services before they would allow their loved one to engage with services. The two case examples – one of South Asian and another of Hispanic woman – demonstrate pre-engagement work with the families, leading to the clients' engagement with services.

Case example

Safiya, an 18-year-old British-born South Asian young lady of Pakistani background, was referred for CBT by her key worker (a mental health practitioner) who suggested that she may benefit from this intervention following a deterioration of her mental health and increase in deliberate self-harm behaviour.

When Safiya was offered CBT, she asked for consent to be discussed with her father. Hence, an invitation to talk to her parents about CBT and how it might address her distress caused by her symptoms was extended. Her first session was at home with both her parents present in the session, and she deferred to her mother for responses to therapist questions. Safiya's mother expressed concerns about the efficacy of the therapy and her fears of it interfering with medication management. The therapist validated her concerns and provided a rationale for therapy being offered including the concern that therapy would interfere with medication. The therapist discussed the evidence for the effectiveness of the therapy in their culture and provided written material for the family to review. Following work with the family for a couple of sessions, Safiya's father disclosed information that he had taken his daughter to Pakistan to seek help from traditional healers. He admitted to spending over £3,000 on treatments from various healers without success and then approached their family physician in England who subsequently referred Safiya to the mental health service. At the end of the session, Safiya and her parents readily agreed to her participating in therapy.

Case discussion

The therapist accommodated his own individualistic approach to adapt to the collectivist one of the client's family and understood the importance of involving the parents in decision making. The therapist met with the entire family at their home, thereby reducing the fear and stigma that families experience when they have to come to a mental health centre. In addition, the therapist let the parents take the lead and be more active than the client in the first couple of sessions. He showed his interest and knowledge about their culture by sharing information he had about that culture as well as giving them written material. Explanation about the benefits of talking and supporting this with relevant evidence helped in harnessing hope and promoting engagement with the family. As a result of the therapist's interventions, the father was able to trust him and gave consent for his daughter to participate in therapy. With her parents being on board with therapy, Safiya was more comfortable engaging with the therapist.

Case example

Elsie, a 35-year-old Hispanic female with a diagnosis of schizophrenia, lived with her mother (Norma) and three children after her husband separated from her. Following hospitalization, Elsie was referred to case management, and her case manager was of Hispanic background. Her son was in therapy for behavioural problems, and his therapist suggested that Elsie may benefit from cognitive behavioural therapy (CBT) for her illness. However, both Norma and Elsie were very hesitant about therapy. They decided to take counsel of the case manager, who they trusted more because of their shared cultural background. Norma wanted to protect Elsie and she was the first person to make contact with the centre and requested information about CBT. She also wanted to find out if they could invite the case manager to be in session. The therapist agreed to meet with Norma, Elsie, and the case manager to address their concerns. In the presence of the case manager, Norma and Elsie raised questions relating to the following main themes: (a) they had seen providers from other cultures who did not understand them and discriminated against them, and (b) therapy was more personal than medication management and they would be misunderstood and judged. The therapist addressed their concerns by being honest and explained that he knew only a little bit about the Hispanic culture but was willing to be open to hearing more from them. He validated their feelings about cultural biases and verbalized his intent to be watchful for such biases. He presented the therapy as being a collaborative effort of two experts. The therapist was the expert in the process of therapy, while Elsie and the mother were experts in the symptoms bothering her as well as the Hispanic culture, and the two experts would make a strong team (collaborative empiricism). The feedback component of CBT was emphasized where the client would have opportunity to 'correct the therapist.' Both Norma and Elsie were satisfied and they consented for therapy.

Case discussion

This particular example demonstrates the principle of family loyalty, reciprocity, and solidarity. The mother took on the role of a carer for her daughter and her grand children following her daughter's mental breakdown. She was also protective of her daughter and wanted to evaluate the therapist before she brought her daughter. The therapist's flexibility in talking with the mother even though she was not the patient helped in gaining her trust and bringing the client to therapy. They felt safer when the case manager from their cultural background was allowed to sit in on the session at their request. As a result, they could express their feelings about prior negative experiences from other providers. The therapist's explicit statements about them being experts in the symptoms and their culture reduced the power differential in the relationship. The therapist communicated sensitivity and respect by being honest about his limited knowledge of the Hispanic culture and willingness to learn from them. The regular feedback, an integral component of CBT, made them feel empowered to correct any misunderstandings on the part of the therapist. All these steps in the pre-engagement and engagement phase helped to get Elsie to therapy.

Exercise: Spend a few minutes to think about the community your agency or service serves. Identify the two ethnic minority groups in your community. Find a staff member from that minority group and discuss with them the steps you can take for wider engagement of the community. Use the framework of steps at the individual, family, and community level to come up with strategies to engage these communities.

Setting of Therapy and Cultural Issues

In the United States and United Kingdom, the locus of care of severely mentally ill has moved to community settings through the establishment of community mental health centres (CMHCs) in the 1960s. With the current emphasis on recovery and community integration, care is moving into integrated systems such as medical homes or to the natural setting of clients' homes (Catty et al., 2002). Many mental health staff such as community psychiatric nurses (CPNs) in the United Kingdom and case managers in the United States see individuals with SMI primarily in the community settings as opposed to office-based settings or hospitals. Similarly, therapists treating individuals with SMI often choose to conduct sessions in client's homes in order to facilitate engagement and reduce barriers to accessing care. Hence, staff working with severely mentally ill cultural minority clients should be aware of the different issues that may arise when dealing with client's in their homes as opposed to their offices.

Technical adjustments for office-based sessions

The initial impressions that people have about the place where they are seen are important, and steps can be taken to make it welcoming by ensuring hiring of ethnically diverse staff in areas that have a large population of ethnic minorities. However, hiring staff from ethnic minority groups may not always be feasible due to the significant shortage of trained staff from ethnic minorities (Council on Social Work Education, 1998; McGoldrick et al., 2005) especially in those communities where ethnic populations are in the minority. Alternatively, attention should be paid to making the physical layout and features of the workplace or office more friendly and welcoming to minority cultures. For instance, there could be magazines and information leaflets in the main languages of the catchment area of the clinic or office. This may seem obvious but often, in practice, does not happen. Ensuring that this occurs and is maintained can make a significant difference and convey positive messages before the client even meets a therapist. The decorative pieces in the offices can include pieces representing other cultures. The therapists can keep track of important holidays for different cultural groups and prominently display signs for these holidays. The welcoming signs are likely to make the clients feel more welcome. They set the stage to build a positive relationship and also give the therapist and client an opportunity to engage in non-threatening small talk specially with clients from different minority groups. Below, we describe an example of a Chinese woman's engagement being facilitated using the discussion about the signs depicting Chinese holiday in the lobby.

Case example

Jing, a 20-year-old female, was brought to the services by her parents with complaints that she had failed her college grades and was isolating herself. Jing herself was withdrawn, did not want to speak much, and felt ashamed to be in the office. Her parents described that they emigrated from China when Jing entered high school. She had problems adjusting to school but managed to graduate with B+ grades. Problems intensified in college and she got a failing grade. This was a source of embarrassment for the entire family.

The therapist worked in an office where there was a diversity group consisting of staff who dealt with cultural diversity and put up signs celebrating diverse cultural holidays. When Jing's family came in, there were signs wishing all visitors a Happy Chinese New Year – it was the Year of the Tiger. During the initial part of the interview, Jing was very uncomfortable being there and would hardly speak. She gave one-word answers to questions despite some encouragement from her parents.

The therapist noticed her discomfort and decided to move the discussion to a topic that could be less threatening to Jing. He asked if she noticed anything in the lobby when she came in. Jing nodded yes with a smile on her face. When the therapist asked as to what brought on the smile, she said, 'the huge sign of the Year of Tiger.' The therapist asked her to explain to him what the significance of the Year of the Tiger was and Jing did so enthusiastically. She also talked about her mother being born in the Year of the Tiger. This was the icebreaker for Jing, and following that, she became more open to answering questions about herself.

Case discussion

In this particular instance, the signs posted in the lobby of the office indicated to Jing and her parents that the staff were sensitive towards their culture. They felt respected and valued as members of that cultural group. In keeping with their cultural norms of differing to the authority of the therapist and not initiating a topic, the family did not spontaneously talk about those signs. The therapist's introduction of that topic gave Jing permission to talk about the subject of Chinese year and facilitated her participation in the assessment process.

Considerations for sessions in community

Staff who primarily work in communities and see clients in their natural environments can be at a disadvantage of not being able to create an environment that is welcoming but, on the other hand, have the advantage of being able to learn a lot more about the clients, their living situations, and family dynamics. In addition, there are also many clients particularly in the initial phases of therapy who are unable, for example, through amotivation or social anxiety, or simply unwilling, for example, if they do not agree that help is relevant, to come to see therapists in their offices. For female clients with young children, permission from families, childcare, and transport can be issues. Therapists should be aware that latent misperceptions and biases could be activated in the environments that clients live. Some members of minority cultures may be socio-economically dis-advantaged and live in segregated housing which is associated with social prob-lems such as high unemployment, reduced economic development, concentrated poverty, suboptimal education, and diminished access to health and mental health care (Primm et al., 2010). Staff visiting these neighbourhoods may be quick to jump to conclusions about the client and the family based on the neigh-bourhood they live in. Staff members should be aware of their own reactions and biases and not let those influence their assessment of the client. A strength- and resilience-based approach to these difficult living conditions is the best way to counter the biases. An empathic approach of the staff member putting them-selves in the situation of the client and thinking of the degree of courage and resilience that is needed to survive in these difficult environments can increase their respect for the humanity of the client and their families. Some advantages of seeing clients in their natural environments are that there is opportunity to see the living circumstances of the client first-hand and get a much clearer view of their living situation. They can meet with a variety of family members, observe the family dynamics, and be in a position to engage multiple family members in the assessment process. The burden on the clients and their families to find the time and logistical resources to visit office is reduced, and thereby, clients are more likely to be engaged in the assessment process. In addition, many clients and their families are more comfortable on the natural turf of their homes as opposed to the therapists' office.

However, sometimes, clients and families may feel more stigmatized, and their standing in the community compromised when a mental health provider visits their home. The setting of the therapy can become either a key enabler or disabler. Culturally acceptable adjustments have shown to be successful. An excellent example of such adjustment is reported by the SITARA trial in the United Kingdom that demonstrated greater satisfaction in participants of the social intervention group that was specifically adapted for depressed and socially isolated Pakistani women living in the city of Manchester, in the north of England. The women travelled to and from the venue in a group taxi, accompanied by a female Pakistani transport facilitator, in order to tackle stigma and to provide some cultural sanction for the intervention; there were childcare facilities and food after each session, and the setting of the behavioural exercises was chosen with care, for example, a museum or shopping mall. The authors explain that social groups are more akin to their own culture of sharing, doing things together, and mutual social support provided through the extended family and a more communal way of life.

Exercise: Reflect on your service environment and consider whether it is culturally welcoming.

Technical Adjustments in Engagement and Assessment

Assessment goes hand in hand with engagement and relationship building. It starts from the very first contact with the client or the family or the first piece of information a therapist gets from a referral source and does not end until therapy is terminated. Assessment is not a linear process and the purpose of assessment is to:

- Understand the person's present issues, background, and expectations
- Gather information in order to develop a cognitive formulation
- Establish a baseline to measure change

Cultural issues are of major relevance to any attempt to understand the person's present issues, early experiences, background, and expectations as these heavily influence them. While an individual collaborative approach is necessary and will help, understanding or being able to find out the prevalent and relevant beliefs, attitudes, and traditions from the individual's culture can make assessment more accurate and empathic. Interpreting the information gathered can then be used to develop a cognitive formulation, but again, ensuring that this is consistent with the individual's beliefs, assumptions, and attitudes is essential. A baseline to measure change can be established, and rating instruments can help in this process. There are now instruments validated for use with many cultural backgrounds so these should be used or it be established that familiar instruments have validity. For details of the assessment areas that are usually covered and process used in CBT, the reader is referred to textbooks that deal with this topic in more detail (Kingdon & Turkington, 2005; Wright, Turkington, Kingdon, & Ramirez Basco, 2009).

Even though engagement and assessment occur simultaneously, at any given point, the focus may be more on information gathering or relationship building. The factors that interfere with the therapeutic alliance can be described under five different categories shown in Table 4.1. Symptomatic factors such as paranoia are universal and affect the therapeutic relationship in all cultural groups, while cultural factors such as specific but differing attributions of illness impact on therapeutic alliance in cultural minority groups. The detailed case description that follows illustrates the various cultural factors and their role in help seeking, engagement, and therapy.

Exercise: Think of a client who did not engage well in therapy. List the factors that influenced this process. What were the cultural issues if any? With a better understanding of the issues, what could you have done differently?

Table 4.1 Factors influencing therapeutic alliance.

Symptomatic issues
- Paranoia
- Hyper-vigilance and hostility
- Grandiosity
- Thought disorder
- Cognitive impairments such as attention and memory problems
- Somatic delusions: a focus on physical symptoms
- Substance misuse
- Withdrawal/high levels of negative symptoms
- Relationship issues: "personality disorder – emotionally unstable/antisocial/dependent/ schizoid".

Personal circumstances
- First episode
- Trauma (either recent or remote)
- Uncommunicative: teenage, catatonic, institutionalized
- Dysfunctional beliefs such as: "expressing feelings is wrong; accepting help implies weakness"
- Literacy issues such as language barrier

Cultural/family issues
- Cultural attributions to illness
- Knowledge, beliefs about system of care
- Attitudes of family and friends about mental illness such as shame, stigma
- Experience of being stereotyped/racism and lack of trust in system of care

Therapist issues
- Inexperience
- Lack of knowledge and awareness of cultural issues
- Lack of confidence in dealing with diversity
- Stereotyping

Service issues
- Alienated from services, for example, negative experiences with staff, lack of efficacy of prior treatments
- History of hospitalization especially if detained, involuntary commitment

Below is a detailed description of a case where assessment was completed while strong relationship was built with a British South Asian Muslim woman. We have used this example to discuss the technical adjustments used in the process of engagement and assessment.

Hamida initially identified with the culture of her country of origin as a Bangladeshi Muslim woman but showed a degree of acculturation relating to issues of gender equality, gender roles, and feministic beliefs. Acculturation in this particular area helped her to break away from a traumatic and oppressive

Case example

Hamida, a 19-year-old second-generation British Asian Muslim woman of Bangladeshi parentage, was referred to the mental health services by her parents with a main complaint of 'bizarre behaviour at home.' The family told the practitioner assessing her that Hamida, a practising Muslim, believed in one God Allah and his holy prophet Mohammad as the last prophet. She prayed five times a day and fasted during the holy month of Ramadan. She offered goods to charity and had faith in God. Hamida's parents elaborated on the main complaints in relation to her behaviour and reported their concerns around her anger, irritability, isolation, and arguments with family and her comments to the family that 'things did not feel right.' The family expressed their shame and guilt about the situation and described how their relatives had been talking about her. Hamida's verbatim statements discussed across a number of sessions are included here under different subheadings to help better delineate the various cultural issues in engagement and assessment.

As part of the assessment, Hamida was encouraged to write a narrative as she initially struggled to discuss her concerns. She wrote:

> My culture and my religion are a big part of my life. My parents brought their culture and religion over from Bangladesh and Bengali is my first language. I have visited Bangladesh twice in my life and I have been to Saudi Arabia with my family for the religious purpose of engaging in 'Ummrah.' At home (in the UK) I wear traditional clothing (Salwar-Kameez) so that I look respectful in front of elders. I believe that respecting and supporting the elderly and the poor is part of our duty and needs to be passed on to future generations.

The therapist was flexible and utilized the client's comfort in writing down her thoughts and feelings and was able to obtain a lot more information than the traditional interview method.

> My family means a lot to me. They have supported me through everything in my life including my illness and I am grateful for that from the bottom of my heart. There were occasions when due to illness I would be left behind from family functions and I did not understand. When relatives came to see how I was getting on, I would react by being upset and run to my room and mess up my room. This was embarrassing for my family, but they continued giving me support and help during my illness.

My life was busy and I found it confusing and hard for a whole year. This was due to a stressful life and partly me being disorganized in general. I believed that I had brought this upon myself. As a result, I would spend most of my time when home in my bedroom sleeping and crying myself to sleep. There was a time when I saw life differently from my family when I grew up, especially when I had to get married to a man double my age through arranged marriage. He came from Bangladesh and I did not like him. My marriage was a disaster and I learnt how men could be evil and controlling towards women. He tried to abuse me too. As result I am now a feminist and believe in female dominance. I understood that men get what they want in my culture and make others suffer because of their ill-mannered behaviors and attitudes towards women.

At the time of assessment, Hamida was still blaming herself for the abuse and argued that *'in a way maybe it is God's way of punishing me for all the bad things I have done in my life and that I may have been a victim in this case but 'Inshallah' it never happens to me again or any other person.'*

Hamida described how she was keen to help Muslim girls who might need support coping with such experiences and had difficulties trusting others.

After my experience of an awful marriage, I started to get depressed and felt very lonely. I stayed in my room crying most the time and thinking to myself as to how life is so unfair to me and wondering why bad things always happen to me. My family did notice a change in my behavior and would ask why I looked sad. Over time things got worse. I let everything get to me, my work and studies. I didn't know what I was doing and I lost myself in thoughts and became angry. I could not talk to anyone as I was sad and felt guilty. I guess I just didn't want to bother anyone about troubles in my life. I didn't want people sticking their nose into my business, especially the doctors, nurses and the college. Screaming and crying during my classes didn't help, wanting to go home all the time without any reason was frowned upon. I was very sad and confused so my parents came to college and spoke to my teachers who suggested that I could take a break from college. Consequently I lost two months of college time due to how I had become.

My first contact with the team was through a nurse visiting at home. I never knew why they were in my home and why they were there to see me. I was scared and would run to my bedroom or go hide in the other room until she had left. When my dad was at home I had to see her when she came again and she would ask me a lot of questions and I would sit quietly and stare at her and be like that every time she visited. Regular visits to the doctor, who was a man, was difficult for me due to my experience with my ex-husband and I would run away from him into the car park. My dad would chase after me and I would scream and hit as I was led back to the outpatient room to see the doctor. A lot of things happened when I was ill, running outside screaming, breaking cutlery and refusing my medication, not sleeping and not wanting to attend college. Therefore the nurse would deliver and monitor my medication to make sure that I was taking it and that it would make me feel better and get well again. My family thought I might need to see someone else like an Imam [Islamic religious leader] because they thought someone had cast an evil eye. My parents decided to take me to this place where we visited this professional Imam who looked very scary. It felt like he was going to kill me or my parents just had enough of me and wanted to sell me in the black market. So, I ran away. A man chased after me in the streets and dragged me back to the house. The Imam then came in with knives in his hands and cut my hair with the knife [which is a traditional ritual performed by the Imam]. During this time I was screaming helplessly. The Imam gave me a gift to wear for the rest of my life, a taveez [a locket worn either on the waist or arm, to ward off evil spirits], one around my waist and the other on my wrist. I will never forget what happened to me that day [traumatic experience]. I visited this place twice and hated it every time. It scared me and to this day I have nightmares about that place and I have imagined 'what if my family had left me there and what it would have been like to live there on my own and how scary it would have been for me.'

Exercise: What is Hamida's philosophical orientation? Discuss the practical considerations that will have an impact on therapy. Think of the technical adjustments required in developing a therapeutic alliance.

marriage and develop a self-assertive and self-affirming belief. Her parents and other older members of the family may not have shared her beliefs, and Hamida felt that she had let them down. The degree of acculturation shows generational variation and could be a source of emotional conflict. Generally, younger generations are more acculturated compared to the parents. The degree of acculturation would determine their involvement and acceptance of psychotherapy. The acculturation differences are also a potential source of conflict between parents and children. Hamida, raised in the United Kingdom, was fluent in Bengali and English and could express her symptoms well in both languages. She spoke in Bengali with her family and in English with clinicians. Sometimes, emotional distress can be difficult to accurately convey in a second language, but in this instance, the therapist did not have difficulty with her language (Figure 4.1).

Hamida was living within an extended family. This can be common practice in South Asian families and is not only acceptable but also regarded well, due to religious and cultural traditions. From a therapeutic point of view, there are pros and cons to be considered when dealing with such a family set-up. Her parents decided

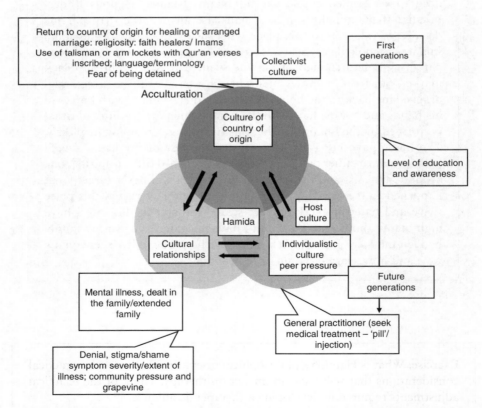

Figure 4.1   Acculturation process for Hamida. Adapted from Rathod and Kingdon (2009). © 2009 Elsevier Ltd 'Printed with permission.'

her partner in life. Hamida went along with her parents' decisions but found herself with a man who was controlling and abusive. Her parents also made the decisions to take her to a traditional healer who subjected her to some rituals that were traumatizing for her. This can be a dilemma for the therapists as they have to work with the permission and consent of the parents while attempting to develop a trusting relationship with the client. The client here respected her parents and elders. She had also suffered negative experiences due to decisions made by the parents. Hamida had developed mistrust for men from her past experiences. Given that her therapist was male, this was discussed at the outset and how she felt working with a male therapist. The issue of gender and choice of venue was given to Hamida.

The therapist emphasized at the outset that he did not expect Hamida to trust him but that trust would be earned. The therapist highlighted examples of varied degrees of trust that Hamida was already demonstrating; he illustrated how small amounts of trust were good enough and this would develop as therapy progressed.

From the 2/3 session, Hamida did not want her parents to attend. She felt that this was her only time where she could talk about her problems. From this stage, family involvement would not help as Hamida did not want it. However, the family had been instrumental in introducing her to the therapist. In other instances, once the therapeutic relationship is established, parents can be helpful in encouraging clients to complete homework assignments and act as co-therapists by reinforcing the therapeutic interventions. Respecting client's wishes enhances engagement in therapy. It is also important for the therapist to convey the message to the parents that decisions are in the best interest of the client so that the family is not threatened by this.

In addition to the family structure, there are specific gender and race issues that are more prominent in some cultures and impact on assessment, for example, females may not be seen as authority figures or even professional figures by South Asian Muslim groups, and this can have an impact on engagement for female therapists. First-generation immigrants often prefer men who have such perceived authority. Second-/third-generation clients become more adaptable. In addition, South Asian women may feel uncomfortable when alone with a therapist from the opposite gender. Some people may avoid prolonged eye contact with the opposite gender out of respect and modesty, and this should not be interpreted as avoidance or anxiety. For some South Asian clients, there may be reservations about white female staff visiting male clients. Families may object as they do not want their neighbours seeing white females due to possible adverse impact on arranging their marriages (Rathod, Kingdon, Phiri, & Gobbi, 2010a).

As her statements indicated, for Hamida, religion was integral to her identity, and the religious rituals provided her with a degree of structure to her day. This was important for her as she was unable to complete her college courses or get a job and hence did not have an external structure to her day. In addition, the religious beliefs gave her a purpose and meaning in life, sense of hope, and coping skills to deal with the ongoing psychological problems. Shared religious beliefs and practices bind family members who may belong to different generations together.

Religious Beliefs and Their Interaction with Culture

Spirituality and religion should be distinguished though they are sometimes used interchangeably. Spirituality is based on and is about experiencing higher states of consciousness and does not require a particular place or a mediator for the same. On the other hand, religion is an organized set of beliefs with its attendant-defined rituals, places of worship, and official mediators (Shanida, 2008). Recent evidence points to the different impacts of religious and spiritual affiliation and practices in an individual's coping and behaviours. Religiousness, including formal religious affiliation and service attendance, is associated with better health habits, such as lower smoking rates and reduced alcohol consumption. Spirituality, including meditation and private prayer, helps regulate emotions, which aids physiological effects such as blood pressure (Aldwin, Park, Jeong, & Nath, 2014). A detailed account of the various religious beliefs and their interface with CBT would be interesting, but an exhaustive account is really outside the scope of this book. Where such accounts would be useful, information from the individual client or members of their faith community combined with individual access to reference material (books or the ubiquitous and easily accessed Internet) can help.

However, it is relevant to discuss the way in which religious beliefs are intertwined with cultural beliefs and thus impact on early experiences, core beliefs, illness manifestations, help-seeking pathways, engagement, and retention in different treatments. In addition, religious institutions are a source of practical and social support for members of ethnic minority and immigrant communities. Studies conducted to investigate the correlation between religiosity and spirituality have concluded that there is a significant relationship associated with psychological well-being and using religion as either a positive or negative coping strategy (Leondari & Gialamas, 2009; Pieper, 2004). A meta-analysis supported this association with a statistically significant effect size (Ano & Vasconcelles, 2005). Studies conducted in the United Kingdom on minority groups concluded that they tend to use religion as a means of coping with their psychological distress (Kalra & Bhugra, 2011). A national survey of African Americans reported that individuals who are more involved with the church are likely to seek out ministers for serious personal problems and that problems involving bereavement were particularly suited for church intervention (Chatters et al., 2011). We know that some people from Hispanic background with SMI may attempt to deal with the stigma of being labelled 'loca' (Spanish for crazy) and may turn towards church and religion to cultivate alternate identities, such as being a church lady, that bestow dignity (Collins, von Unger, & Armbrister, 2008). Asian Americans who were proficient in English and sought help from church were found to be more likely to seek mental health treatment as well. Spirituality-focused groups have been found to be a good antidote to the lack of hope and demoralization that is so often associated with being seriously mentally ill (Revheim & Greenberg, 2007). It is important that therapists do not dismiss or judge the alternate help-seeking behaviours.

Any perception on the part of the client or their family that they are being judged is likely to lead to premature termination.

Therapists are known to be uncomfortable dealing with religious issues and may avoid exploring those (Rathod, Kingdon, Phiri, & Gobbi, 2010a). Fundamentally, the influence of religion and spirituality within minority cultures remains strong despite westernization and acculturation, and therefore, therapists should be prepared to explore and address religious and spiritual beliefs and practices in an objective and sensitive manner taking care not to anthologize culturally accepted beliefs and practices (De Mamani, Tuchman, & Duarte, 2010).

As the aforementioned case example illustrates, clients and families can hold simultaneously contradictory attributions to distress and illness. In Hamida's case, her parents believed that her distress and illness were as a result of casting of an evil eye – hence, they took her to an imam for healing, but at the same time, they allowed the therapist to come into the house and shared sensitive information with him. This example endorses findings from the (Rathod, Kingdon, Phiri, & Gobbi, 2010a) study that different cultural and religious help-seeking behaviours and pathways can be multidimensional and therefore use traditional and conventional pathways. This particular family continued to engage in religious practices such as reciting the Koran and praying five times a day, visiting imam for religious and spiritual support, and using arm lockets [taveez] to ward off evil.

Impact of Cultural Factors on Therapist Approach and Stance

Collaborative empiricism is a fundamental cognitive therapy principle which underpins teamwork and balanced contribution from both the therapist and client. Clients have to be socialized to cognitive therapy as a part of the assessment process. The collaborative model is more difficult to accept in some cultures that are paternalistic and expect the clinician or therapist to be a figure of authority, who will 'solve their problems or tell them what to do.' As a result, in the assessment phase, clients from some Eastern cultures may take a very passive stance that could be misunderstood by culturally uninformed therapists. In the example earlier, Hamida deferred to her parents and let them do the talking for her.

Asian clients may prefer a more structured (fits well with CBT principle) and prescriptive approach (Iwamasa, Hsia, & Hinton, 2006). The latter approach may conflict with CBT approaches involving collaborative empiricism where the client and the therapist work together to understand and develop alternative ways to address the clients' difficulties. The expectation is that the therapist or others would solve their problems just like they would, for instance, go to the mosque to see a priest or imam, who may give them zum zum (holy water), verses from the Koran to recite, or tavees to ward off evil spirits. Exploration of opinions about problems may lead to doubts about the clinician's competences. The therapist therefore needs to be creative and actively engage the client to participate in their own recovery and manage the transition from consultative to collaborative approach:

THERAPIST: So what do you think is the problem?
PATIENT: I don't know; you tell me; you are the expert!
THERAPIST: Ok, I will give you a suggestion; let's test this out together to see if is so...

The therapist can continue to maintain a collaborative empirical approach by working with the client from where they are positioned. The transition from the consultative to collaborative empiricism is crucial in adapting CBT to this client group. A clear agreed summary of the first session can be part of this, outlining briefly the key issues and plans to deal with the issue. Tasks set collaboratively ('homework') after this first and subsequent sessions to develop further understanding or test out beliefs expressed are important to endorse their feeling that 'something happened' and will continue to happen in therapy.

In contrast to paternalist cultures, some clients from African Caribbean backgrounds prefer the collaborative stance and prefer the therapist–client relationship to be viewed as equal. This reinforces the notion that therapy is respectful and the expert therapist and the expert patient are working collaboratively to help ameliorate distress and teach skills to cope with their problems.

The case of Hamida is presented in detail so that the different cultural factors that impact on engagement and assessment could be discussed in some detail. Even though the framework of looking at different cultural factors is helpful, it is important to remember that individuals from the same cultural and familial backgrounds may present differently due to individual factors and various degrees of acculturation.

Therapeutic Self-Disclosure

Staff including therapists and case managers either deliberately or unwittingly may be role models for the clients. From a behavioural perspective, each of us acts as a stimulus for our clients. Our age, gender, height, weight, appearance, clothing, and decoration of office space are all pieces of information that clients may interpret correctly or incorrectly. Hence, we should be aware of this impact on clients and make every effort to model behaviours, attitudes, and emotions that are likely to enhance therapeutic change (Goldfried & Davison, 1976). Self-disclosure can be a way of engaging clients in treatment. The literature about self-disclosure typically considers the therapist as the one who is disclosing or initiating disclosure (Derlega & Berg, 1987). However, our recent study (Rathod, Kingdon, Phiri, & Gobbi, 2010a) showed that self-disclosure may be initiated and sought by clients particularly from some cultural minorities. Clinicians should be aware that clients are doing their own assessment of the clinician during their interactions. It is therefore important to be cognizant of cultural background of clients so that culturally derived behaviours relating to being secretive and mistrust are dealt with appropriately and with sensitivity.

There are various dimensions and interpretations of questions relating to 'self-disclosure' in establishing a therapeutic alliance. In our study (Rathod, Kingdon, Phiri, & Gobbi, 2010a), we found that African Caribbean clients expect the clinicians or therapist to disclose self-information as a sign of respect and trust. African Caribbean service user participants admitted to asking therapists personal questions to encourage self-disclosure and become comfortable that they are treated 'as a person and not a number.' For instance, they would ask questions such as 'Do you have children, or where do you live?' Some questions were so subtle that the therapist was unaware they were being tested. Therapists are not singled out when it comes to seeking self-disclosure. The African Caribbean participants reported that they would do this to their friends as well. Therapists should be prepared for client-initiated self-disclosure. We asked cognitive behavioural therapists in focus group interviews in our study (Rathod, Kingdon, Phiri, & Gobbi, 2010a) how they dealt with self-disclosure as initiated by clients. Some therapist participants reported that they felt secure in themselves and did not find disclosing a personal issue a problem as long as this was appropriate and within therapeutic and professional boundaries. In contrast, those therapists who had responded in a defensive manner to questions of self-disclosure in particular with the African Caribbean participants reportedly found it difficult to engage their clients. Therapists' responses to client-initiated self-disclosure should be sensitive. It is not the content but the context that the response focuses on. So if a therapist tactfully responded to the client without divulging anything personal but was sensitive in their response, the client felt reassured that they were respected by the therapist enough to divulge personal information.

The other reason for therapist disclosure raised by the participants was the way clinicians expect to know much about the clients, when they themselves do not want to self-disclose. Therapeutic rapport can be built based on reciprocity when dealing with self-disclosure issues, bearing in mind that the professional boundary should be maintained.

On occasion, self-disclosure can be about the client assessing the knowledge and experience of the therapist. Some men from South Asian backgrounds may not respect a young female therapist as much as they would mature male. Sometimes, the class system prevalent in cultural societies comes into it. If a therapist is from the same cultural or ethnic background, the client is able to identify the class through names based on which they decide whether to respect the therapist or not. Sometimes, they ask specific questions about this. '*Your name is … does that mean you are from… .*' There is sometimes an issue of 'upmanship' in asking questions about the therapist.

When working with refugees or asylum seekers, they may be wary of the clinicians and therefore may ask personal questions to ascertain that you are genuine and would not jeopardize their legal status. The most common form of self-disclosure involves voluntary disclosure of one's personal situation or illness to another – in this case a patient or client. It is assumed that the role of disclosure will be to instill hope (Fisher, 1986) to clients and hopefully nurture a process of openness and self-disclosure on their part, concurrently reducing any form of stigma and shame resulting from suffering with mental illness (Hyman & Center for Mental Health Services, 2008).

Self-disclosure, while a strength, is not without its potential downside – the most prominent of which is boundary violation. It is important to maintain professional boundaries both for the safety of professionals and clients. Therefore, therapists need to consider the context, costs, and benefits of self-disclosure and the way it is done in order to ensure that it is helpful to their clients. Below is a clinical example of self-disclosure in an Asian male.

Case example

Que, a 33-year-old Asian male with a diagnosis of schizoaffective disorder, lives with his parents and a sister. He goes to a day programme 4 days a week. One constant complaint from his peers at the day programme was that he was malodorous. After multiple complaints from his peers, the supervisor of day programme gave an ultimatum to him to improve self-care or risk being discharged. His case manager talked with Que and his parents and found that Que took a shower only two or three times a month and that was the main reason for him being malodorous. When the case manager questioned Que, he said that the reason he did not take showers more often was because he would get pneumonia from frequent showers. Que's parents believed that getting wet in rain can cause pneumonia but did not hold the same worries about regular showers. The case manager used self-disclosure to inform Que that he takes a shower every single day and in all the 30 years of taking showers every day he never ever contracted pneumonia. He also disclosed to Que that in his culture, cleanliness was very important and gave some examples. He discussed with Que that there was no information that he had been aware of to say that taking showers would lead to pneumonia and he would research further if Que wanted him to do so. Following the self-disclosure, Que agreed to initially increase his showers to twice a week for 1 week and then meet his case manager again. The case manager reached out to a counsellor at the partial hospitalization (day) programme to inform him about this intervention and to give positive feedback to Que when his hygiene was good. Que met his case manager in a week, and they discussed how he did not get sick but had positive experiences in the day programme, and they agreed to increase the goal of taking showers to alternate days. Over the next 8 weeks, his hygiene improved and he was allowed to stay in the programme.

Case discussion

In the example above, culturally shared beliefs about contracting pneumonia by getting wet were generalized to regular showers as a risk for pneumonia. Self-disclosure by therapist helped the client to consider changing his behaviour and experiment with frequent showers and thereby improve his hygiene.

Exercise: Considering the above example, can you think of the kind of self-disclosure you would be comfortable with? Think of one or two cases on your current caseload and the potential use of self-disclosure in those instances. The next step is to utilize self-disclosure and evaluate the impact on the client and your level of comfort.

Technical Adjustments: Engagement Strategies for Therapists and Case Managers

The technical adjustments to CBT described in the following would be useful to therapists working with clients from cultural minority backgrounds. Wherever possible, case managers can also use these techniques to enhance engagement. Case management is widely considered the linchpin of services – where most client contact and support occurs – and acts to coordinate community services for adults with SMI, at least in the United States (Corrigan, Mueser, Bond, Drake, & Solomon, 2008). There are similarities with community mental health teams elsewhere. Case managers tend to have either associates or bachelor's degree and some training in mental health practice but not a specific professional training. Peer workers may work with case managers.

Most individuals with SMI do not have the luxury of working with a therapist at the first assessment, and the case manager (or mental health team member) is the professional they have the most contact with. Case managers need to engage severely mentally ill people and help them address their physical, mental health, and social service needs before and while they can see the therapist. It is therefore crucial that case managers engage clients from cultural minorities so that when available they are ready for therapy. Case management in the United States is looked at as an engagement and linkage service (brokering services) and not specifically as providing therapy, and hence, they require a different set of tools to engage and work with clients. They need to focus on specific interactions that help to enhance the engagement process while removing the barriers to the development of a trusting relationship.

Education, Normalization, Validation, and Problem Solving

Education and normalization are good engagement strategies to provide valid information about mental illnesses and reduce stigma for individuals from minority cultures. We have discussed this in more detail in the pre-engagement section. Population-based health educational and awareness-raising initiatives do not adequately reach minority culture, and the information presented is typically not done in a culturally sensitive manner. In addition, immigrants to a country may have beliefs about illness that are very different from the majority ethnic community. They may lack knowledge of the mental health system and the resources that they can take advantage of. Case managers have the ability to outreach to the ethnic minority communities and educate clients about the mental health issues and available resources and, in many cases, link them with resources and thereby remove barriers to help-seeking behaviours. There are some strategies that make education more effective. One is that case managers can involve members of the ethnic community that clients are likely to heed. We have discussed earlier in this chapter that some of these community members are peers from the cultural minority, church leaders, or advocates for the community. In many cases, it is easier to engage clients by working with family members and respected members of the community.

Educational efforts should go hand in hand with normalization of experiences. There are good examples of where this strategy works, for example, in Thailand, temples are the first port of call when people are unwell. In order to better treat patients with SMI, some psychiatric hospitals have actively integrated Buddha's teachings into community mental health work.

Normalization

Normalization is one of the most important approaches used in CBT (Dudley, Hammond, et al., 2007). Normalization has three aspects to it. The first aspect is educating clients that they are not alone in their experiences which helps destigmatize their experiences and reduce distress. This can be done by providing information about well-known people who are known to have mental illness. This is particularly helpful if the clients are presented with examples of cultural icons who have disclosed mental illness. The second aspect is sharing information as to how symptoms similar to those of the client are seen in normal individuals under some stressful conditions. A good example that explains hallucinatory experiences can be prolonged sleep deprivation:

CLIENT FROM AFRICAN CARIBBEAN BACKGROUND:	I have a mental illness, no one will ever give me a job now... My family think it is my fault...
THERAPIST:	One in four people suffer from symptoms of mental illness at some time in their lives – that does not mean they are all unemployed. It is

CLIENT:

THERAPIST:

CLIENT:

not yours or your families' fault; otherwise, there will be countless families at fault.

Yes, but I will not get better as I am black.

Irrespective of colour, these symptoms can have a variable course in different people. And many illnesses can be chronic like diabetes, asthma, etc. – despite the diagnosis, people learn to manage them and lead a good life. In some cultures, symptoms of psychosis are considered normal.

So do you think I will get better...?

The third aspect is how individuals can function in society and play a variety of roles despite having symptoms using the recovery approach. In this context, 'recovery' refers not just to symptomatic change but to the broader process of enabling people with mental health problems recover their lives and achieve the same personal goals. The key building blocks to achieving recovery are maintaining hope, re-establishing a positive identity, building a meaningful life, and taking responsibility and control (Andresen, Oades, & Caputi, 2003). Self-determination, self-management, and shared decision making are tools that enable this approach. The client's culture is a key enabler in this process. A number of cultures promote self-management, and community support can be positive in this respect.

Validation

This is a powerful technique in CBT which helps in engagement and allows the client to feel valued. It is particularly helpful when working with clients from minority cultures as the fundamental application is in helping clients to fully accept 'themselves and their world' and as they are 'in the moment' (Linehan, 1993). Validation goes beyond empathy in that the therapist attempts to make sense of the clients' thoughts and assumptions within the context and function which again is helpful with different minority cultures (Bhui & Morgan, 2010). The basic tenet in validation is to help the client learn to trust and validate themselves. Through validation, therapeutic relationships can be strengthened, especially in situations where a client is ambivalent about the therapeutic relationship. A number of clients from minority cultures who have experiences of discrimination and marginalization have fears and expectations of similar treatment from the therapist. Through validation, a therapist takes a genuine stance of treating clients as people with equal status rather than just a 'mental patient.' A powerful method of validation is acknowledging that clients are experts in the field of subjective experiences in relation to their life experiences, cultural influences, and their symptoms such as hallucinations or delusion. An example of the therapist verbalizing the expertise of the client is given in Chapter 5 (Elsie).

One specific type of validation that has been found to be helpful in the literature is what is called 'myth,' and it stands for the set of beliefs about the origin and course of the symptoms – a view about effective treatment modalities and consequences of not getting help (Benish, Quintana, & Wampold, 2011). Kirmayer and Young (1998) recommend that clinicians actively validate and accept clients' initial framing (i.e. myths) of the presenting problem. This preliminary validation and communication of respect for the client's initial myth, before any adaptation occurs, are critical for fostering the willingness of the client to consider alternate explanatory models later in treatment. It should be noted that the objective verifiability of the illness myth is less important than whether the client finds it acceptable and culturally compatible (Wampold, 2007). A common thread between universal healing practices and psychotherapy is the quality of non-falsifiability (Frank & Frank, 1993). When psychological suffering is pervasive and involves many areas, the afflicted is less interested in the scientific, objective truth of an explanatory model than in relief of the distress done in a way that is personally affirming and culturally believed, loved, honoured, and valued (Benish et al., 2011). Beyond validation, myth can also be utilized as specific intervention either by (a) introducing an explanatory model based on the cultural belief tendencies of specific ethnic minority groups or (b) the therapist and client cocreate a new explanatory model through a series of interactions (Kleinman, Eisenberg, & Good, 2006).

Case example

Lakshmi, a 60-year-old Indian woman, immigrated to the United States and lived with her only daughter following the death of her husband. The adjustment to a new country while she was going through the grief process was difficult. One thing she complained of was the loneliness. Six months after moving, she started hearing voices of her neighbours in India. These neighbours had been in conflict with her husband, and she always believed that the stress of this conflict was responsible for his heart attack. She became anxious, had insomnia, and was not able to function. When she was seen for assessment, she had the 'illness myth' that all her symptoms were due to a spell of black magic caused by the neighbours. She also believed that the antidote for this was going to India and having certain rituals performed by an expert. She did not want to see a psychiatrist but agreed to this due to pressure from her daughter. Lakshmi wanted to know if the therapist believed her. The therapist professed his lack of any evidence to conclude one way or other about her beliefs and instead focused on the impact of her symptoms on her self-care and social functioning. The discussion was about the options available for her to get relief. Medication was presented as an interim option until she was able to go to India and get permanent relief. She was agreeable knowing that she could stop the medicine once she went to India. Over the next few weeks, she could see the benefits from the medication and agreed to continue taking it. After a couple of months, her sister came to spend a few months with her. The company of her sister and the support removed the big stress of loneliness, and she improved in her mood and functioning. At that time, her illness narrative was that the neighbours had tried black magic but the effect of this was temporary. She did acknowledge the benefit from medication even though she still did not believe that she had had a mental illness as such. She no longer felt the need to go to India.

Case discussion

In this example, Lakshmi had an 'illness myth' that the symptoms came from black magic and that she had to go to India. However, a combination of medication and increased support helped in resolution of the symptoms. She accepted treatment including medication even though it was not consistent with her illness beliefs. Her beliefs about magic underwent some modification, and she also acknowledged the benefits of treatment and incorporated it into her illness myth.

Problem solving

This is another useful approach that can be beneficial to the case manager and therapist when working with clients from minority cultures. In SMI, problem-solving deficits are often numerous and varied. Defining the problem at hand can be problematic for a client with SMI, for example, with hallucinations, delusions, and severe amotivation due to depression. In addition, clients from minority cultures often struggle with their problems due to a lack of confidence in dealing with them and sometimes hopelessness due to their past experiences. The steps in problem solving are identifying and then prioritizing problems, choosing to work on one problem at any point in time, working on them, and then evaluating progress. The case manager can brainstorm with the client the various possible solutions and finally do a pros and cons of different solutions. Many ethnic minority clients such as Asian and Hispanic clients are reported to work well with this direct problem-solving approach (Table 4.2).

Table 4.2   Key points on therapeutic alliance and culture.

Therapeutic alliance is a critical element of therapy
Understand the impact of cultural factors in influencing therapeutic relationship
Adjust stance based on philosophical orientation
Pay attention to therapy environment and make it inviting and welcoming to the diversity
     of population served
Invest in engaging key stakeholders to enhance pre-engagement of minority communities
Understand your own biases and limitations and keep your cultural knowledge current
Admit own limitations and be willing to learn from patients about their culture

Conclusion

One of the critical steps in CBT is developing and maintaining a positive therapeutic relationship. This is very important in the therapy of individuals from
different cultural backgrounds as a variety of client-related and therapist-related
perceptions and beliefs as well as system issues act as barriers in therapy. Many
individuals from minority cultures are marginalized by the majority culture,
and hence, therapists have to take extra steps in order to engage them and keep
them in therapy. The extra steps include pre-engagement through outreach, advocacy, and working with the family and community as the way to reach the client
and promote traditional help-seeking behaviour. During the assessment phase,
a variety of cultural factors should be kept in mind, and the therapist should
be flexible enough to adapt the assessment style to the cultural expectations
and needs of individual clients that informs the formulation. Case managers
have a vital role and can use some of the techniques for engagement and
pre-engagement.

References

Adebimpe, V. R. (1994). Race, racism, and epidemiological surveys. *Hospital & Community Psychiatry, 45*(1), 27–31.

Aldwin, C. M., Park, C. L., Jeong, Y.-J., & Nath, R. (2014). Differing pathways between religiousness, spirituality, and health: A self-regulation perspective. *Psychology of Religion and Spirituality, 6*(1), 9. doi:10.1037/a0034416

Andresen, R., Oades, L., & Caputi, P. (2003). The experience of recovery from schizophre-nia: Towards an empirically validated stage model. *The Australian and New Zealand Journal of Psychiatry, 37*(5), 586–594.

Anez, L. M., Paris, M., Jr., Bedregal, L. E., Davidson, L., & Grilo, C. M. (2005). Application of cultural constructs in the care of first generation Latino clients in a community mental health setting. *Journal of Psychiatric Practice, 11*(4), 221–230. pii:00131746-200507000-00002

Ano, G., & Vasconcelles, E. B. (2005). Religious coping and psychological adjustment to stress: A meta-analysis. *Journal of Clinical Psychology, 61*, 461–480.

Bamatter, W., Carroll, K. M., Anez, L. M., Paris, M., Jr., Ball, S. A., Nich, C.,...Martino, S. (2010). Informal discussions in substance abuse treatment sessions with Spanish-speaking clients. *Journal of Substance Abuse Treatment, 39*(4), 353–363. doi:10.1016/j.jsat.2010.07.005, pii:S0740-5472(10)00158-3

Benish, S. G., Quintana, S., & Wampold, B. E. (2011). Culturally adapted psychotherapy and the legitimacy of myth: A direct-comparison meta-analysis. *Journal of Counseling Psychology, 58*(3), 279–289. doi:10.1037/a0023626, pii:2011-10381-001

Bernal, G., Bonilla, J., Padilla-Cotto, L., & Perez-Prado, E. M. (1998). Factors associated to outcome in psychotherapy: An effectiveness study in Puerto Rico. *Journal of Clinical Psychology, 54*(3), 329–342.

Beutler, L. E., Forrester, B. H., & Hannah Stein, M. (2000). Common, specific, and cross-cutting psychotherapy interventions. *Psychotherapy, 50*(3), 298–301.

Bhui, K., & Morgan, N. (2010). Effective psychotherapy in an ethnically and culturally diverse society. In R. Bhattacharya, S. Cross, & D. Bhugra (Eds.), *Clinical topics in cultural psychiatry* (pp. 337–347). London, UK: Royal College of Psychiatrists.

Boyd-Franklin, N. (2003). *Black families in therapy: Understanding the African American experience* (Vol. 2). New York, NY: Guilford Press.

Catty, J., Burns, T., Knapp, M., Watt, H., Wright, C., Henderson, J., & Healey, A. (2002). Home treatment for mental health problems: A systematic review. *Psychological Medicine, 32*(3), 383–401.

Chang, J., Natsuaki, M. N., & Chen, C. N. (2013). The importance of family factors and generation status: Mental health service use among Latino and Asian Americans. *Cultural Diversity & Ethnic Minority Psychology, 19*(3), 236–247. doi:10.1037/a0032901

Chatters, L. M., Mattis, J. S., Woodward, A. T., Taylor, R. J., Neighbors, H. W., & Grayman, N. A. (2011). Use of ministers for a serious personal problem among African Americans: Findings from the national survey of American life. *The American Journal of Orthopsychiatry, 81*(1), 118–127. doi:10.1111/j.1939-0025.2010.01079.x

Cho, H., Kim, I., & Velez-Ortiz, D. (2014). Factors associated with mental health service use among Latino and Asian Americans. *Community Mental Health Journal.* doi:10.1007/s10597-014-9719-6

Collins, P. Y., von Unger, H., & Armbrister, A. (2008). Church ladies, good girls, and locas: Stigma and the intersection of gender, ethnicity, mental illness, and sexuality in relation to HIV risk. *Social Science & Medicine, 67*(3), 389–397.

Corrigan, P. W., Mueser, E. T., Bond, G., Drake, R. E., & Solomon, P. (2008). *Principles and practice of psychiatric rehabilitation: An empirical approach.* New York, NY: Guilford Press.

Council on Social Work Education. (1998). *Statistics on social work education.* Alexandria, VA: Author.

Cunningham, R. (2002). Living with schizophrenia and thriving in remission: 10 years of stress and crises. *Brief Treatment and Crisis Intervention, 2*, 247–260.

De Mamani, A., Tuchman, N., & Duarte, E. (2010). Incorporating religion/spirituality into treatment for serious mental illness. *Cognitive and Behavioral Practice, 17*(4), 348–357.

Derlega, V. J., & Berg, J. H. (1987). *Self disclosure: Theory, research and therapy.* New York, NY: Plenum Press.

Dudley, R. Bryant, C., Hammond, K., Siddle, R., Kingdon, D., Turkington, D. (2007). Techniques in cognitive behavioral therapy of schizophrenia: Using normalizing in schizophrenia. *Journal of Norwegian Psychological Association, 44*, 562–572.

Evans-Jones, C., Peters, E., & Barker, C. (2009). The therapeutic relationship in CBT for psychosis: Client, therapist and therapy factors. *Behavioural and Cognitive Psychotherapy*, *37*(5), 527–540. doi:10.1017/S1352465809990269, pii:S1352465809990269

Fisher, D. V. (1986). Decision-making and self-disclosure. *Journal of Social and Personal Relationships*, *3*(3), 323–336. doi:10.1177/0265407586033005

Frank, J. D., & Frank, J. B. (1993). *Persuasion and healing*. Baltimore, MD: Johns Hopkins University Press.

Goldfried, M. R., & Davison, G. C. (1976). *Clinical behavior therapy*. New York, NY: Holt Rinehart & Winston.

Horvath, A. O., Del Re, A. C., Fluckiger, C., & Symonds, D. (2011). Alliance in individual psychotherapy. *Psychotherapy (Chic)*, *48*(1), 9–16. doi:10.1037/a0022186, pii:2011-04924-003

Hussain-Gambles, M., Atkin, K., & Leese, B. (2006). South Asian participation in clinical trials: The views of lay people and health professionals. *Health Policy*, *77*(2), 149–165. doi:10.1016/j.healthpol.2005.07.022, pii:S0168-8510(05)00191-0

Hussain-Gambles, M., Leese, B., Atkin, K., Brown, J., Mason, S., & Tovey, P. (2004). Involving South Asian patients in clinical trials. *Health Technology Assessment*, *8*(42), iii, 1–109. pii:98-23-19

Hyman, I., & Center for Mental Health Services. (2008). *Self-disclosure and its impact on individuals who receive mental health services* (DHHS Publication No. SMA-08-4337). Rockville, MD: U.S. Department of Health and Human Services, Substance Abuse and Mental Health Services Administration, Center for Mental Health Services.

Ihara, E. S., Chae, D. H., Cummings, J. R., & Lee, S. (2014). Correlates of mental health service use and type among Asian Americans. *Administration and Policy in Mental Health*, *41*(4), 543–551. doi:10.1007/s10488-013-0493-5

Iwamasa, G. Y., Hsia, C., & Hinton, D. (2006). Cognitive-behavioral therapy with Asian Americans. In P. A. Hays, & G. Y. Iwamasa (Eds.), *Culturally responsive cognitive-behavioral therapy: Assessment, practice, and supervision* (pp. 117–140). Washington, DC: American Psychological Association.

Kalra, G., & Bhugra, D. (2011). Ethnic factors in managing black and minority ethnic patients. *Current Opinion in Psychiatry*, *24*(4), 313–317.

Keijsers, G. P. J., Schaap, C. P. D. R., & Hoogduin, C. A. L. (2000). The Impact of interpersonal patient and therapist behavior on outcome in cognitive-behavior therapy. *Behavior Modification*, *24*(2), 264–297. doi:10.1177/0145445500242006

Kim, B. S. K., Li, L. C., & Liang, T. H. (2002). Effects of Asian American client adherence to Asian cultural values, session goal, and counselor emphasis of client expression on career counseling process. *Journal of Counseling Psychology*, *49*(3), 342–354. doi:10.1037/0022-0167.49.3.342

Kingdon, D., & Turkington, D. (2005). *Cognitive therapy of schizophrenia*. New York, NY: Guilford Press.

Kirmayer, L. J., & Young, A. (1998). Culture and somatization: Clinical, epidemiological, and ethnographic perspectives. *Psychosomatic Medicine*, *60*(4), 420–430.

Kleinman, A., Eisenberg, L., & Good, B. (2006). Culture, illness, and care: Clinical lessons from anthropologic and cross-cultural research. *Focus*, *4*, 140–149.

Leondari, A., & Gialamas, V. (2009). Religiosity and psychological well-being. *International Journal of Psychology*, *44*(4), 241–248. doi:10.1080/00207590701700529

Li, L., & BSK, K. (2004). Effects of counseling style and client adherence to Asian cultural values on counseling process with Asian American college students. *Journal of Counseling Psychology, 51*, 58–167.

Linehan, M. (1993). *Cognitive-behavioral treatment of borderline personality disorder.* New York, NY: Guilford Press.

Martin, D. J., Garske, J. P., & Davis, M. K. (2000). Relation of the therapeutic alliance with outcome and other variables: A meta-analytic review. *Journal of Consulting & Clinical Psychology, 68*(3), 438–450.

Mattis, J. S., Mitchell, N., Zapata, A., Grayman, N. A., Taylor, R. J., Chatters, L. M., & Neighbors, H. W. (2007). Uses of ministerial support by African Americans: A focus group study. *The American Journal of Orthopsychiatry, 77*(2), 249–258. doi:10.1037/0002-9432.77.2.249, pii:2007-07239-010

McGoldrick, M., Giordano, J., & Garcia-Preto, N. (2005). *Ethnicity and family therapy.* New York, NY: Guilford Press.

Miranda, J., Bernal, G., Lau, A., Kohn, L., Hwang, W. C., & LaFromboise, T. (2005). State of the science on psychosocial interventions for ethnic minorities. *Annual Review of Clinical Psychology, 1*, 113–142. doi:10.1146/annurev.clinpsy.1.102803.143822

Nezu, A. M. (2010). Cultural influences on the process of conducting psychotherapy: Personal reflections of an ethnic minority psychologist. *Psychotherapy: Theory, Research, Practice, Training, 47*(2), 169–176.

Pan, D., Huey, S. J., Jr., & Hernandez, D. (2011). Culturally adapted versus standard exposure treatment for phobic Asian Americans: Treatment efficacy, moderators, and predictors. *Cultural Diversity & Ethnic Minority Psychology, 17*(1), 11–22. doi:10.1037/a0022534, pii:2011-03115-002

Park, M., Chesla, C. A., Rehm, R. S., & Chun, K. M. (2011). Working with culture: Culturally appropriate mental health care for Asian Americans. *Journal of Advanced Nursing, 67*(11), 2373–2382. doi:10.1111/j.1365-2648.2011.05671.x

Parra, P. A., & Guarnaccia, P. (1998). Ethnicity, culture, and resiliency in caregivers of a seriously mentally ill family member. In H. I. McCubbin, E. A. Thompson, A. I. Thompson, & J. E. Fromer (Eds.), *Resiliency in native American and immigrant families* (pp. 431–450). Thousand Oaks, CA: Sage Publications, Inc.

Pieper, J. (2004). Religious coping in highly religious psychiatric inpatients. *Mental Health, Religion & Culture, 7*, 349–363.

Pinto, R. Z., Ferreira, M. L., Oliveira, V. C., Franco, M. R., Adams, R., Maher, C. G., & Ferreira, P. H. (2012). Patient-centred communication is associated with positive therapeutic alliance: A systematic review. *Journal of Physiotherapy, 58*(2), 77–87. doi:10.1016/S1836-9553(12)70087-5, pii:S1836-9553(12)70087-5

Primm, A. B., Vasquez, M. J., Mays, R. A., Sammons-Posey, D., McKnight-Eily, L. R., Presley-Cantrell, L. R.,…Perry, G. S. (2010). The role of public health in addressing racial and ethnic disparities in mental health and mental illness. *Preventing Chronic Disease, 7*(1), A20.

Rathod, S., & Kingdon, D. (2009). CBT across cultures. *Psychiatry, 8*(9), 370–371.

Rathod, S., Kingdon, D., Phiri, P., & Gobbi, M. (2010a). Developing culturally sensitive cognitive behaviour therapy for psychosis for ethnic minority patients by exploration and incorporation of service users' and health professionals' views and opinions. *Behavioural and Cognitive Psychotherapy, 38*, 511–533. doi:10.1017/S1352465810000378, pii:S1352465810000378

Rathod, S., Phiri, P., & Kingdon, D. (2010b). Cognitive behavioral therapy for schizophrenia. *The Psychiatric Clinics of North America, 33*(3), 527–536. doi:10.1016/j.psc.2010.04.009, pii:S0193-953X(10)00051-1

Revheim, N., & Greenberg, W. M. (2007). Spirituality matters: Creating a time and place for hope. *Psychiatric Rehabilitation Journal, 30*(4), 307–310.

Shanida, N. (2008). *The blissful brain*. London, UK: Gaia.

Sue, S., Yan Cheng, J. K., Saad, C. S., & Chu, J. P. (2012). Asian American mental health: A call to action. *The American Psychologist, 67*(7), 532–544. doi:10.1037/a0028900, pii:2012-27130-003

Svensson, B., & Hansson, L. (1999). Therapeutic alliance in cognitive therapy for schizophrenic and other long-term mentally ill patients: Development and relationship to outcome in an in-patient treatment programme. *Acta Psychiatrica Scandinavica, 99*(4), 281–287.

Szapocznik, J., Lasaga, J., Perry, P. R., & Solomon, J. R. (1979). Outreach in the delivery of mental health services to Hispanic elders. *Hispanic Journal of Behavioral Sciences, 1*(1), 21–40.

Taylor, B. A., Beatriz-Gambourg, M., Rivera, M., & Laureano, D. (2006). Constructing cultural competence perspectives of family therapists working with Latino families. *American Journal of Family Therapy, 34*, 429–445.

Thompson, V. L., & Alexander, H. (2006). Therapists' race and African American clients' reactions to therapy. *Psychotherapy, 43*(1), 99–110. doi:10.1037/0033-3204.43.1.99, pii:2006-05485-008

Wampold, B. E. (2007). Psychotherapy: The humanistic (and effective) treatment. *American Psychologist, 62*, 857–873. doi:10.1037/0003-066X.62.8.857

Warwar, S., & Greenberg, L. (2000). *Handbook of counseling psychology* (3rd ed.). New York, NY: John Wiley & Sons, Inc.

Wright, J., Turkington, D., Kingdon, D., & Ramirez Basco, M. (2009). *Cognitive behavior therapy for severe mental illness: An illustrated guide*. Washington, DC: American Psychiatric Publishing Inc.

5

General Theoretical Modifications in Orienting Clients to Therapy

We will now discuss techniques and modifications used when beginning therapy that are particularly useful with clients from the range of different cultures. We will focus on issues such as stereotyping and adjusting to the dynamic nature of culture. We describe two types of therapeutic interventions that are likely to work across different minority cultures. We have used examples to discuss these interventions.

Minority cultures are very distinct from one another but at the same time share some common experiences of having to deal with the stressor of adapting to a majority culture. In general, the majority or the dominant culture has stereotyped perceptions about minority cultures that are further perpetuated by the mass media (McGoldrick, Giordano, & Garcia-Preto, 2005). These perceptions are a source of stress for members of the minority culture who feel the pressure to adopt the beliefs and world view of the majority culture. In the process of understanding an individual's life experiences and adaptive capabilities, therapists have to move from the universal human experience to the specific individual experience and reactions. The pathway to understanding an individual is from universal human experience to common experiences of all minority cultures to the experiences of members of individual culture, the family unit, and finally the individual client. We all share certain experiences. It might help to clarify this by describing the perspective of one of the authors of this chapter:

So taking myself, I share something in common with all humanity such as the various positive and negative emotions and existential issues, then when

Cultural Adaptation of CBT for Serious Mental Illness: A Guide for Training and Practice, First Edition. Shanaya Rathod, David Kingdon, Narsimha Pinninti, Douglas Turkington, and Peter Phiri.
© 2015 John Wiley & Sons, Ltd. Published 2015 by John Wiley & Sons, Ltd.

> it comes to being an Indian American, I share some features with all the minority groups, followed by what I share with Indian Americans as a group, then my subculture as a South Indian, followed by what I share with my family and finally my individual beliefs and experiences that are different from anyone and make me unique.

Modifications are largely necessary to address the 'world view' orientation of minority culture clients when working with them. Examples are reflected in differences in the body–mind concept, individualistic versus a collective orientation, self, and ego boundaries among others. The dichotomization of body and mind is a characteristic of Western culture, and many people from Eastern cultures are used to manifesting and communicating their problems through their bodies even though the problems are psychological (Tseng, Chang, & Nishjzono, 2005). Somatization, as we have discussed before, can be understood as an indirect and culturally more acceptable way of communicating distress through the body instead of direct verbal communication. This is a more helpful way of understanding somatization as opposed to the thinking that people are either incapable or not sophisticated to verbalize psychological distress. We have discussed attributions to the soma in many Eastern cultures in Chapter 3. The earlier case example of Lin (Chapter 3) demonstrated this issue. Modifications to therapy to allow for these attributions help with engagement and therefore the process of therapy. We have discussed this further in Chapter 9 which focuses on specific modifications of therapy in depression.

The collective orientation of certain cultures means that individual needs take a secondary seat to the needs and priorities of the collective group (family or community). The self in Western concept is one of the individual and the family is considered a nuclear family. However, in Eastern cultures, the boundaries of self are broader and include the family. In addition, the family is considered more broadly and can include extended family to various degrees. The therapists have to be more open to the involvement of the families in the care of their family members to engage the clients. We have used the earlier example of Shobha (Chapter 3) to demonstrate this difference. Throughout the chapters, we have discussed this concept with modifications to different stages of therapy in detail.

Further modification requires cognizance of personality development needs across different cultures. This includes concepts like prolonged dependence in children from some Eastern cultures due to strong family bonds. We know that the concept of personality development is universal; however, the pace of development and the major themes emphasized at each stage are subject to societal influence. We have mentioned the 4-2-1 syndrome in Chapter 3 which demonstrates cultural and societal determinants of personality development, especially variables like autonomy, dependence, and independence from families. This concept is further demonstrated through examples in the next chapter.

Specific Theoretical Modifications
for Culturally Diverse Groups

Understanding the world view of the client helps the therapist to make technical adjustments and theoretical modifications to therapy. An important factor in the interaction of the therapist and client is the world view of the therapist. This includes their own value systems, beliefs, understanding of different cultures, prejudices, and experiences. These may impact on the therapy sessions, but awareness of the interaction enables the therapist to deal with them.

Two specific aspects related to minority cultural groups are important to take into account:

1. The universal nature of bias and stereotyping
2. The dynamic nature of cultures

As mentioned earlier in the chapter, therapists need awareness that the majority or the dominant culture typically has stereotyped perceptions about minority cultures that are further perpetuated by the mass media (McGoldrick et al., 2005). Although there will always be a wide range of attitudes, stereotyping of the majority culture is also very possible and can itself lead to unintended consequences in therapy.

Stereotyping is a universal human phenomenon that is seen in different countries and cultures and across all time periods. Stereotyping and bias are not only seen across cultures but also within subgroups of the same culture. For example, African American men may be misrepresented as tending to be 'hostile and violent' and women as being 'loose and sexual.' The media, especially through popular films, portrays the image of Italians as frequently criminal, belonging to the mafia; the British as 'stiff upper lipped' with posh accents; and the French as great lovers.

Exercise: Identify the three commonly served minority cultures in your agency or service and write down the common stereotypical assumptions related to these communities. The focus of enquiry can be different topics such as attitudes towards medication and therapy, views about privacy and family involvement, approach towards the therapist, etc. To make the exercise even more helpful and meaningful, speak to a staff member belonging to the minority community and discuss the common stereotypical assumptions from their perspective.

Therapists being members of the larger society may also share some of these stereotypes and perceptions and may not be aware of them unless they take steps to overcome these biases: the growth in diversity training in recognition of this by most health and social care agencies/service has been designed to address such misconceptions. The very first step in doing so is trying to become aware of one's own biases which will often be shaped by personal contact – or the lack of it – with people from different backgrounds. This is a process which was expected of therapists practising most forms of counselling or psychotherapy, and so the skills to reflect in this way may already be present but it has, arguably, become less of a requirement for CBT therapists and so may not be such a familiar process to them.

We are used to looking for the ways in which family and life experiences shape the core beliefs and attitudes of our clients, and so it is not a big step to apply these techniques to ourselves, generally, and in relation to our own cultural attitudes. Having a member of the family or friend who comes from a minority culture can be very influential but can also unconsciously lead to stereotyping of 'all' people from that culture having the positive and negative attributes of that person.

First, examining one's own cultural identity can be a start and then reflecting on views about people especially clients from different specific cultures. Arthur Nezu suggested that all therapists should engage in a similar process of self-understanding of their ethnic status – that is, to contemplate who you are, in what ways are you diverse/different, and how such diversity impacts on your work as a psychotherapist. The purpose of this process is to think about 'me', the impact of 'me on them' ('them' being my clients), and the impact of 'them on me', beyond that which generally occurs within one's professional office (i.e. treatment setting) (Nezu, 2010). The process can be illuminating but also, on occasion, threatening to the therapist but at the same time can lead to an experiential understanding and sensitivity that clients experience when cultural issues are discussed.

The next step is developing an attitude of cultural neutrality. Cultural neutrality is an attitude that considers all cultures as equal and with positive and negative features in every one of them whether it is a dominant or a minority culture. This may not come naturally for therapists or indeed anyone. Culturally sensitive therapists have to be able to develop this attitude and be able to bring it into sessions when dealing with minority cultures. Culturally neutral attitudes can be developed by making conscious efforts to learn about the different cultures that your clients come from with a focus more on adaptive strengths of the cultural group. There are many steps in the process of learning about different cultures and developing cultural expertise. The first and a basic step that can be done by anyone is to obtain historical and factual information about different cultures by turning to the websites (e.g. www.everyculture.com) or books and articles on the specific topics. However, it has to be kept in mind that websites can only give factual information and these are not a substitute for the time and effort needed to learn a different culture. One might, for example, know the actual date of Chinese New Year and that the year is the year of horse. This bit of information is a useful conversation starter but would not help the therapist to have a deeper understanding of the importance of the New Year to Chinese in general and the client you are dealing with in particular. Hence, therapists should be guarded about assuming that they know a culture based on some facts read, especially on the Internet. On the other hand, these facts can be useful when in conversations about culture with clients – and should be validated with them.

The next or third step in one's multicultural edification is to enquire about particular cultural groups, where possible, from colleagues who belong to that culture. The fourth step may be to seek opportunities to interact with other members from other cultures and develop one's knowledge – it may be that they can help identify and overcome any general or specific misunderstandings that you have. Giving a personal example, one of the authors of this book found that they discovered a lot more – specially cultural strengths – when they started working closely with a colleague from an African background. Defying all prevalent stereotypes, they found him to be ambitious, polite, soft-spoken, kind, intelligent, and an achiever.

Clients and their families are experts in their cultures and are an excellent source of information. Many are very willing to share their knowledge and expertise about their own culture. A genuine non-judgemental enquiry to learn about the culture of the clients is enormously validating and reaffirming to them. Many would be thrilled to take on the role of educating and supervising the therapist in the nuances of their culture. Talking about oneself (that would include one's culture) is intrinsically very rewarding and is shown to increase activity in the nucleus accumbens and ventral tegmental area of the mesolimbic dopaminergic system in ways similar to food, money, or sex. Honest questioning by a therapist regarding culture encourages self-reflection and disclosure of one's thoughts and feelings about the impact of culture on oneself. Behavioural experimentation that included fMRI studies has shown that both self-reflection and self-disclosure are independently rewarding and stronger than primary rewards such as food (Tamir & Mitchell, 2012). However, some clients may be put off when the therapist, who is considered an expert, does not have the understanding of their culture. This is particular in some cultures where the therapist is considered to be an expert and the client is not comfortable to take on the role of being a cultural educator to the therapist. In some instances, individuals may not even want to discuss the issue of their culture even when the therapist is utilizing a very supporting stance as the example of Chloe in the following (second case example) shows.

Finally, all therapists who are working with diverse clients would benefit from supervision and consultation with other experts in the culture. It is to be understood that in this fast changing world, it is very difficult to keep up with changes in different cultural groups and consultation with other experts in that culture on a periodic basis is the best way to keep one's knowledge and perspective current. The best example of this is where the therapist has a cultural coach who guides them in navigating the complex issues that might arise during therapy with a client from minority culture.

A final factor to be aware of is the dynamic nature of cultures as they adapt to changing world circumstances. None of the cultures are static. Therapists dealing with diverse cultures should attempt to take the time and make the effort to learn about the changes in the culture of the clients they treat. This is done by using a personal approach to understanding the individual client's culture. Let us discuss the example of Gordon.

Case example

Gordon is a 36-year-old executive in the United Kingdom who emigrated from Zimbabwe about 15 years ago. He had worked extremely hard over the years to achieve success in his career and was proud of his achievements. While in the United Kingdom, he married his wife who was Caucasian, and the couple had three sons. After 10 years of marriage, his relationship broke down. He had to move out of the family house and maintained contact with his sons who stayed with his ex-partner. His mood started deteriorating which also started affecting his work. His confidence was affected and he started believing that 'it was all his fault.' Gordon was not keen on antidepressant medication but wanted to try CBT.

His first appointment with the therapist did not go as planned. The therapist did an assessment and asked a number of questions around perceptions of discrimination, problems at work, and Gordon's social circumstances. Gordon came out of the session feeling that the therapist had stereotyped him into a 'box.' He felt that the therapist was looking to find poor socio-economic status, criminal record, and experiences of racism. He debated whether to return to therapy. On discussion with his general practitioner (GP), he felt encouraged to attend one more session to discuss his thoughts around the assessment session.

At the second session, Gordon openly put his views across. He explained to the therapist that he was aware of workplace discrimination but was proud of his achievements in a very short space of time. The therapist changed course quickly after that as they had realized the influence, although subconsciously, of their own bias. The therapist acknowledged the problem and asked Gordon to highlight the secret of their success. Gordon explained that he had been able to use his greatest cultural strength to his advantage. He told the therapist that not many people were aware that historically minimalism was a norm through choice in his culture. A minimalistic attitude increased the observational strength in their community, and he had learnt to seize opportunities rather than wait for them. This discussion served two purposes: the therapist had a chance to learn something about his client's culture and found tools to work on in future sessions using strengths-based approach, and Gordon was able to talk about his skills which reminded him about his success. In future sessions, the therapist learnt that Gordon enjoyed playing and watching football with his friends and his sons and was an ardent fan of Manchester United club and David Beckham was his idol.

Case discussion

In this example, the therapist had subconsciously made assumptions about Gordon due to his cultural background. He was quick to recognize the issue in order to make amends. He also used Gordon's cultural strengths to build his confidence in future sessions. Secondly, the therapist failed to recognize that Gordon had adapted to the UK culture effectively and had a successful life. His culture may have been different from the traditional native culture where he grew up. He was in a different place through the process of acculturation.

Case example

Chloe is a 42-year-old female whose family immigrated from Greece when she was 7 years old to the United States. She presented with anxiety and depression to a recovery-oriented psychiatric emergency service 2 weeks after her boyfriend broke up with her. This service is based on a living room model of assessment and crisis stabilization and includes individual therapy. Medication management and case management are provided in a client-centred and peer-involved manner. As part of her assessment, the therapist asked her information about her immigration experience and adjustment to new culture. Chloe took a defensive stance and said that her background was a personal matter and the therapist should not judge her based on the background. The therapist explained to her that the questions about her culture were to help him understand her better and that he comes from a perspective that every culture has strengths and he wanted to know how he could utilize the strengths from her culture to help her address current issues. Even after this explanation, the client did not want any more questions about her ethnicity or her immigration history. The therapist moved on to talk about other topics she was comfortable discussing. Next day, the client complained to the supervisor that the therapist was asking her questions about her ethnicity and that people have used this information before against her. She threatened to leave the programme unless the issue was addressed. The supervisor met with the therapist and then came up with a response to the client's concerns. She met with the client and also gave a written response to her concerns. The first point was that it was standard practice to ask questions about ethnicity and immigration status and a blank template of assessment was provided to the client so that she could see for herself that she is not being singled out. Second, it was mentioned that the purpose of questions is to make adjustments to therapy to best suit the needs of the client. Third, the issue of client choice was emphasized and said that client has a right to inform which questions were making her uncomfortable and the team would avoid those questions. Fourth, the team offered her the option to speak to another client of her background who had a positive experience in therapy and was open and willing to share her own experience with the client.

After the meeting, Chloe's anger dissipated and she decided to continue her engagement with the programme. However, she wanted the team to not discuss the issues of ethnicity until she gave them permission to do so. Eventually, this client's crisis was resolved, and she was discharged from the programme one month later but at no time was she ready to discuss any aspects of her ethnicity or immigration status.

Case discussion

In this particular instance, Chloe reacted very negatively to neutral questions about her ethnicity. Even after the therapist explained the purpose of the questions, she remained upset to the point of complaining to the supervisor of the programme. She gave history of very abusive relationship with a previous boyfriend that used to berate her about her ethnicity. This appeared to be the reason for her reactions that were out of proportion to the questions asked. The supervisor, by validating her feelings through her actions and giving an assurance that the team would not discuss the issue ethnicity, helped to heal the rupture in the therapeutic relationship and helped continued engagement and successful resolution of her crisis. However, the client at discharge was still not psychologically ready to discuss her ethnicity, and the supervisor sent this information to the programme she was linked to for follow-up. Therapists should be aware that there may be rare situations where discussion of ethnicity and race could rupture the therapeutic relationship (Table 5.1).

Table 5.1　Key points in developing cultural neutrality.

Reflect in what ways are you different and recognize your own biases towards different cultures

Be mindful that your own speech can reflect attitude and beliefs you hold about other cultures

Develop a better understanding of cultural groups you work with

Seek opportunities to interact with other members of the cultural groups

Use client and family as a source of information

Arrange supervision with cultural experts/cultural consultation groups

Be aware of the dynamic nature of culture and make efforts to keep your knowledge current

Adjustments and Modifications in Response to Cultural Bias

According to Larrison and Schoppelrey (2011), therapists account for 28% of the variance in adverse mental health outcomes for ethnic minorities. In order to improve outcomes, the therapist needs to make a number of adjustments to therapy. A meta-analysis of studies showed that culturally adapted psychotherapy is more effective than unadapted, bona fide psychotherapy by $d = 0.32$ for primary measures of psychological functioning (Benish, Quintana, & Wampold, 2011). The adjustments from therapist are described under the headings of therapist flexibility, reducing the power differential, and changing the focus to the process of therapy.

Therapist flexibility

This is an important element in working with clients from minority cultures. There are three areas of flexibility:

1. Setting
2. Stance
3. Cultural factors

One area of flexibility relates to the setting of therapy, and we have discussed this before in a different context. The therapist should be flexible about the location, length, and frequency of sessions and explicitly empower clients to have input in making these decisions collaboratively. Many clients from minority cultures come from disadvantaged backgrounds, and the burden of making appointments in therapist's office can be significant. Sometimes, even if they come from an affluent background, they may not drive or may not want to be seen in a clinic setting due to perceptions of stigma. A session scheduled in client's home would make it much easier for the client to keep the appointment, help the therapist to have a much better understanding of the client's living circumstances, and also develop positive relationship with the family members. Again, negotiation with clients is the key as there will be clients who prefer that a therapist should not be seen in their home surroundings as 'what would neighbours think?' Many other settings can be considered for, for example, community bases, places of religion if rooms are available, or neutral places in the community where clients feel comfortable.

Case example

Jorge is a 27-year-old Hispanic male with a diagnosis of schizophrenia who came to see the therapist in his office weekly. Jorge had difficulty keeping the appointments as his mother had to drive him and she could not always get away from her responsibilities at home. The therapist scheduled a session at Jorge's home. During the session, he met Jorge's mother, dad, and brother and understood that the family pulled together to share the responsibility of monitoring

Jorge's medicines and supporting him. In addition, it was clear to the therapist that the decisions about Jorge were not made by him alone but the entire family talking about the issue. The home visit significantly changed the quality of interaction with Jorge and his family as they were much more comfortable talking about the burden of dealing with his illness while they were trying to establish a financial foothold in the United States. Seeing the difference in the quality of the interactions and the importance of being able to interact with the entire family, the therapist gave Jorge and his family the option of seeing him once a week in his office or once in 2 weeks at their home. The family preferred sessions at home. The therapy proceeded much smoothly with the family taking an active part in reinforcing the homework assignments given to Jorge.

Case discussion

In this particular instance, a visit by therapist to client's home made a significant change in the quality of interaction with the client and his family. Immigrant families who are trying to be financially independent have difficulty taking time away from work to get clients to appointments. The therapist's visit gave the entire family an opportunity to interact with the therapist. In this case, the therapist's flexibility in scheduling home therapy sessions further removed barriers for family involvement in the therapeutic process. The family here worked together as a team in playing the role of therapy extenders by encouraging Jorge to complete his assignments and get the best out of therapy.

The second area of flexibility relates to the therapeutic stance. Clients from some minority cultures such as Hispanic or Asian cultures expect the therapist to take on an authoritative role, and in these situations, a collaborative stance may need to be developed gradually. An immediate move to collaboration may be misconstrued as the therapist being indecisive or not knowledgeable. Some individuals from Asian or Hispanic cultures may be reluctant to give feedback or express their discomfort or negative emotions. In the sessions, the therapist should be actively monitoring the impact of the different interventions on the client's verbal and non-verbal behaviour and be prepared to move from active interventions that may be causing discomfort and shift to supportive interventions.

The third area of flexibility is to make accommodation for cultural factors during the course of therapy such as family interference and also issues around personal space, for example, Hispanics tend to have a 'contact culture,' that is, personal space is less than other cultures, for example, white. The therapist should expect ruptures in therapeutic relationship due to a variety of reasons such as recurrence of symptoms, family disapproval, change in social circumstances, and alcohol or substance abuse and be mindful of any negative thoughts or emotions relating to the client or his culture that may be contributing to the problems in relationship.

Reducing the power differential between therapists and clients

Choice and finding common ground

There is a significant power differential inherent in the roles of therapist and client – one is coming to the other for help – but this differential can be negated or at least minimized to allow greater development of collaboration and self-efficacy (Gannon, 1982). The difference can though also be magnified in individuals from minority cultures who face cultural and linguistic barriers to effective communication. In addition, some cultures consider the doctors or therapists to be authority figures and expect a paternalistic stance as discussed before.

A mutually respectful and equal relationship should be the goal of therapy although the pace with which the paternalistic stance changes to a collaborative one has to be flexible. At a very basic level, as human beings, we all share similar emotions, dreams, and aspirations and can all face disappointments in life. We can all relate to issues such as grief, loss, anxiety, and fear for the future. Sharing such experiences puts the client and therapist at the same level for a period of time. This is akin to Irvin Yalom describing the therapy process as a journey of two fellow travellers on the road of life (Yalom, 2002). First of all, the therapist should subscribe to this view of seeing themselves as a fellow traveller as opposed to an expert. With this humbling perspective, the therapist can then redistribute the power in the therapeutic relationship through interventions that give a choice to clients, make the therapist more human and genuine, and increase their self-reliance (Gannon, 1982). Clients can be given a choice about all aspects of therapy as described in the flexibility section described earlier. The therapist can be more human and genuine by measures such as finding common experiences with the client and therapeutic self-disclosure.

Changing focus

The power differential in the relationship can also be reduced by changing the focus from the content of the client's life to the 'process of therapy' in the 'here-and-now' situation. The focus on the content is generally about the client's issues and deficiencies, while the focus on the process is about the interaction between the client and therapist. Focusing on the process of therapy in the context of the dyadic relationship and allowing clients to evaluate and give feedback about the approach and style of the therapist can be very empowering for clients as well as very therapeutic. Some clients from minority cultures need to proceed more slowly to be comfortable giving feedback as they may view the relationship hierarchically and hence be reluctant to give feedback. In these instances, consider a stepwise approach to obtaining feedback. The first step in obtaining feedback is one about a specific intervention that is being utilized or a homework assignment. Here, asking questions such as *Do you think that this homework assignment will be helpful?* or *Can you think of problems in doing this homework?* is a good non-threatening way that encourages feedback without client resorting to yes or no answers. The next step is helping the client become more comfortable about giving feedback about the session and finally about the style or effectiveness of the therapist.

Case example

Ca-bo, a 26-year-old Thai male of the Lahu culture, had recently immigrated to Toronto from Thailand. He had been married six months previously and emigrated to take up a good job opportunity. He had found the move difficult, especially as he had found accommodation in an area where there weren't many Thai people or, at least, he had not yet found them. He was still adjusting to the workplace. He had developed symptoms of depression and feelings of guilt. He told the therapist that he felt guilty that he had broken their traditional practice after marriage of not living with his in-laws. He wanted to pray at the temple for his sins. Due to his severe feelings of guilt, Ca-bo's self-confidence had become very poor, and reducing the power differential was proving to be a challenge for the therapist.

The therapist had some knowledge of the marital customs in Ca-bo's culture that he was expected to stay with his in-laws after marriage. However, his feelings of guilt went beyond this and had become a symptom of his depression. The therapist used a stepwise approach to working on the power differential. He started by exploring Ca-bo's relationship with his wife. Ca-bo had met his wife 18 months previously and treasured her. He described how the couple had developed an equal relationship. In subsequent sessions and on exploring further, Ca-bo himself realized that he had felt isolated since he had moved to Canada. Once he started developing some insight, his confidence started improving. The therapist slowly established a collaborative relationship with him in subsequent sessions, and the power differential became less.

Case discussion

In this example, the therapist used a stepwise approach to reduce the power differential. He built on what Ca-bo told him about his customs and equal relationship with his wife. He explored with him and discovered that in Lahu villages the marital partners are equal in status. In discussing the strengths of having an equal partnership, he was able to highlight to Ca-bo that his own relationship in therapy could be equal.

Exercise: Consider a client in therapy where you think the aforementioned adjustments in power differential would be helpful. What would you do differently?

Eastern Philosophy-Based Approaches to Orientation to Therapy

Mindfulness is referred to as a way of 'paying attention to the present.' This concept is derived from the Eastern meditation practices. Jung said the West believes 'in doing,' while the East in 'impassive being' (Jung, 1958). Baer (2003) defined mindfulness as 'the non-judgemental observation of the ongoing stream of internal and external stimuli as they arise.' It focuses on three primary states of the mind, namely, the reasonable mind (logical, analytical problem solving), emotional mind (creative, passionate, and dramatic), and wise mind (integration of both reasonable and emotion minds). A wise mind responds intuitively in a given situation. This helps develop self-trust and decision-making skills. Mindfulness-based CBT is establishing an evidence base in severe mental illness including psychosis (Chadwick, Taylor, & Abba, 2005). Mindfulness-based approaches may be appropriate in minority cultures as their origins derive from Eastern practices – primarily Buddhism but also with Muslim, especially Sufist influences. As discussed in the previous chapter, the concept of balance is acceptable in Asian cultures. It is recommended that therapists should formulate and consider whether and if so when to introduce such techniques.

Eastern approaches to problems may sometimes be at odds with the problem-solving approach presented earlier in the chapters. Whereas Western approaches to problem solving involve direct efforts to change stressors that are seen as the source of the problem, Eastern approaches often involve acceptance of a problem and coping with one's reaction to the problem. Some problems are not necessarily amenable to being solved, including some aspects of severe mental illness. An acceptance-based approach to hallucinations would be to acknowledge their occurrence and not necessarily try to reduce them, but accept that they occur with the understanding that they need not dictate a person's life (e.g. persecutory hallucinations). Therefore, principles from therapies such as mindfulness, acceptance, and commitment therapy may be more accepted (Table 5.2).

Table 5.2   Key adjustments in response to cultural bias.

Offer flexibility in setting of therapy; stance of collaborative versus authoritative; accommodation of cultural factors
Reduce the power differential in therapy
Do not react defensively to clients who may be resistant in therapy – understand their philosophical orientation
Use a holistic approach, for example, mind and body techniques or mindfulness-based approaches

Conclusion

Stereotyping and bias are universal and are the strongest barriers to strong therapeutic relationship with cultural minority clients. Therapists have a personal responsibility to take steps to become culturally neutral and thereby more effective. These steps are delineated. An example is presented of Western and Eastern approaches to a problem as complementary and not contradictory.

References

Baer, R. A. (2003). Mindfulness training as a clinical intervention: A conceptual and empirical review. *Clinical Psychology: Science and Practice, 10*(2), 125–143.

Benish, S. G., Quintana, S., & Wampold, B. E. (2011). Culturally adapted psychotherapy and the legitimacy of myth: A direct-comparison meta-analysis. *Journal of Counseling Psychology, 58*(3), 279–289.

Chadwick, P., Taylor, K. N., & Abba, N. (2005). Mindfulness groups for people with psychosis. *Behavioural and Cognitive Psychotherapy, 33*(3), 351–359.

Gannon, L. (1982). The role of power in psychotherapy. *Woman and Therapy, 1*(2), 3–11.

Jung, C. G. (1958). *The collected works of C. G. Jung* (Vol. 2). Princeton, NJ: Princeton University Press.

Larrison, C. R., & Schoppelrey, S. L. (2011). Therapist effects on disparities experienced by minorities receiving services for mental illness. *Research on Social Work Practice, 21*(6), 727–736.

McGoldrick, M., Giordano, J., & Garcia-Preto, N. (2005). *Ethnicity and family therapy.* New York, NY: Guilford Press.

Nezu, A. M. (2010). Cultural influences on the process of conducting psychotherapy: Personal reflections of an ethnic minority psychologist. *Psychotherapy: Theory, Research, Practice, Training, 47*(2), 169–176.

Tamir, D. I., & Mitchell, J. P. (2012). Disclosing information about the self is intrinsically rewarding. *Proceedings of the National Academy of Sciences of the United States of America, 109*(21), 8038–8043.

Tseng, W.-S., Chang, S. C., & Nishjzono, M. (2005). *Asian culture and psychotherapy:Implications for East and West.* Honolulu, HI: University of Hawaii Press.

Yalom, I. D. (2002). *The gift of therapy.* New York, NY: Harper Collins Publishers Inc.

6

Individualized Case Formulation

We have discussed how culture influences the engagement and assessment process and how the therapist can adjust their stance to enable and adapt to minority cultures. An assessment leads directly on to case formulation. Formulation should be understood as a very dynamic and fluid process that is modified continuously as therapy progresses and does not end until it is completed – when an agreed summary can be extremely helpful in maintaining therapy gains. Unfortunately, what sometimes happens is that a formulation is drawn up early in therapy and remains static, not revisited and revised as new information emerges. In working with clients from different cultural minorities, frequent revision of the formulation is extremely important as therapists rarely if ever understand the cultural influences on client's symptoms and functioning at the beginning of therapy. Indeed, many individuals from different cultural backgrounds may need to be educated about the concept of formulation. Formulation serves as a great vehicle for communicating with other members of the client's treatment team such as the case manager, care coordinator, psychiatrist, or primary physician; the members of the client's family; and other caregivers. It also helps the different members of the client's treatment team as well as their social circle (if they wish to share) to get on the same page. It may be that some areas of the formulation are too sensitive to be shared with everyone, but even then, a negotiation around the parts that can be discussed can usually lead to some agreement on sharing and result in improved understanding and support for other professionals and client's support system.

Cultural Adaptation of CBT for Serious Mental Illness: A Guide for Training and Practice, First Edition. Shanaya Rathod, David Kingdon, Narsimha Pinninti, Douglas Turkington, and Peter Phiri.
© 2015 John Wiley & Sons, Ltd. Published 2015 by John Wiley & Sons, Ltd.

Individualized collaborative case formulation is akin to a map or even a Global Positioning System (GPS) to help us work out where we are now and then guide our journey to a new destination. Clinically, it serves a variety of purposes:

1. Formulation validates the client's experiences and normalizes the presenting issues. Normalizing presenting issues is an effective method to place the client's experiences in context of human reactions to difficult situations, reducing the stigma and catastrophic fears. It serves to enhance self-esteem and strengthens adaptive coping skills (Kingdon & Turkington, 2005).
2. Formulation enhances client engagement, instills hope, and makes the client's complex problems more manageable.
3. Formulation also guides the client and therapist in choosing the sequence of interventions to anticipate potential problems in therapy and address them (Kuyken, Padesky, & Dudley, 2009).

Our understanding of the aetiology of severe mental illnesses (SMI) continues to evolve, and SMI is currently thought to be due to a combination of biological, cognitive behavioural, and social cultural factors – the modified stress–vulnerability model (Wright, Turkington, Kingdon, & Ramirez Basco, 2009; Zubin & Spring, 1997) that we have discussed in Chapter 2. These different factors influence the onset, course, and outcome of the illnesses. For all SMI, biological treatments are important, that is, medication management remains a critical part of the overall illness management although there are studies emerging which suggest that clients who refuse to accept medication can still benefit from CBT (Morrison et al., 2014). However, cognitive behavioural interventions are currently considered complementary to medication and are offered to help them cope with distressing symptoms and reduce the likelihood of relapse of symptoms (Dixon et al., 2010; National Institute of Health and Care Excellence, 2014; Turkington et al., 2006). CBT can also aid medication management by improving attitudes to treatment (Rathod & Turkington, 2005).

There are a number of formats utilized for case formulation, and while no one format is universally accepted for case formulation, there are significant overlaps between them. The core of each approach is the linking of thoughts, feelings, and behaviours with significant events and underlying belief systems as discussed in Chapter 2. The case formulation approaches described in this chapter are based on principles of CBT with cultural adaptation for different cultural groups using the framework that we have described. It is therefore not a DSM-based cultural formulation – which is more focused on the diagnoses – but is consistent with it. An outline for cultural formulation was first introduced in DSM IV based on the recommendations of an independent National Institute of Mental Health (NIMH) workgroup on culture (Mezzich et al., 1999), but there was no method for collecting the required information. Subsequently, guidelines and practical approaches to develop a cultural formulation were proposed (Mezzich, Caracci, Fabrega, & Kirmayer, 2009). DSM 5 expands on prior approaches and describes 5 aspects of culture that need to be taken into account in the formulation of any case:

1. Cultural identity of the individual
2. Cultural conceptualization of illness
3. Psychosocial factors and cultural stressors
4. Cultural features of relationship between the individual
5. Overall cultural assessment

Clinicians who are familiar with the cultural aspects of assessment in DSM 5 would find the associations with Chapters 4–7 in conducting therapy with minority cultural groups helpful.

The formulation used here is described by Beck (2011) and by Wright et al. (2009). The main elements of the format are retained, and where technical adjustments and theoretical modifications are made to address culturally relevant issues, those are described in the following sections. More extensive coverage of the different formulations can be found elsewhere in textbooks and articles that cover the topic more comprehensively (Grant et al., 2012; Kingdon & Turkington, 2005; Perivoliotis et al., 2011; Ramirez Basco, & Rush, 2005). We start with the case example of an African American male and describe the cultural factors of significance and adaptations made in the development of case formulation. We will then discuss relevant cultural issues in the formulation for major ethnic minority groups and practical implications for Hispanic and Asian cultures.

Case example

Eric, a 26-year-old African American male with eight admissions in the last 2 years to psychiatric institutions, was recently enrolled in assertive community treatment (ACT) due to his history of non-engagement with other services. The ACT team is a comprehensive self-contained programme in the United States that meets the medical, psychosocial, and case management needs of the most difficult-to-engage patients by providing all psychiatric treatment, rehabilitation, and social services (Stein & Santos, 1998). The ACT team is available around the clock, 365 days a year, and services are provided lifelong or for an indefinite period of time (Drake, Merrens, & Lynde, 2005). Individuals who are unsuccessful in engaging with other less intensive treatment programmes such as partial hospitalization and case management are referred to ACT teams.

Presenting issues/Symptoms/diagnosis: Eric presented with main symptom of anxiety and that 'people were not letting him do God's work.'

He believed that he was the chosen one to spread God's message and that the devil was working through people trying to treat him. He also heard the voice of the devil threatening him, but saw that purely as a religious issue and not a symptom of mental illness. He believed that anxiety is normal in his situation considering the obstacles that people were putting in this path. His mother and grandmother were concerned about his behaviours of trying to preach to people, not making an effort to get a job, and getting into trouble with the law for minor offences such as trespassing into other people's property. He carried a diagnosis of schizophrenia.

Current situational issues (including family issues, culture and community issues, and treatment by dominant cultural groups): He lived with his mother and maternal grandparents in a neighbourhood that was run down and considered a drug-infested area. The family subsisted on social security.

Formative influences (including migration experience, adaptation to new culture, and language issues): Eric's family lived in the state of Georgia and moved to New York (NY) State when he was 10 years old. Growing up, Eric witnessed his dad abusing drugs and being violent to his mother. In addition to being a witness of the violence, he was also a victim of violence as his dad was verbally and at times physically abusive to him. Eric's mother finally took a restraining order against his dad and then moved away from him to NY. This internal migration across state lines protected Eric from his father's physical and emotional abuse but also had some unintended negative consequences in making Eric's adjustment to new environment more difficult. Eric had a lot of peers of his background and colour in school in Georgia and felt one among the peers, but in his new school in NY, he was among the handful of African American kids and felt that he was not part of the dominant white culture. Being new to school, he did not have friends, was not part of any group, and was subjected to racial taunts in the playground and lunch room. When he was in high school, his mother suffered a mental breakdown and diagnosed with schizophrenia, and his grandmother took up the parenting responsibility.

Eric graduated high school and enrolled in a community college. He was a loner in college, could not handle the pressures of college, and dropped out in the first year. His first psychotic breakdown was when he was 23 and he was involuntarily hospitalized for trying to enter the neighbour's house, acting on the delusional belief that the neighbour's wife was being harassed and not allowed to go to the church and he had to rescue her. He was hearing God's voice giving him commands.

Biological, genetic, and medical Factors: Eric had biological vulnerability for mental illness and substance abuse problems based on the history of mental illness in his mother and substance abuse in his father.

Strengths/assets (include individual strengths, strengths and resilience in the family, strengths relating to ethnic community, and religious and spiritual strengths): Despite witnessing drug use by his dad and being genetically vulnerable, Eric never experimented with drugs. His mother was very involved in the local church, and from a very young age, Eric spent a lot of time with church activities. The supportive environment of the church and the teachings that drug use was against God's teachings helped Eric to stay away from drugs. One of the benefits of moving to NY was him connecting with his grandmother and extended family consisting of two aunts and uncles and five cousins. Two of his uncles were positive male role models for him and were substitute paternal figures. Multiple members of his family had experiences of overt racism and discrimination, and it was a regular topic of conversation at the family dinner table. Eric had strong African American cultural identity and viewed his group as being disadvantaged and discriminated against. His own experiences in school of being racially taunted reinforced these beliefs. The pastor of his church was an activist and a strong advocate of African American rights and was a good support for Eric.

Treatment goals: The goals that Eric verbalized were that (a) he should be allowed to do God's work and his treatment providers should stop people who had been obstructing him from engaging in God's activities (b) he wanted the devil to stop bothering him and was going to place his faith in God and church to do this. He did not express any vocational or educational goals as doing God's work was more important than working on something that was selfish. The family goals were that he should recognize being mentally ill, accept treatment including medication for his emotional problems, and find a job.

Exercise: What are the philosophical orientation and practical settings to consider when drawing up the formulation?

Building Block Approach to Formulation

Case formulation for SMI should take a building block approach where the therapist starts with the development of a mini formulation to identify cognitive and behavioural responses that are maintaining, worsening, or in some cases mitigating individual symptoms and thereby identify meaningful targets to work on. The next step is the development of a cross-sectional formulation with connections between multiple symptoms and client beliefs and behaviours.

The final step is the longitudinal formulation that explains the formative influences on symptoms and takes account of the client's philosophical orientation and practical settings. This approach has been described before (Wright et al., 2009). The building block approach is particularly useful in clients from minority cultural groups wherein the stepwise progress depends on the individual's ability to understand and accept the formulation as the example of Eric demonstrates.

Mini formulation

In Eric's case, the mini formulation explains one of Eric's symptoms, that is, auditory hallucinations. The triggers for his voices are usually boredom and anxiety. The voices trigger thoughts of the devil persecuting him, and he engages in behaviours that he considers God's work to counter the effects of the devil (Table 6.1 and Figure 6.1).

Cultural contribution to the formulation

Eric's attribution of the malevolent voice to the devil and his reaction to counter it by doing God's work come from his formative experiences of being involved in the church from a young age. His philosophical orientation involves his family including the mother and grandmother's shared beliefs about God and the devil and engaging in religious rituals such as praying to ward off troubles. They believed in and encouraged Eric to be involved with voluntary and other social activities in the church. Where they differed with Eric was that they recognized the auditory hallucinations and his behaviours as part of illness and that he needed to take medication to help him. They saw the medication as complementing prayers and did not see any conflict in him praying while also taking medication. Regarding the practical considerations, they shared his distrust of the mental health system but were willing to engage with it, while Eric expressly rejected any offers of help. The therapist presented the mini formulation to Eric, his mother, and grandmother.

Cross-sectional formulation

Developing the formulation occurs collaboratively with clients in most cases. Once the client understands and accepts the mini formulation, the next step is to develop the cross-sectional formulation which identifies the different symptoms the client is experiencing in the present, the various triggers (predisposing) and mitigating (precipitating) factors, as well as the support systems and coping skills that help the client deal with symptoms. In Eric's case, the therapist was able to develop the cross-sectional formulation slowly as Eric started engaging and trusting the therapist. During this step of formulation, it is important to focus on the strengths of the individual and bring to the fore the various coping skills that

Table 6.1 Cognitive model to explain the symptoms for Eric.

Situation	Voices threatening him	Phone call from doctor's office reminding him about an appointment	Van arriving to pick him for day programme
Automatic thoughts	This is the devil's voice The devil wants to destroy me	They want to give me medicine I cannot trust the doctors	They think I am crazy It is the devil working through them
	Doing God's work is the way to stop the devil I should go around spreading the word of God	They use people as guinea pigs My mother was used as guinea pig	They want to get money by calling people mentally ill
Meaning of automatic thoughts	I am the chosen one	I am not safe with the doctor	I am not safe around them
Emotions	Anxiety Anger	Anxiety Depressed	Anxiety Anger
Behaviours	Making unsolicited phone calls to strangers to talk about God Knocking on doors in the neighbourhood to preach God's word	Wandered off when case manager came to pick him up	Refused to get on the van

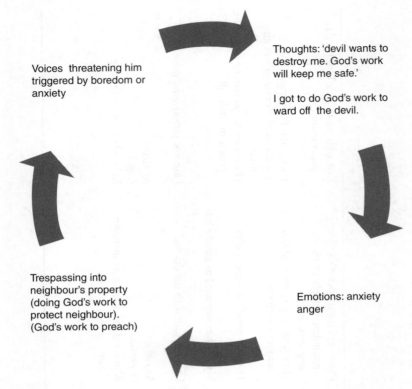

Voices threatening him triggered by boredom or anxiety

Thoughts: 'devil wants to destroy me. God's work will keep me safe.'

I got to do God's work to ward off the devil.

Emotions: anxiety anger

Trespassing into neighbour's property (doing God's work to protect neighbour). (God's work to preach)

Figure 6.1   Mini formulation for Eric.

the individual has developed and utilized. Strengths can be internal qualities like determination, hopefulness, self-awareness, self-responsibility, pride, a strong work ethic, family values, and spiritual faith or external resources like money, family, community, stable and safe housing, mentors, and friends. Strengths can be discovered (or rediscovered) or newly developed (Ragins, 2012). More often than not, the therapist has to take time and have the patience to identify and tease out these strengths from the client. In Eric's case, his ability to not use drugs even though he saw his father use them is a significant strength that the therapist decided to bring to his attention. His mother and later grandmother played a part in him developing the strength of faith and being involved in church activities, and this was conveyed to them. Many minority cultures have strong family support systems or community support systems that help mitigate and/or cope with symptoms of the illness, and therapist should actively look for the strengths of the culture and convey it to client and families.

For Eric, the cross-sectional formulation is depicted in the figure with interactions between the symptoms, triggers, mitigating factors, and his coping mechanisms (Figure 6.2).

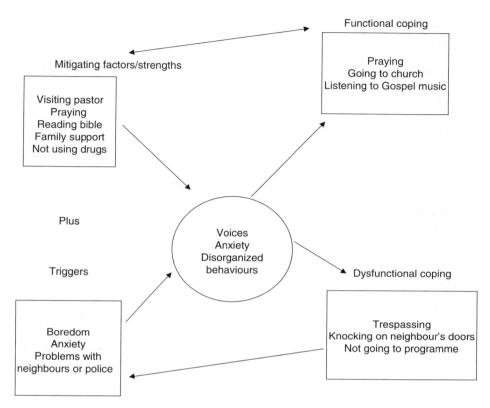

Figure 6.2   Cross-sectional formulation for Eric.

Longitudinal formulation

The third step is a longitudinal formulation that explores the developmental history and helps the individual and their families to understand the various biological, psychological, and sociocultural factors that may have played a role in the onset of the symptoms and may be contributing to the maintenance of symptoms and functional impairment. This again takes into account the client's world view and practical considerations that influence the predisposing, perpetuating, precipitating, and protective factors. Eric's longitudinal formulation is described in Table 6.2.

Eric had a genetic vulnerability to psychotic breakdown and substance abuse based on his family history. He developed psychological vulnerabilities due to the trauma of witnessing his mother being abused and also being a victim of abuse himself. He developed negative beliefs about himself that he was not worth the love and caring of his parents. The social cultural factors that were important in his case in developing his worldview were the internal migration (movement within a country) that separated him from his friends and racially and culturally

Table 6.2 Longitudinal formulation for Eric.

Predisposing factors	Precipitating factors	Perpetuating factors	Protective factors
Genetic vulnerability	Racial discrimination	Misinterpretation of religious beliefs	Family – uncles
Abusive/traumatic childhood	Inability to cope at college	Non-compliance with medication	Church
Internal migration			Personal resilience and resolve to not use drugs
Racial discrimination			
Loss of peer group			

Current concerns
1. Grandiosity, hallucinations, and delusions
2. Preaching and trespassing
3. Poor insight
4. Non-concordance
5. Doing God's work in response to hallucinations and delusions

Thoughts	Feelings		Behaviours
Grandiose beliefs of being the chosen	Urge to do God's work		Preaching to people
Dysfunctional thoughts about medication	Anxiety, anger		Trouble with law
			Trespassing into others' property
			Unsolicited phone calls

Social		Physical
Lives with mother and grandmother		
House in drug-infested area		

Underlying concerns
Negative self-image
Feelings of being discriminated

similar peer group and made his acculturation adaptation difficult. As Casas and Vasquez (1996) reported, changes in racial or ethnic demographics of a community can lead to difficulties related to acculturation. When acculturation occurs in an environment that does not have the resources to provide social support from teachers, friends, or counsellors, it can create stress and loss of self-esteem resulting from the clash of cultural values and norms. His extended family was a tremendous source of strength for him as is the case with many African American families. Despite this and the relief from the abuse, he lost the support of his peer group and his group identity by moving to a new cultural environment. Discrimination and conflicts between students of colour and white students have been reported to contribute significantly to the acculturative stress experienced by the former on predominantly white campuses (Saldana, 1994). The racism and discrimination that Eric experienced in the new state increased his stress and reinforced the negative beliefs he had about himself. Grandiose beliefs of being the chosen one were probably the result of the negative beliefs about himself and the sense of being helpless in the face of the difficult situations coupled with the strong religious beliefs. Grandiose delusional beliefs are said to have their origin from underlying core beliefs of worthlessness and helplessness (Kingdon & Turkington, 2005). Eric not possessing marketable skills and being involved in spiritual activities played into his beliefs to be a preacher. Doing God's work gave him a sense of higher purpose in life and counteracted the negative beliefs about himself. He would internally reframe the reasons for his hospitalization with beliefs such as *I was put in hospital by God to minister to the mentally ill in hospital. By being in hospital and not fighting the system, I was showing forgiveness and thereby living God's word and doing God's work*. He would take medication when in the hospital and be pleasant and cooperative but stop medicine as soon as he left the hospital. He also had a combination of dysfunctional beliefs relating to medication. He believed that the medication was similar to the drugs his dad used and would make people lose control. Also, taking medication meant that his faith in God was not strong as he was relying on artificial chemicals made by man and not by God. His experiences as a member of African American minority and hearing the stories of discrimination from his family members caused him to distrust the mental health providers as they represented a system that has discriminated against his cultural background and repeatedly held him in hospital against his will.

Care plan (including involvement of family and community resources)

The main goal was to build a working relationship with Eric to the point where he could trust the team and would be willing to engage and discuss his symptoms and beliefs. Eric had never developed a long-term trusting relationship with any provider and viewed anyone who represented the mental health system as an adversary. Hence, it was important to work with his support system including his case manager, his grandparents, and his pastor to engage Eric.

The aforementioned case template and the one discussed in Chapter 3 for Hamida are applicable for different illnesses but may need to be complemented with additional formulation for some symptoms such as positive and negative symptoms in schizophrenia or the mood cycling in mania. The goal is to develop a comprehensive formulation, but the process has to be guided by the individual client and his or her ability as well as readiness to develop such a formulation.

> **Exercise:** Think of two current clients from the minority cultural background that had issues with medication adherence. Did you look at the cultural factors playing in to medication adherence? What cultural supports and strengths can you draw on in these two cases to enhance adherence? Can you implement the strategies and review your response and compare with what it was with Eric.

Case Formulation and Specific Issues for Various Cultural Groups

In the following section, we discuss the cultural factors that are relevant for different minority groups as they relate to individualized case formulation followed by technical adjustments to address these factors (Table 6.3).

African Americans

African Americans can be broadly divided into two groups: those who have been in the United States for generations and recent immigrants from other countries particularly the African Diaspora. The African Americans continue to experience discrimination, negative stereotyping by the media (Coltraine & Messineo, 2000), inferior health services (Hollar, 2001), and higher morbidity rates (Hines & Boyd-Franklin, 2005). In addition, a higher proportion of African Americans are socially disadvantaged compared to the rest of the population. The perception and/or the experience of discrimination can lead to low self-esteem and reduced sense of optimism about their future and that of their children and distrust of the mental health system. Experiences of racism and discrimination are significantly associated with substance abuse (Kwate, Valdimarsdottir, Guevarra, & Bovbjerg, 2003) and also with demoralization, negative beliefs about oneself, and an external locus of control (Hines & Boyd-Franklin, 2005). These beliefs are internalized and may play out as anger or hostility towards therapists that are seen as part of the dominant culture. Distrust of the system is associated with negative attitudes towards therapists, unwillingness to seek mental health services, poor engagement, and premature termination. According to some authors, lack of planning for the future in some African American clients results in excessive lateness and missed appointments (Hardy & Laszloffy, 1995). However, the alternate viewpoint is that lateness and missed appointments are generally a function of their lack of resources such as transportation to keep appointments. Therapist's level of colour blindness (viewpoint that ethnicity and colour do not matter) was directly related to their capacity for empathy and also to their attributions of responsibility for the solution to the problem with an African American client but not with a European American client (Burkard & Knox, 2004). When therapists come across these behaviours, they (a) have to be aware of their internal biases and

Table 6.3   Key points in culturally individualized formulation.

Individualize case formulation based on an individual's philosophical orientation and practical consideration that can guide therapy

Take a stepwise approach to building formulation

Conceptualize thinking of client rather than correct them

From the beginning, use cultural factors and particularly strengths as part of the formulation

Keep the formulation dynamic by updating or adding to it based on new information available

Make modifications in how the formulation is shared with minority culture clients and their families

Religion and spirituality can be positive coping mechanisms and consider this in developing the formulation

(b) should enquire from individual client the reasons for excessive lateness or missed appointments and not assume the reason.

African American culture provides many positive experiences that should be kept in mind when developing a strengths-based formulation. A minority culture can contribute to changes in the values and systems of the majority culture. For example, one of the significant contributions of the black culture to the United States is the egalitarian family model in which neither husband nor wife is always in charge (Willie & Reddick, 2003). The extended family system is prevalent in African American culture and is an important source of strength and support. As discussed in earlier chapters, the extended family has a broader definition in African American culture and in addition to including blood kin such as cousins does include 'fictive kin' such as members of a church family or play mama (Boyd-Franklin, 2003). The extended families can play a variety of roles such as mediators in problems, provide temporary shelter in times of hardship, and prepare children for race-related struggles (Neighbors, Hudson, & Bullard, 2012). Another source of strength for African American is a greater level of religiosity and the associated religious institutions and spiritual beliefs (Chatters, Taylor, Bullard, & Jackson, 2008; Taylor, Chatters, Mattis, & Joe, 2010). Churches help individuals to develop support networks, be involved in constructive activism for the community, achieve status, and give a meaning and purpose to their lives' activities. A positive racial and cultural identity in African American families is associated with coping, mastery, and optimism and acts as a buffer against the negative effects of discrimination and racism (Wong, Eccles, & Sameroff, 2003). As mentioned earlier, African American immigrants from other countries have different experiences than the African American clients in United States. Most of them have not experienced the same degree of racism, are generally more educated and more resourceful, immigrate voluntarily, and have the option of returning home. In addition, first-generation immigrants have a minimalistic lifestyle with limited needs and hence are able to create a more secure future for their children. On the other hand, second-generation African Americans develop racial identities and stances that are more similar to those of African Americans who have been in the United States (Stephenson, 2004).

An important factor and variable to keep in mind in developing formulations with cultural minorities is the degree of stress associated with the process of immigration as we have discussed previously in Chapter 3. On this count, it is also important to differentiate immigrants from refugees. The former desire and plan to move, can have higher education, have greater financial resources, and have the ability to go back to their country of origin. They usually have support and housing when they arrive and usually settle in or near an established community. Refugees have no previous interest and experiences; they leave without planning, are less well educated, and can be poor as they do not come with many possessions. They often do not speak English and live in communities where poor ethnic minorities live. The stressors that refugees face are significantly greater than the immigrants. Even when one is an immigrant and not a refugee, a variety of pre-immigration and post-immigration stressors can be contributory factors in psychopathology as highlighted previously (Bemak & Chung, 2014).

> **Exercise:** Think of two African Caribbean/black African clients from your case load and list the strengths that you had identified at the time of assessment. What are the other strengths that you can discuss with these clients? Can you incorporate evaluation of culture-related strengths in your assessments?

Technical adjustments in formulation

For those African American clients who have had experience of racism and discrimination, it is very important for therapists to consider the role of racial bias and discrimination in the formulation of psychopathology. The therapist can bring up this topic in a supportive and non-judgmental way as the client may perceive feelings of shame or guilt in addressing them directly. Some open-ended questions are helpful such as the following: *are there aspects of your race and culture that may be important for us to talk about? Do you have cultural or religious beliefs that may be impacting on how you feel or in the way problems are bothering you?* However, many individuals may not be comfortable addressing racial issues with a therapist from different cultural background particularly early on in therapy. In those instances, the therapist should back off but leave the door open for the client to bring this issue with a statement such as *We do not need to talk about this issue of racial discrimination at this time. However, I will be open to discussing this issue any time when you are comfortable doing so. It may be that you feel that I will not understand your experience which may be partially true, but I do understand discrimination. All of us have experienced discrimination at some level – due to appearance, gender, age, or other reasons.* When clients are given choices by the therapists or people who provide care, they interpret that they are being respected – as described by Ellen Saks in her personal autobiography - dealing with psychotic illness (Saks, 2007). If engagement with an individual from African American cultural background is challenging, premature dropout can be reduced by focusing the conversation on the cultural strengths that reduces the stigma and enhances positive coping skills (Hall & Sandberg, 2012). Identifying and enhancing the spiritual and religious coping skills can increase the repertoire of coping skills and reduce the barriers with therapist. Therapists who work in areas with predominance of African Caribbean/black African/other black clients should engage the community by developing interventions tailored to the community such as keeping open lines of communication with advocates and influential members of the community who can in turn identify and refer appropriately (Zúñiga, Strathdee, Blanco, Burgos, & Patterson, 2010).

Exercise: Consider the case example of Aida from Chapter 3, which is restated below. Identify the cultural aspects of her philosophical orientation and practical consideration. Based on this, develop her longitudinal formulation (Appendix 2).

Aida, a 36-year-old woman of Nigerian descent, was raised by her grandmother in Nigeria until age 16, when she migrated to the United Kingdom to live with her aunt. From a very young age, she aspired to be a singer and practiced at the church choir regularly. According to tradition, when baptized at 14 years of age, she was meant to start serving the Lord, but instead, she had been going to parties with friends and enjoying herself. She started smoking cannabis from age 15 onwards. At age 25, she had been in an abusive relationship for 2 years. When this relationship ended, she started hearing the voices of her ancestors, as she described them, telling her, 'you will serve the Lord.' She started reading the bible, was fasting for long periods of time, and was ministering to the Bible on the bus.

Her treating psychiatric team appreciated the importance to her of her religious beliefs and agreed that many people pray and get comfort from their religious practice. She explained that she was not religious but her ancestors sent messages from a tree near her residence and she understood it as 'read the word' when the branches tilted in a certain direction. She therefore stayed on the bus, reading the bible until she received another message to stop, often after several hours of being on the bus. She explained that she needed permission to eat and therefore fasted for long periods, sometimes needing hospital admission.

Aida agreed that her quality of life could be better but refused to believe that she was mentally unwell or needed treatment. At best, she was willing to attend a session with a 'Yoruba healer.' Her reasoning was that she was being punished or was under a Voodoo spell.

Hispanic population

The Hispanic population has their origins in different countries of South America and Spain. Hispanic people as a group deal with issues of poverty, illegal immigration, language barrier, and low educational level. The term Latino is now commonly used by Latinos and non-Latinos to refer to both immigrant and US-born Americans of Latino ancestry (Hays & Iwamasa, 2006). Hispanic or Latino values differ from mainstream American values in the following ways: their identity is collectivist as opposed to the individual identity fostered by mainstream America. For Latinos, life is more about being part of a family and community and not just about being an individual. For many, relationships are hierarchical with older generation and male members accorded more respect. Communication style is based on deference to those in higher status, and the goal is for smooth and non-confrontational relations. Feelings are not expressed verbally and there is a degree of stoicism and resignation. As opposed to professional relationships that are task oriented in mainstream culture, the Latino values emphasize personal dimension of all human relations.

Technical adjustments in formulation
Many dimensions of CBT are consistent with the social and cultural characteristics of Latino clients. The educational and didactic part of CBT is helpful in orienting Latino patients to therapy by educating them about how mental disorders are conceptualized. This also helps to counter the belief that mental health services are reserved for *personas locas* (crazy people) in mental institutions. In addition, the Latino clients are comfortable referring to therapy as a class, and use of homework, worksheets, and in session chalk boards helps them to look at this as a class (Hays & Iwamasa, 2006). Many Latinos see physicians as authority figures and expect them to be more directive, which may interfere with them being collaborative and active in their participation. A significant proportion of Latinos are from low socio-economic status and deal with real-life issues related to external circumstances, and the problem-solving component of CBT fits in very well to address these problems. This can help individuals perceive therapy as being responsive and meaningful in their lives.

Therapists can utilize the Latino value of *personalismo* to engage clients. This means that the first focus should be on relationship building and the presenting problems take a back seat to relationship building. Therapists may have to engage in small talk, find areas of common interest, and sometimes be open to engagement strategies such as having a cup of coffee with client when in community before starting to develop a formulation. Where therapists have limited or no Spanish skills, some self-deprecating humour about one's difficulty in learning a new language can lower the hierarchical barrier between the therapist and the client.

Wherever possible, the therapist should make additional effort to involve the family with the permission of the client. There are some individuals who prefer to keep their issues private even from their family members, and those wishes should be respected. The involvement of family members should be from the very first session onwards, and they can be included in the formulation, education, and homework assignments. Many Latino family members take on a caregiver role for the seriously ill family member and do it with a sense of duty. It is important to validate the caregiver role and address this as a positive aspect of the culture. Formulation and cognitive restructuring should not label thoughts as irrational or distorted, and the preferred method is to consider these thoughts as half-truths by using 'yes, but' technique (Organista, 1995). 'Yes, but' technique can be used by asking clients to complete a sentence such as '*the voices are very bothersome and at times very strong but... .*' With regard to termination, the approach should be perceived as not breaking the relationship. One way to do this is leave the door open for the client to call back, and there are some therapists who even allow them to drop by and say 'hello' (Hays & Iwamasa, 2006).

Case example

Elsie, as discussed in earlier chapters, is a 35-year-old Hispanic female. Briefly, her symptoms had been auditory hallucinations with derogatory content, suicidal ideation with two attempts, and paranoid thoughts. She and her three children lived with her widowed mother, Norma, aged 73. The two main issues of concern for Norma had been that Elsie stopped medication, became sick, and was hospitalized and she undermined her mother's disciplining of children by allowing them to break the rules.

Elsie did not want to be in therapy and was there because her mother wanted her to be there. Developing a therapeutic relationship was difficult as the therapist was from a different culture and therapy was seen as 'another thing' that mom was forcing on her. The therapist found himself in a challenging situation when attempting to build a therapeutic relationship. The mother drove Elsie to every visit and expected to be in the session, and alienating the mom would have led her to terminate therapy prematurely, while the mom being in session led Elsie to be withdrawn and not engaging with therapy. For the therapist, building a relationship with Elsie was of critical importance, but losing the logistical support of mother was not an option. The therapist decided to modify the session by allotting most of the session to talk individually with Elsie and then bring her mom in for the last 10 min to address her concerns. Before the mother was called in, the therapist would discuss with Elsie as to what she was comfortable with being discussed with the mother. That way, the therapist helped Elsie have control over the material that could be discussed with the mom while not giving the sense to the mother that she was being left out. In the session with Elsie, the approach that was taken was to focus on relationship building by trying to understand her philosophical orientation. This was done by starting the discussion about Elsie's migratory experience and issues in adjusting to a new country. The approach helped the therapist to develop a formulation with Elsie.

Elsie immigrated to the United States when she was 10 years old, long before her illness started, and she became more enthusiastic talking about that experience. The narrative of migratory experience can be extremely therapeutic for most individuals with history of immigration. It also helps individuals to place their life in long-term perspective while helping the therapist to build a longitudinal formulation. The therapist also utilized judicious self-disclosure about his own experiences with immigration to the United States. The shared experience of immigration helped to build a positive therapeutic relationship, and Elsie was able to articulate her dreams when she came to the United States and how the illness squashed her dreams. She had limited aspirations now and wanted her children to be successful. She wanted to play her role as a mother to the children. The therapist decided to address the issue of non-adherence from the perspective of her either facilitating or impeding life goals. The therapist helped Elsie draw a life line in order to develop a formulation with the periods of adherence and non-adherence, and collaboratively, they examined the correlation of non-adherence and periods of hospitalization. Elsie was able to recognize that non-adherence was a barrier in reaching her goals. There was an added influence of a cousin who would tell her that medications were for *personas locas* (crazy people). The issue was addressed by enlisting the mother's help to find a community activist that was respected and had some understanding of mental illness. Elsie trusted this lady and agreed to visit her and get her opinion about medication and mental health treatment. That was a positive visit for Elsie as the activist was able to share stories of people in the community who went to treatment for mental health problems and were doing well.

Elsie came back from the visit with a positive view about taking medication and continuing with therapy. Thus, a combination of relationship building, formulating and addressing non-adherence from life goal perspective, doing a timeline and developing a correlation between non-adherence and hospitalization, and enlisting the mother's help in getting the perspective of a community activist all helped Elsie to remain medication adherent.

The conflict between her and her mother was that Norma saw Elsie as not respecting her, while Elsie viewed her mother as treating her like a child in front of her own children. Elsie would have angry outbursts against the mother which made her mother frustrated. The therapist drew up a formulation with Elsie and addressed the issue of angry outbursts in a culturally informed way of teaching assertiveness skills for Elsie. When she addressed the issues with her mom, she would first ask permission with a statement such as '*Can you allow me to say something about how I feel.*' Such assertiveness techniques are consistent with the Latino value of '*simpatia*' *or* smooth and less confrontational communication (Comas-Díaz & Duncan, 1985). In turn, the mother agreed to give any feedback to Elsie when she was by herself and not in front of the children.

In this instance, a number of cultural factors informed the relationship building and formulation. Identifying her philosophical orientation and practical setting was the first step and actually helped break the ice. Elsie's migratory experience was a good topic for her to discuss and moved the focus away from her current disability to her dreams and aspirations and the way she coped with different stressors. The therapist was able to identify a number of positive coping skills that Elsie utilized to deal with her stressors and draw her attention to them. The focus of the therapist on strengths increased her self-efficacy, helped her to look at herself more as a 'survivor and not a failure,' and improved the relationship with the therapist. In many members of the Hispanic culture, it is normal for a parent to take responsibility of ill children and grandchildren. What might also come along with this is the expectation that they would like to know what occurs in therapy. Sometimes, it requires creative solutions to maintain the privacy of the therapy without the parent feeling alienated. Utilizing cultural concepts of smooth communication helped address the conflicts between the mother and her daughter.

Asian populations

The term Asian includes Chinese, Korean, Japanese, Asians from the Indian subcontinent (Indians, Pakistanis, Bangladeshi, Nepalese, Burmese, etc.), and Vietnamese. Asian groups in the United States and elsewhere are clearly not from one homogenous culture because of different geographical countries of origin, different waves of immigration, and different natural histories. There is a dichotomy with respect to educational qualifications of Asian populations. Asian groups, especially Indian, Chinese, and Japanese, are more likely than whites to have earned a college degree, but on the other hand, some subcultural groups such as Laotians and Cambodians are more likely to have a less than ninth-grade education (Burgess, Ding, Hargreaves, van Ryn, & Phelan, 2008). Religious beliefs and spiritual practices vary greatly with many Chinese people being Buddhist or Christian, Indian people being predominantly Hindu, Thai and Sri Lankan being mainly Buddhist, and Pakistanis being predominantly Muslim. Asian groups on the one hand are held as model minority and on the other hand are targets of racism, discrimination, and hate crimes. After generations of domicile in the United States and United Kingdom, the accents and cultural traditions may fade, but the skin tone and the shape of eyes do not and hence make them a target of racism (Chang, 2003). The effects of specific or community racism is evidenced by keeping secrets to hide family shame, as well as stories of coping that strengthen survival.

The Asian American/UK/European groups though not homogenous share a number of characteristics. Like other cultural groups, they have a collectivist as opposed to individual identity, and the collective may range from the nuclear family to the extended family, an entire village, or even a country. The focus is not on the rights of the individual but rather on what is good for the group (Marin & Gamba, 2003). It is not uncommon for three generations to live in one house with many relatives living within walking distance (Uba, 1994). The family roles are clearly defined, and there is patriarchal authoritarian system. The father and to a lesser extent the mother make decisions for the family often without the input of the children, and it is assumed that parents have greater wisdom and will be able to make better decisions, even after the children reach adulthood (Tien & Olson, 2003). The strongest emotional attachment for a woman is often to her children, especially her sons. Most parents demand filial piety, respect, and obedience from their children. In terms of emotional expression, Asian parents are variable among different groups in open display of affection or emotions. Parents put their interests aside to focus on the education of the children, and at the same time, they expect to be cared for in old age. When the children get treatment from mental health system, parents expect to be informed about the treatment and may even try to make decisions for the children.

One of the major themes in Asian religions is the concept of balance. Hindu scriptures emphasize the need for balance or 'santulan,' discipline or 'sanyam,' and moderation. In China, the balance between yin (passivity) and yang (activity) permeates different domains from conception of the body, emotions, society, and the environment. To achieve balance, the individual is expected to have moderation in all things. As opposed to the reductionist view of medicine, the Asian view of health is more holistic, with the belief that spiritual aspects of life are important and have a bearing on physical and mental health. The focus is on indirect or remote causes as opposed to direct and immediate causes (Shiraev & Levy, 2001), and their locus of control is external. This integrated approach to health is strength of the culture and should be highlighted and used in formulations.

In many Asian countries, religious organizations are highly respected and a priest, minister, yogi, imam, or a Buddhist monk may be the first person people go to instead of a mental health professional (Lee et al., 2009). Mental health services are underutilized because of the stigma and belief that it brings shame to the entire family, lack of financial resources, differing conceptions of illness and health, and lack of culturally competent services (McGoldrick,

Giordano, & Garcia-Preto, 2005) as we have already discussed in previous chapters. Emotional problems can be presented with somatic complaints as discussed in Chapter 3. When in treatment, Asian families often expect the clinician to 'fix it' with immediate results, and the problem-solving approach aspect of CBT with education to modulate expectations is likely to work well in these situations, and similar strategies have been suggested in family therapy of Chinese families (Iwamasa, Hsia, & Hinton, 2006; Soo-Hoo, 1999). In terms of language, some words or concepts are different in native language compared to English. For example, in Mandarin, there is no differentiation between him, her, or it, and when Mandarin speakers use English, there can be confusion about the gender pronoun.

Case example

Min, a 20-year-old female, came in due to voices, paranoia, and anxiety as well as intrusive memories of a sexual assault by her friend's stepdad. She had strong thoughts of guilt and suicide and made two prior attempts. She immigrated to the United States from China at the age of 12. She lived with her parents who spoke very limited English and a sister who was 2 years younger. Min had a rough transition to the US schooling system, going from a confident, well-liked, and straight. A' student in China to struggling with grades, not having many friends, and being very diffident about herself. When she was 16, her friend's stepdad sexually assaulted her. Her parents were ashamed of this and decided to keep it in the family and not inform anyone. It was a topic they did not like to talk about. Her parents did not even confront the abuser. She never processed the trauma that was associated with guilt, depressed mood, and suicidal ideation with attempt. Min came to the attention of mental health services when she was in crisis following a suicide attempt. She chose to come to therapy as medication alone was not helpful and her parents let her make the decision as long as it was not known in the community.

In therapy, Min's demeanour was more of a passive one, waiting for directions from the therapist. Her view of the therapist as superior and hence deserving of her respect was a barrier to therapeutic relationship. The therapist's view was to address the power differential in the relationship and increase Min's assertiveness in the here and now of therapy so that he could understand her philosophical orientation. The therapist used a number of interventions to accomplish this. The first ones were education and socialization to therapy. Next, the therapist found situations where he obtained specific explicit feedback from her during the session. It was clear that she had great difficulty saying anything that might seem negative. This was addressed in the 'here and now' of therapy by specifically enquiring about her thoughts and beliefs towards therapy in the sessions. She was able to verbalize her core belief that she should respect and not criticize the therapist because he was older than her and was her therapist. The therapist utilized self-deprecating humour and worked on cognitive restructuring of the belief that she should not criticize him. Gradually, she was able to work with the therapist on formulation and express critical elements about the formulation, interventions, and therapist's style. This breakthrough of a psychological barrier helped her to discuss her beliefs about the trauma including her parents' response to 'shove it under the rug.' Collaboratively, a formulation was discussed, and she recognized that the self-blame and guilt for the incident were to a significant extent tied to her core belief that older people are not wrong and that somehow she was responsible for the sexual assault on her. She was able to overcome the guilt, and consequently, there was improvement in her depressed mood, and suicidal ideation became less frequent and less intense.

The therapist reached out to the parents to address their concerns and invite them to a meeting. The father did not want any part in the session, and the only thing they wanted was for the therapist to help their daughter in the best manner he saw fit. Combinations of significant language barrier as well as a strong sense of shame were barriers to the parents being engaged in therapeutic process. Towards the end of the individual therapy, Min felt comfortable to join a trauma support group for women and was able to process her trauma in a group setting. She was able to reduce the dosage of her medication and remained free of self-harm behaviours.

Technical adjustments to formulation

In Min's case, the cultural belief that elders should be obeyed and not criticized had played a significant part in self-blame and guilt for sexual abuse and was part of the formulation. The therapist's interventions to give her permission to be critical in sessions about him helped her overcome this strong psychological barrier to not think critically of elders. This case is an example of family not being involved due to linguistic barrier and a sense of shame about mental illness.

Indian groups

The immigration of Indian population to the United States started to a significant degree in the 1960s. Although some differences exist in the United Kingdom because of the lengthy and often troubled links from when India was part of the

British Empire and eventually secured independence, the similarities generally outweigh the differences.

Indians as a group are among the most highly educated and better off immigrant groups in the United States and the United Kingdom. Due to their educational status and exposure to American culture before immigration, they tend to be fairly well adjusted http://www.pewsocialtrends.org/asianamericans-graphics/indians/. However, a number of cultural factors have to be kept in mind when dealing with Indian clients. For many Indian clients, family plays a vital role in all major decisions in an individual's life including their treatment and care. They bear the major burden and take responsibility of care of the persons with illness and dampen the effect of limited resources as the example of Rakesh in the following section demonstrates. The family involvement may not give privacy for the client to discuss therapeutic issues with the therapist .The American Health Information Portability and Accountability Act (HPAA) clearly gives primacy to client privacy irrespective of their dependence on the family. Also, many clients, particularly the younger ones, value their privacy and independence and do not want the parents to be part of decision making about their lives. The therapist can sometimes be in a bind when a client does not like the family involvement and is afraid of losing their support and hence would like the therapist to address the issue with the family. Therapists have to tread the fine line of promoting client independence in a way the family who is supporting the client do not feel excluded and thereby disengage from therapy.

Case example

Rakesh, a 27-year-old Asian Indian male with schizophrenia, was referred to individual therapy by his mother. He lived with his parents and was the younger of two siblings, and his older brother had a steady job as an engineer. Rakesh was from a very young age 'mom's boy.' His mother was very strong willed, while Rakesh was the docile one in the family, and usually, he went along with his mom's decisions. Rakesh's mother was the one who pushed him and at times made decisions for him. Rakesh's parents were first-generation immigrants to the United States from the northeastern part of India. Coming from a background where their peers were more educated and successful, they put tremendous pressure on their children to succeed. Rakesh had great difficulty in reconciling the expectations of his parents with the attitudes and beliefs of his peer group. His peers made decisions about their lives, and the parents allowed them to make their own decisions. The way he was treated compared to his peers was an unresolved issue for Rakesh, and before he could resolve the issue of becoming independent and charting his own life course that was separate from his parents, he had a psychotic breakdown. The deficits from his illness including his inability to sustain a regular job made him more dependent on his parents, and his mother became even more protective of him. As part of his psychotic episode, Rakesh exercised poor judgement and made poor financial decisions. Rakesh did not fully accept his illness and would stop his medication regularly. In his mother's mind, he could not be trusted to make decisions about his illness and his life. She was the one who enquired about the therapeutic options, called to speak with the therapist before informing the son, and then drove him to the appointments. She cooked for him, cleaned his room, and was involved in every aspect of his life. She also had expectations that he would be as successful as her older son who was not mentally ill. Rakesh was ambivalent about therapy as evidenced by his reluctant engagement in therapy. However, he attended because he both feared his mom and also did not want to disappoint her. At times, Rakesh resented being treated like a child but had difficulty being assertive for fear of losing the financial and other support of his mother.

Exercise: Identify the cultural influence on Rakesh's philosophical orientation and practical considerations. How would you develop a formulation?

The main issues that the therapist had to deal with were to (a) help Rakesh resolve the ambivalence about therapy and help him gain a better understanding of his illness, (b) help Rakesh be appropriately assertive towards his mom and place limits on her involvement in his life, and (c) help his mom give some time and space for Rakesh to live his life while being there to support him. The therapist was from the same ethnic background as the client, and that helped him to be more comfortable about the therapy. On the other hand, it also created some issues in that the mother would expect the therapist to go out his way of normal practice and accede to her requests. For example, the mother would sometimes call before the appointment and would give information about her son and would ask the therapist to not divulge where the information came from. The therapist addressed this issue by informing her that it was extremely important to establish a positive therapeutic relationship with Rakesh and such a relationship could only be built by being open and honest with him. He validated her motivations to help Rakesh but disagreed with the approach of treating Rakesh as a child and withholding information from him. He also informed her that the information shared about Rakesh would be divulged to him. The therapist went ahead and informed

Rakesh about his mother's request as well as the therapist's response. This intervention had a positive impact in Rakesh's attitude towards the therapist, and he became more open and trusting of the therapist. The mother was not pleased with the therapist's response but came around when she started noticing that she did not have to drag Rakesh to the appointments and that he was showing some interest in therapy himself. The way the therapist approached his mom and placed limits on her involvement was a good model for Rakesh when he later on in the therapy started working on being assertive towards his mom.

When the therapist started working with Rakesh on ambivalence towards illness, he found that the high expectations for success that his mother and the rest of his community had from Rakesh were the source of most stress. Rakesh found it easier to deny his illness than face the stigma from a community that is focused on financial success. The therapist helped Rakesh understand the stress–vulnerability model of his illness and the negative impact of the stress of high expectations on his illness. Over the course of therapy, Rakesh was able to distance himself from the high expectations, and the change in his self-expectations helped him to resolve some of the ambivalence around treatment. The next part in his therapy was teaching assertiveness skills to effectively yet respectfully limit his mother's involvement in his life. One issue that came about in therapy due to the similar cultural background of the therapist and the client was the possibility that the client may meet with the therapist in a social setting. This was a possibility because the client and the therapist were from the same geographical area and Indian background and there was a small Indian community in the area. This issue was brought up by Rakesh as part of the discussion of severe degree of stigma towards mental illness he experienced from the community. The therapist acknowledged that this was a possibility and that the client should be absolutely assured of his confidentiality. This issue of extra concern about confidentiality comes into play when therapists are practicing in rural areas that are less densely populated and people seem to know everyone's business. So the therapist is more likely to encounter his own clients in a social context. When these possibilities exist, the therapist should bring these topics for discussion and address the concerns that may arise.

Case discussion

The aforementioned case example illustrates the differences in self-construal between Rakesh and his mother. Rakesh had acculturated to a larger extent and like his peers endorsed the independent view of the self, promoted by the individualistic society he was raised in. The independent view emphasizes an individual's internal attributes and separateness from the interpersonal context fostering assertiveness, autonomy, and the promotion of one's goals. On the other hand, his mother had an interdependent self-construal, which emphasizes connectedness with the social context, harmonious interpersonal relationships, and conformity over individual assertiveness and uniqueness (Markus & Kitayama, 1991). Belonging to a community that is successful and has high expectations is a source of stress for Indian students, and part of therapist's focus is to help families modulate their own expectations. Some researchers have suggested that therapist has to help the parents understand that their children are Americans/British of Indian origin as opposed to Indians in America or Europe (Chakrabarti, 2009).

Islam and implications for CBT

Muslims in the developed countries come from 60 different countries, and hence, there are no single set of beliefs that represent the entire population of Muslims (Williams, 1998). There has been an increase in religious intolerance and Islamophobia in the United States following the 9-11 attacks, and Muslims are fearful and feel very misunderstood (Giger & Davidhizar, 2002) as we have discussed in Chapter 1. Hence, they are likely to expect the therapist to misunderstand them and their religious beliefs. In a study of clients and the providers, 93.8% of Muslim women reported that the providers did not understand their religious or cultural needs, and in the same study, 83% of providers reported challenges when providing care for a Muslim woman (Hasnain, Connell, Menon, & Tranmer, 2011). It would help if therapists know at least the basic constructs of Islam as this would help them to allay their concerns. Muslim families may seem conflicted by Western standards because of the contrasting emphasis on group cohesion and a more collectivist identity. Muslim families, however, seek more connectedness in marital relationship and between members of extended family (Daneshpour, 1998). Confrontation, or even direct communication, can be considered selfish and insulting to the community. Similarly, clients may – at least on the surface – conform to requests, treatment plans, and so forth, as disagreement might be perceived as confronting the therapist.

Muslims may be particularly open to holistic, ecological interventions that incorporate members of the family and the broader community (Daneshpour, 1998). In addition to imams (Muslim priests), other elders in the community can be utilized as resources in therapy process.

Recent immigrants, as well as other Muslims, may not be aware of the range of organizations that have been developed over the past two decades to provide social support to Muslim communities. This is particularly the case with mosques, which often provide services of a completely different character than Muslims typically enjoyed in their country of origin (Hedayat-Diba, 2000). It is important to explore the spiritual belief system when working with Muslim clients.

Sincerely inquiring about peoples' spiritual beliefs and practices sends the implicit message that their spirituality is respected and deemed important in the counselling dialogue (Mahmoud, 1996). Religiosity has been shown to moderate the effects of job stress (Jamal & Badawi, 1993) and discrimination for Muslims (Byng, 1998). Some scholars interpret the principles of CBT as consistent with the religious concepts of Islam: *Allah (God) will not change the condition of people unless they start changing what is in themselves* (Surat Ar-Ra`d, 11). This particular dictum encourages individuals to be self-reflective and evaluate their mental experiences and work with formulations. When dysfunctional beliefs are identified, they should be modified or replaced with beliefs derived from the shari'a, particularly the Quran (Hodge, 2005).

Conclusions

Psychological distress is culturally interpreted very differently, and it determines the pathways to help-seeking behaviour. Individual case formulation is a critical element in CBT, and cultural factors significantly inform and guide the formulation. Cognitive behavioural formulation for cultural minority groups should take a building block approach proceeding from mini formulation to cross-sectional and finally to longitudinal formulation. The formulation should take into account the individual cultural background and perspective of the patient and their communities. Interventions that are culturally appropriate have to extend beyond the therapy dyadic situation and involve parents, other family members, religious leaders, community activists, and communities. Modifying the formulation to fit the culture of the client leads to the choice of culture-specific interventions.

References

Beck, J. (2011). *Cognitive behaviour therapy: Basics and beyond* (2nd ed.). New York, NY: Guilford Press.

Bemak, F., & Chung, R. C.-Y. (2014). Immigrants and refugees. In F. T. L. Leong, L. Comas-Díaz, G. C. Nagayama Hall, V. C. McLoyd, & J. E. Trimble (Eds.), *APA handbook of multicultural psychology, Vol. 1: Theory and research* (pp. 503–517). Washington, DC: American Psychological Association.

Boyd-Franklin, N. (2003). *Black families in therapy: Understanding the African American experience* (2nd ed.). New York, NY: Guilford Press.

Burgess, D. J., Ding, Y., Hargreaves, M., van Ryn, M., & Phelan, S. (2008). The association between perceived discrimination and underutilization of needed medical and mental health care in a multi-ethnic community sample. *Journal of Health Care for the Poor and Underserved*, *19*(3), 894–911. doi:10.1353/hpu.0.0063

Burkard, A. W., & Knox, S. (2004). Effect of therapist color-blindness on empathy and attributions in cross-cultural counseling. *Journal of Counseling Psychology*, *51*(4), 387–397. doi:10.1037/0022-0167.51.4.387

Byng, M. D. (1998). Mediating discrimination: Resisting oppression among African American Muslim women. *Social Problems*, *45*, 473–487.

Casas, J. M., & Vasquez, M. (1996). *Counseling the Hispanic* (4th ed.). Thousand Oaks, CA: Sage.

Chakrabarti, L. (2009). *Educational experiences and academic achievement of Asian Indian American students in a Midwestern University town in the United States: A multiple case study* (69), ProQuest Information & Learning, US. EBSCOhost psyh database. Retrieved from http://search.ebscohost.com/login.aspx?direct=true&db=psyh&AN=2009-99031-414&site=ehost-live (accessed on September 18, 2014).

Chang, I. (2003). *The Chinese in America: A narrative history*. New York, NY: Viking.

Chatters, L. M., Taylor, R. J., Bullard, K. M., & Jackson, J. S. (2008). Spirituality and subjective religiosity among African Americans, Caribbean Blacks and Non-Hispanic Whites. *Journal for the Scientific Study of Religion*, 47(4), 725–737. doi:10.1111/j.1468-5906.2008.00437.x

Coltraine, S., & Messineo, M. (2000). The perpetuation of subtle prejudice: Race and gender imagery in 1990s television advertising. *Sex Roles*, 42, 363–389.

Comas-Díaz, L., & Duncan, J. W. (1985). The cultural context: A factor in assertiveness training with mainland Puerto Rican women. *Psychology of Women Quarterly*, 9(4), 463–475. doi:10.1111/j.1471-6402.1985.tb00896.x

Daneshpour, M. (1998). Muslim families and family therapy. *Journal of Marital and Family Therapy*, 24(3), 355–368. doi:10.1111/j.1752-0606.1998.tb01090.x

Dixon, L. B., Dickerson, F., Bellack, A. S., Bennett, M., Dickinson, D., Goldberg, R. W., Lehman, A., Tenhula, W. N., Calmes, C., Pasillas, R. M., Peer, J., & Kreyenbuhl, J.; Schizophrenia Patient Outcomes Research Team (PORT). (2010). The 2009 PORT psychosocial treatment recommendations and summary statements. Schizophrenia Bulletin, 36(1), 48–70.

Drake, R. E., Merrens, M. R., & Lynde, D. W. (2005). *Evidenced based mental health practice: A textbook*. New York, NY: Norton and Company.

Giger, J. N., & Davidhizar, R. (2002). Culturally competent care: Emphasis on understanding the people of Afghanistan, Afghanistan Americans, and Islamic culture and religion. *International Nursing Review*, 49(2), 79–86.

Grant, P.M., Huh, G.A., Perivoliotis, D., Solar, N., & Beck, A.T. (2012). Randomized trial to evaluate the efficacy of cognitive therapy for low-functioning patients with schizophrenia. *Archives of General Psychiatry*, 69, 121–127. DOI: 10.1001/archgenpsychiatry.2011.129

Hall, C. A., & Sandberg, J. G. (2012). "We shall overcome": A qualitative exploratory study of the experiences of African Americans who overcame barriers to engage in family therapy. *American Journal of Family Therapy*, 40(5), 445–458. doi:10.1080/01 926187.2011.637486

Hardy, K. V., & Laszloffy, T. A. (1995). Therapy with African Americans and the phenomenon of rage. *In Session: Psychotherapy in Practice*, 1(4), 57–70.

Hasnain, M., Connell, K. J., Menon, U., & Tranmer, P. A. (2011). Patient-centered care for Muslim women: Provider and patient perspectives. *Journal of Women's Health*, 20(1), 73–83.

Hays, P. A., & Iwamasa, G. Y. (2006). *Culturally responsive cognitive-behavioral therapy*. Washington, DC: American Psychological Association.

Hedayat-Diba, Z. (2000). *Psychotherapy with Muslims*. Washington, DC: American Psychological Association.

Hines, P. M., & Boyd-Franklin, N. (2005). African American families. In M. McGoldrick, J. Giordano, & N. Garcia-Preto (Eds.), *Ethnicity and family therapy* (3rd ed., pp. 87–100). New York, NY: Guilford Press.

Hodge, D. R. (2005). Social work and the house of Islam: Orienting practitioners to the beliefs and values of Muslims in the United States. *Social Work*, 50(2), 162–173.

Hollar, M. C. (2001). The impact of racism on the delivery of health care and mental health services. *Psychiatric Quarterly*, 72(4), 337–345.

Iwamasa, G. Y., Hsia, C., & Hinton, D. (2006). Cognitive-behavioral therapy with Asian Americans. In P. A. Hays, & G. Y. Iwamasa (Eds.), *Culturally responsive cognitive-behavioral therapy: Assessment, practice, and supervision* (pp. 117–140). Washington, DC: American Psychological Association.

Jamal, M., & Badawi, J. (1993). Job stress among Muslim immigrants in North America: Moderating effects of religiosity. *Stress Medicine*, 9(3), 145–151.

Kingdon, D., & Turkington, D. (2005). *Cognitive therapy of schizophrenia*. New York, NY: Guilford Press.

Kuyken, W., Padesky, C. A., & Dudley, R. (2009). *Collaborative case conceptualization: Working effectively with clients in cognitive-behavioral therapy*. New York, NY: Guilford Press.

Kwate, N. O., Valdimarsdottir, H. B., Guevarra, J. S., & Bovbjerg, D. H. (2003). Experiences of racist events are associated with negative health consequences for African American women. *Journal of the National Medical Association*, 95(6), 450–460.

Lee, S., Juon, H.-S., Martinez, G., Hsu, C. E., Robinson, E. S., Bawa, J., & Ma, G. X. (2009). Model minority at risk: Expressed needs of mental health by Asian American young adults. *Journal of Community Health: The Publication for Health Promotion and Disease Prevention*, 34(2), 144–152. doi:10.1007/s10900-008-9137-1

Mahmoud, V. (1996). African American Muslim families. In M. McGoldrick, J. Giordano, & J. K. Pearce (Eds.), Ethnicity and family therapy (2nd ed., pp. 122– 128). New York: Guilford Press.

Marin, G., & Gamba, R. J. (2003). *Acculturation and changes in cultural values*. Washington, DC: American Psychological Association.

Markus, H. R., & Kitayama, S. (1991). Culture and the self: Implications for cognition, emotion, and motivation. *Psychological Review*, 98, 224–253. doi:10.1037/0033-295X.98.2.224

McGoldrick, M., Giordano, J., & Garcia-Preto, N. (2005). *Ethnicity and family therapy*. New York, NY: Guilford Press.

Mezzich, J. E., Caracci, G., Fabrega, H., Jr., & Kirmayer, L. J. (2009). Cultural formulation guidelines. *Transcult Psychiatry*, 46(3), 383–405. doi:10.1177/1363461509342942, pii:46/3/383

Mezzich, J. E., Kirmayer, L. J., Kleinman, A., Fabrega, H., Jr., Parron, D. L., Good, B. J., ... Manson, S. M. (1999). The place of culture in DSM-IV. *The Journal of Nervous and Mental Disease*, 187(8), 457–464.

Morrison, A., Turkington, D., Pyle, M., Spencer, H., Brabban, A., Dunn, G., ... Hutton, P. (2014). Cognitive therapy for people with schizophrenia spectrum disorders not taking antipsychotic drugs: A single-blind randomised controlled trial. *The Lancet*, 383(9926), 1395–1403.

National Institute of Health and Care Excellence (2014, February). Psychosis and schizophrenia in adults: Treatment and management. Clinical guidelines, CG178. London, NICE.

Neighbors, H. W., Hudson, D. L., & Bullard, K. M. (2012). The challenge of understanding the mental health of African Americans: The risks and rewards of segregation, support, and John Henryism. In E. C. Chang, & C. A. Downey (Eds.), *Handbook of race and development in mental health* (pp. 45–66). New York, NY: Springer Science + Business Media.

Organista, K. C. (1995). Cognitive–behavioral treatment of depression and panic disorder in a Latina client: Culturally sensitive case formulation. *In Session: Psychotherapy in Practice*, 1(2), 53–64.

Perivoliotis, D., Grant, P., & Beck, A. (2011). Advances in Cognitive Therapy for Schizophrenia: Empowerment and Recovery in the Absence of Insight. *Clinical Case Studies*, 8(6) 424–437.

Ramirez Basco, M. & Rush, J. (2005). Cognitive-Behavioral Therapy for Bipolar Disorder. Guildford Press, New York.

Ragins, M. (2012). *Recovery: Changing from a medial model to a psychosocial rehabilitation model.* Retrieved from http://mhavillage.squarespace.com/storage/06RecoverySevereMI.pdf (accessed September 26, 2014).

Rathod, S., & Turkington, D. (2005). Cognitive-behaviour therapy for schizophrenia: A review. *Current Opinion in Psychiatry, 18*(2), 159–163.

Saks, E. R. (2007). *The center cannot hold.* New York, NY: Hyperion.

Saldana, D. (1994). Acculturative stress: Minority status and distress. *Hispanic Journal of Behavioral Sciences, 16,* 116–128.

Shiraev, E., & Levy, D. (2001). *Introduction to cross-cultural psychology.* London, UK: Allyn and Bacon.

Soo-Hoo, T. (1999). Brief strategic family therapy with Chinese Americans. *American Journal of Family Therapy, 27*(2), 163–179. doi:10.1080/019261899262041

Stein, L. I., & Santos, A. B. (1998). *Assertive community treatment of persons with severe mental illness.* New York, NY: W. W. Norton & Co.

Stephenson, E. (2004). The African Diaspora and culture-based coping strategies. In J. L. Chin (Ed.), *The psychology of prejudice and discrimination: Racism in America* (Vol. 1, pp. 95–118). Westport, CT: Praeger Publishers/Greenwood Publishing Group.

Taylor, R. J., Chatters, L. M., Mattis, J. S., & Joe, S. (2010). Religious involvement among Caribbean Blacks in the United States. *Review of Religious Research, 52*(2), 125–145.

Tien, L., & Olson, K. (2003). Confucian past, conflicted present: Working with Asian American families. In L. B. Silverstein, & T. J. Goodrich (Eds.), *Feminist family therapy: Empowerment in social context* (pp. 135–145). Washington, DC: American Psychological Association.

Turkington, D., Kingdon, D., Rathod, S., Hammond, K., Pelton, J., & Mehta, R. (2006). An effectiveness trial of a brief cognitive behavioural intervention by mental health nurses in schizophrenia: Clinically important outcomes in the medium term. *British Journal of Psychiatry, 189*(1), 31–35.

Uba, L. (1994). *Asian Americans: Personality patterns, identity, and mental health.* New York, NY: Guilford Press.

Williams, R. B. (1998). *Asian Indian and Pakistani religions in the United States* (Vol. 558). Thousand Oaks, CA: Sage Periodicals Press.

Willie, C. V., & Reddick, R. J. (2003). *A new look at Black families* (5th ed.). Walnut Creek, CA: AltaMira Press.

Wong, C. A., Eccles, J. S., & Sameroff, A. (2003). The influence of ethnic discrimination and ethnic identification on African American adolescents' school and socioemotional adjustment. *Journal of Personality, 71*(6), 1197–1232. doi:10.1111/1467-6494.7106012

Wright, J., Turkington, D., Kingdon, D., & Ramirez Basco, M. (2009). *Cognitive behavior therapy for severe mental illness: An illustrated guide.* Washington, DC: American Psychiatric Publishing Inc.

Zubin, J., & Spring, B. (1997). Vulnerability: A new view on schizophrenia. *Journal of Abnormal Psychology, 86,* 103–126.

Zúñiga, M. L., Strathdee, S. A., Blanco, E., Burgos, J. L., & Patterson, T. L. (2010). Community HIV preventive interventions. In J. M. Suls, K. W. Davidson, & R. M. Kaplan (Eds.), *Handbook of health psychology and behavioral medicine* (pp. 381–396). New York, NY: Guilford Press.

7

Individualized Treatment Planning

This chapter focuses on devising a treatment plan that is drawn up collaboratively and individualized to the particular client based on the formulation and adapted to a minority culture. Individualized treatment planning is a universal requirement of therapy, but there are specific modifications that need consideration when working with minority cultures. These take into account the formulation based on the philosophical orientation and practical consideration of the client. Culture should not be assumed to be homogenous. Although people from one particular culture are very similar in many ways, there are many individual differences based on linguistic ability, degree of acculturation, connections to the country of origin, education levels, and membership of ethnic organizations. In this regard, different members of the same minority cultural group can vary in their presentation of psychological distress, pathways to care that they choose, their engagement with services, and response to different interventions. We have explained these variables in earlier chapters. Additionally, illness pathology and personality issues can coexist, further complicated by cultural influences. An individualized treatment plan takes into account the unique circumstances of the client's life story, culture, and the influence of those experiences in moulding the belief systems.

We start this chapter with an overview of basic techniques of CBT although an in-depth discussion is presented in the individual chapters of psychosis, depression, and mania. We have discussed cultural adaptations to techniques such as normalization, validation, education, and problem solving in Chapter 4. In this chapter, we will then discuss individualization of treatment using three case examples.

Cultural Adaptation of CBT for Serious Mental Illness: A Guide for Training and Practice, First Edition. Shanaya Rathod, David Kingdon, Narsimha Pinninti, Douglas Turkington, and Peter Phiri.
© 2015 John Wiley & Sons, Ltd. Published 2015 by John Wiley & Sons, Ltd.

Theoretical Modifications to CBT Techniques

In this chapter, we describe modifications to therapy using three case examples of individualization:

1. Individual differences between members of same cultural background
2. Individualization of a case where co-morbidity of illness and personality coexist in a client from a mixed racial background
3. Individualization of treatment planning in an individual with advanced levels of acculturation

Case example

Carlos, a 46-year-old Hispanic male, born in Puerto Rico immigrated to the United States when he was 2 years old with his parents. He, along with his two sisters, was raised in New York. He attended a predominantly African American school where he was picked on. He decided to join a gang to belong to a group and also for survival. He started abusing drugs, dropped out of school, married a person with drug addiction, and was estranged from his family. He developed florid psychotic symptoms, and following an accidental overdose of heroin that nearly killed him, he joined a church group and decided to turn his life around. He separated from his wife because she was not ready to join his journey of sobriety and started reaching out to his family. He recognized the need for individual therapy and made enquiries to find out the places where such therapy was available for him and joined a research study of CBT. From the very beginning of therapy, he was very motivated to change, formed a good therapeutic relationship with the therapist, and reconnected with his sisters. He moved in to live with her sister and helped her work through grief when his brother-in-law died and then with drug addiction of his nephew.

Case discussion

This case illustrates the difference in philosophical orientation, practical considerations, and presentation from the case of Elsie described in previous chapters who also belonged to a Hispanic background. Elsie was older when her parents migrated to the United States, and the migratory experience was very traumatic for her unlike Carlos who was 2 years old and hence had no memories of the migration. Elsie and Carlos responded very differently to the stress of cultural discrimination. She became more withdrawn and isolated while he took up a rebellious path and joined a gang and got into drugs. When Elsie became psychotic and separated from her husband, her mother accepted her into her household and became the de facto parent for the grandchildren. Carlo's family disowned him attributing all his problems to drug use, and even when he developed psychosis, they did not want anything to do with him. The above two examples illustrate how two families from the same cultural background can respond very differently to mental illness in a family member. The pathway that Elsie took to care was through the crisis centre, and this was in part due to her lack of knowledge and understanding of mental illness. However, Carlos took the traditional path of going to his primary care physician as he had grown up in the United States and was comfortable with the system of care. For Elise, support for individual therapy came from her child's therapist who recognized the need for individual therapy, and the case manager from Elsie's cultural background supported it. Carlos himself recognized the need for individual therapy and made concerted efforts to eventually find a research study and enrol in it.

There are differences in the therapy modifications in both cases. Elsie took a very passive stance in her therapy, and the therapist had to use a variety of culturally informed interventions to build therapeutic relationship. Carlos was much acculturated and hence did not need specific adaptations. Termination process in the two cases differed with Elsie's mom deciding that she had enough therapy and asking for termination, while Carlos ended the therapy when therapist completed the therapy process (Table 7.1).

Therapists should be aware of the significant individual differences in presentation, engagement, and the process of therapy between clients belonging to same minority cultural groups. The need for technical adjustments and modifications in therapy that are adapted from Tseng's model (Tseng, 2001) described in Chapters 4–6 varies very widely between clients of same cultural minority group. The flexibility of therapist described in Chapter 5 will help in tailoring the interventions to the individual needs of the clients (see Appendix 3 on setting goals).

Exercise: Think of two individuals from the same minority cultural background with different philosophical orientations. Consider if your interventions differed based on these differences. What would you do differently if you see them again?

Table 7.1 Differences in philosophical orientation and technical adjustments for two Hispanic clients.

Therapy phase	Elsie	Carlos
Pathways to care	Did not take traditional pathway of accessing through primary care physician	Went through primary care physician
	Presented in crisis as she did not access services	Crisis presentation due to accidental overdose
	Referred to cognitive therapist by her child's therapist	He sought out help and had no family support
Pre-engagement/ engagement	Required pre-engagement work with mother	Did not require pre-engagement work
Assessment/ formulation	Cultural identity	Cultural identity
	Hispanic cultural identity at home and in therapy environment	Very well acculturated in therapy situation
	Migratory experience is very important and was traumatic	Migration was not important factor
	Responded to ethnic discrimination by isolation and withdrawal	Rebelled due to discrimination and joined a gang
	Husband broke up after illness	Family disowned him
	Language: some limitation in expressing emotions	Language: Not a barrier in assessment or therapy
	Illness attributions: to traumas in life	Biomedical attribution of illness
Therapy issues	Required cultural adaptation to make shift from authoritarian mode to collaborative mode	Was easily socialized to the collaborative style
	Family involvement: mother wanted to be part of therapy process	Families were available if therapist saw the need to involve them
	Termination: decision made by mother to terminate therapy	Termination: agreement reached collaboratively between therapist and client

Individualization and Adaptation in a Case with Comorbidity

There is some evidence to say that personality disorders are probably under diagnosed in minority cultures (McGilloway, Hall, Lee, & Bhui, 2010) and therapists should be more open to the diagnosis of personality disorder in minority cultures where appropriate. Psychopathology of illness and personality issues coexist in a substantial proportion of clients ('traumatic psychoses'), and the relative importance may vary (Wright, Turkington, Kingdon, & Ramirez Basco, 2009). There are some authors who question the validity of personality disorder in ethnic minority clients as cultural factors are not adequately addressed in conceptualizing and diagnosing personality disorders (Ryder, Dere, Sun, & Chentsova-Dutton, 2014). Therapists should be open during the assessment phase to focus on the particular problem or diagnosis that is most distressing or causing the most functional impairment to the client and then slowly build on the formulation.

Although CBT is proven to be effective in reducing symptoms of depression and preventing relapse, its treatment of complex clients with personality problems frequently shows reduced response rates. Borderline personality disorder is a construct that encompasses three factors representing the different features of this disorder. The three factors are disturbed relatedness, affective instability, and behavioural dyscontrol, and they underlie the different diagnostic criteria (Calvo et al., 2012).

Case example

Pamela, a 38-year-old single mother of two children aged 8 and 11 years old, divorced following a volatile relationship involving emotional abuse. She had been working as a public employee. She had a younger brother aged 33 years but had not maintained contact with him since her dad's funeral 3 years ago. She lived in a three-bedroom house, and mortgage was being paid for by her ex-partner.

Pamela, a bicultural female born to Hispanic father and Caucasian mother, was referred to the cognitive therapy service following her enrolment in assertive community treatment team. She presented with a long history of periods of depressed mood, hypochondriacal delusions, self-referential delusions, and auditory hallucinations of her mother's voice putting her down. She also described periods of emotional dysregulation without clear-cut manic and depressive periods with strong negative thoughts about herself, deliberate self-harm behaviour of cutting wrists with razors, and two prior overdose attempts. At the time of her presentation, she was struggling to meet her work commitments alongside her responsibilities as a mother to her two kids. Her beliefs about medication swung as a pendulum from *I cannot survive without them to they do not do me any good*, and she would often stop her medication.

Case Discussion

This particular case has an added layer of complexity in that Pamela belonged to a bicultural household and suffered from a combination of symptoms of a depressive disorder and a borderline personality disorder. The diagnosis used here is the DSM-5. Pamela's presentation was consistent with the earlier description of borderline personality due to her dichotomous thinking that she was inherently flawed, inadequate, and a failure. These negative thoughts affected her mood and triggered self-harm behaviours.

Affect: Pamela presented with intense feelings of anger and frustration. She described feeling lonely and unsupported. Her belief was that she 'is inherently flawed, inadequate, not lovable' and therefore hated herself. Her view of people was that they were critical and judgmental and the world a harsh place to live in.

Physical: She reported being tired and lethargic and often unable to eat. Sometimes, she binged on food. She described her sleep pattern as erratic with initial insomnia and early morning awakening. She reported difficulty with concentration, particularly trying to organize her thoughts and prioritize.

Cognitive: She had ruminations about not having friends and thoughts that other people disliked her. She did not have a strong cultural identity due to mixed cultural heritage of her parents. A strong cultural identity is associated with a positive self-image (Smith & Silva, 2011). She believed that people had been talking about her and that her neighbours were conspiring to get her evicted and make her homeless. She was convinced that she was 'dying of terminal illness.' She believed that she was worthless, unlovable, and a failure. She described thoughts in the extremes and demonstrated dichotomous thinking which resulted in intense emotional arousal and extremes of behaviour.

Behaviours: Pamela coped by avoiding painful emotions through self-harm behaviour by cutting her wrists superficially. She spent money to gratify her impulsivity. She avoided dealing with problems and coped by 'burying her head in the sand.' Consequently, she was in debt and had problems with bailiffs. She was unable to cope with work and daily stresses. She reacted in anger and had outbursts at work. She sought relationships with emotionally cold or unavailable men. Sometimes at work, she flirted with men and then felt embarrassed when her gestures were not reciprocated.

Cultural issues for consideration

A number of cultural issues need consideration. These include Pamela's philosophical orientation and practical considerations. How does Pamela's bicultural identify influence her symptoms, presentation, and family members' response to her illness and behaviours? Are there cultural differences in how her psychopathology is conceptualized and addressed? How does one separate the symptoms of depression and personality disorder from the moderating influence of culture? According to Tseng's model of cultural adaptation, even though the concept of personality development is universal, the pace of development and the major themes emphasized at each stage are subject to cultural influences (e.g. the stage for autonomy is much delayed, and the theme of independence is less emphasized in many collectivist cultures).

Diagnosis

Pamela met the diagnostic criteria for affective disorder (depression) as diagnosed by her psychiatrist. She met the DSM criteria for borderline personality disorder (American Psychiatric Association, 2013).

Goals for therapy

Pamela and the therapist worked collaboratively to develop goals for her therapy. It was important for the therapist to recognize Pamela's sensitivity about her cultural identity and need for validation and work within those constrains to develop specific measurable goals.

Pamela's goals
1. To be able to cope with workload and reduce stress levels to 25–30%
   - I will have regular supervision with line manager.
   - I will attend necessary team and management meetings.
   - I will not procrastinate or back-stab colleagues.
   - I will not use others to pass messages to management.
   - I will take my lunch breaks as per policy.
2. To be a better person to be around (interpersonal relationships)
   - I will be interacting better with people.
   - I will establish and maintain relationships.
   - I will not seek unavailable men.
   - I will be assertive with my children.
3. To improve mood and reduce negative thoughts
   - I will engage in meaningful social and leisure activities such as taking children climbing and going to church.
   - I will be able to challenge negative thoughts and beliefs about myself.
   - I will be more compassionate towards self and less critical.
4. To address self-defeating behaviours
   - I will be able to tolerate distress and use alternative ways of coping.
   - I will be able to prioritize and manage my finances.
   - I will be able to cope better and not self-harm.

Therapist goals
- To develop a therapeutic rapport based on trust and collaboration
- To improve her self-awareness about her cultural identity and develop strengths-based approach of hope and resilience

- To support Pamela to identify schema modes and enable her to nurture and develop healthy adult mode in order to weaken maladaptive schemas
- To validate her feelings and emotions
- To help her be more self-reliant through positive behaviour change

Initial Assessment

Personal history

Pamela described memories of a difficult childhood due to an emotionally abusive mother and a dad who was very distant. In addition, she was constantly in the middle of cultural conflicts between her parents. The family did not have support of grandparents due to her parents not being from the same culture. At school, she was very ambivalent about being a part of Hispanic or Caucasian ethnic click. Consequently, she did not have friends and was bullied at school. She described herself as *I'm mental, I am the black sheep of the family*. She reported memories of being told off, blamed, and punished by her parents who would jump on anything negative in her grades and conveniently ignored her accomplishments. At 17–19 years, she started abusing cannabis and LSD. Her father was intolerant of the drug use behaviour and asked her to leave the family home while at college, while the mother had more permissive opinion of drug use. Her mother suffered from anxiety and depression. Following the loss of her father 3 years ago, Pamela stopped contact with her mother and sibling brother.

Discussion

Pamela's world view was influenced by the bicultural nature of her family. Social support including support from extended family members acts as a buffer against emotional distress and mental illness in cultural minority clients. However, the bicultural nature of her parents robbed Pamela of the support that many minority cultural children get from extended family members. Clients from bicultural families can have difficulty developing cultural identity as the above example of Pamela illustrates.

Past psychiatric history

She suffered postnatal depression after her first child. She also reported a past history of eating disorder, namely, bulimia. A year later, she was seen by a clinical psychologist. She thought that the episode was triggered by feelings that her partner was unsupportive, and she became preoccupied with her physical health fearing that she might contract hepatitis C or cancer.

Current relationships

Pamela was a lone parent with two children. She was separated from her ex-partner and father of her children about 4 years ago due to emotional abuse. Since the separation, he has disengaged from the children, adding to her responsibilities as a parent and her frustrations. She was socially isolated and found it difficult to establish and maintain relationships. Her parents being from two different cultures led to the extended family being disengaged from her, and hence, Pamela had limited interaction or support from other family members.

Discussion

Normally, extended family members provide both logistical and emotional support and can help in raising grandchildren. Unfortunately, for Pamela, the extended family was disengaged, and she was left to fend for her children herself.

Education and employment history

Despite feeling a 'misfit' at school, she managed to leave graduate school with good grades and progressed to a high national diploma and a university degree. She had been employed as a public servant for over 2 years. She had recently increased her working hours to full time, motivated by the debts she had acquired along the way. She had been avoiding dealing with debts and had not opened or responded to any letters. At the time of the assessment, she was anxious of bailiffs. Although she enjoyed her work, she reported finding it difficult to cope and maintain workload.

Risk history

She took two overdoses when she was a teenager. She had also been cutting her arms since she was 17 years old, superficially with a razor. She denied any suicidal intent/plans. Low mood was associated with feelings of guilt, worthlessness, and low self-esteem. When distressed, Pamela tended to experience strong urges to self-harm. According to Pamela, the function of self-harm was to stop emotional pain. Pamela identified her children as a protective factor against suicidal urges.

Initial Formulation with Technical Adjustments

The 5-part model (Padesky & Mooney, 1990) was used at session one to socialize Pamela to the cognitive model. This can be used with clients of diverse cultures. Pamela accepted the cognitive model at an intellectual level without much difficulty and was willing to engage with the therapist. She showed the motivation and

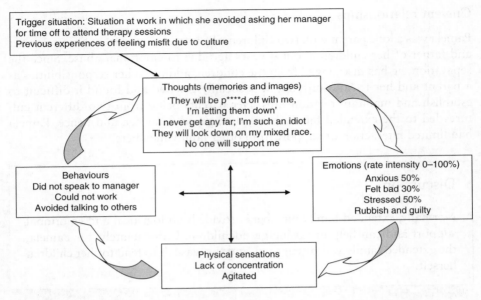

Trigger situation: Situation at work in which she avoided asking her manager for time off to attend therapy sessions
Previous experiences of feeling misfit due to culture

Thoughts (memories and images)
'They will be p****d off with me,
I'm letting them down'
I never get any far; I'm such an idiot
They will look down on my mixed race.
No one will support me

Emotions (rate intensity 0–100%)
Anxious 50%
Felt bad 30%
Stressed 50%
Rubbish and guilty

Behaviours
Did not speak to manager
Could not work
Avoided talking to others

Physical sensations
Lack of concentration
Agitated

Figure 7.1 5-part model for Pamela. Copyright 1986, Center for Cognitive Therapy, www.padesky.com.

a degree of self-reflection to engage in therapy. Standard cognitive behavioural techniques are emphasized (Beck & Freeman, 1990) in the initial management of symptoms (Figure 7.1).

Schema Therapy Case Conceptualization

This is a broader formulation developed following initial assessment (Young, Klosko, & Weishaar, 2003):

Relevant schemas

1. Emotional deprivation
2. Abandonment
3. Mistrust/abuse
4. Social isolation
5. Defectiveness/shame
6. Social undesirability
7. Failure
8. Vulnerability

Current problems (as identified by her)

Problem 1: Work-related stresses and inability to cope with demands and work commitments
   Schema links: failure, social undesirability, and defectiveness/shame

Problem 2: Relationship problems: seeks unavailable relationships and can be flirtatious and uninhibited
Schema links: emotional deprivation, mistrust/abuse, abandonment, social isolation, and vulnerability
Problem 3: Self-harm by cutting wrists superficially with a razor and somatic
Schema links: emotional deprivation, mistrust/abuse, and defectiveness/shame

Schema triggers (M = male and F = female)

- Ongoing problems with ex-partner M (as continues to have sporadic access to children)
- Work-related stresses, when she feels she is being excluded or asked to do more work (M/F)
- Difficulties in managing children
- Debts and bailiff notices. Feeling tired, alone, and depressed

Severity of schemas, coping responses, and modes: risk of decompensating

Schemas and coping responses are similarly strong. Pamela described strong urges to self-harm by cutting superficially.

Possible temperament factors

Pamela described that she can be volatile and moody. When irritable, she can feel very angry, and this usually results in outbursts.

Developmental origins

- Mother was abusive and dad was emotionally distant
- Father was critical and judgmental
- Cultural identity issues due to her mixed racial background
- Mixed parental message with mother who emphasized autonomy while father did not
- Mother suffered with anxiety
- Young brother favoured
- Estrangement from extended family and lack of the protective social support

Core cognitive distortions

- Dichotomous thinking style
- Personalization
- Emotional reasoning

Surrender behaviours (freeze)

- Buries head in the sand

Avoidance behaviours (flight)

- Comfort eating (addictive self-soothing)
- Pamela seeks excitement or distraction through flirting, shopping, and spending money
- Deliberate self-harm to numb emotional pain and past memories
- Social withdrawal. Exaggerated focus on independence and self-reliance rather than involvement with others

Overcompensating behaviours (fights)

- Passive/aggressive
- Buys kids unnecessary things to make up for time spent at work

Therapeutic relationship

Pamela started off therapy expecting to be rejected, put down, and discriminated due to her cultural background and mental illness. However, a positive relationship was built by making adjustments for her emotional sensitivity and validation of her experiences. In addition, the therapist brought up the topic of cultural differences between them and how that could interfere with therapy. Pamela was hesitant to talk about cultural and racial issues and tested out the therapist by sharing some of the problems she had in fitting with any ethnic group in school. The therapist validated her thoughts and beliefs and also helped her to better understand the contribution of her mixed racial heritage to the overall level of stress and her psychopathology. She was then able to make connections in cognitions, affect, and behaviours from an intellectual level without expressing emotions. Pamela understood and bought into the ultimate goal of therapy to become self-reliant and 'become her own therapist.'

Discussion:

Developing a therapeutic relationship is extremely important but challenging for someone with the degree of complexity of problems that Pamela presented. The therapist had to create an environment where she felt safe enough and her thoughts and feelings were validated. By helping Pamela understand the role of her mixed racial heritage on symptoms, the therapist helped her to distance from the feelings and start working on reframing her beliefs.

Treatment plan

Twenty-four sessions with review of therapy at 12 sessions were negotiated. It was discussed that long-established dysfunctional patterns of her behaviours do require time to change.

Assessment and education phase

- Socialization to the cognitive model
- Education about the schema model. Can use *Reinventing Your Life* book (Young & Klosko, 1994)
- Identification of dysfunctional life patterns and early maladaptive schemas
- Exploration of the childhood origins of the schemas and link to presenting problems
- Identification of coping style modes
- Identification and education about cultural moderators
- Usage of experiential work/imagery and dialogues for assessment

Change phase

- Interpersonal strategies to modify schemas
- Strengthening healthy adult mode
- Here-and-now grounding techniques
- Building a rational and logical case against the schema by testing the validity of a schema, reframing the evidence supporting a schema, and evaluating the pros and cons of coping schemas
- Conducting a dialogue between the schema side and the healthy side
- Constructing schema flash cards
- Filling out schema diary forms
- Behaviour pattern modification
- Relapse prevention work

Anticipated barriers in therapy

Pamela scored high on mistrust/abuse schema, and it was anticipated that the therapist would have to overcome the mistrust and build a positive relationship. Padesky (2005) emphasizes that the therapist accept distrust and address this by discussing and identifying signposts of trustworthiness and engaging patient to look at these. The therapist used this approach to build a trusting relationship.

Technical Adjustments to CBT Techniques Used

Thought records

Use of thought records (Beck, 2011) helped Pamela identify her cognitive biases, affect, and subsequent behavioural responses. She would eagerly identify rational responses but not transfer to emotional level. She explored what was stopping her from putting this to practice and explored pros and cons to help her make informed decisions. The therapist explored this in the context of cultural influences and used her philosophical orientation to explain her behaviour.

Schema education

She was given relevant chapters from *Reinventing Your Life* (Young & Klosko, 1994) book to read about life traps relevant to her problems and cultural influences. Feedback from Pamela showed that she made sense of the life traps and could relate to some of the characters described (Young et al., 2003). This was helpful in normalizing her problems that she was not alone.

Schema diary sheets

Other interventions to bring about some change in Pamela's beliefs were employed. Pamela discovered that reading homework material such as schema diary sheets was much less threatening than discussion in therapy. Schema diary sheets (Young et al., 2003) were used. Pamela found these very useful in identifying the triggers, affect, and behaviours and the life traps activated. She was also able to identify the cultural influences and early life experiences the life traps were related to for a completed schema diary (Table 7.2).

She was encouraged to complete schema diary sheets so that she could work out a general rule for such situations and use a schema flashcard (Morrison, 2000; Young et al., 2003). Through learning to question and test out how she interpreted information, Pamela was learning how to re-evaluate her beliefs and experiences in ways that were enabling her to develop a new relationship with herself and the world around her (Padesky, 2005).

As therapy progressed, Pamela was able to identify and relate to schema activation in several situations. Imagery was used to trigger emotions connected to early maladaptive schemas (Young et al., 2003). She identified how her behaviours and

Table 7.2   Schema therapy flashcard for Pamela.

Right now, I feel upset, angry, and frustrated because someone I like does not reciprocate my feelings
However, I know that this is probably my *Abandonment/Emotional* schemas, which I learned through my relationship with my parents. My parents never connected with me emotionally, and now, mom freely admits that she never bonded with me. Also, due to my parents being from two different cultures, both sides of the family did not want to know us
These schemas lead me to exaggerate the degree to which I react to the slightest possibility that someone may like me; this invaluably leads to disappointment, because the hope is based on fantasy
Even though I believe that no one is ever going to love or care for me, the reality is that my children love me. Therefore, the reason that I am on my own isn't because I am hideous or crap; it's the situation
The evidence in my life supporting the healthy view includes my children telling me they love me
Therefore, even though I feel I want to punish myself because it's what I think I deserve for not being good enough, I could instead self-care and nurture myself. Hold my guinea pig, have a bath, and read a book. I am OK – no matter what my parents think of me

patterns were self-fulfilling prophecies, especially in choosing unavailable or committed men in relationships. Once Pamela felt understood and validated, she moved on to reality testing of schema-driven distortions. Schemas were activated in therapy which the therapist dealt with in a supportive manner.

Behavioural experiments

Behavioural experiments to test out assumptions and help Pamela change her cognitive biases were employed at various levels. This included surveys asking colleagues and close friends and observational experiments. This was helpful in weakening the early maladaptive schemas and gradually strengthening the healthy adult mode.

Continuum method

Pamela's failure schema was approached using (Padesky, 1994) continuum method to weaken dichotomous thinking. Pamela initially believed she was '100%' a failure. She was encouraged to keep a core belief data log to enter evidence supporting her new belief and to reframe counteractive evidence.

Experiential work/imagery

When it came to talking about the cultural conflicts relating to her mother and father, Pamela would dissociate. This was a significant source of distress for her. When this behaviour was highlighted, she acknowledged that she found it hard to deal with emotions relating to her cultural identity. The therapist addressed this by validating the difficulty in developing a strong cultural identity in a household where parental expectations were very divergent, not having positive cultural role models and lacking the support of extended family. Pamela was gradually able to talk about her cultural identity issues without dissociation, and therapist's interventions were to promote healing and restructuring of her belief systems related to cultural identity. Through discussions about culture, Pamela was able to recognize that she was more acculturated than her father and became more comfortable in her cultural identity.

Case discussion

The case of Pamela is fairly lengthy due to the complexity of her problems involving the personality disorder, cultural issues, and limited family support system relating to the conflict of cultures. The discussion focused primarily on the dysfunctions attributed to borderline personality disorder. However, the reader should know that Pamela developed positive coping skills that helped her to address a number of issues. She was able to utilize many of these skills in dealing with her psychotic symptoms and in this fashion was able to demonstrate true self-reliance. This was possible after disentangling her assumptions and thoughts linked to her cultural identity.

> **Exercise:** The example of Pamela shows a variety of cognitive therapy techniques and how they were utilized. Go over the list of techniques used and identify a minority culture client where you have utilized the technique. If you have not used these techniques in a minority culture client so far, you can think of your case load of minority clients and see where these techniques can be used.

Individualized Treatment Planning in an Individual with Advanced Levels of Acculturation

In the first scenario, we discussed how treatment planning and adaptations to delivery based on formulation have to be individualized and can vary despite similar cultures. Below, we discuss another scenario through the example of Lincoln who through his level of acculturation and assimilation was able to identify with the majority culture. However, when therapy started, it transpired that there were elements of his distress through low self-esteem that were linked to his experiences through being of minority culture.

Case example

Lincoln is a second-generation African Caribbean born in the United Kingdom from parents originally from Jamaica. Due to relationship problems, his father moved to the United States, while his mother moved to England to join her own mother. Lincoln described his cultural identity as being 'black and of Caribbean origin', and he also held his British identity. He'd always wanted to visit Jamaica and was enchanted by it, but when he actually visited the place, he did not feel at home. He was pleased to note that people there could identify him as someone from England. Back in the United Kingdom, he grew up in a mixed neighbourhood with many people of colour. His close relationships had mostly been with black people, but not exclusively. His best friend was Portuguese. He was sensitive to and aware of discrimination, and this angered him, but was not a theme in his own narrative of his life. Although he was rewarded for best all-round pupil in his mixed elementary school, he later dropped out of secondary school and attributed this to personal distresses not related to minority status or discrimination. He succeeded in returning to school and eventually obtained a university degree. His aspirations and family, education, and comfortable material lifestyle had been mainstream and also very Caribbean. For a while, he attended the centre for black men with mental health problems based in his local community.

Lincoln was diagnosed with a schizoaffective disorder. He had suffered numerous episodes of psychosis in the past. They would begin with a few bright and glorious hours of confidence, energy, and belief in himself, his mission, his special powers, his plans, and his voices leading him on followed by an immediate great 'black crash' and overwhelming feelings with ruminations on themes of worthlessness and guilt, with a conviction others were looking at him as he was black, talking about him, seeing how contemptible and inferior he was, and reading his useless thoughts. After the first episode, he struggled to make sense of what had happened. He thought the annunciation of power and religious mission might be true. In time, he concluded this was not the case, and they represented disorder and breakdown. Usually, Lincoln's symptoms stabilized fairly quickly with medication, but he continued to experience symptoms of residual anxiety. Feelings of derealization, self-rejection, lack of confidence, anxiety about being judged by others due to his colour, hypersensitivity to and great over perception of criticism, and rejection which he had experienced since late childhood had grown more intense. He often found himself looking at the mirror saying *I hate you, I hate you* aloud. He felt despair that he will *never lead a normal life*. Consequently, he had been isolating himself to avoid experiencing terrible social evaluative anxiety. This was sometimes accompanied by experiences of thought broadcasting. Lincoln's goal in therapy was to stop self-loathing. The therapist and Lincoln were able to relate many of his negative thoughts about himself to his relationship with his family and to things they had said to and about him. The therapist and Lincoln set goals to work on self-attacking thoughts, increasing activity and social contacts. As sessions progressed, Lincoln identified that he felt offended by the bias in the media that had left an impression that *black people are more violent than other cultures* (Sears, 2008). This impacted on his confidence and perceptions of others.

As part of the pre-engagement and engagement phase, the process of alliance building, formulation, treatment, and review seemed to proceed with ease as would with a predominantly white patient. Possible explanations about this included Lincoln's level of acculturation and adjustment. The therapist was also an immigrant in the United Kingdom: being from New York and having lived in England for the past 10 years, the therapist was able to draw from own experiences of American culture and was used to working with people from diverse cultures. The therapist could relate to overexposure of ethnic groups in the cosmopolitan city and use of heuristic subtypes to get by.

The therapist shared a provisional formulation with Lincoln focusing on making sense of his low self-esteem using the general self-esteem model. This information was drawn from the assessment sessions. Lincoln was well acculturated to his British Caribbean background. Language was not an issue for him as he spoke English fluently.

General self-esteem model

Childhood experiences

- Mother blamed him for her problems although he was only a child.
- Physically and emotionally unsafe: an absence of positive experiences children need for development; he did not get affection, respect, emotional validation, encouragement, and love.
- Father never wanted to know him; no father figure.
- Belonged to a group that is subject of racial prejudice and negative stereotypes (i.e. black British).

Core beliefs

- I'm useless, worthless, bad, inferior, not good enough, and unlovable.

Rules for living

- If I accomplish a lot and make myself acceptable to everyone, maybe I can be okay; otherwise, people will see I am useless.
- I must always get it right (that way maybe my mother and others would love and respect me).
- People will hurt or reject me if they see the real me that is different to them.
- I shouldn't expect other people to like me or treat me well; that way I won't be disappointed.
- Nothing I do is worthwhile unless it's recognized by others.

Feelings

Self-hatred, rage against self, shame about self-helplessness, and hopelessness

Thoughts and perceptions: prejudice against yourself (compare to racial prejudice)

- Don't notice all the good things about you and very conscious of weaknesses.
- Good things about you and what you do are unimportant, down to luck, and exceptions.
- Failures, mistakes, difficulties, and rejections aren't just part of life; they are proof you are useless, inferior, and bad.

Unhelpful behaviours

- Avoidance of situations where you might have social contacts or be looked at by strangers.
- Overwork and preparation for tasks – or – avoiding situations where he would feel he needed to perform and could fail.

- Self-attacking thoughts.
- Berating self for mistakes instead of giving self-constructive criticism.
- Slow to become angry with others and putting up with a lot. When he finally gets angry, wrongs have built up, and letting go of anger is difficult.
- (He also had helpful behaviours! Setting goals, working hard despite obstacles, persistence, getting help when he needs it.)

The following diagram shows a typical maintenance cycle of Lincoln's low self-esteem (Figure 7.2).

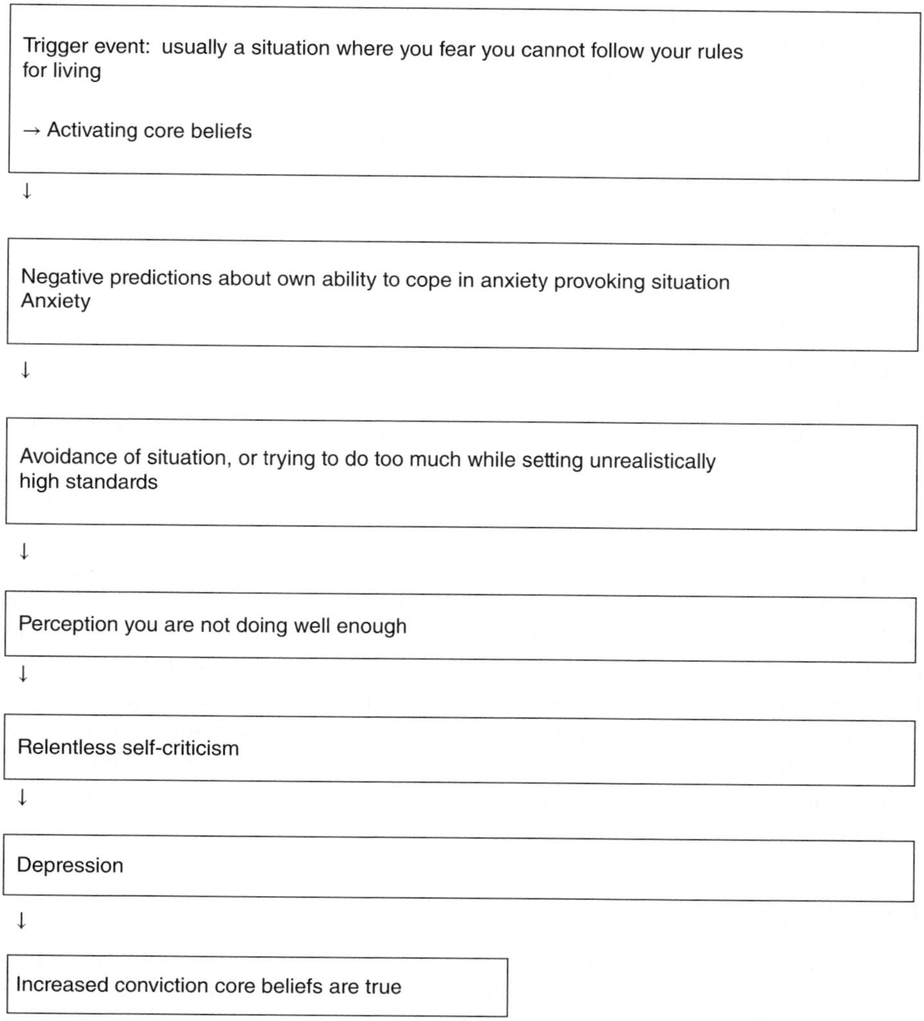

Trigger event: usually a situation where you fear you cannot follow your rules for living

→ Activating core beliefs

↓

Negative predictions about own ability to cope in anxiety provoking situation
Anxiety

↓

Avoidance of situation, or trying to do too much while setting unrealistically high standards

↓

Perception you are not doing well enough

↓

Relentless self-criticism

↓

Depression

↓

Increased conviction core beliefs are true

Figure 7.2   Maintaining cycles of low self-esteem.

Below is an example the therapist and Lincoln collaboratively worked out about how the low self-esteem maintaining cycle may have contributed to his first episode:

Rule: 'I must accomplish and excel or people will see I am useless.'

Trigger: 'Far from home; feeling isolated; only black person at work; (emphasis here) felt rejected, used and humiliated by girlfriend; time and demand pressures at work consequently; finding self struggling to maintain high standards of performance; fear I will violate the rule by not being up to snuff.'

Core belief activated: 'I am useless; no one will accept me.'

Self-critical thoughts begin

Rule reactivated: 'I must accomplish and excel so people do not see I am useless and black people are accepted.'

Emotional response: 'Increased anxiety. Prediction, I will fail.'

Action: 'work harder and longer, take work home weekends.'

Increased anxiety; self-critical thoughts; overwork → insomnia, exhaustion, harder to work.

Self-critical thoughts increased → low mood feelings of hopelessness.

Rule: 'I must accomplish and excel' → fantasy of great success which offers relief from depression and feeling of escape

Mood suddenly shoots up; supreme confidence; great plans; and soar out of touch with reality

---

Below is the formulation and then agreed treatment plan that was devised based on the assessment information and shared formulation. Although Lincoln had a diagnosis of schizoaffective disorder treatment focused on the intense chronic self-critical ruminations and self-isolation as these problems seemed to have the most impact on his present quality of life. Setting therapy goals should be done collaboratively and drawn from the problem list following an assessment. CBT principles apply here that the goals must be specific, measurable, and achievable within a set time. In most cases, patients tend to set general goals; here, the therapist can help fine-tune general goals for more specific goals.

Formulation: Making sense

The longitudinal formulation detailing the 4 Ps – namely, predisposing factors, precipitating factors, perpetuating factors, and protective factors (Kingdon & Turkington, 2005) – was utilized to help Lincoln make sense and gain understanding of his presenting problems and what helps and maintains them.

Predisposing factors (issues that make a person more sensitive to stress and more vulnerable to developing mental health problems)	Precipitating factors (events that happened just before a problem began or got worse)	Perpetuating factors (circumstances, beliefs, behaviours that recovery harder or relapse more likely)	Protective factors (strengths and resources which can aid recovery)
Critical angry rejecting mother who remained upset all the time since moving to country due to impact of immigration	Puberty-precipitated self-consciousness and intrusive negative thoughts about self	Contacts with mother (important)	Loved and appreciated by grandmother
Unsafe as a child: alcoholic stepfather abused mother, mother kicked out of house	Manic episodes preceded by periods of low mood and stress. Precipitants of 'highs' and lows include:	Very high demands and expectations of self (important)	Intelligent, thoughtful, reflective
Ethnic background, experiences of being different standing out, negative stereotyping, having to prove something	Sleeplessness	Noise, undesirable activities in a lot adjacent to apartment	Persistent – stuck with goal of finishing university despite lack of confidence, no emotional support from mother, and external obstacles
Sensitive moody person by nature	15–31 years – cannabis a few times a week for many years. Once skunk	Withdrawal and isolation	Willing to try new things
First episode not precipitated by drug use or period of heavy using generally. (One brief psychotic reaction to skunk after first break after which never smoked again)	Stress at work: performance demands Shift work Social isolation – away from friends or family, *only black person*	Not enough to do Finances limited	Good at seeking and using help intelligently when needed

Current concerns: Things that are bothering me on my daily activities

Relationship with mother (but realizes he can only work on changing himself in therapy, not changing her)

Low self-esteem, hate myself, intrusive self-critical thoughts all the time***

No confidence, not assertive

Very anxious when outside with people, especially crowds and at social events; therefore stays at home; it will be bad if I'm noticed by others

Difficulty in sleeping and anxious

Frequent long-lasting low moods; sudden mood arousal, where everything seems different, which are usually short-lived (few hours to a few days); usually pleasant, bring relief from low mood but believe odd things, convinced special powers and importance, out of control. Occasionally unpleasant, not sure what is real or unreal, frightened and disorient

The next column describes thoughts, feelings, and actions that go with current concerns

Thoughts	Feelings	Actions
Everything my mother said about me is true (I'm ugly, I'm useless, I'm gay)	Ashamed, embarrassed	Only go out to public places when not likely to be crowded
I don't like what I see in the mirror	Fearful	Stay at home most of the time
I should have more confidence	Unsure of yourself	Say bad things to self out loud: for example, 'I hate you, I hate you, I hate you'
It's too late for me to accomplish anything in life or marry and have a family	Lonely	Sought help when realize have gotten very low or high
People who make eye contact with me may hurt me in some way	Angry (at self)	Use medication, think about psychology sessions, do homework
People can read my thoughts	Angry at others and then guilty	Keep up with some family members
That person talking to her/his friend or looking in my direct is talking about and saying negative things about me	Suspicious	Worked at MIND, checked out gym membership, went to men's group and other day services
If I don't speak well, people will think 'what's wrong with him…he's an idiot'	Sometimes sad and hopeless	

(Continued)

Thoughts	Feelings	Actions
I will not be able to handle social contacts without falling apart (unless I have a drink)	High episodes – 25, few hours or days: usually feel happy, powerful, important, supremely confident – a few times feel unsure what is real, frightened, disoriented	
I was out of order when I expressed anger at/to my mother, father, girlfriends	Afterwards concern, alarm	

Relevant social circumstances	Relevant physical issues
Close to one brother, some contact family	Insomnia
Casual contact with friends	Difficulty in concentrating
Long-term relationship ended 2008 amicably: gone out little since	When outside physical anxiety, sweating
Attended day service programme no longer offered and had job at MIND, which has finished	Feel out of shape and heavy

Underlying concerns: Issues, beliefs, and behaviours that may be behind some of current concerns

Will I be able to marry and have a family?

Keeping work

Stigma

I can never be happy until my mother loves me

Something is fundamentally wrong with me; I am not worthy

If I were different, if I accomplished more, my mother would love me (I'm doing this for my mother)

I can't trust women

Goals and values

Values: relationships and feeling connected with others, making something of myself, bettering myself, making a difference

Activities: enjoying music, working out, cycling, eating, and surfing

Short term: losing three stone, becoming more confident and assertive

Long term: marriage, family

Treatment summary

Problem 1: Self-critical

Constant self-criticism – 'treat self as an enemy on the alert (hypervigilant) for everything wrong with you constantly think about bad past events and catastrophic thoughts about the future.'

Origins: mother's constant criticism of you and her anger towards you and others—mother upset a lot of the time since immigration.
Discrimination as a child.

Function of self-criticism (what it does for you)

- Escape feelings of fear and sadness about being without love and protection by imagining your mother (children turn to their mothers for help even when their mothers aren't very nice).
- Protect self from mother by criticizing self first.

But: feeling awful about self, anxious and despairing about the future, unhappy, and stuck.

Treatment goals: Learn to be compassionate and loving towards yourself.

Steps to goals

- Use thought diaries to develop compassion-focused alternatives to self-critical thoughts.
- Practise positive affirmations
- Have successful people from same cultural background.
- Practise creating and strengthening compassionate images (safe place in Hyde Park, grandmother as guardian spirit, memories of Paolo, of good encounters with people).
- Cook for yourself (self-nurture).
- Practise relaxation and mindfulness to keep your focus in the present.
- Increase pleasurable activities and absorbing activities.

Problem 2: Retreating from others

Stay in, self-isolate, and don't do much – avoid life because other people share it.

Origins: mother's criticism of you → internal shame, worry about how you look to others, and external shame.

Worry → physical symptoms of anxiety → concern how symptoms anxiety make you look to others; your appraisal of fear symptoms is that you are 'going mad'; sometimes, he feels that others are reading his thoughts – shame and panic.

Function of retreating from others and avoiding social situations (what it does for you)

- Avoid perception people are looking at you, judging you, or reading your thoughts.
- Avoid situations that make me realize I am black.
- Avoid associated anxiety and vicious circle of anxiety (anxiety leads to fear of relapse; fear of being rejected by others because of anxiety symptoms results in heightened anxiety).

But: you are lonely and bored.

- Being home alone all day increases self-critical thoughts, feeling the world is unreal, and belief your life is empty and will not get better.
- Believing your life is empty is more likely to come true if you avoid other people and going out.

Treatment goals

- Get more activity into your life.
- See more people more often.
- Learn to accept bad feelings without judging yourself and return attention and focus to what's important.

Steps to goals

- Walk daily/use the library regularly.
- I will try to have a social contact in person once a week with people I am already in touch with or know well (call aunty, my brother, and old friend twice a month and one live encounter once a week).

Graded exposure plan: use local centre

- Break circle of anxiety around public places/fear of relapse: distinguish anxiety symptoms and relapse symptoms and exposure with acceptance of anxiety symptoms.

Sub-goal: part-time job

- Walk to workplace and back, rehearse visit in my mind, and phone/email contact.
- Go to workplace and learn about options.
- Attend a group.
- Enter job programme.

Sub-goal: go to gym

- Walk to gym daily.
- Exercise at home with DVD.

Table 7.3 Summary of key considerations in therapy process.

Be mindful of pitfalls in therapy including over-identification, sameness, identification
    with oppressor, and colour blindness
Avoid misinterpretation of patient behaviour – do not make cultural assumptions
Be aware that core beliefs or schemas are strongly influenced by culture
Listen carefully and consider ways in which a client's culture influences formulation
    and treatment goals
Use culture as a strength in therapy
Use techniques like validating and normalizing and be non-judgmental
Use culturally appropriate metaphors

- Imagine rehearsal of going to gym in which everything is going well.
- Imagine rehearsal of going to gym in which something is not going the way I'd
  like and coping with it.
- Go in gym (Table 7.3).

Conclusion

The engagement, assessment, and case conceptualization flow into development
of a treatment plan which is individualized to the person, their role in the family,
the cultural background they belong to, and the social–cultural circumstances.
The individualized plan guides the choice and sequence of interventions utilized
in therapy. The chapters that follow discuss in-depth individual diagnosis and
adaptations associated with them.

References

American Psychiatric Association. (2013). *Diagnostic and statistical manual of mental dis-
orders* (5th ed.). Washington, DC: Author.
Beck, A., & Freeman, A. (1990). *Cognitive therapy of personality disorders*. New York,
NY: Guilford Press.
Beck, J. (2011). *Cognitive behavior therapy: Basics and beyond* (2nd ed.). New York, NY:
Guilford Press.
Calvo, N., Andion, O., Gancedo, B., Ferrer, M., Barral, C., Di Genova, A., ... Casas, M.
(2012). Borderline Personality Disorder (BPD) diagnosis with the self-report
Personality Diagnostic Questionnaire-4 + (PDQ-4+): Confirmation of the 3-factor
structure. *Actas Españolas de Psiquiatría*, *40*(2), 57–62.
Kingdon, D., & Turkington, D. (2005). *Cognitive therapy of schizophrenia*. New York, NY:
Guilford Press.
McGilloway, A., Hall, R., Lee, T., & Bhui, K. (2010). A systematic review of personality
disorder, race and ethnicity: Prevalence, aetiology and treatment. *BMC Psychiatry*, *10*,
33. doi:10.1186/1471-244X-10-33

Morrison, N. (2000). Schema-focused cognitive therapy for complex long-standing problems: A single case study. *Behavioural and Cognitive Psychotherapy*, *28*, 269–283.

Padesky, C. A. (1994). Schema change processes in cognitive therapy. *Clinical Psychology and Psychotherapy*, *1*, 267–278.

Padesky, C. (2005). Constructing a new self: cognitive therapy for personality disorders. Workshop presented in London, England, 23–24 May 2005.

Padesky, C. A., & Mooney, K. A. (1990). Clinical tip: Presenting the cognitive model to clients. *International Cognitive Therapy Newsletter*, *6*, 13–14. Retrieved from http://padesky.com/clinical-corner (accessed on September 19, 2014).

Ryder, A., Dere, J., Sun, J., & Chentsova-Dutton, Y. E. (2014). The cultural shaping of personality disorder. In F. T. L. Leong, L. Comas-Díaz, G. C. Nagayama Hall, V. C. McLoyd, & J. E. Trimble (Eds.), *APA handbook of multicultural psychology, Vol. 2: Applications and training* (pp. 307–328). Washington, DC: American Psychological Association.

Sears, D. (2008). The American color line 50 years after Brown v. Board: Many 'peoples of color' or Black exceptionalism? In G. Adams, M. Biernat, N. R. Branscombe, C. S. Crandall, & L. S. Wrightsman (Eds.), *Commemorating Brown: The social psychology of racism and discrimination* (pp. 133–152). Washington, DC: American Psychological Association.

Smith, T. B., & Silva, L. (2011). Ethnic identity and personal well-being of people of color: A meta-analysis. *Journal of Counseling Psychology*, *58*(1), 42–60.

Tseng, W. S. (2001). *Handbook of cultural psychiatry*. San Diego, CA: Academic Press.

Wright, J., Turkington, D., Kingdon, D., & Ramirez Basco, M. (2009). *Cognitive behavior Therapy for severe mental illness: An illustrated guide*. Washington, DC: American Psychiatric Publishing Inc.

Young, J. E., & Klosko, J. (1994). *Reinventing your life*. New York, NY: Plume.

Young, J. E., Klosko, J. S., & Weishaar, M. E. (2003). *Schema therapy: A practitioner's guide*. London, UK: Guilford Press.

8

Psychosis: Cultural Aspects of Presentation and Adaptations to Treatment

Culture significantly impacts on all aspects of psychosis from its commencement, psychopathological manifestations, course, treatment approaches, and outcomes. This chapter will cover culture and its relationship to the incidence, prevalence, aetiology, and course of psychosis with a discussion of practical considerations including societal and service issues and the emphasis on promoting recovery. Technical adjustments and theoretical modifications used in the adaptation of cognitive behavioural therapy (CBT) will be described and illustrated.

Epidemiology of Psychosis and Culture

The incidence and prevalence of schizophrenia were at one time thought to be the same across a variety of different cultures. This is now known to be unlikely the case (Murray, Jones, Susser, van Os, & Cannon, 2003). Certain societies seem to have significantly lower levels of people suffering from schizophrenia while others have a higher incidence.

The prevalence of non-affective psychosis (bipolar disorder and schizophrenia) has been estimated at 1 to every 250 at any one time in the United Kingdom (HSCIC, 2009). But this prevalence varies across the world (Jackson et al., 2007; Selten, Slaets, & Kahn, 1997) and within countries (Kirkbride et al., 2006). In an attempt to investigate the variability in the incidence of psychotic disorders, AESOP study (Kirkbride et al., 2006) conducted in three quite different centres in England concluded that migrants were more vulnerable to developing psychosis and highlighted that risk factors such as living in urban areas (van Os, 2004)

Cultural Adaptation of CBT for Serious Mental Illness: A Guide for Training and Practice,
First Edition. Shanaya Rathod, David Kingdon, Narsimha Pinninti, Douglas Turkington, and Peter Phiri.
© 2015 John Wiley & Sons, Ltd. Published 2015 by John Wiley & Sons, Ltd.

which included social deprivation among other unknown contributants contributed significantly to the remarkably high incidence rate of psychotic disorders. General socio-economic factors impact on such problems as poverty and discrimination; hence, a combination of these stressors with the impact of migration can result in high levels of distress, making individuals vulnerable and susceptible to mental illness. Concurrently, stigma associated with mental illness and racism can result in isolation, unemployment, and subsequent dependence on statutory benefits with its own associated stigma. Ethnic minority groups therefore have a higher risk of psychoses in comparison to the predominantly white group: specifically, the African Caribbean and black African groups had a significantly higher risk of both schizophrenia and manic psychosis (Fearon et al., 2006). We have discussed stresses surrounding migration and described in Chapter 3 how there is a then further negative effect on access to services and psychological treatment.

Risk in other groups is variable with no increase apparent in Asian populations, but there remain issues about treatment (discussed previously and later), specifically in relationship to psychosis.

Culture and the Aetiology of Psychosis

Crucial factors in the aetiology of schizophrenia include genetic predisposition (multiple small genes appear to be acting together), quality of obstetric care, trauma, life events, and degree of attachment, substance use, maternal viral infection, and urban upbringing. A genetic predisposition to develop schizophrenia may be present in as many as 7–10% of the population. There is now no significant known difference in the genetic predisposition for schizophrenia across cultures because there are so many genes involved, each contributing a small and cumulative contribution to vulnerability. However, the genetics of voice hearing raises some interesting cultural issues as the vulnerability for voice hearing specifically is said to be genetically more robust (Sanjuan, Molto, & Tolosa, 2013) although there is also a clear link with environmental factors, especially trauma (see in the following). Complications before and around the time of birth appear to double the risk. There is obviously massive variation in the quality of antenatal and perinatal care across cultures and countries. Improvement in this area is reported as contributing approximately 5% to the perceived reduced incidence of schizophrenia in the United Kingdom/United States in the last 50 years. However, the contribution is assessed to be only in the order of 20% of a risk reduction even if all obstetric and antenatal care was perfect (Warner, 2000). Unfortunately, obstetric and antenatal care in many areas of the world remains far from optimal.

Those cultures with mothering styles which breed suboptimal attachment styles might be expected to produce increased levels of psychosis – which might conversely suggest that cultures which have more robust and enduring family networks would tend to be protective. Adequate levels of maternity and paternity leave might be pertinent in relation to achieving sound attachments. In cultures where mothers are working very long hours or where children are intentionally removed from mothers' presence to be placed in very early nursery environments, this might lead to an increase in levels of psychosis although there is no evidence demonstrating this. The one-child policy in China might have implications for attachment, and in the CBT study that we have completed in Beijing (submitted for publication), there was some suggestion only that expectations on the son or daughter could be high and consequently pressure to meet parental goals and aspirations with consequences for management of psychosis.

The effect of trauma in the genesis of psychosis is complex, and a very sensitive area as families can understandably believe that they are being blamed for causing psychosis in their offspring where general evidence on the incidence of trauma is presented. It is very important to distinguish different groups presenting with psychosis, and we have published data in relation to this (Kingdon, Selvareji, Kinoshita, & Turkington, 2008). There are many clients for whom family support has been excellent and continues to be so, but there are a small number, possibly around 20–30% (Kingdon et al., 2008), who have far more difficulties in childhood and, because of a range of circumstances, have experienced physical and emotional abuse.

Case example

Michelle had been the victim of childhood sexual and emotional abuse at the hands of a babysitter. She never disclosed this but always believed that she must have done something wrong for this to have happened to her. At the age of 23 years, she was the victim of a sexual assault outside a nightclub and shortly thereafter began to hear multiple voices commenting on her actions in a derogatory way. She reported somatic hallucinations of 'a raping sensation,' olfactory hallucinations of aftershave, and visual hallucinations of a disembodied head, which leered at her. Unfortunately, antipsychotic medication produced little benefit until she disclosed the nature of her traumas. At that point, she was given information about how common psychotic symptoms are in adult survivors of childhood abuse. She was taught coping strategies and was able to stop blaming herself. It took many sessions of CBT using schema modification work with a female therapist before Michelle's self-esteem began to improve. Cognitive restructuring was done around the issue of the abuse and attempted rape, and schema-focused therapy was focused on the 'I am to blame' core belief. A disclosure was made to the police and charges were brought once Michelle was able to face her abuser. All symptoms were improved by the CBT input, and the medication regime was rationalized and hospitalization delayed and reduced in terms of time spent in the hospital.

Emotional abuse is an important issue in terms of vulnerability to later psychosis (Arsenault et al., 2011). Physical abuse and sexual abuse are strongly over-represented in the childhoods of people who go on to develop schizophrenia. Read, van Os, Morrison, and Ross (2005) also report a dose–response effect in terms of positive symptoms, particularly hallucinations, and a tendency for the emergence of psychosis following a trauma-related trigger event. Interestingly, thought disorder and negative symptoms tended not to dominate these clinical presentations. Again, in our recent study, we found that Chinese clients with psychosis tended not to report trauma histories or, also, experience hallucinogenic drug abuse (Li et al., submitted for publication). This leads to presentations of schizophrenia dominated by delusional systems, negative symptoms, and cognitive deficits within China. However, it may be that emotional, physical, and sexual trauma is more common than that which is reported, as has been the case in the past in the United States and Europe, due to fear of 'losing face' and presents as depression and demoralization in association with psychosis.

Case example

Li, aged 24 years, the child of a lawyer and office worker, developed schizophrenia in his adolescence with cognitive deficits in attention and short-term memory. The predominant picture was of negative symptoms with poor self-care, alogia, blunting, and reduced motivation. He did have some ideas of reference that people spitting in the street were referring to him. Drive for achievement and a very strong work ethic are powerful cultural factors in Chinese society. Li, because of his symptoms, had completely given up trying to do anything as he was trying to do too much too quickly. Li started treatment and after several sessions did start to improve when working with a graded activity schedule with mastery and pleasure recording. The therapist had to work at his pace acknowledging pressures of his cultural beliefs. He came to start to experience small successes and pleasures as being worthwhile and began to slowly become more sociable and to take more care of his appearance. He then began to consider other possible reasons as to why people might be spitting in the street and his ideas of reference receded.

Views about the use of addictive and hallucinogenic drugs traditionally vary within different cultural settings. Heroin and other opiates have a low potential to produce hallucinations but can lead to dependence and sedation and therefore a strong likelihood of worsening negative symptoms. Drug misuse of hallucinogenic drugs is much less in some Eastern cultures (China, Japan, and Korea) although opiates are much more common. Drugs which can cause hallucinogenic experiences are however acknowledged as a contributory factor in African Caribbean cultures where they can be culturally sanctioned with individuals even expected to use certain drugs especially marijuana. The tendency in certain cultures to use strong 'skunk' cannabis has been linked to an increase in paranoia and an increase in negative symptoms particularly reduced self-care, reduced motivation, and a long-term effect on short-term memory. The new designer drugs such as ketamine and PCP are the most psychogenic drugs yet developed and may increase psychosis rates in Western societies where these are experimentally used, often as part of hallucinogenic drug cocktails. Similarly, LSD in Western societies can cause psychedelic states, a form of long-term psychosis with visual hallucinations, delusions, thought disorder, and reduced self-care. Initially, it was unclear whether these drugs were simply bringing forward psychotic episodes of illnesses that would have occurred in any case. While there are some people who experience a psychotic episode which remits and does not persist or return, there now seems little doubt that the use of these drugs has directly led to people developing persistent psychotic illnesses who would not have done so otherwise. There have been some differences demonstrated between the group of people with drug-related psychotic illness and other with psychosis; this includes higher levels of positive symptoms, lower levels of negative symptoms, greater socialization, and, unfortunately, increased risk of hostile/criminal behaviour towards others especially with continuing substance misuse.

Grief has been linked to hallucinations and potentially the emergence of psychosis. However, hallucination of the presence of the deceased is a component of normal grief. In terms of grieving, certain cultures seem better at this than others. The cultural response to grief is crucial in relation to this as in some cultures grieving is expected and honoured and expression of pertinent emotions of despair and anger is facilitated. In other societies, the 'stiff upper lip' is expected which often leads to failed bereavement and increases the likelihood of psychotic experiences of grief. The psychotic symptoms, which are particularly caused by failed bereavement, are auditory hallucinations and delusions of thought possession including thought broadcasting and thought insertion.

In a number of cultures like the African Caribbean, it is believed that spirits and ghosts of the deceased protect families by residing in trees near the home or as dragons in Chinese culture. This can mitigate the sense of loss and allow resolution, but it can also be manifested as a theme when psychosis emerges, and understanding of the association with grief helps in understanding the possible source of the symptom.

Case example

Gill from Texas, United States, had found it impossible to grieve following the death of her mother. She had looked after her mother during her last illness and eventually had to agree to her admission to the hospital. She arrived 5 min late for the first visiting session only to find that her mother had just died. Wracked with shame and guilt, she did not enter a normal grieving process and never moved beyond the denial phase. There were no despair and no anger. Within 1 month after the death, she started to believe that she was shouting out in public and that her thoughts were being broadcast to others. An examination of the antecedents of the psychosis revealed that the stress of looking after her ill mother, sleep deprivation, and failed bereavement were the crucial precipitants. Behavioural experiments were used to realty test the issue of thought broadcasting, and alternative explanations were generated. Gill suggested that possibly people might be reacting to her distress and poor self-care. The link was made with her mother's death and a normalizing approach used to show how often carers blame themselves for something that wasn't their fault. She then wrote a letter to her mother explaining why she was late and then gradually entered a phase of appropriate grief. Belief in thought broadcasting and 'shouting out' diminished, and she began to show signs of social recovery.

Philosophical Orientation and Theoretical Considerations

Cognitive models of psychosis

Delusions

Theories underpinning cognitive therapy assume that unhelpful or negative thinking is related to the distress experienced by people and consequently CBT was initially developed as a comprehensive theory of depression (Beck, Rush, Shaw, & Emery, 1979). However, it has since been extended to relate to the explanation of a range of other disorders (Blackburn & Twaddle, 1996) including personality disorders (Beck, Freeman, & Associates, 1990) and psychosis (Garety, Kuipers, Fowler, & Beddington, 2001; Kingdon & Turkington, 1991; Morrison, 2001; Tarrier, Harwood, & Yussof, 1990) as we have discussed in Chapter 2. There was a pause in the development of cognitive approaches to psychosis until the early 1990s when work on psychosis began to emerge. While quite pragmatic in its development, theoretical understanding has also proceeded.

The current advances in cognitive therapy for psychosis generally emphasize the importance of emotions on influencing cognitive processes (Freeman et al.,

2004). Maher's (1988) theory of delusions suggested that delusions can be explained by the application of normal reasoning processes to abnormal experiences. He argued that delusions reflect rational attempts to making sense of anomalous experiences. Simply put, he sees delusions as explanations. The premise of this model is based on two assumptions.

Firstly, anomalous 'strange' experiences drive a search for meaning. This meaning is affected and biased by pre-existing beliefs and assumptions about the self, others, and – of particular relevance to cultural adaptation – the individual's world view (Maher, 1988) or philosophical orientation. Basically, Maher argues that there are no significant differences between the inferential reasoning of normal and deluded individuals.

Secondly, delusions do not come about through biased reasoning processes. This has been questioned (Garety & Hemsley, 1994; Garety & Freeman, 1999; Coltheart Longden, & McKay, 2010). Basic cognitive disturbance has been linked to data gathering biases such as a 'jumping to conclusions' style of thinking: clients with psychosis tend to reach decisions with less evidence resulting in delusional interpretation. This factor implies bias by deluded individuals in their ability to evaluate for beliefs; however, it is not clear whether this is an enduring characteristic of people who develop psychosis or a consequence of it or of the circumstances leading to the psychosis. Anxiety can lead to a 'search for meaning,' which is relieved as soon as acceptance of an explanation – a meaning – is reached and so anxiety avoidance may be a factor. This has been explored by work on 'need for closure,' which has however come to inconclusive results.

Persecutory beliefs may be the consequence of genuine persecutory experiences (Bentall, Corcoran, Howard, Blackwood, & Kinderman, 2001), and particular environmental conditions, for example, social deprivation and racism, are associated with paranoid thinking (e.g. Fuchs, 1999; Harris, 1987; Mirowsky & Ross, 1983). Delusions have also been suggested to result from a psychological defence against underlying negative emotion and low self-esteem (Hassan, 2011), projecting these distressing feelings and beliefs outwards towards others rather than towards the self. An attempt to make sense of anomalous experiences may result therefore in 'blaming others' (Bentall et al., 2001).

Persecutory delusions may occur when information is accurately perceived and then misinterpreted due to faulty self and social knowledge and influenced by threat beliefs or traumatic experiences rather than it is being due to faulty perceptions (Morrison, 2001). Therefore, individuals may experience auditory hallucinations following misattribution of intrusive thoughts to an external source in order to reduce the feeling of discomfort resulting from a discrepancy between their experiences and their own beliefs and behaviours. Of particular interest is the probability of misinterpretations in the ways that behaviours are considered to be culturally unacceptable. This explanatory framework can consider and incorporate cultural influences, but although it has been widely adopted by clinicians, its empirical basis is still limited.

There is more evidence supporting differences in the recall of autobiographical information between individuals with symptoms of schizophrenia and nonclinical populations (Corcoran & Frith, 2003). Theory of mind refers to an individual's ability to understand that other people have desires and mental states and explains how individuals comprehend the knowledge and intentions of others. Frith (1992) argued that deficits in theory of mind could be implicated in the formation of persecutory delusions due to, for example, difficulties arising from monitoring other's thoughts and intentions resulting in paranoid ideation and delusions of reference (Bentall et al., 2001; Corcoran, Frith, & Mercer, 1995; Frith & Corcoran, 1996). As stated earlier on by Corcoran and Frith (2003), autobiographical memory differences may be implicated in schizophrenic individuals resulting in the recall of negative or traumatic events.

Vulnerability to developing psychosis can be explained through bio-psychosocial factors (Freeman & Garety, 2004). The formation and maintenance of psychotic phenomenon at onset derive from significant life events leading to cognitive deficits such as attention, perceptual, and jumping to conclusions biases (Garety, Hemsley, & Wessely, 1991). The role of emotion is central to this process, in particular threat arousal as a contributory factor to processing of anomalous experiences (Freeman, Garety, Kuipers, Fowler, & Beddington, 2002). Integrating multiple factors in this approach makes it ideal for use with ethnic groups as it emphasizes the impact of social background, in particular traumatic experiences as contributory factors that can exacerbate negative self-schemata and predisposition to psychosis. Furthermore, it considers that threat beliefs could result from a number of cognitive biases that the authors implicate in the maintenance cycle such as prejudices that may maintain biased belief systems.

Any individual with a 'jumping to conclusions' bias from any culture is likely to be influenced by the changing beliefs held by the members of that culture, as reflected by the changes in the content of delusion. Normalization can be used to explain this process and target emotion through re-evaluation of the threat beliefs. Safety behaviour and avoidance (e.g. Dugas & Robichaud, 2007; Papageorgiou & Wells, 2003) can also reinforce these negative biases.

Cognitive interpersonal approaches complement these theoretical positions and have focused on attachment issues (discussed earlier). Consideration of these can be very relevant to threat beliefs and their impact on paranoia and subsequently to recovery (Gumley & Schwannauer, 2006).

Auditory hallucinations
There remains limited understanding of the pathophysiology of auditory hallucinations related to psychotic phenomenon (Lennox, Bert, Park, Jones, & Morris, 1999), but an implicit premise or working hypothesis places origin in the region of auditory cortex subserving language. Clients with diagnoses of schizophrenia

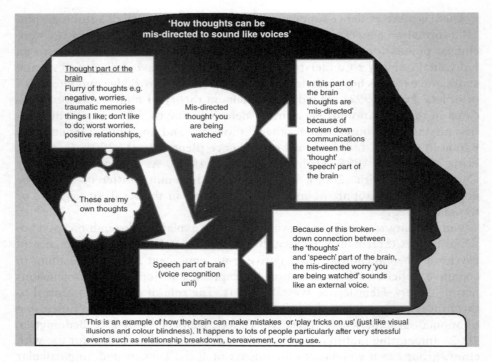

Figure 8.1   How thoughts can be mis-directed to sound like voices. Adapted from Keen (2009). Reproduced with permission from N. Keen.

experiencing auditory hallucinations have been investigated using brain-imaging scans, and conclusions reached that there was a strong association of the right middle temporal gyrus with the experience of auditory hallucinations. Voices seem to reflect abnormal activation of auditory cortex.

Normalizing this phenomenon in CBT is best described in Figure 8.1; originally from Nelson (1997, pp. 184–187), the diagram illustrating this is adapted from Keen (2009) BABCP case presentation. The figure describes how one's thoughts can be misdirected to sound like voices due to an abnormal activation of the auditory cortex in the brain – they are experiencing 'inner speech.'

Lennox et al. (1999) further elucidate this abnormality of language function in individuals with psychotic experiences, in particular the left hemisphere (associated with language) with the right hemisphere (associated with emotional tone of speech as well as auditory). Accordingly, in patients with this brain abnormality, the right-side activation associated with emotional and memory arousal can be a plausible explanation in the retrieval of emotional verbal memory in hallucinating individuals (Lennox et al., 1999).

This reattribution strategy can be used with clients who experience 'voices' – auditory hallucinations. Using this explanation with clients with psychosis as an alternative view of their phenomenon was plausible with CBT participants. In line with this hypothesis, examples like '*talking to someone on a landline telephone and suddenly having another line crossing over*' (i.e. hearing another person talking in your line) are one way of helping patients make sense of what is going on. Another illustration used was explaining how the brain sometimes plays tricks on us by asking a client whether they have ever had an experience of other people or family members asking them whether they had called their name out. On the other hand, a commonly used illustration to normalizing this illusionary blind spot relates to assumptions that '*if you ask a man to find an item in the refrigerator, he may report that it is not there, but when his wife opens the fridge they find it.*' Some clients can relate to such illustrations aimed at normalizing anomalous experiences subsequently find reductions in distress caused by their previously catastrophic appraisals of anomalous experiences (Freeman et al., 2004), instead of believing it is the mafia out to kill them or neighbours poisoning them, it may be that the voices originate inside – and their mind is playing 'tricks on them.'

A particularly useful analogy is that with dreams and nightmares where speech from other people occurs but is recognized as being internal in origin. Sleep deprivation is known to produce voices and other psychotic phenomena so a clear relationship exists and can be helpful in explaining distressing experiences.

These approaches come together in stress–vulnerability models initially developed by Zubin and Spring (1977) and further modified by Nuechterlein et al. (1994). These are readily explainable, incorporate cultural dimensions, and so have been effective in enhancing therapeutic rapport and developing understanding. We have discussed in Chapter 2 the basic model proposing that psychotic symptoms occur as a result of a combination of vulnerabilities and strengths in the presence of stressful experiences (Kingdon & Turkington, 2005). Therefore, by learning skills and developing alternative ways of understanding and dealing with stress, it can allow the symptoms to abate and make relapse less likely. The impact of illness can produce further stresses, for example, job loss and effects on self-esteem, which complicate return to full functioning but which can be identified and managed in their own right. The model can be over-simplistic and linear, and it can readily be vulnerability focused rather than taking a strengths approach. It can also be used to misrepresent stress as 'bad' leading to inappropriate avoidance – it is however the management and perception of stress that is the focus.

The fundamental premise in psychological frameworks within cognitive therapy is working collaboratively and the development of shared formulations of individual experiences. An experiential approach is used to modify beliefs and developing alternative explanations of psychotic phenomenon. This can result in the patient learning new coping strategies or enhancing helpful strategies and weakening the potency of hallucinations through such strategies as reality testing and behavioural experiments in session and in-between session activities ('homework'). The fundamental premise of CBT for psychosis is to reduce distress and disability associated with psychotic symptoms (Birchwood & Trower, 2006). Where a client is asymptomatic, therapy may focus on developing social skills and relapse prevention.

Culture and course of psychosis

The results of the International Pilot Study of Schizophrenia that was conducted by the WHO (de Girolamo, 1996) revealed that presentations of psychosis in developing countries are more acute with more florid positive symptoms and more catatonia and have a shorter duration than in Western societies such as Europe or North America. Those very acute presentations of psychosis tend to have a shorter, more severe but briefer course and a better prognosis in terms of recovery. In terms of the duration of untreated psychosis, this is also very different in the way it is dealt within different cultures. Cultures with an overt belief in the illness model may be more likely to recognize at least positive symptoms of psychosis earlier and respond with psychoeducation and antipsychotic medication. In cultures where the illness model is not predominant, these symptoms may be more likely to still be recognized at an early stage but normalized and worked with within a family and cultural setting. The International Pilot Study of Schizophrenia (Leff, Sartorius, Jablensky, Korten, & Ernberg, 1992) seems to point towards the latter approach being less stigmatizing and more facilitative of recovery although its findings have proved very difficult to interpret. This also impacts on help-seeking behaviours (discussed in Chapter 3) that therapists need to recognize.

Culture and phenomenology of psychosis

While the form of psychotic symptoms is broadly the same from culture to culture, the content is strongly moulded by the cultural setting and by chronology. Current ideas resonating in society are extremely powerful in terms of the genesis of delusional content. These include conspiracy theories particularly surrounding the assassination of President Kennedy, the 9/11 attacks, and the death of the Princess of Wales. There are currently delusions linked to UFOs and aliens along with new religious ideas and technological advances, for example, silicon chips – often implanted in the person's body. The table below has been drawn up in consultation with colleagues from different countries and describes, very tentatively, delusional content within a variety of different cultures and how this has changed over time (Table 8.1).

The content of phenomenology does seem closely linked to the cultural setting in which the psychosis develops as well as deriving from the individual's personal experience. The context in which the delusion arises and the beliefs prior to their origin seem to be critical.

Table 8.1   Examples of cross-cultural themes for delusions.

Spain: originally, the vast majority of delusions were linked to religion and persecution by spies from other nations. Currently, religion is estimated to form about half of delusional content with the other half being made up of technological content

Italy: delusions were again originally described as being almost entirely of religious content with a small amount linked to persecution by foreign nations. Currently religious content has fallen to half, maybe a quarter being linked to Mafia and other criminal persecutors and a similar proportion to technology

United Kingdom: in the United Kingdom, the religious content has fallen very dramatically and currently, only a small proportion are due to religion, perhaps half due to microchips and computer technology and the remainder due to aliens and other suspected persecutors

China: in China, this seems to have changed relatively less over the past few years, and currently, perhaps half are estimated as linked to possession by spirits of the ancestors and some to conspiracy theories, and a significant proportion were encountered as erotomanic or delusions of jealousy

West Africa: again, the delusional content has changed slowly: maybe half in relation to the ancestors and similarly in relation to conspiracies or witchcraft including delusions of possession

India: the delusional content seems to have religious and supernatural delusions prominent. Delusions of possession can be prominent in rural settings where clients feel they have been possessed by the goddess

South Asian Muslims: predominantly religious delusions, conspiracy, and supernatural

---

Case example

Samuel arrived in the United Kingdom as an asylum seeker and very quickly became socially isolated and began to hallucinate. Samuel believed that these were the voices of his ancestors discussing his difficulties in the United Kingdom. As such he indicated that there was a certain type of herbal tea available from his faith leader, which could help placate the voices. He had no concept of an illness model or of relating his voices to his asylum-seeking status and the stress linked to that situation. He agreed to monitor the frequency and intensity of the voice-hearing experience in a voice diary (see Appendix 4) to see if the herbal tea produced any benefits. When this didn't seem to work, Samuel became more agreeable to consider a vulnerability–stress explanation and to begin low-dose antipsychotic medication.

Practical Considerations

Culture and services

Inequalities in the provision of mental health services for black and minority ethnic (BME) patients when compared to the majority of white population continue to be a subject of debate (Audini & Lelliott, 2002; Bhui, Stansfield, Hull, Priebe, & Feder, 2003) in the United Kingdom and elsewhere. As we have discussed in Chapter 1, when compared to their white counterparts, patients from minority ethnic groups with schizophrenia are likely to be misunderstood and misdiagnosed (Fernando, 1988; Sashidharan, 1989), and African Caribbeans were more likely to be treated with medication and/or brought into the hospital under compulsory legal provisions (Bhui, 1997; Bhugra, 1997; Dunn & Fahy, 1990), and this has been echoed in the Healthcare Commission's report (Count me census, 2008). Furthermore, dissatisfaction of statutory health-care provision by ethnic groups is common (Keating, 2007). Race and its impact on establishing contact with services and developing therapeutic rapport are clearly significant. A lack of understanding of BME cultural backgrounds and application of 'West-centric approaches' on the migrant population has previously been highlighted as problematic (Lewis, 1965; Thomas & Sillen, 1972). Other factors include limited family supportive structures brought about in some instances by family fragmentation resulting from migration. A study conducted in the United States on African American groups and the United Kingdom on African Caribbean groups identified and thus confirmed the impact of isolation and loneliness as contributory factors to elevated levels of vulnerability in the migrant population (Banks, Kohn-Wood, & Spencer, 2006; NIMHE, 2004).

Concerns that psychological needs of BME groups were not being met have been highlighted in the literature before and more so now. For example, African Caribbean people are just as likely as white people to consult the family doctor for psychological problems but actually less likely to receive medication, for example, antidepressants (Nazroo, 1997). African Caribbean and South Asian women were least likely to be diagnosed by their doctor as having a psychological disorder in comparison to their white counterparts (Cochrane & Sashidhran, 1996). However, this is likely to change given the current drive by the government on improved access to psychological therapies especially for people from minority ethnic groups. It does seem however that self-referral routes are more successful at achieving access by BME groups and so these are being actively encouraged.

Common stereotypes have been used to explain the under-representation of the South Asian and the over-presentation of the African Caribbean people from ethnic minority backgrounds in mental health services (Bhui, 1997). The notion that Asians are more likely to somatize than any other group and the assumption that Asian people perceive general practitioners to treat only physical complaints, as a reason for under-referral, are not supported by evidence.

Cultural Aspects of Delivering CBT

CBT is now a treatment of choice for schizophrenia and associated psychotic symptoms (APA, 2004; NICE, 2014), but CBT for psychosis is not simply the use of standard CBT developed for psychopathology, in people with psychosis. It requires adaptation for positive and negative symptoms (Kingdon & Turkingdon, 2005). What's more, cognitive therapy techniques need to be modified in order to deal with some of the specific issues resulting from psychosis (Turkington, Kingdon, & Weidon, 2006). There are four key therapy stages: (i) developing a therapeutic alliance based on the patient's perspective, (ii) developing alternative explanations of psychotic symptoms (through techniques like thought records, schema modification), (iii) reducing the impact of positive and negative symptoms, and (iv) offering alternatives to traditional medical approaches to address adherence.

Technical Adjustments and Theoretical Modifications

Building a therapeutic alliance (specific aspects related to psychosis)

First impressions can count for a lot especially as there is evidence that clients with psychosis have a tendency to 'jump to conclusions.' Therapists may be judged quickly as this quote from a service user in our qualitative study illustrates:

> so it will help, seriously help because first impression counts. And if you blow it then you ain't getting back, you seriously ain't getting and then you end up wondering why that person is being aggressive towards you or whatever it is, because of what you triggered off in the first place without even knowing it yourself... [interview with African Caribbean service user]

By contrast, in certain cultures, for example, China and Japan setting up a therapeutic alliance can be very difficult as the psychiatrist/therapist is viewed as a highly respected authority figure to be learnt from, not as a collaborator to work with, and where there is inherent suspicion as a result of paranoid ideas or anxiety related to social interaction, these problems can be multiplied. This combining of issues is a very clear problem in the early stages of engaging people from minority cultures. It is believed to be disrespectful for the client to contribute much by way of conversation or comment during a CBT session. Cognitive therapy's collaborative empiricism can be a challenge where a client takes a passive role as they probably would with their traditional expert, for example a guru or healer. Similarly, an overtly directive style could result in the client viewing the therapist as a controlling agent of the dominant culture. How might a therapist address this collaborative versus paternalistic stance?

THERAPIST: So what seems to be the problem?
CLIENT: I don't know; you tell me; you are the expert.
THERAPIST: Ok, I will give you a suggestion; let's test it out together to find out if that is so.

The use of culturally appropriate stories or metaphors to emphasize key concepts is helpful to keeping client engaged and can be used at different stages of therapy. See Munoz and Mendelson (2005) for examples of Latino metaphors.

Exercise: Think of a patient from a different cultural background who you have seen. Can you identify any culturally relevant metaphors, terms, concepts, or stories that you can use to facilitate introducing key CBT principles with your local diverse groups?

Asian clients may prefer a more structured and prescriptive approach (Iwamasa, 1993). Exploration of opinions about a problem may lead to doubts about clinician's competences. Therefore, harnessing hope and ensuring client leaves session with something, for example, a clear summary of discussion or a statement of new insights or therapeutic gains, are encouraged. Consider individualist and collectivist concepts when working with diverse cultures as we have discussed in earlier chapters. Without sensitivity to cultural norms and explanations of the phenomenon, culture could create obstacles in the cognitive and behavioural change processes, especially if the explanations used for change do not match or agree with cultural models of illness. Take, for instance, the concept of 'self and the collectivist cultures' that we have discussed before. The self is defined in terms of group identity and interdependence with group members (Owusu-Bempah, 2002). Accordingly, group goals, have primacy of individual goals and the needed emphasis is that of the group they belong to. Consider the recent disasters in the United States (Hurricane Katrina in 2005 and the subsequent looting) and the Japanese tsunami disaster with orderly reaction in line with collectivist needs. This is in stark contrast to individualist concepts; consequently, therapists should be cognizant of these throughout the therapeutic process and adapt intervention accordingly. In addition, many cultures use antipsychotic medication as a first-line therapy usually linked with support and a degree of psychoeducation although there are other societies in which medications are much less available and psychological treatment might be more accessible as a monotherapy. There has been recent support for CBT where antipsychotics are not being taken (Morrison et al., 2012, 2014) and that this might be a reasonable and safe strategy. This study involved clients who actively refused to take medication, and, as yet, there are no investigations where CBT has been offered as an alternative to medication although these are now being considered – especially for first episode clients.

CBT has been used also successfully in people at risk for psychosis but who have not had definitive diagnoses.

In developing a CBT dialogue with African Caribbean clients with schizophrenia, fixed appointment times are often viewed flexibly and this requires therapist's diaries and schedules that are open to change and the ability to stretch working hours on occasion. Attitudes towards the use of time differ according to cultures, for instance, in the West, time is seen as a commodity and as such is valued (i.e. 'time is money'); in contrast, there is a stereotypical assumption that African cultures tend to have a very flexible attitude towards time; this tends to be seen in patients talking too much or turning up late for therapy and still expecting to be seen for the hour. As a talking therapy, CBT can be adapted to this group because they accept that talking is their 'mantra.' However, this may cause challenges when rigid time is set and clients feel they are being rushed in therapy. Flexibility in session structure and agenda setting is recommended. Here, the therapist will need to socialize client to the cognitive model and adapt a flexible approach as opposed to a more rigid structure. Similarly, the use of a more conversational style of communication is favourable; the therapist should be mindful of not digressing but keeping therapy focus on the main problems rather than peripheral issues. It is also clear that in early to middle sessions with African Caribbean, client's emotions are rarely acknowledged and may in fact never be disclosed during the course of the therapy. Demonstration of respect and acknowledgement of their difficulties, for example, racism, are important strategies and make them feel 'heard.' Talking about racism in therapy can be an anxiety-provoking process for some. Some clients may prefer to talk to someone of the same background or colour about race issues, as illustrated by this excerpt from an African Caribbean client talking to a therapist of colour:

> You don't know the half of it mate… I am glad I got a chance to speak now. I can speak to you because you are a man of my colour and I can explain {meaning racial issues} – so that I don't feel no shame.

There is an assumption that talking to a white therapist about racial issues, they may be misunderstood and ignored. Therefore, to work well with clients from different ethnic backgrounds, therapists will need to recognize the potential significance of the experience of everyday racism for mental health itself, for uptake of services, for therapeutic relationship and for the outcome of therapy. When addressing racism in therapy, therapists should not walk on 'eggshells,' but validate client's feeling of their experience and explore this with sensitivity, that is, acknowledge their difficult position. Kluckhohn and Murry's (1953) observation that 'every person is in certain respects like all other persons, like some other person, like no other person' articulates this identity of similarity with others yet holding on to our differences. The non-specifics of the interaction need to be correct for the culture. As discussed, the ideal way to do this would seem to be for

Table 8.2   Key adjustments in building a relationship.

1. First impressions count
2. Keep a flexible approach in settings and timings
3. Understand your client's philosophical orientation and practical settings
4. Have a prescriptive approach if needed before developing a collaborative stance
5. Use culturally appropriate metaphors where appropriate
6. Consider your client's group identity
7. When appropriate, do not be afraid to discuss client's difficult experiences like perception of racism

the cognitive behavioural therapist to be of the same culture. However there are the problems described with this in earlier chapters, and where this is not possible, the cognitive behavioural therapist should endeavour to receive specific training about cultural aspects of psychosis and the role of mental health professionals (Table 8.2).

Formulation with Psychosis in Different Cultural Settings

Teaching of the CBT model is usually acceptable to most societies. In its basic form, the 'activating event–belief–consequence' (ABC) model is usually a powerful technique, which is readily grasped. Appropriate and sensitive personal disclosure, responsive to client needs, can be used and valuable with clients with psychosis and especially paranoia. It is powerfully useful in some Western societies, African Caribbean cultures, and people from the Indian subcontinent but could be deemed inappropriate in China or Japan. The ABC model might be less effective, even acceptable, where there are strong cultural beliefs about the voices of the ancestors. This is particularly the case in Native Australian culture. In such instances, it can still be used in relation to the stress of the experience, that is, 'they shouldn't be doing this to me,' which is pertinent to the emotional and behavioural reaction to the experience. Problem lists and target setting in some cultures might deferentially be responded with a 'you decide.' The use of lifelines can be problematic if the client feels he/she is disclosing highly personal information which could be 'disrespecting' the family background, for example, some South Asian Muslim cultures.

The use of a mini formulation (as described earlier) is usually acceptable, as the client will usually agree that they are using safety behaviours in relation to their hallucinations or delusions and the veracity of these behaviours can be questioned and tested out in behavioural experiments. Similarly, mental behaviours such as worry and rumination appear to be good metacognitive CBT targets in most cultures as a potential means of boundary setting psychotic experiences using postponement techniques.

Table 8.3 Formulation with psychosis in different cultural settings.

1. Use mini formulation to begin with
2. Consider the client's cultural identity, cultural reference group, language, cultural developmental influences
3. Consider their philosophical orientation – level of acculturation, beliefs about illness and help-seeking preferences
4. Consider the influence of religion

When helping clients make sense of their psychosis, formulations should embed relevant cultural factors (see list below). These will vary with individuals and ethnic groups:

- Cultural identity.
- Cultural reference group(s) – this may include the ethno-cultural and religious groups the individual client identifies in addition to parental background.
- Language, as spoken at home given that these groups may be bilingual or multilingual – assessing the level of literacy may be helpful as this may inform the degree to which adaptations may be necessary, for example, clients that are illiterate and not speaking English eliciting cognitions, emotions, and behaviours may be a challenge for the therapist.
- Consider cultural factors in the early and late childhood development.
- Involvement with the host culture and their experience of this given that where an individual has more than one culture, they may oscillate between the culture of country of origin, host culture, and community or societal culture in an attempt to resolve a problem (acculturation).
- Explanations of illness models (discussed in earlier chapters) – consider idioms of distress and help-seeking behaviours and pathways.
- Often neglected factors include the impact of migration and acculturation stress.
- Religion and spirituality should be considered (Table 8.3).

Work on medication concordance

CBT for antipsychotic medication concordance within different cultures will always need to address the issue of the health belief model within that culture, personal and family schemas about medication use, and also cultural schemas about medicines. In China, for example, beliefs in traditional Chinese medicine are strong though it is combined increasingly with beliefs in 'Western' practices. There is nevertheless actually little in the way of overlap between these two cultural medication schemas. When treating someone with a belief in traditional Chinese medicine, it is often efficient to discuss a traditional remedy first to see if it is helpful for paranoia, anxiety, or hallucinations before attempting a trial of a Western-style antipsychotic medication. Also, certain cultures, for example, South Asian Muslims and Hispanic, are particularly keen on depot medication rather than tablet medication as they seek a quick cure.

Case example

Juan forgot to take the vast majority of his antipsychotic medication even with a pillbox and reminders. He suffered repeated relapses and prolonged periods of hospitalization. At the day hospital, he was asked by a fellow client why he wasn't having injections. He therefore requested this from his consultant, and this did impact his poor compliance.

It seems that attending for an injection is more acceptable or certainly used more in some countries, for example, Spain and England, than in many other countries, for example the United States. There is also great variability in the acceptability of clozapine around the world; this in particular may relate to the perceived dangerousness of the treatment due to the need for regular blood testing which is used internationally. The therapist should understand the orientation of the client in relation to medication. A discussion of obstacles and solutions could be helpful.

CLIENT: Taking drugs is against my religion, and people will think I am mad if they find out.

THERAPIST: Can you remind me what the reason you were in the hospital recently for was?

CLIENT: I had been worried that I was being watched, and this was stopping me from going out.

THERAPIST: What helped you when you were in the hospital?

CLIENT: Taking time out and maybe the medication helped me sleep.

THERAPIST: How were your symptoms affecting your plans for the future?

CLIENT: I could not go out and could not go to work.

THERAPIST: So how does treatment fit in with this?

In this case, the therapist set up the next session with the local priest with the client's permission to discuss misconceptions about religion and medication. Coping cards, written adherence plans, and discussion of alternatives like discussion about side effects and simplification of medication schedules can be helpful.

Exercise: Think of a client that you are currently working with or have worked with. What have been the cultural barriers to medication concordance? How can you use their culture and philosophical orientation to improve adherence?

Working with cultural stigma

Stigma is a powerful variable that is different between cultures as we have discussed in Chapter 3. There has been a strong lobby for the retention of the highly stigmatized diagnostic label of schizophrenia in the United States. When clients perceive therapeutic pessimism through a diagnostic label, recovery can be more difficult to achieve. However, a proportion of people in Western society receive the diagnosis of schizophrenia, and a substantial proportion of clients and families attest to the importance of receiving a diagnosis in empowering them to find out more about coping with the condition and reduce the blame that is sometimes incurred from having a mental health problem; understanding it as an illness which is caused by something physically malfunctioning – in the brain – can help self-perception and perception of others. It can lead to improved insight, better concordance, and improved stress management.

The perception of stigma is important when determining treatment choices in cultures where the community spirit is strong, for example, in South Asian Muslim cultures. Stigma must be understood in the context of the individual and family in the respective minority groups. Mental illness is still seen as a taboo even by those living in Western societies. A therapist visiting the home for weekly sessions could be considered stigmatizing due to shame and guilt brought to the family and community due to mental illness. Therapy as part of a social group in a community centre or near a religious place could be less stigmatizing. Again, in those cultures where arranged marriage may still be occurring, the stigma impacting on prospects for marriage can determine whether the client and family accept CBT. Engaging community leaders in educating communities is often a way forwards as we have discussed in earlier chapters.

Case example

Ben became psychotic and ran away from home becoming a vagrant and becoming involved in alcohol abuse and substance misuse. During a period of imprisonment, he was able to receive some antipsychotic medication and was given a diagnosis of schizophrenia. Although initially angry and then saddened by this, he was able to contact his family again who organized his transfer back to a local hospital. Eventually, during CBT sessions, he wrote a timeline of his survival from acute schizophrenia. He found the diagnosis very helpful in reintegrating with his family.

On the other hand, the change of diagnostic name to integration disorder in Japan is deemed to have had some impact on stigma. Stigma always worsens the outcome of schizophrenia, and in certain cultures, it is seen as not only a disgrace for the person but also for their whole family and community as discussed earlier. Destigmatizing cultural milieu such as those set up in Stavanger in Norway, Manchester in the United Kingdom, and Melbourne in Australia has led to earlier detection of psychotic prodromes and earlier intervention leading to the hope of reduced transition, delay in transition, or reduced severity of symptoms.

Developing coping strategies

Eastern, especially Buddhist, cultures may have inbuilt mechanisms which assist coping with, for example, auditory hallucinations. Where mindfulness approaches are routinely practised, these may be more readily adopted to reduce the distress associated. Mindfulness is a metacognitive coping style (involving thinking about thinking) which is showing itself to be effective in managing voice hearing. Voices can be culturally normalized in those societies where voices are more acceptable. However, within such cultures, when the experience is distressing, cognitive behavioural approaches and work on safety behaviours, meaning, and enhanced coping strategies can be very helpful. Voice hearing may be less well coped with, in stressful Western societies where coping practices often include the use of loud music and strong cannabis. Delusions can also be less well tolerated in less liberal societies. In liberal societies where freedom of speech is taken to be important, a diversity of opinion is usually already accepted. Confrontation and collusion both worsen delusions, and certain cultures are more likely to practise either type of approach leading to entrenchment of delusional beliefs due to inability to vocalize symptoms from fear of being confronted. Spirituality and religion are used as coping strategies in most cultures. Spiritual development is a vital part of most cultures, and Laungani (2004) emphasizes this in Asian cultures. Both work as a locus of control and can provide support and networking.

Consider the following biblical texts:

"I can do all things through Christ who strengthens me"
"I have the mind of Christ"
"I am fearfully and wonderfully made"

If a client with a psychotic disorder uttered one of the above statements in your session, the therapist might want to think about:

What goes through their mind? What would they imagine and why? How would a CBT therapist or practitioner address this? What are the implications of their response?

The influence of religion and spirituality (belief in the supernatural) remains strong despite westernization and acculturation (Williams, Foo, & Haarhoff, 2006).

Work with voices

Work with voices involves improving understanding and ability to cope and combating negative beliefs associated with them. The understanding and acceptability of the experience of hearing voices vary culturally. In white populations in the developed world, it has generally become associated with mental illness with exceptions in some religious communities. These communities, for example, evangelical Christian churches, value the experience of communication with God, hearing his voice, and sometimes that of his saints or angels, or conversely, they may experience the devil speaking. But for the most part, 'hearing voices is a sign

Table 8.4 Example of diary of conversations with voices and coping strategies.

Situation	Voices present	What did the voices say?	Loudness 1/10	How did I feel?	What did I do?
While eating with family, especially with the father	Yes	'Stop eating, leave'	All 7–8	It was annoying and I was slightly nervous that I might make it obvious that I wasn't feeling comfortable/normal, which would probably lead to my father getting angry as I am not allowed to challenge him	I tried to finish my food and leave as quickly as I could
Pretty much every time my mom brings me my medication	Yes	'Turn the light off' Telling me to challenge my father 'Don't touch the fish, it's poisoned' 'Just take your food to your room, you shouldn't be here' Orders to do strange things, for example 'Pour your drink on your head' 'Spit in the bowl' 'Don't swallow them' 'Hide them under your tongue and spit them out later' 'These pills are what's hurting you the most'	7–8	I was also worried that I would do some of the strange things I was being told It makes me feel unsure about the medication, which can lead to me not taking it some days	When I got to my room, it got better and the voices stopped for an hour or so Sometimes, I hold the pills under my tongue and wait until my mom leaves the room to spit them out

of madness.' This causes fear and stigmatization and may cause distress in its own right amplifying the voices and leading to unnecessary distress. The fear of being labelled mad can impair presentation to services, which may be able to offer help. However, these services may themselves have negative beliefs about voices, assuming that these represent long-term problems and over-medicating.

As discussed, the increased use of illegal drugs that can induce hallucinations and paranoia is one other situation in which these experiences are explained by phenomena other than mental illness. They may lead on to persistent problems but still remain easier to explain. The process of inducing these states was popular in the 1960s and 1970s but less so now, possibly because the dangers are recognized – the very negative effects on creative musicians such as Sydney Barrett (Pink Floyd) and Peter Green (Fleetwood Mac) highlighted these to a broad population. Hearing voices has been viewed and experienced as a much more benign process in other cultures where it has also been associated with religious and cultural ritual. Shamans who clearly hear voices are venerated because of their holy status and ability to communicate with God.

Response to commands is a particularly important issue and in association with mental illness tends to be seen as negative although it is accepted that friendly positive voices often exist. However, response to God's commands or those associated with other religions can go beyond this in being required but often supportive and constructive and acting as a guide through life in a very positive way reflecting good rather than as can be the case with mental health issues, evil. Therefore, any work with voices needs to reflect a full understanding of their context and content.

Normalization of voices should therefore be consistent with the culture of the individual. In CBT for psychosis, it is now a common place to teach a client how to engage in a dialogue with voices in particular keeping a voices' diary of what the voices say, how loud there are, and how distressing they are; are they commenting or commanding in nature? What strategies the client used to cope with the distress caused by the voices (see voices diary in the following and Appendixes 4 and 5) (Table 8.4).

As part of exploring the nature and power of the voices over the individual, it is worth finding out whether the source of the voice is internal or external and whether others can hear them.

Case example

Hafad believed that the voices he heard were the devil and that the devil caused him to harm himself and significant others. This was contrary to his Muslim faith. During the month of Ramadan, he attended a therapy session and was upset that when this was explored in detail, it sufficed that he believed that during the Ramadan, the devils are locked up, according to the Koran, and was surprised and upset that he could still hear the voice of the devil.

Case discussion

This presentation gave the therapist leverage to explore the belief and opportunity to consider alternative explanations. As part of Hafad's homework, he was tasked with checking for scriptural evidence to support his beliefs, and the therapist also as part of his homework explored the same. In the following session, during homework review, both client and therapist shared their findings. Hafad confirmed that the Koran mentioned that during Ramadan, the devils are locked up; the therapist had gone a step further and researched what the Koran Hadiths' commentaries about this were and shared the varied viewpoints from different scholars and interpretations thereof. Using the ABC model, Hafad was able to consider alternative viewpoints from the Hadiths and also alternative view that the voices he was hearing maybe were not from the devil after all.

The therapist used the illustration about how our thoughts can be misdirected to sound like voices, and he found this explanation more plausible resulting in the reduction of distress. Hafad adopted a gradual move from voices to '*these are my thoughts which sound like voices.*'

Basic CBT techniques can be modified and used with diverse groups. Clients, initially baffled by this anomalous experience, are often surprised by the outcome when a reality testing behavioural experiment is used to test whether the voice is internal or external by using a tape recorder. They then can only hear their own voice on the recorded excerpt when it is played back. The impact of this experiment tends to reduce distress and weakens assumptions that others can hear what the voices are saying.

Case example

A young Iranian Muslim who experienced derogatory voices resulting in social isolation and avoidance of social activities or spending time with family in fear of what the voices were saying about his family members conducted this behavioural experiment, that is, recording a dialogue with the voices and then playing this back. When he next met in a session with the therapist, he reported that he had bad news and good news. Curious as to what the bad news was, the therapist asked him to relate this first:

CLIENT: I am cross that no one did this experiment with me when I first
               presented in the services; if I had done this 2 years ago, this
               would have solved many of my problems and made my life
               easier.
THERAPIST: validated his feelings and asked about the good news.
CLIENT: When I played the recording on my laptop, I could only
               hear my voice and nothing else. So all the time, I thought
               my parents could hear them [voices] and that they were
               pretending or lying to me when they denied this I was
               horrible to them. I apologized to my parents for my behaviours
               and yesterday sat down and watched a game of football
               with my dad.

This behavioural experiment was simple to complete; however, the impact and
new insights gained were massive. Clients can use a smartphone or recording
device to carry out this experiment (Table 8.5).

Work with delusions

The experiential side of beliefs needs exploring in the cultural context – how
did they develop and what are the relevant experiences of the individual. The
explanations and systematization of delusions and hallucinations may be based
on cultural beliefs. For example, delusions of possession by a ghost or spirit in
African Caribbean patients can be based on a cultural belief that ancestor's
spirits are protective of native tribes. CBT with these delusions would need to
rationalize and normalize using the cultural beliefs while addressing any distress that may be caused. Similarly, in South Asian Muslim patients, psychotic
symptoms may be related to 'casting of evil eye/spirits or magic' as we have
described.

Addressing hallucinations and delusions in this instance will require therapists'
cognizance of both cultural and religious background of patient involved.

Table 8.5 Key points when working with voices.

---
1. Explore the voices and their content in the context of culture and philosophical
   orientation of client
2. Normalization of voices should be consistent with the culture of the individual
3. Diary of conversations with voices and coping strategies can be helpful
4. Use cultural metaphors or religion appropriately to develop alternative explanations
5. Use behavioural experiments like reality testing using people from the same culture
   like family and friends
6. Use culture consistent coping strategies

Validation of the distress is emphasized with a focus on reducing distress. Developing shared formulations based on a model such as stress–vulnerability (Zubin & Spring, 1977) as described before has been useful in conceptualizing and explaining this. In other cases, therapists report working collaboratively with the patient to test the client's idiosyncratic formulation of their presenting problem with a proposed cognitive hypothesis through reality testing and behavioural experiments more appropriate. Furthermore, the use of mind and body models specific to person's culture is recommended.

The following case example describes how a BME therapist worked with a client who felt persecuted by a fellow client who she believed was a witch.

Case example

...the formulation based on my cultural understanding helped in really dealing with the problem, by that I mean the challenges that we were facing because she had the delusion that there was another resident in the hostel … She thought this resident; she didn't even use the word witch. But she was attributing so much to this woman that she was so scared of this woman. Nobody could understand why she was scared. But this is a tall black woman being afraid of this little white woman. She was so scared that even she wouldn't want to see her at a distance. But eventually looking at how she described her, it gradually hit me. Because she looked at the white woman and the way she dresses. It was the image that an African child would actually give to a witch (laughter). Hair all about the place, I mean her makeup was all over red and bangles that way. And I just cracked it. Oh-ok 'she is seeing a witch.' And that's why she believed this woman can even influence her at a distance because they live in separate blocks. But she would say 'she beat me in my room, she does that.' Nobody could make sense as to why this other woman would hit her. And then I could understand that she was actually "beating" meant doing witchcraft to this woman. So the lesson of the day was to work with the social workers to help … this other woman to dress down a bit because her makeup and everything was quite scary to everybody. They worked on the other woman's self-image and I told them my understanding of the situation, how my client was attributing all those thoughts and beliefs to her. The staff was able to respond to her in a very positive way. When she came up with those ideas and I mean her intense anger towards this woman … So we managed to reduce the violence that this woman was directing towards this other person.'

Case example

Here, the therapist describes a client attributing cause of distress to *jinns* and how she explored with the patient cultural norm and the meaning to the individual:

> I am just thinking about someone that is Iranian who lives here who has *jinns*, you know these ghosts that harm him in the night, kill him or something. I suppose you can work on the understanding that is a belief held by his culture ... how do other people (from his culture) cope with *jinns*? Why for him has it become distressing and obviously there is something psychologically based. Why for him it has become more extreme and something about his beliefs, about them and other people's culture don't worry about, you know why has it become more distressing for him to have these experiences if they happen in his culture.

Examining the evidence

Working with delusions does, of course, not mean trying to convince the person that they are wrong. It involves collaboratively understanding their perspective and then working with the implications of the belief. It may be that they need to address particular issues in their lives which the therapist or family or community can assist them with. Delusions may have arisen because of difficulties in communicating distress – *'if others agreed with you or fully accepted what you said, why would that matter to you.'* It may well be that issues such as loneliness or lack of respect are expressed and these can be directly worked with. There is also some current work suggesting that working on worry about delusional beliefs can be helpful, which can be applied cross-culturally. Beliefs that others have malicious intentions and intend to harm us are common even in the general population.

Developing alternative perspectives/schema modification

Exploring evidence for and against such beliefs is crucial in helping clients to consider more evidence before making rash conclusions. Any threatening assumption is likely to invoke worry and anxiety that can be maintained by such thinking errors as 'turning a mole hill into a mountain' or inflating the sense of danger.

The therapist can facilitate client to explore alternative views and test these out as part of homework.

THERAPIST: What do you think your friend would think about your explanation about jinns?

Thought records can be helpful in developing alternative explanations.

Case example

A 50-year-old Guyanese American woman with a diagnosis of schizophrenia manifesting a systematized persecutory delusional system and multimodal hallucinations and acting out behaviour on delusions of running on to the streets to get away from her persecutors was referred for therapy. In the sessions, she was so emotionally charged about the delusions that it was difficult to shift her attention to any other subject. Multiple attempts by the therapist to move the discussion to other topics were of no avail. The therapist shifted the discussion by asking her questions about Guyana and how it contrasted with life in the United States. She started talking about Guyana, her arousal came down, and she became more relaxed. For the next 15 min, she was engaged in enthusiastic discussion about the cultural differences between the United States and Guyana. During the entire discussion, she did not once bring up her delusions. At the end, her feedback was that this session was very enjoyable because she had the opportunity to talk about her country of origin.

Case discussion

In this particular instance, a shift in her mental schema occurred when the therapist changed the discussion from the present to talking about her native country. She went from being a client talking about her symptoms to being an expert in her culture and educating the therapist about her culture. This shift was very therapeutic. So while none of the traditional CBT techniques were used, this session was very productive and formed the foundations for future work through engaging her (Table 8.6).

Table 8.6   Key points when working with delusions.

1. Identify the cultural influence on development of delusions
2. Rationalize and normalize using cultural beliefs while addressing any distress
3. Develop shared formulations using cultural strengths
4. Examine the evidence – targets like distress and worry are good starting points and may be linked to experiences like discrimination
5. Develop alternative explanations in line with cultural beliefs

Work with negative symptoms

Negative symptoms are frequently missed or ignored, yet there is good evidence that they can be substantially helped by CBT. They can vary in prevalence cross-culturally and seemed particularly prevalent in work in China and the United States with which we have been involved. The existence of large mental hospitals also appears to be relevant in institutionalizing clients; this can also happen in family and social care homes, which become demoralized and have little opportunity for normal social interaction increasing secondary negative symptoms. Excessive medication levels are known to lead to demotivation, sedation, and blunted affect.

The interrelationship with positive symptoms, anxiety, and depression is an important one, and treatment of these in their own right can benefit negative symptoms, but clients may also develop a tendency to avoid increasing the intensity or cause relapse of these symptoms contributing to apparent negative symptoms. Such protective mechanisms seem to be prevalent in all societies, but isolation and criticism possibly and also overprotection tend to increase them. Criticism and overprotection may be occurring for positive reasons – to motivate or support the individual – but can entrench symptoms – and can be counterproductive although working with them needs to take into account cultural norms of behaviour and communication.

The main emphasis in working with negative symptoms is empowerment of the individual so they feel back in control of their own lives, and this may mean letting them relax, 'take time off,' and reduce their striving to achieve goals, which are out of their reach currently. In the meantime, they can work on managing positive symptoms and anxiety so that they can feel more positive about life and re-engage with targets to meet long-term goals. Again, families and they themselves can find it difficult to accept reducing activity to ultimately achieve more, but often, they have actually 'driven themselves to a standstill' affecting concentration, attention, and general functioning. A psychiatrist from Pakistan explained how he discussed this with families by using the following story:

> A family are trying to return home and they go to the main City railway station. They ask which trains are leaving and are told that there are two that will be going at some time. One will leave soon but is not going to their hometown. The other is going at some time in the future, not sure when, but it will reach their home eventually. Which one do you think they chose?

Long-term goals which may be quite general – 'I want to get married and have my own home' – are important to set even if they may seem distant as they can instill hope and provide direction. Sometimes, these may seem unrealistic and even delusional – a Chinese client set the goal of abolishing world poverty which he was going to do by selling his artwork. This did allow a discussion of the first steps towards this – getting some art materials – if this is what he was

Table 8.7 Key points when working with negative symptoms.

1. Empower your client using cultural strengths
2. Manage anxiety of carers and families
3. Reset short-term and long-term goals collaboratively
4. Identify pleasurable activities that would be culturally acceptable
5. Behavioural activation through activity scheduling is useful
6. Other techniques like cost–benefit analysis and problem solving can be used successfully

determined to do. So when the clients themselves feel ready, they can then set for themselves – with assistance as necessary – small achievable targets which can start them on the journey towards their long-term goals.

Behavioural activation is recommended through the utilization of the activity schedule initially to get an overview of how your client spends their time and identifying themes that emerge from the overview and linking these to the formulation. Brainstorming to identify and list pleasurable activities that would be culturally acceptable to the individual and family and adding these to the weekly activity schedule rating masterly and pleasure can be helpful in breaking the negative spiral and improving mood and meaningful activities.

Other useful strategies such as the cost and benefits analysis can promote decision making based on analytic consideration of pros/cons rather than on how one feels. Practical approaches such as problem solving can promote confidence when working with diverse groups. Where individuals are overwhelmed by stress, setting realistic goal and taking small steps towards the mark are recommended. In some instances, the period of convalescence may be what the client needs. Psychoeducation both to individual and family members, where appropriate, may help reduce stress (Table 8.7).

Blocks to therapy

Managing blocks in therapy is an art. Therapists need to develop skills in handling blocks by discussing the issues with client and exploring any perceived dysfunctions in therapist and client behaviour and of its effects. These may be a result of a lack of understanding of the client's culture. Emphasizing the impact of such behaviour outside of therapy and linking it to relationships are important. Therapists need and should not react defensively and validating client's concerns helps. Validating the client's feelings and exploring pros and cons of behaving in a certain way need to be addressed. Therapists need to explore normative blocks that reflect norms of client's culture rather than individual's idiosyncrasies. A typical example is where people just agree with figures of authority but do not do what was talked about or seemingly agreed or when moderators such as shame or guilt prevent someone from discussing their fear of dishonour or shame.

Conclusion

Culture will contribute a substantial component of the aetiology to psychosis through a variety of vulnerability and resilience-enhancing factors. It will also mould the content and the form of the psychotic symptoms, but once psychotic symptoms have emerged, culture can also act as a protective or exacerbating factor. It is important for all mental health professionals, particularly in metropolitan areas, to learn culture-specific aspects of CBT for psychosis in order to effectively engage and work with individuals from diverse cultures.

References

APA. (2004). *Practice guideline for the treatment of patients with schizophrenia* (2nd ed.). Washington, DC: American Psychiatric Association Press.

Arsenault, L., Cannon, M., Fisher, H. L., Polanczyk, G., Moffitt, T. E., & Caspi, A. (2011). Childhood trauma and children's emerging psychotic symptoms: A genetically sensitive longitudinal cohort study. *American Journal of Psychiatry, 168*, 65–72.

Audini, B., & Lelliott, P. (2002) Age, gender and ethnicity of those detained under Part II of the Mental Health Act 1983. *British Journal of Psychiatry, 180*, 222–226.

Banks, K. H., Kohn-Wood, L. P., & Spencer, M. (2006). An examination of the African-American experience of everyday discrimination and symptoms of psychological distress. *Community Mental Health Journal, 42*(6), 555–570.

Beck, A. T., Freeman, A., & Associates. (1990). *Cognitive therapy of personality disorders.* New York, NY: Guilford Press.

Beck, A. T., Rush, A. J., Shaw, B. F., & Emery, G. (1979). *Cognitive therapy of depression.* New York, NY: Guilford Press.

Bentall, R., Corcoran, R., Howard, R., Blackwood, N., & Kinderman, P. (2001). Persecutory delusions: A review and theoretical interpretation. *Clinical Psychology Review, 21*, 1143–1192.

Bhugra, D. (1997). Setting up psychiatric services: Cross-cultural issues in planning and delivery. *International Journal of Social Psychiatry, 43*(1), 16–28.

Bhui, K. (1997). London's ethnic minorities and the provision of mental health services. In S. Johnson, R. Ramsay, G. Thornicroft, L. Brooks, P. Leliott, E. Peck, … D. Goldberg. (Eds.), *London's mental health.* London, UK: Kings Fund.

Bhui, K., Stansfield, S., Hull, S., Priebe, S., & Feder, G. (2003). Ethnic variation in pathways to use of specialist services in the UK. *British Journal of Psychiatry, 182*, 105–116.

Birchwood, M., & Trower, P. (2006). The future of cognitive behavioural therapy for psychosis: Not a quasi-neuroleptic. *British Journal of Psychiatry, 188*, 107–108.

Blackburn, I. M., & Twaddle, V. (1996). *Cognitive therapy in action.* London, UK: Souvenir Press.

Boydell, J., van Os, J., McKenzie, K., Allardyce, J., Goel, R., McCreadie, R. G., & Murray, R. M. (2001). Incidence of schizophrenia in ethnic minorities in London: Ecological study into interactions with environment. *BMJ, 323*, 1336.

Cochrane, R., & Sashidharan, S. P. (1996). Mental health and ethnic minorities: A review of the literature and implications for services. In *Ethnicity and health* (pp. 105–126). CRD Report No. 5. York, UK: University of York.

Coltheart, M., Longdon, R., & McKay, R. (2010). Delusional belief. *Annual Review of Psychology, 62,* 271–298.

Corcoran, R., & Frith, C. (2003). Autobiographical memory and theory of mind: Evidence of a relationship in schizophrenia. *Psychological Medicine, 33,* 897–905.

Corcoran, R., Frith, C. D., & Mercer, G. (1995). Schizophrenia, symptomatology and social inference: Investigating "theory of mind" in people with schizophrenia. *Psychological Medicine, 26,* 521–530.

de Girolamo, G. (1996). WHO studies on schizophrenia: An overview of the results and their implications for the understanding of the disorder. *Psychotherapy Patient, 9*(3/4), 213–231.

Dugas, M. J., & Robichaud, M. (2007). *Cognitive behavioural treatment for generalized anxiety disorder: From science to practice.* New York, NY: Routledge.

Dunn, J., & Fahy, T. A. (1990). Police admissions to a psychiatric hospital. Demographic and clinical differences between ethnic groups. *British Journal of Psychiatry, 156,* 373–378.

Fearon, P., Kirkbridge, J. B., Dazzan, P., Morgan, C., Morgan, K., Lloyd, T., ... Murray, R. M. (2006). Incidence of schizophrenia and other psychoses in ethnic minority groups: Results from the MRC AESOP Study. *Psychological Medicine, 26,* 1–10.

Fernando, S. (1988). *Race and culture in psychiatry.* London, UK: Billings and Sons Ltd.

Freeman, D., & Garety, P. A. (2004). *Paranoia: The psychology of persecutory delusions.* Hove, UK: Psychology Press.

Freeman, D., Garety, P. A., Fowler, D., Kuipers, E., Beddington, P. E., & Dunn, G. (2004). Why do people with delusions fail to choose more realistic explanations for their experiences? An empirical investigation. *Journal of Consulting and Clinical Psychology, 72,* 671–680.

Freeman, D., Garety, P. A., Kuipers, E., Fowler, D., & Beddington, P. (2002). A cognitive model of persecutory delusions. *British Journal of Clinical Psychology,* 41:331–347.

Frith, C., & Corcoran, R. (1996) Exploring theory of mind in people with schizophrenia. *Psychological Medicine, 26,* 521–530.

Frith, C. D. (1992). *The cognitive neuropsychology of schizophrenia.* Lawrence Erlbaum Associates, Hove, UK.

Fuchs, T. (1999). Life events in late paraphrenia and depression. *Psychopathology, 32,* 60–69.

Garety, P. A., & Freeman, D. (1999). Cognitive approaches to delusions: A critical review of theories and evidence. *British Journal of Clinical Psychology, 38,* 113–154.

Garety, P. A., & Hemsley, D. R. (1994). *Delusions: Investigations into the psychology of delusional reasoning.* London, UK: Oxford University Press.

Garety, P. A., Hemsley, D. R., & Wessely, S. (1991). Reasoning in deluded schizophrenic and paranoid patients: Biases in performance on a probabilistic inference task. *The Journal of Nervous and Mental Disease, 179,* 194–258.

Garety, P. A., Kuipers, E., Fowler, D., & Beddington, P. (2001). Theoretical paper: A cognitive model of the positive symptoms of psychosis. *Psychological Medicine, 31,* 189–195.

Gumley, A., & Schwannauer, M. (2006). *Staying well after psychosis.* Chichester, UK: John Wiley & Sons, Ltd.

Harris, T. (1987). Recent developments in the study of life events in relation to psychiatric and physical disorders. In B. Cooper (Ed.), *Psychiatric epidemiology: Progress and prospects* (pp. 81–102). London, UK: Croom-Helm.

Hassan, F. (2011). Paranoid delusions: A review of theoretical explanations. *ASEAN Journal of Psychiatry, 12*(1).

Health & Social Care Information Centre. (2009) Adult Psychiatric Morbidity in England - 2007, Results of a household survey http://www.hscic.gov.uk/pubs/psychiatricmorbidity07

Healthcare Commission 'Count Me in census' (2008). *Results of the 2008 national census of inpatients in mental health and learning disability services in England and Wales.* Commission for Healthcare Audit and Inspection, London, UK.

Iwamasa, G. Y. (1993). Asian Americans and cognitive behaviour therapy. *Behaviour Therapy, 16,* 233–235.

Jackson, J. S., Neighbors, H. W., Torres, M., Martin, L. A., Williams, D. R., & Baser, R. (2007). Disentangling mental health disparities: Use of mental health services and subjective satisfaction with treatment among Black Caribbean immigrants: Results from the National Survey of American Life. *American Journal of Public Health, 97*(1), 61–67.

Keating, F. (2007). *African and Caribbean men and mental health.* Better Health Briefing Paper 5. London, UK: Race Equality Foundation.

Keen, N. (2009, July). The voices tell me to do it…but are they all mouth and no trousers? *BABCP annual conference: Symposium.* Exeter, UK.

Kingdon, D., Selvareji, V., Kinoshita, Y., & Turkington, D. (2008). Destigmatising schizophrenia: Does changing the name reduce negative attitudes? *The Psychiatric Bulletin, 32,* 419–422.

Kingdon, D., & Turkington, D. (1991). Preliminary report: The use of cognitive behavioural therapy and a normalising rationale in schizophrenia. *Journal of Nervous & Mental Disease, 179,* 207–211.

Kingdon, D., & Turkington, D. (2005). *Cognitive therapy of schizophrenia.* New York, NY: Guilford Press.

Kirkbride, J. B., Fearon, P., Morgan, C., Dazzan, P., Morgan, K., Tarrant, J., … Jones, P. B. (2006). Heterogeneity in incidence rates of schizophrenia and other psychotic syndromes: Findings from the 3-Center AESOP Study. *Archives of General Psychiatry, 63*(3), 250–258.

Kluckhohn, C., & Murry, H. A. (1953). Personality formation: The determinants. In C. Kluckhohn & H. A. Murray (Eds.), *Personality in nature, society and culture* (pp. 35–48). New York, NY: Knopf.

Laungani, P. (2004). *Asian perspectives in counselling and psychotherapy.* New York, NY, Brunner-Routledge.

Leff, J., Sartorius, N., Jablensky, A., Korten, A., & Ernberg, G. (1992). The international pilot study of schizophrenia: Five year follow up findings. *Psychological Medicine, 22,* 131–145.

Lennox, B. R., Bert, S., Park, G., Jones, P. B., & Morris, P. G. (1999). Spatial and temporal mapping of the neural activity associated with auditory hallucinations. *The Lancet, 353,* 644.

Lewis, A. (1965). Chairman's opening remarks. In A. V. S. De Rueck, & R. Porter (Eds.), *Transcultural psychiatry* (pp. 1–3). London, UK: Churchill. From Fernando, S. (1991). *Mental health, race and culture.* London, UK: Mind Publication, Macmillan Press.

Li, Z., Guo, Z., Wang, N., Xu, Z., Qu, Y., Wang, X., Sun. J., Yan, L., Ng, R., Turkington, D., & Kingdon, D. Cognitive-Behavioural Therapy for Patients with Schizophrenia: A Multicenter Randomised Controlled Trial in Beijing, China. (Under review).

Maher, B. (1988). Anomalous experience and delusional thinking. The logic of explanations. In T. Ottmanns & B. Maher (Eds.), *Delusional beliefs*. New York, NY: John Wiley & Sons, Inc.

Malik, N., Kingdon, D., Pelton, J., & Turkington, D. (2009). Effectiveness of brief cognitive behavioural therapy for schizophrenia delivered by mental health nurses: Relapse and recovery at 24 months. *The Journal of Clinical Psychology*, 70(2), 201–207.

Mirowsky, J., & Ross, C. (1983). Paranoia and the structure of powerlessness. *American Sociological Review*, 48(2), 228–239.

Morrison, A. P. (2001). The interpretation of intrusions in psychosis: An integrative cognitive approach to hallucinations and delusions. *Behavioural and Cognitive Psychotherapy*, 29, 257–276.

Morrison, A. P., Hutton, P., Wardle, M., Spencer, H., Barratt, S., Brabban, A., … Turkington, D. (2012). Cognitive therapy for people with a schizophrenia spectrum diagnosis not taking antipsychotic medication: An exploratory trial. *Psychological Medicine*, 42, 1049–1056.

Morrison, A. P., Turkington, D., Pyle, M., Spencer, H., Brabban, A., Dunn, G., Christodoulides, T., Dudley, R., Chapman, N., Callcott, P., Grace, T., Lumley, V., Drage, L., Tully, S., Irving, K., Cummings, A., Byrne, R., Davies, L. M., Hutton, P. (2014). Cognitive therapy for people with a schizophrenia spectrum disorders not taking antipsychotic drugs: A single-blind randomised controlled trial. *The Lancet*, 383 (9926)1395–1403.

Munoz, R. F., & Mendelson, T. (2005). Toward evidence based interventions for diverse populations: The San Francisco General Hospital prevention and treatment manuals. *Journal of Consulting and Clinical Psychology*, 73, 790–799.

Murray, R., Jones, P. B., Susser, E., van Os, J., & Cannon, M. (Eds.). (2003). *The epidemiology of schizophrenia*. Cambridge, UK: Cambridge University Press.

National Institute for Health and Care Excellence (NICE). (2014 February). *Psychosis and schizophrenia in adults: Treatment and management* (Clinical guidelines, CG178), London, UK.

Nazroo, Y. (1997). *Ethnicity and mental health*. London, UK: Policy Studies Institute.

Nelson, H. E. (1997). *Cognitive behavioral therapy with schizophrenia*. Cheltenham, UK: Stanley Thorne.

National Institute for Mental Health (NIHME). (2004). *Celebrating our cultures: Guidelines for mental health promotion with the South Asian Community*. Gateway Reference: 2560. Leeds, UK: Author.

Nuechterlein, K. H., Dawson, M. E., Ventura, J., Gitlin, M., Subotnik, K. L., Snyder, K. S., … Bartzokis, G. (1994). The vulnerability-stress model of schizophrenic relapse: A longitudinal study. *Acta Psychiatrica Scandinavica. Supplementum*, 382, 58–64.

Owusu-Bempah, K. (2002). Culture, self and cross-ethnic therapy. In B. Mason, & A. Sawyer (Eds.), *Exploring the unsaid: Creativity, risks and dilemmas in working cross-culturally*. London, UK: Karnac.

Papageorgiou, C., & Wells, A. (2003). An empirical test of a clinical metacognitive model of rumination and depression. *Cognitive Therapy and Research*, 27(3), 261–273.

Read, J., van Os, J., Morrison, A. P., & Ross, C. A. (2005). Childhood trauma, psychosis and schizophrenia: A literature review with theoretical and clinical implications. *Acta Psychiatrica Scandinavica*, 112, 330–350.

Sanjuan, J., Molto, M. D., & Tolosa, A. (2013). Candidate genes involved in the expression of psychotic symptoms. In R. Jardri, A. Cachia, P. Thomas, & D. Pins (Eds.), *The neuroscience of hallucinations*. New York, NY: Springer.

Sashidharan, S. P. (1989). Race and mental health 2: Schizophrenic or just black? *Community Care, 783*, 14–15.

Selten, J. P., Slaets, J. P., & Kahn, R. (1997). Schizophrenia in Surinamese and Dutch Antillean immigrants to the Netherlands: Evidence of an increased incidence. *Psychological Medicine, 27*, 807–811.

Tarrier, N., Harwood, S., & Yussof, L. (1990). Coping strategy enhancement (CSE): A method of treating residual schizophrenic symptoms. *Behavioural Psychotherapy, 18*, 643–662.

Thomas, A., & Sillen, S. (1972). *Racism and psychiatry*. New York, NY: Brunner/Mazel. From Fernando, S. (1991). Mental health, race and culture. London, UK: Mind Publication, Macmillan Press.

Turkington, D., Kingdon, D., & Weiden, P. J. (2006). Cognitive behaviour therapy for schizophrenia. *American Journal of Schizophrenia, 163*, 365–373.

Van Os, J. Does the urban environment cause psychosis? (2004) *British Journal of Psychiatry 184*, 287–288.

Warner, R. (2000). *The environment of schizophrenia*. London, UK: Routledge.

Williams, M. W., Foo, H. K., & Haarhoff, B. (2006). Cultural considerations in using cognitive behaviour therapy with Chinese people: A case study of an elderly Chinese woman with generalised anxiety disorder. *New Zealand Journal of Psychology, 35*(3), 153–162.

Zubin, J., & Spring, B. (1977). Vulnerability: A new view on schizophrenia. *Journal of Abnormal Psychology, 86*, 103–126.

9

Depression: Cultural Aspects of Presentation and Adaptations to Treatment

There are many excellent texts on CBT for depression, and most cognitive thera-pists receive extensive training in this area prior to accreditation by the relevant professional bodies (e.g. Academy of Cognitive Therapy, British Association for Behavioural and Cognitive Psychotherapies). However, cultural adaptation of CBT to diverse cultures is not always integrated in this training, and so this chapter reviews relevant research and good practice. General principles have been laid out previously, so here, we will provide information on specific adaptations. This chapter discusses theoretical and practical issues which necessitate modification of approaches affecting engagement and therapy in the management of depres-sion in a multicultural context.

There are limited research on CBT specifically for non-white populations and just one randomized controlled trial outside the West in which CBT was used to treat depression (Wong, 2008). There are other studies which have used compo-nents of CBT as part of a psychological intervention (Araya et al., 2003; Sumathipala, Hewege, Hanwella, & Mann, 2000). Research on non-white clients in the West has mainly been carried out in the United States. Ancis (2004) has described culturally responsive interventions, while Hays and Iwamasa (2006) have described CBT for different cultural groups in the United States. Other authors (Barrera & Castro, 2006; Hwang, 2006; Lau, 2006; Tseng, 2004) have provided guidelines or frameworks for developing culturally sensitive interven-tions for clients, and we have discussed these in Chapter 2. Guidelines suggested by Tseng (2004) and Hwang (2006) refer to Chinese American clients. Kohn, Oden, Munoz, Robinson, and Leavitt (2002) have described adapted CBT for depressed African American women. How much clients of diverse cultures living

Cultural Adaptation of CBT for Serious Mental Illness: A Guide for Training and Practice, First Edition. Shanaya Rathod, David Kingdon, Narsimha Pinninti, Douglas Turkington, and Peter Phiri.

in the West might differ from those living in their country of origin has not been formerly investigated although theoretical frameworks describing acculturation have been described (see Chapter 3). Our group has published qualitative and quantitative work on CBT in black and minority ethnic groups in the United Kingdom, China, and Pakistan, and this has been referred to previously and will also be in this chapter.

The relevance of social factors and context is well established in the genesis of depression as we have discussed in Chapter 3. From a CBT perspective, thoughts about specific events shape feelings and behaviour – while some events are universal, the distinct nature of key culturally determined factors needs to be taken into account. As an example, social factors associated with depression in Pakistan (Javed & Mirza, 1992; Mirza & Jenkins, 2004) were found to include lack of an intimate, confiding relationship – as has been found in the white populations (Roy, 1988). Another study (Husain, Creed, & Tomenson, 2000) found severe financial and housing difficulties, large number of children, and low educational level to be particularly closely associated with depression – again similar to in white groups. More specifically, Rabbani and Raja (2000) found that women in the older age group in Pakistan and those with longer duration of marriage are more likely to be mentally distressed. Arguments with husband or in-laws, husband's unemployment and therefore not having a permanent source of income, and lack of autonomy in making decisions significantly contributed to mental illness. Other studies from Pakistan (Husain, Chaudhry, Afridi, Tomenson, & Creed, 2007; Husain, Gater, Tomenson, & Creed, 2004) found the following factors to be associated with anxiety and depression: low educational status, not having a confidant, having four or more children, being older, not being married, living in a house with more than three people per room, and housing and financial difficulties. A study of upper- and upper-middle-class urban population (Niaz, Izhar, & Bhatti, 2004) in Pakistan found that depression in single women was associated with parental conflicts (4.3%), conflicts with boyfriends (3.3%), adjustment problems (2.3%), and father's alcohol abuse, whereas in married women, it was associated with marital conflicts (31%), bereavement (9.8%), domestic violence (3.6%), work stress (3.2%), daughter's marriage (1.3%), and traumatic experiences (7%). There is evidence that South Asian women living in the United Kingdom, particularly of Muslim family origins, have a higher prevalence of depression, suicide, and self-harm than white women. Research indicates that British Pakistani women with depression lack social support and experience marked difficulties particularly in marital and close relationships (Gater et al., 2009). They may also lack fluency in English and the resources to obtain help.

Often, cultural differences in parenting can have an impact on how people cope with distress, identify themselves, and interact in their social surroundings. Family stress and authoritative parenting styles have been found as significant predictors of depressive symptom expression (Diaz, 2009). In Denmark, Hendin (1964) noted that guilt arousal was the major disciplinary technique employed by Danish mothers to control aggression, resulting in strong dependency needs in their sons.

This marked dependency has been noted as the root of depression and suicidality after adult experiences of loss or separation. Reunion fantasies with lost loved ones have been common in those committing suicide. In Sweden, pressure on children to succeed has been linked to depression (Durrant, 1996). Similarly, many Asian families have academic expectations of their children, and when these expectations are not met, it can lead to symptoms of anxiety or depression (Lee, 1997). Rickel, Williams, and Loigman (1988) reported that African American mothers can exercise high levels of behavioural control and exhibit a stricter parenting style than do Caucasian mothers and this may be an attempt to mediate between their children and a society that is perceived to be racist and discriminatory. Cohesive families are regarded as a resource protecting against distress in adolescents (Harris & Molock, 2000), and adolescents from communal cultures such as Asian Americans have been found to value well-being of others which is protective in depression (Lee, 1997).

So while some social factors may be universally associated with depression, specific factors (including protective factors) may be important in some cultures over and above others, and these may differ from people from other cultural backgrounds in their places of origin or in adopted environments. Community and faith leaders or representatives of their communities can provide indications of key issues, which can then be used in recognizing these factors – and their significance – when they emerge in therapy. A collaborative, receptive style of working can ensure that the issues are sensitively and appropriately managed.

Philosophical Orientation and Practical Considerations

CBT involves exploration and attempts to modify dysfunctional assumptions. People with depression and anxiety usually have beliefs towards self, others, and the world that are unhelpful. Such core beliefs, underlying assumptions, and even the content of automatic thoughts might vary with culture (Padesky & Greenberger, 1995) as we have discussed in Chapter 2. Tam and Wong (2007) from Hong Kong looked into dysfunctional attitudes of depressed Chinese clients and found 10 domains; (1) vulnerability, (2) need for approval, (3) roles of performance within family hierarchy, (4) familial harmony, (5) relational harmony, (6) imperatives, (7) fate, (8) face, (9) fairness, and (10) success–perfectionism. The most dominating themes were 'vulnerability' and 'need for approval.' Role performance within family, familial harmony, fate, face, and fairness were described as culture-specific themes.

It has been suggested (Laungani, 2004) that there are four core value dimensions that distinguish Western culture from the Asian culture. Although not entirely dichotomous, these can be considered as (a) individualism–communalism, (b) cognitivism–emotionalism, (c) free will–determinism, and (d) materialism–spiritualism. It is postulated that Asians are more likely to be community oriented, to make less use of a reasoning approach, to be inclined towards spiritual explanations, and to be prone to a deterministic point of view of life. An emotional approach towards problem solving, for example, not only affects how people cope with their emotional and day-to-day difficulties but also the long-term development and maintenance of problems. It is also relevant to how people communicate with each other especially during a conflict. Similarly, it has been suggested that Western societies are work and activity centred, while Asian societies are relationship centred (Pande, 1968). This has important implications in delivering therapy in that the therapy may need to involve family members as well. The notion of the 'script of life' being already written has enormous implications. Spiritual development is an important part of many Asian cultures (Laungani, 2004), and discovery of the self and self-awareness is a vital part of the spiritual development. This world view can affect life in many ways, starting from the help-seeking behaviours to the way people harbour their feelings of guilt and shame as discussed in Chapter 3. Buddhism on the other hand takes a non-linear view of the life. It is possible that the Western concepts of psychotherapy, for example, taking responsibility for one's own life experiences, might cause conflict in Asian clients.

One of the features of most Asian cultures is the importance of social hierarchies (Laungani, 2004), often based on cast, sect, race, language, or even colour, thereby conferring certain advantages and disadvantages to people from some groups. It can also lead to the ideas of purity, pollution, and genetic superiority of the races and the resultant identity. The implications of these beliefs are significant when coping with stress and distress or issues of self-esteem and assertiveness. The hierarchies are sometimes reflected in how Asian clients see their therapists in a respectful position and also imply that the therapist cannot go wrong. But on the other hand it could also be a disadvantage for a therapist from the same culture. The knowledge can however be used by therapists to the client's advantage.

Attitudes people hold towards health and the health systems affect their health-seeking behaviours as discussed in Chapter 3. It is common for Asian clients to see more than one doctor for a problem (Laungani, 2004). Asian clients may tend to look for cures – it is common for clients to say things like *doctor give me a medicine which will eradicate the illness at its roots*. Such attitudes obviously leave them open to exploitation by some faith healers as well as health professionals. But more importantly, it has implications for follow-up in psychotherapy. However, if Asian models of health-seeking pathways follow Asian models of spiritual leadership – the concept of guru or pir, who is followed throughout one's lifetime – it is possible that clients might go to their therapists for the reasons of faith rather than reason. So if the client is engaged by the therapist, they might follow advice more vigorously. Common strategies to treat and reduce mental health problems in Asia include advice from religious leaders or faith healers and religious activities, like saying prayers; going to religious places, pilgrimage, etc.; or even marriage. This knowledge allows therapists to accept that the client may seek support from different sources in addition to therapy.

But the literature in this area is full of ambiguities and is based on observations rather than empirical evidence. For example, it has been suggested that Asian clients prefer a more structured and directive approach (Iwmasa, 1993). They may not feel very comfortable in discussing ideas with the therapist who is trying to ask for their opinion and might even develop serious doubts about his/hers competence. Some authors have suggested that Asian clients might use an emotional approach in solving their problems, while others say that Asian clients like focusing on thoughts rather than emotions. Sue and Zane (1987) have proposed that Asian clients find it helpful if the presenting problem is addressed directly and some progress is evident in the first session. This relates to the expectation of cure.

Traditional healing practices

In a research in Pakistan (Naeem, Gobbi, Kingdon, & Ayub, 2012), psychologists who were interviewed felt that seeing traditional healers (e.g. faith healers) causes hindrances in therapy. However, this was not confirmed during interviews with the clients as none of the clients admitted to seeing a traditional healer! However, this seemed in part due to client's fear that psychologists and doctors do not want to hear about traditional healers, rather than due to an actual lack of contact. Informal discussions with mental health professionals did indeed confirm this, that they do not like involvement of traditional healers. While there are stories of negative outcomes for clients by the traditional healers, there are more success stories. Our discussions also revealed that people follow traditional healers faithfully (in the literal sense of the words) for lives. The fact remains that the number of mental health professionals is too small to cope with psychiatric problems if the faith healers stop working and community support was taken away. It seems that at the moment two systems are operating parallel to each other in most parts of the world. How traditional systems of mental health support compete or complement newer 'evidence-based' practices remains an unanswered question but one that needs exploring.

> **Exercise:** Take a few minutes and think about your own views regarding traditional healing practices. Do you see them as conflicting or complementary? How does this influence your stance as a clinician?

Technical Adjustments and Theoretical Modifications

Engagement

The therapist–client relationship is the foundation on which the building of therapy is built irrespective of culture but may need to be developed in different ways. However, courtesy, careful listening, warmth, and genuineness are universal. Some cultures accept advice giving more readily. Cognitive therapy can be adapted to suit clients in this regard, and therapy can be delivered in a counselling/psycho-educational style while ensuring understanding and collaboration is occurring. Sometimes, clients may not express disagreement with the therapist due to respect but then express it in actions, for example, they might not turn up for the next appointment. It is the duty of the therapist to pay attention to these indications of lack of agreement and ideally pick them up before such ruptures of the relationship occur by noting changes in clients' body language and language and expression. We have discussed these issues in details earlier.

Structure and agenda of sessions

Cognitive therapy has been developed as a relatively short-term therapy. Sessions are structured with an agenda agreed at the start. This immediately raises issues around cultural expectations and norms; while such an approach may be very familiar and anticipated in high-income countries, it may be less familiar to clients and therapists elsewhere. Later in this chapter, we will discuss the case example of Banto. You will note after reading the example that the therapist had to adapt the agenda of the sessions to allow Banto to discuss her interpretation of the symptoms of somatization and therefore the therapy work started in later sessions. Similarly, in some situations, due to lack of resources, a well-established social security system, and poverty, improving daily functioning might be more important for the client than freedom from depression – although the interaction between the two remains important. This means therapists would need to focus on behavioural techniques to improve functioning like structured daily routine and tasks, which focus on mastery and pleasure. Indeed, psychologists have reported that clients in Pakistan find behavioural techniques especially useful and they use these techniques at the start of the session (Naeem et al., 2012).

Gender

Gender is of considerable significance in most communities as discussed in earlier chapters. Women may have differential dropout rates to men as in some areas of the world. Women are dependent on men to be brought to the hospitals. They may also have to seek permission from the man in the house. Men on the other hand can often travel more, are in control of finances, and may be more educated than women (Gater et al., 2010). Women however are more likely to suffer from depression and anxiety. Depression among women not only has negative effects on children but also the whole family. Including the accompanying person during the assessment and thereafter talking to him on how the mental health of the woman can have an effect on the health of the family might be useful in this regard. Domestic violence is also an unfortunate issue cross-culturally but may present in very different ways – or be particularly well concealed in some circumstances.

CBT involves work between sessions, assignments or homework, reading informational material, or writing diaries. These require reading and writing skills. In developing countries and immigrant communities, clients in younger age groups are tending to be better educated, and older clients are also educated at least in reading Holy Books, for example, Koran, and so can have basic literacy skills. But it is still common to come across clients, especially female clients, who are not literate or are unable to communicate in the language of the therapist. This needs to be sensitively assessed so that alternative methods can be used, for example, audiotapes and audio diaries (as cassette recorders are widely available), beads, counters, or symbols for writing diaries. Clients can be provided with audiotapes of therapy session, information, or assignments. Beads and counters are commonly used in, for example, Islamic cultures for repeating religious verses or words. Counters can be used to count thoughts. Help from a family member can be useful in this regard. Use of pictures and diagrams may also be helpful. Detailed recall can also be used to identify key issues – where literacy is an issue, clients have sometimes developed memorizing techniques to compensate, for example, for the inability to write down lists.

Interview process

It is always important to understand the client's frame of reference but particularly helpful in making cultural adaptations – and difficult if the therapist is from a very different background. Key questions around the client's philosophical orientation include the following: what do they think about their illness? What do they think is the cause of the illness and what can treat (heal) it? Do they know that non-medical treatments exist and do they feel that they might work? What is their model of illness? Is it biological, psychological, social, religious, or spiritual or related to some or each of these dimensions?

Clients may be unable to name an illness to describe their condition – in some languages, words used to name emotions may not exactly approximate to those usually used in CBT. Physical expressions may be used like 'weakness of brain or illness of brain, some sort of physical illness, illness of suffocation, illness of poor sleep and illness of tension.' Clients may describe problems in carrying out their daily activities, but may not be able to report stopping his or her duties or responsibilities. What clients think about the cause of depression has important implications in terms of not only the medical and psychological treatment but also with respect to compliance with treatment and follow-up. We have already discussed this in Chapter 3.

There may be issues around expectations in that clients from many cultures may expect medication as the main treatment or a brain test to find out the cause of their illness. Clients will use culturally accepted interventions, for example, 'dum' (blowing air with reading of holy verses), but may not admit to seeing a non-medical healer. While such interventions may not have the evidence base of Western psychological treatments, their continued use over many centuries indicates that they have value to people, and being able to convey to the client that you accept this – even if on this occasion they haven't been successful – can improve engagement and collaboration in therapy.

Working with emotional presentations

Clients in most cultures find it difficult to recognize moods and emotions. The word 'moody' is commonly used in many cultures to mean someone with emotional fluctuation, especially if angry or irritable. Emotional expression can vary in cultures as well, for example, public display of emotion and grief; sometimes wailing following death of a dear one is acceptable in many Asian cultures like Indian and Pakistani cultures. In fact, lack of such display is questioned by friends and family. Japanese on the other hand focus less on emotions and exhibit distress through difficulties in interpersonal relations (Marsella, Kinzie, & Gordon, 1973). It is therefore an important part of therapy to teach about emotions and their meaning using culturally relevant measures. Clients can be asked to measure their emotions using a visual analogue scale. For example, people usually use the example of rupee (which has 16 anas) in Pakistan and are asked to rate how sad they feel – where 0 ana is normal and 16 anas is very depressed (Table 9.1).

Clients with depression often present with diverse emotions, which can vary in their cultural acceptability, for example, guilt, anger, and shame. The therapist therefore needs to have some knowledge about management of different emotional issues to assist underlying depressive symptoms. Shame and guilt are important emotions in the lives of some people from Asian cultures. Shame can also lead to feelings of intense guilt. Shaming is seen as the most effective method of social control (Lewis, 1971). Speaking to an elder in a loud voice or even disagreeing with an elder and dressing in a particular way can be a sign of 'shamelessness.' Clients might feel ashamed of not being able to do what they are expected to do. Similarly, a family member might use shame to make the client do things. It may therefore be that in some circumstances, a 'normal' level of shame exists and therapeutic involvement is unnecessary or even to be avoided. Similarly, anger is

Table 9.1   Recognizing emotions.

These questions can help patients in recognizing their emotions by labelling them and also in differentiating one emotion from another. Ask the patient how he/she might feel when in these situations:

You had an accident
Someone shouted at you for no reason
You have lost your job
You are in your bed and you hear a noise on the roof
You have been caught while stealing from a shop
Your friend has told you off for no reasons
You have been offered a job
Your mother-in-law shouted at you

From Naeem, Ayub, McGuire, and Kingdon (2013). Reproduced with permission.

another emotion that needs considering within the context of Asian cultures. Anger might be due to a person's inability to express him-/herself. It can become common since the concept of 'respect of elders' means contradictory opinions are not expressed in situations of conflicts. We have discussed cultural betrayal and shame attached to it in Chapter 3. Finally, cultures with a strong religious component are likely to be associated with issues concerning sin and guilt.

Guilt is a common symptom of depression. It has been suggested that people from Western cultures, which are based on Christian religious traditions, might experience more guilt than other cultures. There is a lack of research studies comparing guilt among different cultures – however, at least in Muslim cultures, the feeling of guilt might be similar due to the similar concepts of sin. Clients with depression often feel guilty because of real or imagined mistakes or shortcomings. One common complaint is feeling guilty due to inability to perform one's role. This is often linked to expectation, pressure from families, and hence shame. Obsessional ruminations also commonly occur along with depression. These will be shaped by culture, for example, obsessive ruminations will often be of a religious nature, which inevitably lead to guilt. A common complaint by clients is of a feeling of being unclean: in Islamic culture – *napak* – there is also a religious aspect to this concept of cleanliness. Explanation regarding these symptoms can be of help. Clients need to be informed that as their depression improves, these thoughts tend to reduce and disappear. Informing clients that people do not have control over their thoughts can help. It is therefore not their responsibility if they have thoughts – which they feel might be punishable – and that the thoughts are not the same as actions. The hot cross bun linking thoughts, emotions, physiological reactions, and behaviours can be used to emphasize the point. Reattribution (develop a more reasonable and acceptable way of thinking) can then be used to develop further strategies. It can be difficult in some circumstances to judge, and it may be that intervention or lack of it is determined by whether these are simply thoughts or expressions as opposed to being contributors to significant distress (Table 9.2).

Self-harm in South Asian women is often a symptom of distress due to cultural factors rather than a personality disorder. Precipitants of self-harm include interpersonal disputes (Burke, 1976; Cooper et al., 2006); marital problems, arranged

Table 9.2 Cultural adaptation techniques when working with emotions.

Identify the core assumptions surrounding the emotion

Understand the cultural influence, that is, philosophical orientation and practical considerations

Help client to understand the formulation using hot cross bun technique

Use culture-congruent alternative explanations for reattribution

Use behavioural experiments to support strategies

Identify strengths

Use cognitive methods to develop coping and strategies that are culturally congruent like visiting temple/religious place marriages or rejections of arranged marriage proposals, and cultural conflict (Merril & Owens, 1986); or gender role expectations (Bhugra, Baldwin, & Desai, 1999). It is documented that South Asian women are at an increased risk of self-harm and their demographic characteristics, precipitating factors, and clinical management are different than whites (Husain, Waheed, & Husain, 2006). For instance, suicide may be permitted in Hindu religious scripts but is shameful among Chinese cultures and a sin among Samoans. Hindu mythology describes suicide in relation to honour when Lord Shiva's wife burnt herself alive following a dispute with her father, Daksha, regarding her husband's honour; in another example, the Hindu deity Sita, Lord Rama's wife, had to burn in fire – 'agnee pareeksha' – to prove her purity. Self-harm and suicide linked with 'honour' are known custom in South Asian countries; as an example, 'sati' has been a ritual that has been prevalent in India for generations – although now recognized as a criminal activity by law (Javed, 1996). This is a ritual where a woman is burnt alive upon her husband's death. Suicidal ideas or self-harm is not usually considered a mental illness and has been more acceptable to protect one's honour as described earlier, specially when the stigma of mental illness is so high and news would spread through the community 'grapevine.'

Suicidal thoughts and pathways can differ between subcultures of the same culture, and there may also be differences between individuals in how much they identify with cultural values. An example is the Maori view of suicide which can be different from non-Maoris and among Maori. Risk factors contributing to Maori suicide in addition to general factors often include negative impact of colonization. Conflict about cultural identity, and loss of identity, language, and land (Ihimaera & MacDonald, 2009). Samoans believe that only God has the right to give and take life, and therefore, there is a perception of stigma attached to the act and for the family (aiga). The importance of spirituality and its inclusion in therapy discussions along with a discussion of heritage as a strength is helpful in these cases (Faleafa, Lui, Afaaso, Tuipulotu, & Skipps-Patterson, 2007). Therapy needs adjustment accordingly to the views of the client in relation to their distress and behaviour of self-harm. The therapist should start with an understanding of how much the client identifies with their cultural beliefs and how this can be used as strength in therapy. Distress management and problem-solving techniques acknowledging the cultural beliefs can be helpful. Use of myths and mindfulness are also acceptable techniques as they resonate with cultural backgrounds in Eastern cultures. Work on behavioural assignments that may promote change.

Exercise: Think of a client from a different cultural background who you have seen or are seeing currently with thoughts of self-harm and suicide. Identify if there are any cultural issues/myths around their thinking. Find out more from your own research how these are associated. Using the adaptation framework, write a strategy to work with these thoughts.

Working with somatization

Therapists focus on the problems and symptoms which are prominent in the client's mind. This may be distress or depressive symptoms, but more commonly, in many cultures, it will be pain or fatigue. Primary presentation of physical symptoms of depression is very common in all cultures but disproportionately so in some, and the link between depression and sleeplessness, fatigue, and pain may be much less well recognized. If a client does not feel that the therapist is addressing their concerns, that is, keeps talking about depression rather than the pain and fatigue they experience, they may not return for therapy or engage effectively in it. This was an identified issue in a research in Pakistan where dropout rates from CBT sessions were very high and seemed to relate to clients finding that the therapist focus did not seem to be addressing their needs (Naeem et al., 2012). It may mean that explanation of the links between pain, fatigue, and depression need attention very early in therapy and demonstrations of how these interact should be provided. Explanation of how somatic symptoms develop from lifestyle and emotional issues may assist – ideally drawn out using Socratic questioning from the person affected, for example, *can we discuss the sort of experiences that can cause the pain you get or tend to make it worse?* Usually, this dialogue commences with a discussion of how pain can be caused by physical illness but can then be moved towards discussion of how pain can be caused by accidents, for example, twisting an ankle, and then on to pain from overuse, tension, and stress. For example, pain and tiredness from repeated or continuous use of muscles can cause discomfort and cramp and can then in turn be related to the muscular tension common in anxiety and depression. Similarly, the feeling of hopelessness and negativity from depression can take away the drive to do normal tasks and be manifest as low drive and fatigue (Table 9.3).

The therapist was able to discuss a number of cultural issues with Banto. This included her expectation that her son and daughter-in-law would look after her and her daughter-in-law would be subordinate to her. When Banto's health had

Table 9.3 Working with somatization.

Structure sessions to discuss the primary focus of distress while assessing underlying core assumptions

Understand the cultural influence, that is, philosophical orientation and practical considerations

Explain how somatic symptoms develop from lifestyle and emotional issues and draw links to clients' own stressors

Use examples to normalize, for example, pain from a fall or upset stomach from virus

Explore formulation with client using cultural explanations

Develop cognitive and behavioural strategies to work with symptoms

Case example

Banto, a 56-year-old Hindu woman, had been struggling with symptoms of depression for some time. She had been with her husband for 36 years, and the family had immigrated to the United Kingdom from India 30 years ago. She had raised three children and her youngest son had been living in their home with his wife. Banto did not get on well with her daughter-in-law, and this had created an unpleasant environment at home. Over time, her daughter-in-law stopped talking to her, but this meant that Banto felt excluded in her own home. She stopped helping with day-to-day chores and spent most of her day either in her bed or on the living room sofa. She lost weight and kept complaining that her *heart felt numb and was sinking.* Her husband took her to her general practitioner and the accident and emergency department of the general hospital on a number of occasions. All investigations including an ECG were normal. Banto's symptoms had been deteriorating. At their 10th visit to the accident and emergency department, it happened by chance that she was triaged by a nurse of Banto's background. Banto enjoyed speaking to her in Punjabi, a language they both knew. Banto used the same words in Punjabi, but this time, the nurse understood that in Punjab, a province in India, symptoms of anxiety were often expressed as 'sinking heart.' The nurse explored Banto's situation further and understood that Banto had been struggling with symptoms of anxiety and depression probably triggered by her family situation, but she herself thought that she had a heart condition and therefore kept presenting to the general hospital. A referral to psychiatric services was made.

Case discussion

This example highlights that symptoms of depression and anxiety can present as somatic symptoms and can often be difficult to recognize and treat. Banto received CBT from a therapist. For a number of sessions, the therapist did not challenge her main symptom of 'her sinking heart.' He worked around it and explored the impact of her symptoms on her life. He then explored her family situation. Once he had worked on a formulation with her, he was able to ask her questions like *how do you feel when your daughter in law ignores you* and *how do you feel every morning when your husband and son go to work.* Banto herself realized through the sessions that she had feelings of dread every morning at the prospect of being alone with her daughter-in-law in the house and being ignored. She realized that she suffered with symptoms of anxiety, which caused palpitations.

started deteriorating and the family thought she had a heart condition, she had been getting some attention from her family which propagated her sick role. Banto worked on a plan of coping strategies for when she experienced feelings of dread and graded task assignments with the therapist. The aim of the behavioural assignments was to socialize her into the community and reduce reliance on family using a step-by-step approach. This started with phone calls to her sister who lived close by and over time developed to visiting the local temple.

Working with self-esteem

Following a worldwide survey (Becker et al., 2014) of more than 5,000 teenagers and young adults, launched in 2008 and covering 19 countries in Eastern and Western Europe, the Middle East, South America, Africa, and Asia, researchers suggested that self-esteem is based in all cultures on four key factors: controlling one's life, doing one's duty, benefitting others, and achieving social status. The authors noted that the relative importance of each of these items for individual self-esteem varies between cultures. For example, participants in the survey who lived in cultural contexts that prized values such as individual freedom and leading a stimulating life (in Western Europe and certain regions of South America) were more likely to derive their self-esteem from the impression of controlling their lives. On the other hand, those living in cultures that valued conformity, tradition, and security (certain parts of the Middle East, Africa, and Asia) were comparatively more likely to base their self-esteem on the feeling of doing their duty. Many academics (Konrath, in press) define personal self-esteem as applying to individual characteristics and abilities, whereas collective self-esteem is a feeling of self-worth that is based on group memberships (e.g. family, occupation, gender). They therefore argue that even though people from collectivistic cultures have lower personal self-esteem, they do tend to have high collective self-esteem, and they also selectively self-enhance on collectively relevant attributes. Cultural orientation can predict self-esteem; for example, Tsai, Ying, and Lee (2001) reported that self-esteem was related to pride in Chinese culture for Chinese American women, whereas for Chinese American men, it was about proficiency in English and Chinese language.

In some cultures (e.g. Asian), girls are often treated as inferior and are socialized to put themselves last and view themselves as second to their brothers and subservient to their husbands, thus undermining their self-esteem. This can initiate a lifelong downward spiral of humiliation and a sense of self-worth around the men in the family. Adverse social experiences like discrimination, isolation, and racism then further impact on self-esteem. This may be another insult in a series of perceived disappointments in life leading to feelings of lack of achievement or being valued.

The therapist needs to identify the key cognitions that define the clients' self-esteem and the cultural influences in their perception. Normalization can be a helpful technique to avoid embarrassment for the client. Following an understanding of their philosophical orientation, level of acculturation, automatic thoughts, and assumptions related to self-esteem, the underlying schema should be explored with the client in the form of formulation. Some of the cultural influences can be subtle and may take some time to uncover. Identification of repetitive patterns linked to emotional distress and despondency can be helpful. For instance:

CLIENT: I will never be good enough to get a promotion.
THERAPIST: Can you help me understand this?
CLIENT: Every time I applied for a promotion, I was turned down, so I have not applied for 5 years.
THERAPIST: Can we discuss the times you applied, what happened, and what was the feedback?
CLIENT: Each time I was up against a white person and was not successful.
THERAPIST: I can understand that there are biases, but let us explore each occasion a bit more in detail to see what happened.

Reality testing, use of thought diary, and log of successes and achievements can be helpful techniques when addressing low self-esteem and helping the client in building a healthy self-concept through further reattribution. Behavioural change through building on strengths is helpful. Use of humour and examples from the clients own culture can help:

THERAPIST: So why did your parents expect you to look after your brother?
CLIENT: Because he was always special to them.
THERAPIST: Have you considered that they thought you were more able?
CLIENT: (Laughs...) Never thought of it like that!

Working with families

The number of nuclear families in the developing world is rising, especially in big cities. However, it is still common for people to live within the extended family. We have discussed in earlier chapters that the family is an important resource when considering therapy for all clients and can be used effectively to help them. Paradoxically, where people from migrant communities have left their families to come to higher-income countries, this can therefore be a major emotional and practical loss. The family can especially assist in the following areas:

• Information gathering
• Supporting the client (there is usually no support system from therapists after office hours)
• Reinforcing work done in therapy sessions in the short and long term
• Bringing the client back for follow-up

Family can be a cause of conflict and stress as well as a valuable resource to help and support the clients. Some conflict may be directly relevant to the client's problems as in any community, for example, arguments and disagreements involving them, ruptures of relationships, and separations. Family secrets may also exist and interfere by leading to the suppression of relevant information. Some families might discuss the secrets among themselves, but they might not be allowed to do so in the open – and there can be cultural influences on this. Secrets and expectations around them can especially concern family members who have been mentally ill. Sometimes, families hide clients with severe mental health problems even from their close relatives, leading to important implications for disclosure to therapists and for family and group interventions.

Often, clients talk freely only when they are seen on their own and may not express themselves when a family member is around. Ideally, the family needs to be involved from the start and when diagnosis, treatment options, and cognitive therapy are being discussed. You can discuss future involvement of the family and in particular which member of the family is going to attend the sessions in the future along with the client. This is a highly sensitive area and the therapist should be very careful in dealing with the family. In hierarchical family systems, there is usually one key decision maker in each family – often not the person accompanying the client who may younger and with better language fluency or able to interpret. Therapists should find out early in therapy who is the family's decision maker. Approaching the decision maker directly or through the family member accompanying the client can ensure that the family's key concerns are understood and cooperation is developed enabling future follow-up.

While it makes sense to involve the family members of the clients in therapy if the client and family are agreeable, at least one individual session relatively early on in therapy, with their confidentiality assured, is also needed. This can need very sensitive handling and issues such as the gender of the therapist can be relevant – it may be that offering a chaperone of the client's gender to be present can overcome objections. Explanation of why it is necessary needs to be carefully described; otherwise, the family may influence or simply withdraw the client from continuing therapy. An honest but acceptable reason is that seeing the client for an independent assessment is offered to all clients on the basis that, while the support may be helpful, sometimes people do express themselves differently if they are on their own. The independent session may only be for a few minutes to explore whether it is necessary for the client to be seen independently – and paradoxically, the more protest there is by the family members about the individual being seen alone, the more necessary it may be. But discussion to minimize their concerns is key to making therapeutic progress with the individual.

Working on communication and language

Clients with depression and anxiety often need help with communication and social skills. Their inability to manage conflicts at home and at work can be a possible source of anxiety and distress. It is therefore helpful for the clients and their families if they receive at least some information and advice on communication and social skills and simple tips on how to manage conflicts within their relationships, if this is a problem area. People are usually expressive and talking too much can be sometimes a problem. However, people generally do not take much interest in writing. This is evident when you are getting into a contract (e.g. a tailor, an electrician, or a plumber). It certainly has implications in terms of homework. Respect is an important part of most cultures but can vary in degree and expectations among different cultures, especially Asian cultures. Respect can sometimes mean that a son cannot disagree with his father or that an employee cannot express his opinion when their 'boss' is around. As a result, it leads to a triangulated approach to communication, often causing more misinterpretation and conflicts. Communication styles therefore differ across cultures, for example, expressing your opinion when talking to a senior or an elder, until and unless you are in agreement, is not seen as a positive value. This can cause issues in therapy where agreement rather than equal collaboration can occur – the client agrees with what is said or asked whether they agree or not leading to passive non-compliance ('forgetting homework') and lack of belief in models of illness being described. Communication may then need to ensure that closed questions are avoided (easily answered 'yes') and open questions, or techniques like role-play, which explore issues are used. Assertiveness may also be seen as inappropriate in dealing with conflict or disagreement – however, sometimes, there are culturally accepted ways of politely questioning seniors, for example, by prefacing any statement with apologies and self-deprecating statements of humility.

In Asian cultures, for example, good communicators use an apology technique. In this technique, the person begins the sentence with *with a big apology; I would like to seek your permission to disagree; if you allow me to express myself; with due respect I would like to say that my opinion is…* . People using this technique not only say this but will also look humble and lower their eyes. Clients can develop this through instruction or practice using role-play. Similarly, making a list of excuses rather than straight refusal as a starting point for learning to say no can be helpful.

Case example

Abdul, a 32-year-old man, lived with his parents and younger brother. He had an engineering degree but was working as a project manager in a small firm for 2 years. He presented with constant headache, anxiety, low mood, and disturbed sleep. He had been seen by two psychiatrists who prescribed him antidepressant medication. However, in spite of being on different antidepressants and anxiolytics as well as mood stabilizers and small doses of antipsychotics for 6 months, there was no change in symptoms. During the assessment sessions, it emerged that Abdul was not happy with his job.

He felt that his job was not up to his standard and that this could not help him to achieve his full potential in life. He had no friends left in the city and wanted to return to the big city where he had his university education. He felt that he will also have more opportunities and could work as an engineer. However, he could not talk to his father who was a strict and powerful man. When he talked to him for the first time 2 years ago about returning to big city, his father dismissed the idea.

The therapist helped Abdul in dealing with symptoms of anxiety and further probed into his conflicting views about going to the big city. Assertiveness training failed since Abdul was not ready to try any techniques. He felt guilty because his father had told him that it was not only against religion but also his family and cultural values to leave them and it will bring shame to his parents (even though one brother lived with parents). The therapist worked on his feelings of shame and guilt related to cultural and family values by exploring various scenarios with him and thereby allowing Abdul to consider options himself before referring the young man to a local faith healer (he was a retired teacher and the therapist had met him a few times before and had discussed the issue with him in detail). Meeting with the religious leader was helpful in clarifying his mind – he was told that a man is allowed to express his opinion and disagree with his parents, as long as he is not rude to them. He was also told that he has duties as well as rights as a son. Finally, Abdul was able to discuss the issue with his father, and in the end, they both agreed that it will be better for him to move to the city but to visit his parents regularly.

Psychological concepts are difficult to translate in some non-European languages. Psychologists in Southeast Asia said clients find it difficult to understand concepts of therapy, for example, cognitive errors. The first step in providing therapy in a non-English-speaking culture therefore may be the translation of terminology and reading material in that language. Translation using a focus group approach can be helpful, and clients find the colloquial expressions easy to understand when these are described along with examples from local people.

Working on coping strategies

Enhancing or sometimes even building new coping skills can be valuable to manage stress and depression. Common examples of such coping skills include talking to a friend, going out for a walk, saying prayers, going to mosque or temple, or reading a book. The range of successful coping skills varies widely, and clients may find it helpful to discuss what works for them (see Appendix 6). Sometimes, people can use alcohol or drugs to cope with problems, which provide a short-term relief, but in the long term, they can be dangerous and lead to conflict because of cultural prohibition. Mindfulness techniques have been derived from Eastern religions and traditions and so may be very relevant and acceptable. Evidence is developing that they can also be highly successful in managing and preventing relapse of depression.

Activity scheduling can be very helpful cross-culturally, as it is simple to explain and has a clear rationale and so can be used early in therapy. Tracking feelings of depression alongside activity can assist in exploring and combatting depressive passivity and inactivity. Exploring and explaining how depressed people tend to stop doing pleasurable activities can motivate, instill hope, and lead to increase in the weekly number of pleasurable activities (see Appendix 6).

Exercise: Look at and explore the environments that your service serves. What are the opportunities to develop coping strategies for minority cultural clients?

Conclusion

Culture influences the aetiology, course, and presentation of symptoms of depression. Some symptoms can easily be ignored if the therapist does not possess this knowledge. Culture also presents opportunities for recovery. It is therefore so important for all clinicians to understand the impact of culture and how to adapt stance and technique to work effectively with clients from minority cultures.

References

Ancis, J. (2004). *Culturally-responsive interventions: Innovative approaches to working with diverse populations.* New York, NY: Routledge.

Araya, R., Rojas, G., Fritsch, R., Gaete, J., Simon, G., & Peters, T. J. (2003). Treating depression in primary care in low-income women in Santiago, Chile: A randomised trial. *The Lancet, 361,* 995–1000.

Barrera, M., & Castro, F. (2006). A heuristic framework for the cultural adaptation of interventions. *Clinical Psychology: Science and Practice, 13,* 311–316.

Becker, M., Vignoles, V. L., Owe, E., Easterbrook, M., Brown, R., Smith, P. B., ... Koller, S. H. (2014). Cultural bases for self-evaluation: Seeing oneself positively in different cultural contexts. *Personality and Social Psychology Bulletin, 40*(5), 657–675. doi:10.1177/0146167214522836

Bhugra, D., Baldwin, D. S., & Desai, M. (1999). Attempted suicide in West London. I. Rates across ethnic communities. *Psychological Medicine, 29,* 1125–1130. doi:10.1017/S0033291799008910

Burke, A. W. (1976). Attempted suicide among Asian immigrants in Birmingham. *British Journal of Psychiatry, 128,* 528–533.

Cooper, J., Husain, N., Webb, R., Waheed, W., Kapur, N., Guthrie, E., & Appleby, L. (2006). Self-harm in the UK: Differences between South Asians and Whites in rates, characteristics, provision of service and repetition. *Social Psychiatry and Psychiatric Epidemiology, 41*(10), 782–788.

Diaz, D. M. V. (2009). *The relations among parenting style, parent–adolescent relationship, family stress, cultural context and depressive symptomatology among adolescent females* (Psychology Dissertations). Georgia State University Paper 60.

Durrant, J. (1996). The Swedish ban on corporal punishment: Its history and effects. In D. Frehesse, W. Horn, & K. Bussman (Eds.), *Family violence against children: A challenge for society*. New York, NY: Walter de Gruyter.

Faleafa, M., Lui, D., Afaaso, B., Tuipulotu, M., & Skipps-Patterson, S. (2007). *Paolo "O o'u Paolo out e malu ai" "It is my people that give me shelter": Embracing our Samoan communities. Suicide prevention for people working with Samoans in Niu Sila*. Auckland, New Zealand: Mental Health Foundation of New Zealand.

Gater, R., Tomenson, B., Percival, C., Chaudhry, N., Waheed, W., Dunn, G., … Creed, F. (2009). Persistent depressive disorders and social stress in people of Pakistani origin and white Europeans in UK. *Social Psychiatry and Psychiatric Epidemiology, 44*, 198–207.

Gater, R., Waheed, W., Husain, N., Tomenson, B., Asseem, S., & Creed, F. (2010). Social intervention for British Pakistani women with depression: Randomised controlled trial. *British Journal of Psychiatry, 197*, 227–233.

Harris, T. L., & Molock, S. D. (2000). Cultural orientation, family cohesion and family support in suicide ideation and depression among African American college students. *Suicide and Life Threatening Behaviour, 30*, 341–353.

Hays, P., & Iwamasa, G. (2006). *Culturally responsive cognitive behavioural therapy: Assessment, practice and supervision*. Washington, DC: American Psychological Association.

Hendin, H. (1964). *Suicide and Scandinavia*. New York, NY: Grune & Stratton.

Husain, M., Waheed, W., & Husain, N. (2006). Self-harm in British South Asian women: Psychosocial correlates and strategies for prevention. *Annals of General Psychiatry, 5*, 7.

Husain, N., Chaudhry, I. B., Afridi, M. A., Tomenson, B., & Creed, F. (2007). Life stress and depression in a tribal area of Pakistan. *British Journal of Psychiatry, 190*, 36–41.

Husain, N., Creed, F., & Tomenson, B. (2000). Depression and social stress in Pakistan. *Psychological Medicine, 30*(2), 395–402.

Husain, N., Gater, R., Tomenson, B., & Creed, F. (2004). Social factors associated with chronic depression among a population-based sample of women in rural Pakistan. *Social Psychiatry and Psychiatric Epidemiology, 39*(8), 618–624.

Hwang, W. (2006). Psychotherapy adaptation and modification framework: Applications for the Chinese Americans. *American Psychologist, 61*(7), 702–715.

Ihimaera, L., & MacDonald, P. (2009). *Te Whakauruora. Restoration of health: Maori suicide prevention resource*. Wellington, New Zealand: Ministry of Health.

Iwmasa, G. Y. (1993). Asian Americans and cognitive behaviour therapy. *Behaviour Therapist, 169*, 233–235.

Javed, M. (1996). Suicidal symptoms in depressed Pakistani clients. *Journal of the Pakistan Medical Association, 46*(4), 69–70.

Javed, M., & Mirza, T. (1992). Risk factors for depression. *Journal of the Pakistan Medical Association, 42*, 57–59.

Kohn, L., Oden, T., Munoz, R., Robinson, A., & Leavitt, D. (2002). Brief report: Adapted cognitive behavioral group therapy for depressed low-income African American Women. *Community Mental Health Journal, 38*(6), 497–504.

Konrath, S. (2012). Self-esteem, culturally defined. In *Cultural sociology of mental illness: An A-to-Z guide*. Sage.

Lau, A. (2006). Making the case for selective and directed adaptations of evidence based treatments. Examples from parent training. *Clinical Psychology: Science and Practice, 13*, 295–310.

Laungani, P. (2004). *Asian perspectives in counselling and psychotherapy*. New York, NY: Brunner-Routledge.

Lee, E. (Ed.). (1997). *Working with Asian Americans: A guide for clinicians*. New York, NY: Guilford Press.

Lewis, H. B. (1971). *Shame and guilt*. New York, NY: International Universities and Press.

Marsella, A., Kinzie, D., & Gordon, P. (1973). Ethnic variations in the expression of depression. *Journal of Cross-Cultural Psychology, 4*, 435–458.

Merril, J., & Owens, J. (1986). Ethnic differences in self-poisoning: A comparison of Asian and White groups. *British Journal of Psychiatry, 148*, 708–712.

Mirza, I., & Jenkins, R. (2004). Risk factors, prevalence, and treatment of anxiety and depressive disorders in Pakistan: Systematic review. *BMJ, 328*(7443), 794.

Naeem, F., Ayub, M., McGuire, N., & Kingdon, D. (2013). *Culturally adapted CBT (CaCBT) for depression*. Lahore, Pakistan: Pakistan Association of Cognitive Therapists.

Naeem, F., Gobbi, M., Kingdon, D., & Ayub, M. (2012). Views of depressed patients in Pakistan concerning their illness, its causes, and treatments. *Qualitative Health Research, 22*(8), 1083–1093. doi:10.1177/1049732312450212

Niaz, S., Izhar, N., & Bhatti, M. (2004). Anxiety and depression in pregnant women presenting in the OPD of a Teaching Hospital. *Pakistan Journal of Medical Sciences, 20*(2), 117–120.

Padesky, C., & Greenberger, D. (1995). *Clinician's guide to mind over mood*. New York, NY: Guilford Press.

Pande, S. (1968). The mystique of western psychotherapy: An eastern interpretation. *The Journal of Nervous and Mental Disease, 146*, 425–432.

Rabbani, F., & Raja, F. F. (2000). The minds of mothers: Maternal mental health in an urban squatter settlement of Karachi. *Journal of the Pakistan Medical Association, 50*(9), 306–312.

Rickel, A. U., Williams, D. L., & Loigman, G. A. (1988). Predictors of maternal child rearing practices: Implications for intervention. *Journal of Community Psychology, 16*, 32–40.

Roy, A. (1988). Vulnerability factors and depression in women. *British Journal of Psychiatry, 133*, 106–110.

Sue, S., & Zane, N. (1987). The role of culture and cultural techniques in psychotherapy: A critique and reformulation. *American Psychologist, 42*, 37–45.

Sumathipala, A., Hewege, S., Hanwella, R., & Mann, A. H. (2000). Randomized controlled trial of cognitive behaviour therapy for repeated consultations for medically unexplained complaints: A feasibility study in Sri Lanka. *Psychological Medicine, 30*(4), 747–757.

Tam, P. W. C., & Wong, D. F. K. (2007). Qualitative analysis of dysfunctional attitudes in Chinese persons suffering from depression. *Hong Kong Journal of Psychiatry, 17*, 109–114.

Tsai, J., Ying, Y., & Lee, P. (2001). Cultural predictors of self esteem: A study of Chinese American female and male young adults. *Cultural Diversity and Ethnic Minority Psychology, 7*(3), 284–297.

Tseng, W. (2004). Culture and psychotherapy: Asian perspectives. *International Journal of Mental Health, 13*, 151–161.

Wong, D. F. (2008). Cognitive behavioural treatment groups for people with chronic depression in Hong Kong: A randomised wait-list control design. *Depression and Anxiety, 25*(2), 142–148.

10

Bipolar Affective Disorder: Cultural Aspects of Presentation and Adaptations to Treatment

This chapter discusses background information about diagnosis, epidemiology, and symptoms relevant to management of mania in a multicultural context. It focuses on culture-specific work on engagement, symptom monitoring, interventions to deal with impulsivity, family work, and collaboration over medication issues and developing structure to the day.

Bipolar disorder (BD) remains among the 10 most disabling disorders according to the World Health Organization causing a significant amount of disability (0.93% of total). Lifetime prevalence is 1.3–1.65% and the suicide rate among the group is 10–20% (Alloy et al., 2005). The lifetime rates for major depression vary widely across countries, ranging from 1.5 cases per 100 adults in the sample in Taiwan to 19.0 cases per 100 adults in Beirut. By contrast, the lifetime rates of BD are more consistent across countries (0.3/100 in Taiwan to 1.5/100 in New Zealand); the sex ratios are nearly equal and the age at first onset is earlier (average, 6 years) than the onset of major depression. Less than half of those with lifetime BD received mental health treatment, particularly in low-income countries, where only 25.2% reported contact with the mental health system. The illness causes considerable distress to individuals through the direct effect of depressed mood and the more indirect effect of mania and hypomania on relationships, self-esteem, and social and financial circumstances. Caregivers report the most distressing aspects of behaviour to be hyperactivity, irritability, sadness, and withdrawal (Baldassano, 2006). Co-morbidity is very common and includes anxiety and substance abuse (Baldassano, 2006). Three-quarters meet the criteria for at least 1 other disorder, with anxiety disorders (particularly panic attacks) being the most common co-morbid condition. Family history is frequent. Cognitive

Cultural Adaptation of CBT for Serious Mental Illness: A Guide for Training and Practice,
First Edition. Shanaya Rathod, David Kingdon, Narsimha Pinninti, Douglas Turkington,
and Peter Phiri.
© 2015 John Wiley & Sons, Ltd. Published 2015 by John Wiley & Sons, Ltd.

impairment has been demonstrated when patients are euthymic increasing with the frequency of episodes (Martinez-Aran et al., 2004). The presentation is heavily influenced by cultural context and exuberant speech and behaviour, which is quite appropriate in one cultural setting and can be interpreted as mania in another. There are therefore key cultural issues in relation to diagnosis and management.

Philosophical Orientation and Practical Considerations

Diagnostic issues: The cultural context

Diagnostic ratings of patients are markedly affected by the raters cultural back ground (Mackin, Targum, Kalali, Rom, & Young, 2006). Videos of American patients with mania were rated quite differently by US, UK, and Indian psychiatrists. Alexithymia and cultural attitudes to elation might seem potentially relevant with more emotionally 'repressed' individuals and nationalities more likely to overreact with manic outbursts. However, there is little evidence for this, and national figures for BD simply suggest lower incidence rates in the developed world than elsewhere (World Health Organization Burden of Disease Project, 2002) and relatively little variation across the developed nations (Weissman et al., 1996) despite cultural differences. Presentation of manic symptoms especially disinhibition, for example, spending excessively, may not be diagnosed as an illness in people from non-white backgrounds but castigated as wilful behaviour and the criminal justice service involved.

The fifth edition of the *Diagnostic and Statistical Manual* describes very clear criteria for BD, but in practice, these have proved difficult to implement consistently and reliably. Diagnosis of bipolar I disorder is relatively straightforward where the criteria are consulted and adhered to. However, interpretation of the criteria for bipolar II has been much more problematic, and over-diagnosis is common with patients who might meet borderline personality disorder (BPD) or primary substance misuse criteria often included. This can be very understandable: Who wants to be diagnosed as having a 'personality disorder'? It is quite a derogatory term and an overgeneralization. However, the answer relates to reducing stigmatization and the misuse of language, dealt with by using more acceptable mutually agreed terms (e.g. complex PTSD or severe emotional difficulties (possibly qualified by 'rapid cycling')). It is not helpful to misdiagnose as this can lead to inappropriate medication usage and therapeutic intervention (e.g. dialectical behaviour therapy can be effective for BPD, but there is no evidence of its effectiveness in BD). **BPD** appears to be much less prevalent in some cultures, for example, in the Far East, for unclear reasons, and so it may well be that the difficulties in differential diagnosis will arise less.

There can also be a tendency to use BD instead of psychosis (e.g. schizophrenia) wherever possible, because of the perception that psychosis is a more serious long-term and intractable disorder. This is not necessarily the case although the term schizophrenia does seem to be much more stigmatizing than BD and replacement of it has been debated. There has already been a change made in Japan from schizophrenia to 'integration disorder' inspired by client and carer organization, and a similar change is being considered in South Korea.

The misdiagnosis of BD instead of substance misuse can also be problematic for similar reasons although the cause may be not be because of stigmatizing associations but because it can allow avoidance of dealing with the key problem, that is, substance misuse, and the need to manage it effectively. In some cultures, it may be more acceptable to have a diagnosis of BD than substance misuse and justify misuse of substances. The use of inappropriate medication and management approaches then compounds the problem. Conversely, cultural use of alcohol and drugs can complicate diagnosis as the interpretation of acceptable usage varies considerably in different settings. Cannabis use is positively endorsed, for example, by Rastafarians or accepted by some ethnic groups, for example, many British African Caribbean, in an equivalent way to the use by white populations of alcohol. Cross-cultural conflicts about drug use, for example, between clinician and client, can lead to increased agitation – on both sides – and behaviour which can be interpreted as hypomanic or even manic. Use of stimulants, such as amphetamines and cocaine, is however more likely to have a direct effect leading to manic behaviour, but negative interaction with others can then lead to persistence of agitated and overactive behaviour and, possibly, precipitation of enduring manic episodes. Resentment about prohibition of alcohol and drugs by others can also complicate, leading to conflict and agitation and non-cooperation with support and treatment. These issues were demonstrated in Leroy's case (see later).

The above issues have cultural dimensions, as there is a perception that BD has become a white middle-class/professionals disorder. Under-diagnosis may be occurring in other cultural groups although empirical evidence for this is very limited as discussed above.

Case example

Leroy spent his early years in Jamaica but then moved to the United Kingdom with his family when he was 9. His mother, to whom he was very close, unfortunately died when he was 16, and contact with his father was limited by the very long working hours that he did. He has two younger sisters who have over the years tried to keep some contact with him, but his extended family have remained in Jamaica and he has lost contact with them. He had troubled teenage years, getting into conflict with the police regularly and having some brief prison sentences. His presentation to mental health services occurred eventually when it was suspected that his behaviour might be a manifestation of BD although his use of illicit drugs made diagnosis difficult. He was assessed in a hospital – although occasionally getting hold of speed and cannabis, he was sufficiently free from their influence for a diagnosis of mania to be made as disinhibited and grandiose behaviour persisted. He spoke of having superior knowledge to hospital staff and powers to control the climate and financial flows on the stock market. He made a recovery from the initial episode but retained some grandiose ideas and disinhibition although interpretation of his behaviour could be difficult, for example, white neighbours complained that he would go to empty his bins in only his boxer shorts. Such behaviour might not be as unacceptable to his peer group. Some of his reactions were responses to overt racist statements and stigmatization, and some seemed – although interpretation was often difficult – to be perceived racism where behaviour, for example, aggressive outbursts, was unacceptable by any cultural norms. His use of drugs continued partly because he was vulnerable to exploitation by other drug users and dealers and also because his social support and network of friends were very limited. His cooperation with services and use of medication was poor, but over the years, relationships with an assertive outreach team who could spend time with him developing interests and contacts did improve his situation and reduce a pattern of repeated negative contacts with the police, failed accommodation placements, and admissions to hospital.

Case discussion

In this case, while Leroy did have a diagnosis of bipolar affective disorder, some of his behaviours and stressors were linked to the cultural context and therefore precipitated the illness. Recognition of symptoms patterns and stressors and managing the illness are key interventions in mania. Therefore, recognition of the cultural context is important in that respect.

Causation of BD and Culture

Current theories of the causation of BD have recently been summarized (Mansell, 2007), and a new enhanced model has been proposed: initial theories explained it as due to individuals being vulnerable because of more sensitive and reactive regulatory systems leading to more extreme mood variations. 'Goal-attainment life events' may be more likely to trigger this, resulting in increases in manic symptoms. Dysfunctional beliefs relating to extreme goal attainment, perfectionism, and need for approval may interact with these life events and further raise the risk of an episode. Disruption of circadian rhythms, that is, biological cycles governing sleep, activity levels, and other drives, has been thought to be relevant with stressful life events leading to elevated arousal and psychomotor agitation. The manic defence hypothesis has recently been revived with mania being seen as the process of trying to avoid the experience of depression. Both depressed and bipolar clients may have a similar ruminative style of coping with depression, but people with the latter also tend to employ the additional strategy of behavioural risk-taking contributing to the development of mania. Mansell's model (2007) considers attempts at affect regulation to be disturbed because of the multiple and conflicting extreme personal meanings that are given to internal states. They prompt exaggerated efforts to enhance or exert control over internal states, which paradoxically provoke further internal state changes, thereby feeding into a vicious cycle that can maintain or exacerbate symptoms.

Unfortunately, these theories currently seem more descriptive than explanatory. Individuals with BD are undoubtedly more sensitive to triggers which lead to swings into depression or mania, and disruption of sleep cycles interacts with, occurs as a result of, or exacerbates the swings. Frantic overactivity and distraction may certainly be a way of avoiding depression – and clients with mixed affective states frequently describe this. There is evidence of different personality attributes associated with BD than with depression alone, and this may be significant in the coping styles adopted to stress. Whether affect regulation is disturbed by extreme personal meanings given to internal states – and whether this is culturally influenced – remains to be demonstrated but, if so, would be a focus for cognitive interventions.

These theories have been and are being used to influence therapeutic strategies with, as described in the following, varying effectiveness.

Effectiveness of current interventions

Effective pharmacological and psychosocial interventions exist but they have been limited in impact. Patients with bipolar I disorder are symptomatically ill nearly half the time (Judd et al., 2002) and have a high probability of relapse; bipolar II disorder is more chronic, more depressive, and associated with more anxiety and emotional fluctuation between episodes than bipolar I (Keller, 2004). Adherence to medication is poor with 'non-compliance as much the norm as the exception'(Basco, Merlock, & McDonald, 2004). Psychosocial approaches have been developed which tend to focus on improving adherence and early intervention to prevent relapse (Scott, 2006). These include interpersonal and social rhythm (Frank et al., 2005) and family therapies (Miklowitz, George, Richards, Simoneau, & Suddath, 2003). Simon and colleagues (Simon, Ludman, Bauer, Unutzer, & Operskalski, 2006) used a systematic care programme and improved mania but not depression; however, adherence to the programme was a problem: 59% completed the first phase of five weekly group sessions and 51% the full

12 months. Cognitive behavioural therapy has been successful with a range of conditions and showed promise in early studies in BD (Lam et al., 2003; Scott, Garland, & Moorhead, 2001). It is well established in treating depression in unipolar disorder and, in some studies, has shown effects on depression in BD (Ball et al., 2006) with varying effects on mania (Lam et al., 2003). Early intervention strategies have had some success with mania but not with depression (Perry, Tarrier, Morriss, McCarthy, & Limb, 1999). Moreover, a large UK Medical Research Council-funded study of cognitive behavioural therapy gave very disappointing results with no demonstrable impact on depression or mania (Scott et al., 2006). Treatment therefore in practice remains predominantly psychopharmacological. Guidelines in the United States and United Kingdom primarily focus on this area with limited reference to psychological and social treatments (National Institute for Health and Care Excellence, 2006).

Rethinking psychological approaches to BD therefore needs to be considered particularly in relation to environmental and cultural circumstances. Currently, clinical interactions of psychiatrists, case managers, and psychologists with patients and caregivers draw upon the ways of working so far evaluated, to a lesser or greater extent, for example, by attempts to intervene early, stabilize social rhythms, and improve adherence to medication. Many relevant assumptions are made about bipolar affective disorder, and it is timely to explore and, where appropriate, challenge them. The concept of bipolar affective disorder in itself needs to be reconsidered, and management consequent on current approaches may even be counterproductive and impair collaboration with clients and their families. Alternative approaches are possible which could form the basis of future intervention strategies.

What can we conclude about the evidence base?

The evidence for effectiveness of cognitive therapy in BD therefore seems to be limited at the moment although there are clear support for relapse prevention work and family work and some support for stabilizing daily living patterns. Work on beliefs about BD holds promise not yet substantiated. There is an absence of work on the influence of culture on the use of CBT in this area. It is possible to extrapolate from other areas, for example, depression and psychosis, but it is important at this stage to progress cautiously while looking to new research to develop in this area in the future. Such research may be of help in the near future, but currently, there are few ongoing intervention studies, and therefore, treatment is based on general principles of good practice, for example, developing a strong therapeutic relationship, rather than clinical trial data. This means that the advice given in this chapter is drawn from experience and case study material rather that hard evidence about management of mania in general and in diverse population groups. However, there is a theoretical basis to a cognitive behavioural approach to BD. There are assumptions made about how BD develops and should be managed which are worth considering.

Assumptions underpinning the concept of bipolar affective disorder

BD is primarily a disorder of affect

While mood change is a component of BD, is it necessarily primary? Mood variation may be related to cyclothymia (cycling mood patterns) which commonly predates episodes (Howland & Thase, 1993). It has been described as a prodromal form of the illness, part of the pathological process, but it could equally be argued that it is simply a risk factor, as many with cyclothymia do not go on to develop frank BD (Howland & Thase, 1993) and therefore as a component of the individual's underlying temperament. Depression may, at least in part, be reactive to the consequences of manic episodes and negative perceptions of the illness. As depression is a common condition, it may also occur independently of the BD preceding or succeeding its diagnosis. In bipolar II, low self-esteem and chronic dysphoria (persistent low mood) may also contribute (as may primary substance misuse and BPD – as described earlier). Spiralling anxiety and frustration could be a factor in precipitation of mania. Elation, on the other hand, cannot be described in itself as an abnormality and indeed to most people is a desirable state (although fear of elation can emerge where it is seen as an indicator of incipient mania).

An alternative position to describing BD as primarily an affective disorder would be to focus on behaviour associated with BD as it coexists with and maybe primarily a disorder of impulse control (Moeller, Barratt, Dougherty, Schmitz, & Swann, 2001). Impulsivity is an important component of mania and forms a part of the diagnostic criteria for it. Habit and impulse disorders, separately described in DSM 5, may also be symptoms of mania, at least transiently. Impulsivity leads to the damaging behaviour that causes distress to caregivers and subsequently the individual themselves. Diagnosis of the disorder without the occurrence of damaging behaviour can occur, especially in bipolar II disorder, but this is unusual in bipolar I. Focusing management directly on avoiding damaging behaviour may be more acceptable to patients, albeit this requires impulse control, than attempts to control mood, especially elation. This may mean considering whether restricting the diagnosis of BD to those circumstances where damaging behaviour results rather than the current tendency for extending it, which has a dubious evidence base. The British Association of Psychopharmacology guidelines underline this despite recommending that prescribers should '...consider extrapolating the advice concerning bipolar I to bipolar II disorder, albeit in the absence of adequate evidence from clinical trials' (Goodwin & Consensus Group of the British Association for Psychopharmacology, 2003, p. 147). Bipolar II may certainly warrant intervention but with a focus on the treatment of depression, low self-esteem, substance abuse, and coping skills for emotional lability. A dual diagnosis programme for substance misuse and BD recently reported positive results for the former but not the latter (Weiss et al., 2007). Describing BD as primarily a disorder of impulse control therefore would be significant in refining diagnosis and may be of particular importance in management.

BD is a bipolar condition

Although the contrast between moods – elation at one pole and depression at another – seems self-evident, the classic pattern of discrete episodes of mania, cycling with euthymia, and then depression is relatively rare (Paykel, Abbott, Morriss, Hayhurst, & Scott, 2006). Episodes are frequently mixed and patients spend much of their time near the depressed pole at a syndromal or sub-syndromal symptom level with other moods, for example, irritability and anxiety, frequently occurring, alternatively or coexisting. Moreover, as previously mentioned, cyclothymia or, as Lange described back in 1939 (Lange, 1939), a cycloid type of temperament seems common. This also has implications for diagnosis and management as it would seem inappropriate to diagnose BD on the basis of previous cyclothymia and any attempts to moderate mood swings need to take into account, understand, and allow for these underlying personality characteristics.

Manic and hypomanic behaviour can be objectively defined

Disinhibition, overactivity, and irritability are subjective concepts which are judged very differently by individuals; social classes and, especially, cultures; and psychiatrists from different countries (Mackin et al., 2006). Clashes between different viewpoints are common in the diagnosis of mania and hypomania. This is especially difficult where these different perspectives involve close family members. Such concepts may be of very limited value in such instances, and reliance on the concept of damaging behaviour may be more reliable, if more extreme. It will still be the case that, for example, the balance between individual rights, other's rights, and the need of treatment will be very difficult to determine.

Elation, sleep disturbance, disinhibition, and overactivity are indicators of relapse

Early intervention strategies tend to target such occurrences (Perry et al., 1999) on the basis that these occurred at the time of the first and often subsequent relapses. Elation may be accompanied by impaired judgment – there is evidence that mild to moderate depression is most conducive to balanced decision making (Bentall, 2004). However, as described earlier, mood elevation may be a feature of the individual's temperament and one that is highly valued (Marlies, 2005). No one would advocate that individuals need to be in a constant state of mild depression to maximize the accuracy of their judgments. Is it any more reasonable to advocate mood control when elation is such a pleasurable state, although appropriate for individuals to take it into account in relation to impulse control?

Variation in sleep pattern is very common, easily reactive to life circumstances, and a very blunt indicator of relapse. Paradoxically, there is good evidence to suggest that sleep deprivation (Parekh et al., 1998) can produce transient increases in mood in unipolar and bipolar patients which can reinforce the attraction of missing sleep. On the other hand, sleep deprivation can lead to confusion, poor judgment, exhaustion, and psychosis. But at what point is it appropriate to intervene? The assumption that an inevitable spiral will develop may not be warranted, and cyclothymic individuals may have a predisposition to variability in their sleep patterns. Events out of the individual's control may disrupt sleep but compensatory strategies, for example, reduction in current commitments, may be possible. Attempting to impose an inflexible sleep pattern, for example, a certain number of hours each night, may paradoxically cause agitation and increased sleep deprivation. Trying to get to sleep can make it more difficult to do so although stepping back from continued activity and taking a period of relaxation may be possible. Disinhibition is a highly subjective judgment (except at the extremes), readily influenced by family and cultural norms, and so its role in early intervention and diagnosis is fraught with difficulties.

In themselves, therefore, these specific signs and symptoms may be simply an expression of the individual's personality, culture, and circumstances, not necessarily part of the chain of events leading to relapse. Describing them as such may become self-fulfilling by raising anxieties in caregivers and the individual. It could be argued that these patterns are identified by individuals themselves and caregivers as 'relapse signatures'; however, the evidence to support the intervention with them is limited and highly influenced by current psychoeducation practices.

Early intervention is appropriate
Early delivery of effective interventions, such as mood-stabilizing or antipsychotic medication, would seem self-evidently appropriate. However, this depends, as described earlier, on the targets selected as indicators of relapse and the objectives established. As described earlier, early intervention focused on mood deflation, reduction of activity, etc., has been limited in effect – some individuals may benefit from increased physical activity releasing tension and anxiety. Focusing on damage limitation might be much more productive in developing common goals and collaboration. Responses, which target the former indicators, may even be counterproductive leading to the individual perceiving this as 'preventing me being happy,' 'blocking my creativity,' and 'controlling me.' The increased frustration from such beliefs and impotency in reducing elation and overactivity may even contribute to arguments with caregivers – formal and informal – and subsequent damaging behaviour through individuals overreacting.

It is not reasonable to expect impulse control in hypomania or mania as it is biologically determined, and only medication and management within protective environments, for example, psychiatric wards, can be effective. The belief that BD is predominantly biologically determined is well established and forms the basis for current intervention strategies, both psychopharmacological and psychological including cognitive behavioural therapy (Basco & Rush, 1996). Because mania is perceived to be biological, impulses are implicitly, albeit wrongly, viewed as not in any way within the influence of the individual. The advantage to holding these beliefs is that the individual is considered to be less likely to blame themselves for the disorder when recovered and therefore less likely to become depressed. The disadvantage is that attempts to or expectations of control of such behaviour are abandoned or learning to control it assumed to be pointless. The belief that biologically determined disorders can only be influenced by biological methods is, of course, incorrect. We often use the analogy of 'stroke' (cardiovascular accidents) in relation to psychosis, but it also applies here. While these are incontrovertibly biological, nevertheless after initial management, it is nursing care, physiotherapy, and occupational therapy that are used to maximize function. Similarly with mania, coping strategies and impulse control are not excluded simply because of putative biological mechanisms. This can also apply to communication: encouragement to control the pressure of speech and clarify the meaning and connections between statements can allow negotiation and discussion to occur.

Abnormal behaviour is a manifestation of the 'manic defence'
Following from psychodynamic theorizing, mania has been conceptualized as a defence against poor self-esteem (Lyon, Startup, & Bentall, 1999). The idea that overly high mood might be a compensation for a reduction or existing low self-esteem and the striving involved to maintain it, through activation of underlying schemas related to feelings of inadequacy, increased irritation, and overactivity, seems to fit well with the clinical picture frequently seen. This especially presents when the individual in a manic episode abruptly dips down into depression and then frantically strives to pull himself out by overactivity and distraction. However, it has yet to be demonstrated that low self-esteem or negative cognition is such a trigger. There have been two studies investigating negative cognitions as a predictor of mania, with evidence for (Reilly-Harrington, Alloy, Fresco, & Whitehouse, 1999) and against (Johnson & Fingerhut, 2004). The difference found may be accounted for by the former using a broader bipolar spectrum group as compared to the latter who used bipolar I patients. Comparing bipolar with unipolar depression, the general finding is no difference (Alloy et al., 2005).

Other abnormal thought patterns in BD have been suggested for many years but proved difficult to isolate. Goal attainment as measured on the Dysfunctional Assumption Scale has been found to be elevated compared with a unipolar group (Lam, Wright, & Smith, 2004), but education levels were not controlled for. Similar reasons may account for 'striving for achievement goals' being linked with increased manic episodes (Lozano & Johnson, 2001). High energy and agitation may lead to an overly positive sense of self and thus elevations in mood and goal-directed behaviour (Mansell & Lam, 2003). Lam and colleagues describe 'a proportion of bipolar patients like being in a state of constant high arousal, positive mood and being behaviorally active – such patients perceive themselves to possess personal attributes associated with being mildly high and value these attributes as desirable – more persuasive, creative, dynamic, entertaining, outgoing and so on.' Then he describes this as aspiring to achieve a 'sense of hyper-positive self' and demonstrates that this group do not do well with cognitive therapy (Lam, Wright, & Sham, 2005). These are the characteristics which feature most in early intervention strategies and are therefore a target for reduction; their presence in abundance could be expected to be associated with poorer outcome, but if these are primary characteristics of personality and temperament, it may be that attempting to modify them is doomed to failure compounded by the conflict activated.

Personality differences have also been a focus of interest. Apart from cyclothymia discussed earlier, researchers reviewing personality characteristics of remitted bipolar patients compared with controls have either concluded that they are similar (Goodwin & Jameson, 1989) or have relatively minor differences from the general population. Reduced persistence with increased harm avoidance and reward dependence has been found (Osher, Cloninger, & Belmaker, 1996), but the authors concluded that the bipolar groups overlapped with the normal population. 'Novelty seeking' was not found to be associated with BD. It is associated with higher educational level, and it has been suggested that its persistence in the population may be derived from its association with creativity demonstrated in many individuals and families. Brothers and sisters of individuals with BD have been demonstrated to be more creative than the general population (Richards, Simoneau, Lunde, & Benet, 1988).

Life events are relevant in some way
While clinicians may take different viewpoints, the personal significance of life events is frequently presented by patients. However, the relevance of life events – environmental precipitants and, in particular, severe trauma such as child sexual abuse and discrimination – remains rather uncertain (Reilly-Harrington et al., 1999). Combination of life events and cognitive distortions may precipitate mania especially where social rhythm disturbance arises (Malkoff-Schwartz et al., 2000). Goal achievement events, for example, exams, with social rhythm disruption may predict mania in predisposed individuals. Child sexual abuse is certainly associated with hallucinations (Hammersley et al., 2003) but whether rates are higher than in the general population or other patient populations is unclear. Interaction with families does seem significant; relapse after an episode of mania occurs in over 90% of people in the subsequent 9-month follow-up period where marital conflict is present (Rosenfarb et al., 2001). Depression but not mania seems responsive to social support (Johnson, Winett, Meyer, Greenhouse, & Miller, 1999).

Technical Adjustments and Theoretical Modifications

A theoretically derived management approach using cognitive behavioural principles that is likely to be effective in BD in people from diverse cultures will consequently focus on:

• Establishing and maintaining engagement between and during any manic episodes
• Assessment which takes full account of cultural influences
• Work with families and the local community
• Work on stabilizing lifestyle
• Work in developing effective coping strategies (which will include use of medication)

- Developing strengths, for example, creativity and social skills
- Reducing the occurrence of behaviour which is damaging to the person's health, reputation, and social circumstances including financially
- Managing and minimizing depressive reactions to illness

Engagement

Establishing engagement with a person experiencing the effects of BD has many similarities to those which relate to any mental health problem including psychosis (see earlier). Cultural issues such as the level of personal disclosure by the therapist that is optimal and the degree or, perhaps, style of collaboration similarly need to be taken into account. People with BD tend to be more gregarious, and intelligence has been found to be higher than in the general population. This favours engagement occurring and in many ways can ease the initial process, provided that they are not currently manic. Establishing a good relationship before relapse can be valuable if such relapse occurs. This may therefore involve a bit more contact, in depth, between episodes in sharing experiences and understanding the person's background, philosophical orientation in relation to culture, current issues, and beliefs about BD.

During depressive episodes in BD, engagement can be impeded by the lack of drive, speech, or motivation accompanying them, but a calm, collaborative presence can enhance the process. This can be complicated if the depression is at part consequent on actions arising from a previous manic episode, for example, financial loss or damage to relationships or simply shame and regret. Working through these issues, problem solving, and putting in place safeguards for the future can provide purpose and hope. If the therapist/mental health worker was part of the care team when the manic episode occurred and damaging behaviour resulted, there can also be an undercurrent of blame towards them for allowing that damage to occur, even where they may not have been aware of the damage occurring, for example, spending, or able to intervene. If such concerns exist, discussion of them can minimize damage to the relationship by sharing of perceptions of what occurred and why actions were or were not taken. The issues of shame and guilt can be managed by recognized cognitive behavioural approaches as discussed in the previous chapter, and an 'illness model' can be relevant. While some degree of control can remain during manic episodes, it is nevertheless very clearly a disorder which seriously interferes with that control, and family, friends, and society in general, in most cultures, are now more accepting that mental health problems of this sort deserve compassion and understanding rather than condemnation and blame.

Engaging during manic episodes is critically important but often considered irrelevant because of their psychotic nature, that is, bizarre beliefs or over-talkativeness of the person. Often, it is assumed that the person is not in contact with reality and that how they are managed is virtually irrelevant to their future progress – the implicit belief is that medication will abort the episode eventually and then it's possible to re-engage and start work again. This is profoundly short sighted as people are very aware of the way they are treated when ill (as they will tell you afterwards), and if they are not taken seriously and there are no attempts made to communicate with them, this increases frustration and consequent agitation and outbursts. In people who already have experiences of discrimination due to their cultural background, this perception can become heightened when unwell, leading to future mistrust and feeling that they are not respected. Collaboration over issues such as problematic behaviour and medication is further affected, whereas friendly discussion can be highly effective in facilitating negotiation. People when they are manic can be very witty and amusing in their speech and have an infectious elation; positively responding and joking with them while gently helping them to avoid behaviours that cause them potential damage are engaging, can promote insight, and can reduce their frustration and substantially improve their cooperation – short and long term. In people who commonly mistrust the system, this may be a good opportunity to form a therapeutic relationship.

Engagement can inevitably be affected by the use of legal powers to detain patients in the hospital, but considering explanations, weighing up the reasons for and against the decision to detain with the person, and then, if necessary, 'agreeing to differ' can minimize agitation and resistance. Even where the mental health worker implicated in the detention remains involved with them in a caring capacity, for example, as a psychiatrist or nurse, it is usually possible to re-engage or maintain engagement. Where controls are in place in hospitals, for example, involving restrictions on leave outside hospital, there is then also an optimal pacing in lifting these restrictions, which reduces frustration while protecting them from negative consequences and maintaining long-term engagement. As we have already mentioned, people from some minority backgrounds have higher rates of detentions and involvement with the police. It is therefore an opportunity to develop and rebuild relationships.

Normalization has been used effectively in psychosis, and its place in BD has yet to be comprehensively explored. In some ways, denial of problems might be increased by an unsophisticated normalization approach – clients are continually stressing that they are 'normal' and it is usually others, family and mental health workers, who are disputing this. However, there is a sense in which it is 'normal' – in fact, desirable – to feel happy and even elated, and appearing to the client to discourage achieving such emotional states can be a source of significant conflict, which is certainly not desirable. Where problems arise, it is because behaviour becomes damaging to the individual and those around them – although here there is a major issue of interpretation determined within a family and cultural context. When does behaviour become embarrassing and disinhibited or when does spending become excessive, irresponsible, or reckless and disinhibited can be culturally determined. When is disagreement between the individual and others acceptable and determined by illness? The association of depression with mania is usually linked although there is evidence (cited by Mansell, 2007) that they may be independent phenomena. Depression is such a common experience that its frequent, though not inevitable, occurrence in people who have experienced mania may be more related to the adverse life events consequent on episodes of mania and the damaging effects on their lives than to an intrinsically lined process.

Assessment which takes full account of cultural influences

Assessment needs to be broad and holistic and, as discussed in previous chapters, needs to set the circumstances arising and leading to concern in a cultural context. The help of people who can interpret behaviour and statements in this context – including often the patient themselves – can make a substantial difference to developing effective care plans.

Whether behaviour is manic or, even more difficult, hypomanic is relative and substantially influenced by personality, family context, and broader cultural issues. Accounting for this is extremely important as disparities between what is an acceptable behaviour in one setting compared with another can be highly influential in determining whether someone is ill or not. Behaviour appropriate to the Mardi Gras or a New Year's Eve party would be seen as disinhibited and over-active in a quiet setting, where such exist, in the Midwest or countryside. This can be problematic where family culture clash, for example, the husband comes from one environment where louder, more disinhibited behaviour is the norm, while the wife comes from a quieter background where such behaviour is not viewed as acceptable. Opposites do sometimes attract, but the resultant clash of cultures can lead to frustration on both sides leading to increased animation in a partner, for example, the husband, while eliciting critical withdrawal in the wife. Complex issues of whether an illness is or is not present can then arise. Therapeutic advice around distancing or 'time out' with gradual rapprochement can be very appropriate – the danger is that such distancing involves admission to hospital and labelling of one member as 'ill' which can have major long-term consequences. Use of the symptom summary worksheet (Basco, 2006) can be useful in develop-ing a sense for the client and therapist as to what is culturally acceptable varia-tion. Use of this diary sheet allows clients to document different symptoms and their presentation when they are well, manic, or depressed.

Exercise: In a client with bipolar affective disorder, reflect on the cultural variations in presentation.

Work with families and the local community

The strongest evidence existing on effective treatment is from studies of family work. This is particularly relevant cross-culturally as family structures and enti-ties have been preserved, generally, in non-white compared to white cultural groups. In the latter, the family have been increasingly difficult to involve because of geographical and sometimes social distance. Some black and other ethnic communities have also seen family fragmentation with immigration, which can inevitably lead to limited family involvement. Work may be with parents and siblings and/or spouses and offspring. People with BD are relatively more likely to have found partners and have married than those with enduring psychosis because of more socially adapted personality attributes and because they have more periods when they have been free of symptoms. Local communities can also have a significant role in providing information to support assessment – by providing detail of times and behaviours which cause concern and then support thereafter. In many cultures, such support is expected and provided – and needs to be mobilized.

Family work may involve the whole family, with or without the person involved, or smaller groups, including simply the person with their partner or a key family member. The family may want to be seen separately, but in most non-white cultures, this is not expected although where a family group meets, in all cultures, the 'patient' can be spoken about as if they don't exist or certainly are not viewed as an active or a legitimate contributor. If manic or hypomanic, this can simply lead to arguments, shouting, or virtually unstoppable flow of speech. If depressed, they may simply be ignored. Involving the person in the conversation is essential to the degree that they can and wish to participate – although assertive chairing may be necessary to ensure each member who wants to contribute does so. In cultures where due to respect the client may normally feel unable to speak in front of elders, when in a hypomanic/manic state, this inhibition may be lost, leading to ruptures in relationships. The therapist may need to explain to the families that this behaviour could be illness related.

Examination of family values, support available, and acceptable behaviour can lead to better understanding and negotiation. Explanation of mental health systems, which may not be familiar cross-culturally, can reassure and lead to early and preventative intervention.

Work on stabilizing lifestyle

Work on social rhythms suggests that stabilization of patterns of sleep, eating, and activity can be beneficial. This is if the person is prepared to cooperate with this approach and maybe a half to a third are unfortunately not able to do so. Cultures differ in the degree to which routine is a part of everyday life – in Islamic culture, the call to prayer does provide such regularity which can be usefully followed to re-establish behavioural stability alongside the spiritual benefits that it may provide. Where someone is unemployed or in further education with relatively few set demands on their time, they have to consider imposing routines – although the very idea of something being forced upon them can be frustrating and often expressed in terms such as 'stifling my creativity.' It may go against their previous and well-established patterns or lack of patterns. The social rhythms proposed also tend to involve sleep at conventional times (11 or 12 at night), which may be a change in pattern from their 'normal' life prior to diagnosis of illness. This is

Table 10.1 Cultural adaptations to stabilizing and managing lifestyles.

1. Use established family and cultural structures to the day, for example, prayer times, family mealtimes
2. Use families and communities to support and plan activities, for example, work at a community centre
3. Use cultural beliefs around medication to improve adherence
4. Use cultural norms to discuss use of substances
5. Develop and discuss strengths based on cultural orientation
6. Use principles of Eastern philosophies to reduce stress – mindfulness

always worth examining in some detail; as this may be a distortion of what actually the case was or where very late nights occurred, these were transient and possibly early episodes of hypomania. In clients from different cultural settings that live in extended families, it may be easier to ensure basic structures like mealtimes, but conversely, disruption to routines due to the illness may upset others in the family.

Setting out a timetable can be part of establishing a settled (although may be viewed as boring!) routine, but negotiation around it – possibly time off at weekends – may be needed. The effects on other household members will be part of this negotiation, and this is not always easy. What is a reasonably time to go to bed or eat? Personal and cultural differences, especially where these differ, will influence the chosen routines. There is certainly a balance to be struck between establishing supportive routines and imposing them, which can simply increase frustration leading to increased agitation and mania (Table 10.1).

Stress management – not avoidance – for the family and the individual seems central to quality of life and maintaining well-being. Avoiding stress is not only impossible but goes against the nature of many people who are prone to BD – excitement is positive 'stress' – the other side of the coin. Avoiding stimulation simply leads to boredom, isolation, and depression so involvement in potentially stressful situations may be necessary to avoid it – but appropriately managed, not 'overdoing' it. Getting 'carried away' with things can lead on to excessive alcohol use, disinhibition, and mania – although the response to an exciting evening can be critical in determining whether mania is precipitated. Arguments are unlikely to help but may keep the agitation going and turn exuberant good nature into frustration, irritability, and persisting problems – when a gentle landing accompanied by exhaustion might alternatively lead to sleep and calm. In clients from Eastern cultures, use of mindfulness techniques which are congruent with their culture may be helpful in reducing stress.

The role of medication and adherence to it while very important is often tricky – across cultures, the belief exists that it is being used to suppress feelings (which in part is true!) and restrict creativity (probably not) by those (psychiatrists and family) who want to control and impose their will on the individual. This can be a particularly thorny issue where doctor and patient are from different cultural backgrounds – especially where one has oppressed the other in the past. Discussion can focus on using medication as a coping strategy within a broad treatment plan to help the person achieve their long-term goals by reducing the likelihood of serious disruption by manic or depressive episodes. Negotiation around type of medication and dosage can be more successful than an approach perceived as authoritarian. Family routines can be used to ensure medication adherence. In many cultures, medication can be preferred by clients as well, and this can be used as a strength.

Often, patient perceptions about medications are culturally defined and open to remediation through cognitive and behavioural interventions. As an example, it has been reported that decreased adherence in African American persons who suffer bipolar affective disorder is due to perceived increases in side effects and slower metabolizing rates of antipsychotics (Bradford, Gaedigk, & Leeder, 1998; Fleck, Keck, Corey, & Strakowski, 2005). Identification of culturally held perceptions about medication help therapist to determine and agree strategies.

Use of drugs and alcohol can be problematic in BD. As previously discussed, it can be a severe persistent problem, and where this is the case, a diagnosis of primary drug or alcohol abuse needs to be considered, and a specific focus on working on that particular problem prioritized. Where it is episodic and seems related to mania or depressive states, understanding the role that it is having in the person's life may help in management. In depression, it is often seen as ways of coping with distress; in mania, it may relate more to elation and socialization. Use of alcohol and cannabis may be seen as an integral part of 'enjoying yourself' and socially sanctioned by companions. It can sometimes be possible to work on a cost–benefit analysis with the individual – what are positives of the use of drugs/alcohol and the negatives. How can you experience the positive feelings without leading to negative consequences? Prohibition doesn't usually work (unless imposed by hospitalization), but damage limitation might – including choosing your companions more carefully and limiting amount of alcohol consumed, including starting later in the evening and alternating drinking nights. Where alcohol is culturally forbidden or disapproved of, part of the reaction may be influenced by this with a mixture of guilt and rebellion causing a complex set of beliefs to unravel.

Early intervention and relapse prevention have been incorporated as key elements in attempting to avoid development of symptoms. There is some evidence to support their value apart from the simple commonsense concept that where problems are developing, treatment should be offered promptly. There does however also need to be a caution about misinterpreting natural exuberance and inappropriately predicting catastrophe, which can bring it about. The balance is difficult as it can become self-fulfilling with predictions of doom leading to conflict in families and precipitation of illness. On the other hand, denial of problems or the gathering storm is also problematic and can mean that intervention occurs too late to abort an episode and serious damage is done.

Exercise: Think of a client with mania that you are/have worked with and who is from a different cultural background to yourself. What is their philosophical orientation in relation to their symptoms. How does that relate to their own unique presentation? How would you use these to work on managing lifestyle?

Developing strengths

Focusing on positive aspects of an individual's life is self-evidently important – even when they are manic – as transient or better, more persistent distraction can be therapeutic alongside other interventions. It can also reduce frustration and increase self-esteem, and simply, the discussion of them can improve engagement and collaboration with teams. Therefore, an approach which seeks to identify and develop strengths needs to be a key part of any programme. An individual's cultural orientation can be used as a strength, and they would be key in identifying as to what they consider would be key strengths.

Reducing the occurrence of behaviour that is damaging

Reconceptualization of BD as being at least as much a disorder of impulsivity as of mood can have significant implications for management. It could however be more stigmatizing although current conceptualizations and terminology seems to be having limited effects on reducing stigma or shame. Depression resulting from stigma and shame remains a pervasive problem (Thase, 2005) and, frequently, is even more damaging than mania. Most clinicians, whether using formal psychosocial interventions or not, do in practice negotiate with patients and their caregivers about their degree of impulse control, what affects it, and how to manage it. So on the one hand, little might change – but on the other hand, undermining the belief that this is a peripheral activity rather than a core therapeutic one which has a strong theoretical basis for it may enhance efficacy. If both therapists and patients and caregivers believe that impulse control is possible – and not just a forlorn hope 'battling against their biology' – it is much more likely to be successful. This has been found to be the case in our own practice, but substantiation is needed from clinical trials.

The focus of early intervention needs to change to damaging behaviour rather than current attempts to curb elation and perceived overactivity. This is more problematic – beliefs are now strong that elation, sleep disturbance, and overactivity are precursors of mania, but the evidence gives at most limited support for intervention at this stage. Some effect on mania has been shown from work on regulating body rhythms, for example, sleep patterns (Simon et al., 2006), but this is quite limited and effects on depression are absent. Alongside such a refocusing, work with caregivers is clearly vital – conflict in relationships is a near-certain predictor of relapse (Rosenfarb et al., 2001; Simon et al., 2006) – and differences in judgments about acceptable behaviour are fundamental. The focus on damaging behaviour is much more likely to be accepted on both sides as clearer and less open to interpretation although there will still be a need for negotiation. For example, as described, some sleep deprivation – a day or two – in bipolar patients is associated with transiently increased mood (Parekh et al., 1998); it is reasonable to consider this therapeutic and simply ignore it as part of the person's normal pattern.

Elation is an enjoyable experience and often makes the individual very attractive to others – it is not inevitably the precursor of mania – and patients often argue, maybe with some justification, that it is interference and concern from others that can change this to mania. Again, a focus on 'not going over the top,' that is, indulging in regrettable behaviour, may be most appropriate. For some individuals and their caregivers, reflection, use of grounding techniques, and mindfulness may have a place at an initial stage, in managing increase in anxiety, racing thought, and frantic overactivity. There will then be circumstances when this fails and damaging behaviour begins – but often initially, this is relatively minor in nature. This may therefore be the appropriate time to intervene. Earlier intervention may run the risk of catastrophization by caregivers and the individual. The fear that this will be intervening too late can be countered by the argument that at this time where evidence of potential damage to self or others is clearer and more definitive, acknowledgement of this by the individual will not be distorted by disagreements over control of non-damaging overactivity or elevated mood. This is not to minimize the profound damage to relationships, financial status, etc. that mania can cause and that repairing the damage afterwards may be very difficult, if not impossible: however, our experience is that a focused approach on damage is more likely to secure a working relationship with the individual and caregivers in these circumstances. This does mean taking into account and monitoring, on a regular and as-needed basis, caregivers' concerns; intervention planning, with a different focus; and frank balanced negotiation between the individual, caregiver, and therapist/psychiatrist. The focus on damaging behaviour can also clarify for all when compulsory measures are required and exactly why. Then, even where the person is manic and hospitalized, negotiating about impulse control can be possible. The use of humour with individuals can enhance collaboration as they readily engage with such an approach – often jokes, puns, and amusing statements emanate from the patient, and they enjoy a dialogue which appreciates and engages with this – and this can allow important messages to be conveyed minimizing irritability and confrontation. The therapeutic environment may also be very important: the availability and use of seclusion and physical, including mechanical, restraint can precipitate fears, agitation, and manic behaviour rather than reducing it. Acute hospital settings where intensive and skilled nursing care is used as an alternative intervention have been, in our experience, much more successful at minimizing damaging behaviour.

Medication management

Adherence currently is very poor especially with those individuals most affected by BD. The refocusing can improve adherence by establishing agreed goals – damage limitation – not mood control. It also reinforces that medication has this goal; any effects on elevated mood are simply a means to this end. 'Mood stabilization' may not be a helpful term. However, this refocusing means negotiation over management when 'early signs' emerge as to whether these are indications for increasing medication, for example, higher dosage or adding another drug. It is possible to have useful considered discussions with individuals as to the point at which they think intervention to limit damage is appropriate. Sometimes, that point may not be the same as that determined by the caregiver or psychiatrist, but supporting the person in their decision is more likely to lead to acceptance of medication and other measures at some point, for example, not going out for an alcoholic drink tonight, than those which are perceived as imposed externally with disruption of the relationship. Differences in values between individual and caregivers may exist and complicate determination of what is an acceptable behaviour. But even where such disagreement occurs, agreement to differ is possible, as inevitably in the long term, the individual will make their own decisions and face the consequences of them, even though short-term compulsory measures are sometimes necessary. Providing assistance in learning from such experiences as part of a maturation process is facilitated by retaining a therapeutic relationship albeit one where disagreements occur.

Depressive episodes need consideration

Their effects can also be very damaging through avoidance, disengagement, negativity, and suicidality, and unlike elation, depression is an undesirable state in itself although may be an understandable one. Depressive episodes may have occurred in response to the consequences of the manic/hypomanic episode or from unrelated life events especially where these have preceded the initial episode. There may also be a major contribution of shame and stigmatization by self and others, negative beliefs about the future, and the adverse effects of mood control to avoid elation. A fear of 'going high' is not uncommon – a fear of indulging in damaging behaviour is more appropriate and potentially more within the individual's control. Such fears can induce mixed conditions where depression, anxiety, and mania occur from the effects of frustration, irritability, and sometimes insight and hopelessness intermingled with elation and grandiosity. Clarification of goals and negotiation around individual's current needs and future ambitions may help with reducing the confusion and underlying distress that often exists. The finding that the proportion of depressive compared to manic/hypomanic relapses experienced by patients is in inverse proportion to levels of lithium used in treatment studies (<0.6, 0.6–0.8, and above 0.8)

(Kleindienst, Severus, Moller, & Greil, 2005) has implications for the levels used in management particularly if there is an increased degree of acceptance of hypomania – at non-damaging levels.

Explanations for individuals and caregivers can usefully draw on vulnerability–stress perspectives: the individual has personality vulnerabilities and strengths that are influenced by culture, which in response to circumstances have lead to a manic/hypomanic episode. Those individual characteristics are likely to have their original basis in their genetic make-up. This may be through genetic determinants of their personality and other characteristics, which also contribute to creativity and impulsivity, and possibly their earlier life experiences. The circumstances when they became manic may have been stress related but may not, and they could have been experiencing positive life events and experiences. However, the consequences of that initial event have been damaging to them, and avoiding such impact on themselves and others in the future is essential. Providing empowering explanations which are evidence based is more likely to enable them to do so.

Managing and minimizing depressive reactions to illness

Depressive reactions to illness are a major cause of disability. Attempts to prevent this emerging need to start while the patient is hypomanic. As they begin to recover, medication management to reduce sedation and immobility can allow a smooth transition back to normal life reconnecting with community supports. At the same time, the reactions of others and the beliefs about self, including self-stigmatization and what has happened to them – including any damage caused – will need monitoring and as far as possible rectifying.

Case example

Shahida grew up in Kenya in a family of Southeast Asian origin before they moved to the United Kingdom when she was in her early teens. She completed school and did quite well. Her family arranged for her to be married, but unfortunately, the relationship proved very difficult, as both partners were quite strong willed, determined, and volatile. They nevertheless had two children although Shahida developed puerperal psychosis – manic in nature – with the second child. The family attempted to manage the situation initially providing substantial time and support, but she eventually required hospital admission. She had developed persecutory beliefs about a 'racist coup,' which would endanger her and her family. She was very overactive and developed grandiose and religious beliefs which the family described as being beyond that of the Koran. She recovered over a period of weeks but was resistant to the idea of taking medication after leaving the hospital. Collaboration with this over the years proved difficult although she did eventually engage in a Socratic dialogue around the pros and cons of collaboration and avoidance of relapse.

Unfortunately, her husband also developed mental health problems soon after she made her initial recovery and required treatment in his own right. Fortunately, family support for the children was available, and this also became very important when Shahida developed severe depressive symptoms. She did not express depressive ideas but spoke of deep fatigue and weariness, poor concentration with headaches, and abdominal discomfort. These persisted despite medication for a few months during which therapy focused on supported behavioural activation before she became euthymic. Once well, she took up the care of her children and her social contacts and also provided support to the older members of the family – she is an excellent cook. Recurrences occurred related to life events, for example, a miscarriage and her older child – daughter – leaving home to go to university. This was compounded by an acrimonious divorce process between himself and Shahida – despite attempts at mediation – which led to a manic episode followed by a lengthy depressive one.

As her life has become more stable with day-to-day rhythms established and she has become more accepting of the value of medication in helping her cope and stay well, episodes have become less frequent. The family, in particular her brother, has remained supportive despite their own busy lives and assisted in managing her affairs when necessary and providing practical support when fatigued. Support from the community mental health team has been given with discussion with her about her needs, particularly those influenced by her cultural background, for example, for a period when she was receiving depot medication injections, a female was allocated at her request.

Conclusion

Management of BD, especially mania, using cognitive behavioural approaches remains at an early stage of development, and there has been very little successful evaluation of them. This is especially the case for culturally adapted methods. However, examining the beliefs, feelings, and behaviours in a systematic way within a cultural context has the potential to allow accurate assessment and effective engagement, collaboration with treatment, damage limitation, gradual recovery, and minimization of depressive episodes (Table 10.2).

Table 10.2   Key points in working with bipolar affective disorder.

1. There is need for further evidence of efficacy of cognitive behavioural approaches in mania
2. Relapse prevention and work on medication concordance are of value
3. Understand the cultural influences on diagnosis and presentation
4. Explore when behaviour becomes embarrassing as this can be culturally determined
5. Involve a bit more contact, in depth, between episodes in sharing experiences and understanding the person's philosophical orientation in relation to culture, current issues, and beliefs about bipolar disorder
6. Begin with work on impulse control rather than elation
7. Focus on damage limitation in developing common goals and collaboration
8. Use cultural strengths and family support in discussing stabilization of lifestyle

References

Alloy, L. B., Abramson, L. Y., Urosevic, S., Walshaw, P. D., Nusslock, R., & Neeren, A. M. (2005). The psychosocial context of bipolar disorder: Environmental, cognitive, and developmental risk factors. *Clinical Psychology Review, 25*(8), 1043–1075.

Baldassano, C.F. (2006). Illness course, comorbidity, gender, and suicidality in patients with bipolar disorder. *Journal of Clinical Psychiatry, 67*(Suppl 11), 8–11.

Ball, J. R., Mitchell, P. B., Corry, J. C., Skillecorn, A., Smith, M., & Malhi, G. S. (2006). A randomized controlled trial of cognitive therapy for bipolar disorder: Focus on long-term change. *Journal of Clinical Psychiatry, 67*(2), 277–286.

Basco, M., Merlock, M., & McDonald, N. (2004). Treatment compliance. In S. L. Johnson & R. L. Leahy (Eds.), *Psychological treatment of bipolar disorder* (p. 246). New York, NY: Guilford Press.

Basco M. R. (2006). *The bipolar workbook: Tools for controlling your mood swings*. New York, NY, Guilford Press.

Basco, M. R. & Rush, A. J. (1996). *Cognitive-behavioral therapy for bipolar disorder*. New York, NY: Guilford Press.

Bentall, R. P. (2004). *Madness explained: Psychosis and human nature*. London, UK: Penguin.

Bradford, L. D., Gaedigk, A., & Leeder, J. S. (1998). High frequency of CYP2D6 poor and "intermediate" metabolizers in black populations: A review and preliminary data. *Psychopharmacology Bulletin, 34*(4), 797–804.

Fleck, D. E., Keck Jr., P. E., Corey, K. B., & Strakowski, S. M. (2005). Factors associated with medication adherence in African American and white patients with bipolar disorder. *Journal of Clinical Psychiatry, 66*(5), 646–652.

Frank, E., Kupfer, D. J., Thase, M. E., Mallinger, A. G., Swartz, H. A., Fagiolini, A. M., ... Monk, T. (2005). Two-year outcomes for interpersonal and social rhythm therapy in individuals with bipolar I disorder. *Archives of General Psychiatry, 62*(9), 996–1004.

Goodwin, F. K., & Jameson, K. (1989). *Manic depressive illness*. Oxford, UK: Oxford University Press.

Goodwin, G. M., & Consensus Group of the British Association for Psychopharmacology (2003). Evidence-based guidelines for treating bipolar disorder: Recommendations from the British Association for Psychopharmacology. *Journal of Psychopharmacology, 17*(2), 149–173.

Hammersley, P., Dias, A., Todd, G., Bowen-Jones, K., Reilly, B., & Bentall, R. P. (2003). Childhood trauma and hallucinations in bipolar affective disorder: Preliminary investigation. *British Journal of Psychiatry, 182*, 543–547.

Howland, R. H., & Thase, M. E. (1993). A comprehensive review of cyclothymic disorder. *Journal of Nervous and Mental Disease, 181*(8), 485–493.

Johnson, S. L., & Fingerhut, R. (2004). Negative cognitions predict the course of bipolar depression, not mania. *Journal of Cognitive Psychotherapy, 18*(2), 149–162.

Johnson, S. L., Winett, C. A., Meyer, B., Greenhouse, W. J., & Miller, I. (1999). Social support and the course of bipolar disorder. *Journal of Abnormal Psychology, 108*(4), 558–566.

Judd, L. L., Akiskal, H. S., Schettler, P. J., Endicott, J., Maser, J., Solomon, D. A., … Keller, M. B. (2002). The long-term natural history of the weekly symptomatic status of bipolar I disorder. *Archives of General Psychiatry, 59*(6), 530–537.

Keller, M. B. (2004). Improving the course of illness and promoting continuation of treatment of bipolar disorder. *Journal of Clinical Psychiatry, 65*(Suppl 15), 10–14.

Kleindienst, N., Severus, W. E., Moller, H. J., & Greil, W. (2005). Is polarity of recurrence related to serum lithium level in patients with bipolar disorder? *European Archives of Psychiatry & Clinical Neuroscience, 255*(1), 72–74.

Lam, D. H., Watkins, E. R., Hayward, P., Bright, J., Wright, K., … Sham, P. (2003). A randomized controlled study of cognitive therapy for relapse prevention for bipolar affective disorder: Outcome of the first year. *Archives of General Psychiatry, 60*(2), 145–152.

Lam, D., Wright, K., & Sham, P. (2005). Sense of hyper-positive self and response to cognitive therapy in bipolar disorder. *Psychological Medicine, 35*, 69–77.

Lam, D., Wright, K., & Smith, N. (2004). Dysfunctional assumptions in bipolar disorder. *Journal of Affective Disorders, 79*(1–3), 193–199.

Lange, J. (1939). Circular insanity. *Handbuch der Erbbiologie des Menschen, 5*, 873–932.

Lozano, B. E., & Johnson, S. L. (2001). Can personality traits predict increases in manic and depressive symptoms? *Journal of Affective Disorders, 63*(1–3), 103–111.

Lyon, H. M., Startup, M., & Bentall, R. P. (1999). Social cognition and the manic defense: Attributions, selective attention, and self-schema in bipolar affective disorder. *Journal of Abnormal Psychology, 108*(2), 273–282.

Mackin, P., Targum, S. D., Kalali, A., Rom, D., & Young, A. H. (2006). Culture and assessment of manic symptoms. *British Journal of Psychiatry, 189*(4), 379–380.

Malkoff-Schwartz, S., Frank, E., Anderson, B. P., Hlastala, S. A., Luther, J. F., Sherrill, J. T., … Kupfer, D. J. (2000). Social rhythm disruption and stressful life events in the onset of bipolar and unipolar episodes. *Psychological Medicine, 30*(5), 1005–1016.

Mansell, W. (2007). The interpretation of, and responses to, changes in internal states: An integrative cognitive model of mood swings and bipolar disorders. *Behavioural and Cognitive Psychotherapy, 35*, 515–539.

Mansell, W., & Lam, D. (2003). Conceptualizing a cycle of ascent into mania: A case report. *Behavioural and Cognitive Psychotherapy, 31*(3), 363–367.

Martinez-Aran, A., Vieta, E., Colom, F., Torrent, C., Sanchez-Moreno, J., Reinares, M., … Salamero, M. (2004). Cognitive impairment in euthymic bipolar patients: Implications for clinical and functional outcome. *Bipolar Disorders, 6*(3), 224–232.

Miklowitz, D. J., George, E. L., Richards, J. A., Simoneau, T. L., & Suddath, R. L. (2003). A randomized study of family-focused psychoeducation and pharmacotherapy in the outpatient management of bipolar disorder. *Archives of General Psychiatry, 60*(9), 904–912.

Moeller, F. G., Barratt, E. S., Dougherty, D. M., Schmitz, J. M., & Swann, A. C. (2001). Psychiatric aspects of impulsivity. *American Journal of Psychiatry, 158*(11), 1783–1793.

National Institute for Health and Care Excellence (2006). *Clinical guideline: Bipolar disorder (CG38)*. London, UK: Department of Health.

Osher, Y., Cloninger, C. R., & Belmaker, R. H. (1996). TPQ in euthymic manic-depressive patients. *Journal of Psychiatric Research, 30*(5), 353–357.

Parekh, P. I., Ketter, T. A., Altshuler, L., Frye, M. A., Callahan, A., Marangell, L., & Post, R. M. (1998). Relationships between thyroid hormone and antidepressant responses to total sleep deprivation in mood disorder patients. *Biological Psychiatry, 43*(5), 392–394.

Paykel, E. S., Abbott, R., Morriss, R., Hayhurst, H., & Scott, J. (2006). Sub-syndromal and syndromal symptoms in the longitudinal course of bipolar disorder. *British Journal of Psychiatry, 189*(2), 118–123.

Perry, A., Tarrier, N., Morriss, R., McCarthy, E., & Limb, K. (1999). Randomised controlled trial of efficacy of teaching patients with bipolar disorder to identify early symptoms of relapse and obtain treatment. *BMJ, 318*(7177), 149–153.

Reilly-Harrington, N. A., Alloy, L. B., Fresco, D. M., & Whitehouse, W. G. (1999). Cognitive styles and life events interact to predict bipolar and unipolar symptomatology. *Journal of Abnormal Psychology, 108*(4), 567–578.

Richards, R., Kinney, D. K., Lunde, I., & Benet, M. (1988). Creativity in manic-depressives, cyclothymes, their normal relatives, and control subjects. *Journal of Abnormal Psychology, 97*(3), 281–288.

Rosenfarb, I. S., Miklowitz, D. J., Goldstein, M. J., Harmon, L., Nuechterlein, K. H., & Rea, M. M. (2001). Family transactions and relapse in bipolar disorder. *Family Process, 40*(1), 5–14.

Scott, J. (2006). Psychotherapy for bipolar disorders – Efficacy and effectiveness. *Journal of Psychopharmacology, 20*(2 Suppl), 50.

Scott, J., Garland, A., & Moorhead, S. (2001). A pilot study of cognitive therapy in bipolar disorders. *Psychological Medicine, 31*(3), 459–467.

Scott, J., Paykel, E., Morriss, R., Bentall, R., Kinderman, P., Johnson, T., … Hayhurst, H. (2006). Cognitive-behavioural therapy for severe and recurrent bipolar disorders: Randomised controlled trial. *British Journal of Psychiatry, 188*(4), 313–320.

Simon, G. E., Ludman, E. J., Bauer, M. S., Unutzer, J., & Operskalski, B. (2006). Long-term effectiveness and cost of a systematic care program for bipolar disorder. *Archives of General Psychiatry, 63*(5), 500–508.

Marlies, ter B. (2005). The strength of the bipolar. *GAMIAN – Europe Newsletter, 7*(18), 9–10.

Thase, M. E. (2005). Bipolar depression: Issues in diagnosis and treatment. *Harvard Review of Psychiatry, 13*(5), 257–271.

Weiss, R. D., Griffin, M. L., Kolodziej, M. E., Greenfield, S. F., Najavits, L. M., Daley, D. C., … Hennen, J. A. (2007). A randomized trial of integrated group therapy versus group drug counseling for patients with bipolar disorder and substance dependence. *American Journal of Psychiatry, 164*(1), 100–107.

Weissman, M. M., Bland, R. C., Canino, G. J., Faravelli, C., Greenwald, S., Hwu, H. G., … Yeh, E. K. (1996). Cross-national epidemiology of major depression and bipolar disorder. *JAMA, 276*(4), 293–299.

World Health Organisation Burden of Disease Project. (2002). Death and DALY estimates for 2002 by cause for WHO member states. Retrieved from http://www.who.int/entity/healthinfo/statistics/bodgbddeathdalyestimates.xls (accessed September 18, 2014).

11

Recovery, Relapse Prevention, and Finishing Therapy

Work on recovery, relapse prevention, and finishing therapy starts at first assessment and continues throughout the therapy sessions. Therefore, the information in this chapter should be used throughout the process of therapy. Severe mental illness by its nature can require long-term management, and when the time comes, smooth termination of therapy with effective relapse prevention strategies is critical to improving and maintaining quality of life and promoting wellness and recovery. Recovery as now formulated does not necessarily mean cure: recovery is about building a meaningful and satisfying life, as defined by the person themselves, whether or not there are ongoing or recurring symptoms or problems (NHS Confederation/Centre for Mental Health, 2012). Cultural factors significantly inform, define, and guide recovery and relapse prevention strategies.

Identifying Indicators of Relapse

Relapse is an increase in or return of symptoms or impairment of functioning following a period of symptom remission or stability. In some clients, this will take the form of a minor and transient setback, and in others, it can become a 'full-blown relapse' which can result in an acute episode of illness with need for a significant increase in support and treatment. An episode of relapse is usually preceded by some signs and symptoms which if identified at an early stage and addressed effectively can often lead to prevention of the full-blown episode. They can appear quite gradually over days or weeks or quite rapidly. The symptoms that are harbingers of relapse are called early warning signs or 'relapse signatures'

Cultural Adaptation of CBT for Serious Mental Illness: A Guide for Training and Practice,
First Edition. Shanaya Rathod, David Kingdon, Narsimha Pinninti, Douglas Turkington,
and Peter Phiri.
© 2015 John Wiley & Sons, Ltd. Published 2015 by John Wiley & Sons, Ltd.

for that individual. Early warning signs are fairly specific for the individual and often occur in a chronological sequential order. One of the tasks of the therapist is to discuss and help their client identify their own early warning signs – or 'relapse signature' – and support them, as well as the family or caregivers where appropriate, to chart the time course of relapse and the guideposts for seeking additional help or intervention. The relapse signatures can range from any of the entire gamut of:

1. Affective symptoms such as anxiety, irritability, depressed mood, mild elation, etc.
2. Cognitive symptoms such as excess worry, preoccupation with bodily symptoms, negative thoughts about self or others, and paranoid thoughts
3. Behavioural symptoms such as social withdrawal, increased motor activity), or impaired functioning such as not caring for self, absenteeism at work, etc.

In the case of psychotic illness, sometimes relapse could be re-emergence of psychotic symptoms which often develop initially with the person retaining full insight (Birchwood et al., 1989). In minority cultural groups, relapse signatures, like psychopathology, can be influenced by their cultural background or experiences as is demonstrated by the following case examples.

Case example

Alberto, a 56-year-old immigrant to the United States, presented to the therapist following three episodes of depression. He engaged well with the therapist and discussed that he had immigrated 25 years ago and had grown up in Naples, Italy. He and his wife had two daughters. When they immigrated, they lived in a segregated Italian community in Chicago. His wife looked after the children and he worked in a factory. As he was a single earner, the family struggled financially, but he did not agree with his wife working as he described his as a patriarchal family. The family tended to follow his cultural traditions and remained integrated in the wider Italian community. His elder daughter, now 24 years of age, had chosen to work at a factory. She defied their cultural tradition, and this was a cause of conflict between them. He described that he came from a generation of traditional Italians where the father took all the decisions. He felt that his role and status was eroded by his children, and this was one of the key reasons for his affective symptoms.

Through the therapy sessions, Alberto had learnt his early warning signs and was working with the therapist to identify them early. He discussed with the therapist that when stressors increased, he tended to ruminate about his role in the family and shame in community due to the cultural betrayal from his daughter. He also explained that when he was unwell, he tended to become more superstitious and with progression of symptoms would stop recognizing that he was unwell. His wife could recognize the signs as she would describe him as irritable about their daughter's job and on occasion lash out at her for no reason. She identified that another early sign was that he would stop going out for fear of what people would say.

The therapist worked on a list of early warning signs which included exacerbation of cultural values and irritability with the family, and they discussed various stressful factors that triggered a relapse.

Case discussion

This example demonstrates a number of cultural factors and their dynamic interplay that influence Alberto's relapse pattern. Alberto, although in the United States for a number of years, was not completely integrated into the host culture. While at one level he had to accept the fact that his children did not want to follow his cultural tradition for want of a better socio-economic life, he struggled with his own perceptions of erosion of his status in the house and felt cultural betrayal. His relapse signatures were influenced by his cultural values which were also stressful for him.

The role of families and the community is important in a number of cultures (as we have discussed in earlier chapters) in intercepting and managing relapse signatures as discussed in Alberto's case. They are able to identify early warning signs, assist in building up the 'relapse signature,' and also identify when symptoms are emerging. However, there is a risk that families become anxious when a behaviour that preceded previous episodes occurs which may not necessarily imply relapse. Genuine physical discomfort, for example, headaches, or assertive or rebellious behaviour can particularly come into this category and may need careful assessment and negotiation.

Case example

Luigi came from rural Sicily and from a modest background. He immigrated to Canada, got married to a Canadian woman, and had three daughters. Luigi, while very traditional himself, allowed his family to follow the traditions that they chose – Italian/Canadian and sometimes mixed. His daughters were not traditional as they had always grown up in Canada. Luigi was proud of his family. He worked in a factory and the family managed financially. Due to recession, he lost his job. Now, the family was under pressure as they had to move house, and their housing condition had become poor. There were water leaks, damp, and mould in some parts of the new house. As he developed symptoms of depression, his behaviour at home became difficult, and he admitted that he started blaming his wife that the house was in this condition. He sometimes mentioned that this may be related as she had made bread in May. His family did not understand what he meant and sought help as they became concerned. They reported that he was irritable and sometimes aggressive and tended to isolate himself at home. His wife could not understand why he was so angry with her while she had adjusted to their situation.

Luigi worked for some sessions with a therapist, and he could recognize that his symptoms had deteriorated and some of his cultural thinking which he may not have believed normally became an issue and influenced him when unwell. He explained that it was an old folk belief that bread made during the first 3 days of May will result in mould and roaches throughout the house. While he was growing up, his family observed this tradition strictly. The origins of this tradition can be traced to a legend about a woman making bread who denied a crumb to a beggar and was generous to devils who had been masquerading as knights. Luigi could make a link that as his mental state had started deteriorating, he was looking for explanations regarding their situation based on old cultural values which normally did not worry him. He also recognized why others may have been concerned about his rationale.

Case discussion

Luigi, a traditional man, held his cultural values but did not impose them on his family. However, his own belief system shaped his automatic thoughts and assumptions. When he became unwell, these culturally influenced thoughts surfaced, and his behaviours changed in response to the assumptions. In therapy, he could recognize that his early warning signs involved him thinking about his traditional beliefs. Such beliefs can also be easily missed or misinterpreted.

> **Exercise:** Think of a client that you are/have worked with from a different cultural background to yourself. How are their early warning signs influenced by their culture?

Philosophical Orientation: Cultural Factors Influencing Relapse

Relapse is often triggered by adverse life circumstances, among other causes. Patterns may be detected and need to be recognized, for example, specific times of the year like anniversaries, substance use or abuse, medication changes, or other individual life stresses like family pressures. In clients from cultures where the shame of mental illness is perceived more than in others, the 'fear of going mad' has been described as frequent even between episodes and in remission which needs to be acknowledged and addressed – it is easy for a vicious circle of increased anxiety in the individual, family, and even community to increase symptoms and lead to the feared outcome. Sometimes, just a sense of unease can begin the cycle, or a physical symptom especially in a number of Asian cultures, including pain, headaches or stomach aches, may begin the relapse.

Due to their experiences, some clients from cultural minorities may attribute their early warning signs to normal responses to life circumstances, and hence, seeking help may be delayed until there is a full-blown relapse or a crisis. On occasion, the relationship to life events may not be clear to the individual or family and indeed the therapist, either because the stress is low key but enduring or positive type of stress such as taking up a job or a specific type of life experience may be occurring to which the person is susceptible, for example, discrimination, isolation, racism, financial difficulties, family pressures, etc. In these situations, it can be difficult to identify any specific stressors, and the cycle may repeat a couple of times before the signs become recognizable.

In some cultures, for example, some South Asian Muslim families where there is an increased emphasis on cure, relapse prevention work can be challenging as the concept of relapse can be difficult, especially for families. Therefore, there may be a level of denial and avoidance to work with the therapist on relapse prevention. In cultures like American Indians, Asian origin clients, and Alaskan natives where the shame and stigma of mental illness is felt acutely and honour is important, denial is an understandable response. The focus of the therapist working towards relapse prevention work needs to be on dealing with normalizing the concept of relapse as a way of dealing with the stigma and shame and at the same time improving insight. A helpful quote from a therapist working with a client *how many times a year on average do you suffer from symptoms of cold and cough? How do you deal with it – do you take vitamins, avoid being cold, being near people who have a cold – what measures do you take?*

Case example

Tulasi, a 32-year-old Indian American woman, lived with her husband and two children in the United States. She was diagnosed with schizophrenia that responded well to antipsychotic medication. Tulasi was working before the illness episode, and she decided to go back to work as soon as symptoms were under control. She came from a cultural background where goal accomplishment was highly valued and all women in her circle were employed. Within 3 weeks of her returning to work, she started feeling anxious, had thoughts that she will fail at work, became irritable, and started neglecting chores at the house. She and her family attributed these symptoms to stress of work until 6 weeks later when she started hearing voices and developed persecutory delusions leading to hospitalization. This cycle of symptom remission followed by return to work and relapse occurred one more time before she came for therapy. The therapist identified and discussed work as a possible trigger for her relapse. Her husband immediately agreed that this was his observation as well, but Tulasi was reluctant to attribute her symptoms to work due to fear that she would be pressurized to stop working.

The therapist normalized her feelings and assured her that it would be normal to fear the consequences and used this as a stepping stone to discuss further outcomes that mattered to Tulasi. She identified that her main goal was to keep her job. The therapist and client came up with a proactive plan to maintain a symptom and work diary the next time she went to work. The diary consisted of a daily rating of identified early warning symptoms. Tulasi was able to identify that work was indeed a stressor that triggered symptoms and decided to scale down her work and go part-time, while her husband agreed to provide more support in taking care of children. With this arrangement, she was able to continue working part-time with a view to increasing in the future.

Case discussion

In this case, the connection between returning to work and relapse of symptoms was not clear to the client or family until the therapist brought it to their attention. Even then, her husband recognized it earlier than her. Her reluctance to acknowledge the impact of her work was due to her cultural expectation of the need to accomplish. However, with a relapse prevention plan including work as a trigger, she was able to understand better and work collaboratively with her therapist and husband to develop a plan.

Marlatt and colleagues in their work on addictions reported finding several types of overt determinants of relapse that cluster in two broad areas: intrapersonal and interpersonal (Larimer et al. 1999; Marlatt et al. 1985). Intrapersonal or environmental determinants include contextual variables, while interpersonal determinants include social/relational variables. The balance between the determinants that determine relapse in different cultural groups may vary. For example, for clients from cultures where the family or community view is important, they may be more sensitive to interpersonal determinants of relapse rather than intrapersonal variants.

Theoretical Modifications and Technical Adjustments

As discussed earlier, relapse prevention work starts when developing a formulation in the cultural context and is often done when the client is 'in remission.' This not only helps them understand what has happened but allows them, or with their permission allows the therapist, to explain to others like their family members who may be key in supporting relapse prevention or recognition of relapse signatures. A relapse prevention plan is an integral part of therapy and includes:

- Strengths (cultural strengths) and helpful strategies learnt during the therapeutic process
- Discussing setbacks (e.g. experiences of racism) and ways of overcoming them
- Encouraging the client to make notes of new discoveries and learning and writing summaries of outcomes of behavioural experiments and alternative ways of coping so that these could be added to a toolkit of helpful strategies, ideas, skills, and techniques
- Evaluating progress of therapy as the client inches towards their goals
- Exploring and discussing the client's concerns about therapy ending, taking into account cultural variations, and involving family where appropriate
- Reviewing what the client has learnt, going through some of the techniques, and relearning where necessary

Case example

Ying Lee, a 37-year-old lecturer with origins from China, lived with a diagnosis of a recurrent depressive disorder. Each of her earlier episodes had been characterized by symptoms of severe depression affecting her functioning. In the last 3 years, she had been able to identify that 2–3 weeks prior to an acute episode, she became preoccupied with personal cleansing and general cleanliness which progressed to an extent that she sometimes stayed awake at night to clean her house and took several showers. She had been drinking excessive amounts of hot water and her visits to the toilet would become very frequent. Normally, she would drink hot water but in moderate amounts.

Ying Lee started therapy but was not keen to discuss or acknowledge the early warning signs. The therapist did not want to disengage her and therefore started giving her homework. One of the activities he asked her to do was to record what her family members said about her activities. He also asked her to keep a diary of her cleanliness activities and amount of fluid she consumed. It took a long time but slowly, the client acknowledged that some of her activities may determine early relapse signatures. Since recognizing this and the stressful triggers that brought these symptoms on, she had been able to seek help early and her last two episodes of depression had not been as severe.

Case discussion

Most cultures value cleanliness, but the extent and remit of cleanliness and methods of achieving it may vary among cultures and individuals. For example, in some Chinese clients, the concept of personal cleansing for cleanliness can be important culturally and in this case manifested as an early warning sign.

Some clients from minority cultures do not like to talk about what has happened or discuss specific incidents. This may include experiences of discrimination, racism, or particular stresses of migration which could be humiliating for them to discuss. While that certainly needs to be respected, other methods can be used to gain their trust. In cultures that place emphasis on the value of tradition and storytelling, this can be a powerful method of influencing them to trust the therapist. Traditional stories can be used to normalize the events and engage clients in sharing information to unpick their relapse patterns. In these clients, relapse prevention work needs to be in a relational fashion rather than in a linear fashion.

Case example

Deepa, a 65-year-old Hindu woman, lived with her son and his wife and their two sons in the United Kingdom. She came to live with them 15 years ago, after she divorced her husband of 28 years. Deepa came from a generation where divorce was considered stigmatizing in her culture. Her first episode of depression occurred after her separation from her husband, and since then, she suffered a number of episodes of depression before she sought a CBT therapist. In each of the sessions, Deepa spent a lot of time trying to justify to the therapist why she had left her husband. The therapist struggled to get past this discussion, and Deepa felt unable to do any other homework. It had become apparent that Deepa's perception of shame through the divorce was a key factor in her multiple episodes of depression.

The therapist consulted his friend – who had a similar background to Deepa – to find out more about cultural thinking around separation of a married couple and divorce. The friend had a religious background. He acknowledged that the stigma of divorce was more pronounced in the older generation of the Hindu culture. He also gave religious examples of separation of Hindu deities like Lord Ram and his wife Sita and Lord Shiva and his wife goddess Parvati as tools to normalize separation and make it acceptable. In the next session, the therapist asked Deepa to expand on what his friend had explained. Deepa had a strong religious background herself. She took a lot of pleasure in explaining the traditional stories to the therapist. In doing so, she herself felt validated. In progressing with therapy, Deepa was able to identify that shame about the divorce and ruminations about it were indeed her early warning signs.

Case discussion

In this case, the therapist used traditional stories to engage Deepa in formulation-based work and identifying relapse patterns.

Due to fear of the person belonging to a different culture, sometimes, therapists may feel that they cannot/or may offend their client by discussing the events leading to and including acute episodes, the antecedents, and experiences leaving the client confused and fearful of future relapse. One way to address this is to discuss relapse prevention as a strategy to help the client to be self-reliant and become their own therapist. A statement such as *I think we need to look at you being*

Table 11.1   Culture and identification of relapse signatures.

Relapse signatures may be culturally determined
It can be easy to miss these signatures if clients are embarrassed by them
Cultural strengths offset against such reluctance, and a number of techniques like
    Socratic questioning, validation, storytelling, and a relational style can be helpful
Families can be helpful in identifying warning signs

your own therapist and helping yourself in future. For you to be able to do that, we need to piece together the information we gathered in different sessions and make a plan for the future. Sometimes going over the past episodes may bring on unpleasant feelings but you may find it worthwhile in increasing your confidence as well as giving you a set of tools to address any future problems would frame relapse prevention work in a positive manner that instills hope. Another way that might be less distressing to some individuals is to complete a blank template for relapse prevention as homework assignment and then discuss that with the therapist. A supportive family member can be part of this assignment as family members can provide objective information that facilitates completion of the relapse prevention plan. See Table 11.1 in the following for relapse prevention plan for Safia from Chapter 4.

Work with Stress–Vulnerability Factors

The stress–vulnerability model of mental disorder describes how both stress and vulnerabilities/strengths including biological factors contribute to symptoms of illness. We have discussed this in Chapter 2. Improving coping skills or altering environmental factors (family, work, experience of discrimination, finance, housing, etc.) and sensible use of medication can reduce vulnerability and build hope and resilience. Part of relapse prevention work is where a client is assisting the therapist to understand stress–vulnerability/strengths interactions and be able to apply this to their own life situation. They are also best placed to identify how their cultural background is a source of strength and resilience. The focus in this model should be on the modifiable resilience building factors. Discussing resilience building factors is empowering to clients and counteracts the demoralization and stigma associated with mental illness. According to some authors (Deegan, 2005), people with psychiatric disorders demonstrate resilience through the use of non-pharmaceutical, personal medicine in the recovery process. Personal medicine is found to be those activities that give life meaning and purpose and that serve to raise self-esteem, decrease symptoms, and avoid unwanted outcomes such as hospitalization. This forms the basis of recovery-oriented work. The therapist supports the client in using cultural strengths in doing this.

Recovery-Oriented Work

The recognition of the concept of 'recovery' first began in the 1980s with first-hand descriptions highlighting the ongoing process of recovery (Deegan, 1988) but has gained momentum again recently. Recovery-oriented therapy begins from the first session and enables the client to develop confidence in skills such as self-determination and management. The therapist supports this by adopting a strengths-based stance instilling hope and motivation. The concept of recovery and relapse management is interlinked as while it may be common to experience relapses in severe mental illness, the recovery approach enables clients to manage their illness, maintain autonomy, and aspire for the future. A client's culture has a lot to offer in terms of strengths when working on recovery and relapse management. For example, sometimes, it is about emphasizing the positives and building on the cultural strengths that enables clients to develop their confidence. This is especially true in clients who have suffered hardships due to their minority status, discrimination, or migration experiences. Their experiences may leave them with embarrassment about their cultural identity. Highlighting the strengths of their culture can be validating. Socratic questioning is an important technique in eliciting culture-based strengths. Coping cards can be used to reinforce the messages.

CLIENT: Every time there is a setback at work, I start dwelling on my past experiences and think of how I have always been discriminated against.

THERAPIST: Can you make a list of all your achievements and what you are proud of?

CLIENT: I am proud of my family, I am a good mother, I have a close community of friends, and we celebrate all festivals together.

THERAPIST: What would you base your achievements on how have your cultural values contributed?

CLIENT: I grew up in a family with a strong work ethic, respect for authority, commitment to tasks, and responsibility to society.

Case example

Ishaq, an 18-year-old man from Pakistan, had suffered bullying and racism through secondary school. He had immigrated with his family 8 years ago to the United Kingdom. His parents were traditional in their outlook and socialized only with others from their community. Ishaq had been in schools where the number of children from minority cultures was few. Due to a number of stressors, Ishaq had presented with signs and symptoms of depression to the therapist.

The therapist used a formulation-based approach and worked on identifying key stressors and early warning signs in the early therapy sessions. In the sessions, it became apparent to the therapist that Ishaq had been struggling with his cultural identity and felt embarrassed every time the therapist approached his cultural issues.

In the fourth session, the therapist asked Ishaq what were his most memorable times while growing up. Ishaq became very animated and described that when he was younger his grandmother lived with the family and every night she used to tell him stories before he went to bed. He treasured those memories. This allowed a window of opportunity to the therapist to build on the cultural strength of close family units.

The therapist further explored his memories of the stories and what they meant to him. He went on to describe that most of the stories his grandmother knew were old folktale with a message. Over the next few sessions, Ishaq narrated some of the stories, and in doing so, the therapist and Ishaq uncovered the richness of his cultural heritage. They collaboratively developed coping cards based on the stories to help Ishaq's confidence.

Case discussion

Ishaq's traumatic experiences had affected his confidence in his cultural identity and also contributed to his symptoms. As the therapist struggled to get Ishaq to speak positively about his culture, he used a strengths-based approach which allowed further work on relapse management.

Medication Adherence

Three aspects of psychotropic medication management that are discussed in the following include cultural influences on attitudes towards:

1. Medication
2. Medication adherence
3. Variable efficacy and side effects of medications

The attitudes of different minority cultures towards psychotropic medication vary in ways similar to the attitudes towards therapy. Those cultures that have a strong herbal tradition may have beliefs that medication dosages are fixed, rapid relief is anticipated, side effects are minimal, and switching to a new regimen is straightforward, and if medication does not meet these, expectations would stop it (Westermeyer, 1989). A number of Asian clients may believe in integrative therapies like Ayurveda and homoeopathy in India or traditional Chinese medicine using herbal remedies and acupuncture in China. Many South Asian Muslim clients prefer an injection or a drip (preferably coloured), and Hispanics may prefer talking therapies as they believe antidepressants can be addictive as we have discussed in earlier chapters. Hence, clinicians should spend adequate time educating the clients about realistic expectations from psychotropic medication from the point of first prescribing it.

There is variation in rates of non-adherence to medication among different cultural groups. In a comprehensive review of the literature, the mean rate of psychotropic non-adherence among Latinos was 44% in studies including only Latinos and was approximately 40% in studies including multiple ethnic groups. This was higher than the mean rate of roughly 30% among Euro-Americans and was comparable to the rate of roughly 40% among African Americans. The effect size of the difference was 0.64 suggesting medium to large effect size. The cultural factors that were found to be related to non-adherence were poor English proficiency, limited degree of acculturation, Spanish-speaking clients, and lack of access of quality care, while protective factors against non-adherence were greater family instrumental and financial support, higher socio-economic status, older age, being married, being more proactive in one's care, having public or private insurance, and having made eight or more visits to a therapist. There is a bidirectional influence of adherence and therapy participation with one positively influencing the other (Lanouette, Folsom, Sciolla, & Jeste, 2009).

Discussion of the role of medication is part of the recovery plan for every individual who is taking medication. Understanding beliefs about medication are important because often people cannot understand the need for ongoing medication compliance when they are well. In these instances, using analogies from physical heath that the client is familiar with can help to normalize. Most clients are familiar with a family member taking medication for high cholesterol or taking vaccines to prevent an illness developing. Explaining that medication for relapse prevention is similar can help them to better understand and accept long-term prophylactic medication. In some clients where somatization is the key symptom and physical illness is more acceptable, this approach is successful.

Culturally constituted cognitive styles affect how patients recognize, label, experience, and report the total drug effect. Cultural attitudes also affect the interpretation of side effects, which may fit into the explanatory models held by the patient. The side effects that are thought by clinicians to be more medically relevant may be ignored by clients, while other side effects can become a focus of their attention. Chinese patients on long-term lithium were unperturbed by polydipsia and polyuria, due to perception that excess removal of toxins from the body is good, but did not welcome fatigue, as it may signify loss of vital energy (Lee, 1993). In enhancing medication adherence, such alternative explanations can help. Coping cards with these explanations can be developed to maintain the gains.

Cultural dietary practices will also directly impact upon the pharmacokinetics of a drug and thereby side effects. Grilling meat over a dry heat also produces polycyclic aromatic hydrocarbons (PAH), which induce CYP1A2, in places where this is common, such as Turkey and many Asian countries. Use of over-the-counter or complimentary medicine can cause side effects due to interactions. Similar reactions can occur to religious rituals such as fasting, which could affect the levels of some medications such as lithium leading to toxicity. Homework using diaries can be helpful to identify these factors.

The pharmacokinetic and pharmacodynamics of some psychotropic medications are different in some ethnic groups, resulting in an increased vulnerability to side effects, reduced efficacy, or both. Hispanics are reported to require half the dose of a tricyclic antidepressant to achieve therapeutic benefit and are more sensitive to side effects (Marcos & Cancro, 1982). With the same dose of haloperidol, Asians are more likely to show extrapyramidal side effects (Lin et al., 1989). African Americans are reported to be at greater risk of developing lithium toxicity, because the lithium–sodium counter-transport pathway, a genetically determined mechanism that exchanges intracellular lithium for extracellular sodium, is less effective (Strickland, Lin, Fu, Anderson, & Zheng, 1995). Clinicians should be aware of the differences in the efficacy and side effects of psychotropic medication in minority cultural groups and as general rule should start with low doses and gradually build the dose (Bhugra et al., 2011).

If it is clear that a relapse is beginning or looks likely, a review of medication makes sense even if not popular. However, if the person assumes that such a review inevitably means increase in doses, or admission, and this is confirmed each time – however effective or ineffective it may be – it can seriously undermine their efforts to use other sensible strategies in a collaborative way. If relapse has led to an increase in medication doses, regular reviews are important so that the dose can be reduced again in remission. Knowing that this is likely to occur can be a positive experience and helps in keeping clients engaged with treatment. For this reason among others discussed, relapse prevention work should start early, as barriers to medication compliance should be identified at assessment and formulation stage.

Identification of Stressors and Coping Strategies

Some stresses are experienced more in migrant populations who have to deal with the stress of the migration, socio-economic pressures, effect of perceived racism, and often isolation. Experiences of discrimination and racism causing low self-esteem can lead to poor coping strategies; similarly, increased family expectation

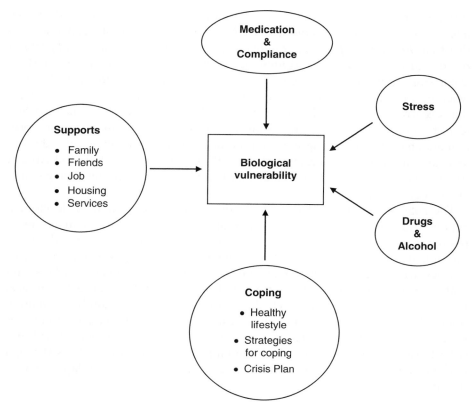

Figure 11.1   Using the stress–vulnerability model to develop coping strategies in relapse prevention.

in some cultures can have the same effect. Even happy events can put people under pressure. The therapist has to work with the client to develop their own coping strategies in the cultural context (Figure 11.1). We have already discussed technical adjustments to do this including strengths-based discussions, using a recovery approach and help from the family where appropriate.

Due to the process of acculturation, people from different cultural backgrounds are often in between two cultures, and work on coping strategies needs to enhance skills in both cultures. The therapist should be aware of the level of acculturation and identification with both cultures in the individual. The role of the therapist is not to try and integrate them into the host culture but to highlight the strengths of their own culture and increase their self-awareness. Analogies can be used from community-based support strategies from their native countries, for example, in a client from China who felt ashamed to join an exercise class as a coping strategy, the therapist asked her of the community dancing sessions in the parks in her native city and whether she had enjoyed them. The client explained that *several forms of community dancing existed, consisting of a large number of women dancing in synchronicity to music played over a loudspeaker.* She expanded further that *the main purpose is not only fitness but is also to continue and perform traditional dance moves, for community spirit and simply for fun.* Similarly, a client from India told the therapist that he benefitted from going to the park when he was back there and particularly cherished the laughter therapy groups that occurred regularly. The therapist was able to build on this in helping him identify coping strategies. There is some literature that successful prevention programmes have taught coping skills to prevent alcohol- and smoking-related problems among Hispanic migrant adolescent (Litrownik et al., 2000) and African American and Hispanic (Botvin et al., 2000) implying that work on coping strategies can be effective.

The role of families and the wider community is important in developing coping strategies in clients from different cultures. In terms of maintaining remission, there is evidence of differences in predictors of mental health in this aspect in different communities. American workers have reported increased self-efficacy which predicted better mental health, whereas Chinese workers said that increased collective efficacy predicted better mental health (Schaubroeck, Lam, & Xie, 2000). Activity schedules for clients can be family/community oriented where appropriate and elders can be used as role models in cultures where they are highly respected. Activities in the community support the cultural collectivism of the community in communities where compatible. Work through faith healers/religious leaders can also be considered part of the relapse prevention plan.

Lifestyle and Management

A healthy, balanced, and structured lifestyle is important in relapse prevention. A regular routine, which allows sufficient sleep and relaxation times in the day, can be very useful. Lifestyle balance would appeal to cultures that believe in harmony, for example, Asian, Chinese, and Buddhist (Sue & Sue, 2003), and mindfulness-based techniques may be useful here. We have already alluded to some of the community activities like community dancing and laughter groups in different countries. There are many ways of staying healthy, and these include regular exercise, balanced diet, personal hygiene, structured daytime activities, and good physical health. Creating a routine for the day will help with motivation and a sense of achievement and avoid boredom. Voluntary or paid employment may be an option but takes time to establish. The idea is to have small and achievable goals and work at the individual's pace. Families can be supportive in achieving this, but on the other hand, in cultures where expectations of the family are high, individuals may feel under pressure to achieve very quickly. The client is best placed to identify their circle of support (see Appendix 9). As stated earlier, community activities may be more acceptable in some cultures.

Drugs and Alcohol

Excessive use of alcohol and drugs is known to trigger relapse, and therapists need to be aware of cultural expectancies around this as we have already discussed. In cultures where there is sanctioned use of substances, abstinence could be a culturally incompatible goal, and harm reduction may be more appropriate. When there are cultural expectancies around alcohol use, it is helpful to involve family members and educate them about the impact of alcohol use in the client. There are instances where families decide to give up alcohol or at least not drink in front of a client to prevent triggers for relapse.

However, it is also very important not to overreact to drug and alcohol use as the increase in individual and family stress, especially if seeming to be judgmental and condemning, can be a more potent cause of relapse than even the drug use itself. The use does not need to be ignored but looking behind why the person is finding drugs or alcohol attractive or how substances are helping them manage stress can enable alternative approaches to be explored. Substance use alone does not inevitably lead to relapse in many individuals – especially if it is being used as a way out of loneliness – but can often be taken as a sign that other supports or social outlets are worth exploring.

Relapse Prevention Plan

This is a plan that aims to build upon what has been learnt and has been helpful to the individual over the months and years. In most clients, there are practices that have been found to help and should be entered onto a staying well plan (see Appendix 7).

One of the techniques that clients find useful is co-production of the relapse prevention plan. 'Co-produced' methods seem to be effective in improving feelings of self-efficacy which, in turn, support a 'fundamental transformation of the clients determination to manage their condition'. This means mutually agreeing the relapse prevention plan based on cultural modifications using the client as the expert in their culture and illness.

The relapse prevention plan needs to be personalized, taking the cultural context into account. This may include:

- Coping strategies that have been helpful
- Dealing with stress
- Role of medication
- Healthy living and structure to the day
- Role of drugs and alcohol
- How to identify early warning signs
- Use of advance directives to deal with relapse
- Minor crisis plan if early warning signs are identified – who to contact

- Major crisis plan – if the minor crisis plan has not brought about a reduction in early warning signs or if there is a major crisis
- Responsibilities of the client, family members, or other providers (What would each person involved with the client do? See Appendix 8)

There is also a very important issue about overreaction to warning signs as discussed earlier. The emergence of early warning signs can sometimes lead to panic – catastrophization – when they can be just normal signs of the 'ups and downs' of life, transient and requiring minimal fine-tuning of lifestyle. They do not inevitably mean that a psychotic episode is imminent and indeed recognition of them could even be a source of relief as by their nature they are early signs to which the person can now make reasonable adjustments and get on with their lives. They can sometimes lead to avoidance of any stressful circumstance and that can be as problematic as relapse itself – 'getting a life' can mean stress, or excitement as it is alternatively known – getting the balance right seems key and learning what can be tolerated and what can be too much.

> **Exercise:** Using the relapse prevention techniques of CBT, can you think of a client where you have used their culture to enhance the plan? How could you have done it differently?

Wellness Recovery Action Plan

Self-management of psychiatric illness is a central tenet of consumer-directed mental health treatment and a key component of recovery-oriented work. In many developed nations, the most widely disseminated self-management programme is the Wellness Recovery Action Plan (WRAP). WRAP sessions are facilitated by peers or staff members, and participation in the sessions is known to improve psychiatric symptoms and instill hope (Fukui et al., 2011). These might include crisis planning, identification of early warning signs of impending psychosis and triggers, and daily maintenance list of things to do to keep well (Copeland, 2002). The WRAP is a tool that allows an individual's cultural strengths to be incorporated and used as part of the care plan.

Finishing Therapy (Termination)

Termination of therapy in an ideal situation should be planned collaboratively by the client and therapist with necessary input from the client's family or other support systems. An ideal therapist would start thinking of termination at the start of the assessment phase in a way similar to a traveller starting a journey with the destination in mind. However, it is important for therapists to be aware of other factors that lead to discharge and termination such as client's psychosocial circumstances, cultural issues, or funding limitations. Termination of therapy can be difficult for some clients who have experienced isolation or low self-esteem and have learnt to trust their therapist and are not fully confident in their ability to cope with their circumstances. In these instances, transitioning them to other community supports can be helpful. Some clients from cultural minorities such as African Americans make the transition from mental health counselling to religious counselling better than straight discharge as they are shown more likely to find spiritual counselling acceptable for treatment (Givens, Katz, Bellamy, & Holmes, 2007). For some people from minority groups, especially asylum seekers, transitory existences may be a way of life, and working with them to manage this and to pick up appropriate supports when they move on should be a part of relapse prevention.

Termination is another opportunity to collaboratively involve the client in decision making. Termination can be planned in one of three ways:

1. Set a date for last sessions and termination without further follow-up.
2. Have a final session and inform client that they can call and set up a booster session if needed.
3. Have a final session but set up a booster or follow-up session in 2–4 weeks. Give the option to call and cancel if everything is going well.

Most clients when given these options are able to make a decision about what works best for them, and in this way, termination can be individualized. Unplanned termination can occur especially where individuals return at short notice to their country of origin for marriage, funerals, or caring for family members, and follow-up is difficult but not impossible. Brief contacts can be made to finalize relapse planning and complete termination discussions or temporarily suspend therapy by phone or video (secure systems may be available or Skype – if the individual accepts that confidentiality cannot be absolutely assured).

> **Exercise:** Consider the two cases of Safia (Chapter 4) and Lincoln (Chapter 7). Draw up their relapse prevention plan (see Appendix 9). What cultural aspects did you consider?

The relapse prevention plans for both cases are in Appendix 9.

Conclusion

Work on relapse prevention and finishing therapy starts at the beginning of therapy. Relapse signatures may be influenced by culture, and triggers for relapse may also be culturally determined. As a therapist, understanding these determinants is important in co-producing a relapse prevention plan with the client.

References

Bhugra, D., Gupta, S., Bhui, K., Craig, T., Dogra, N., Ingleby, J., … Tribe, R. (2011). WPA guidance on mental health and mental health care in migrants. *World Psychiatry*, *10*(1), 2–10.

Birchwood, M., Smith, J., Macmillian, F., et al. (1989). Predicting relapse in schizophrenia: the development and implementation of an early signs monitoring system using patients and families as observers. *Psychological Medicine, 19*, 649–656.

Botvin, G. J., Griffin, K. W., Diaz, T., Scheier, L. M., Williams, C., & Epstein, J. A. (2000). Preventing illicit drug use in adolescents: Longterm follow-up data from a randomised controlled trial of a school population. *Addicitve Behaviours, 25*, 769–774.

Copeland, M. E. (2002). Guide to Developing a WRAP - Wellness Recovery Action Plan. Mental Health Recovery.com. (accessed on 06/11/14 at: http://mentalhealthrecovery.com/wrap

Deegan, P. (1988). Recovery: The lived experience of rehabilitation. Psychosocial *Rehabilitation Journal, 11*, 11–19.

Deegan, P. E. (2005). The importance of personal medicine: A qualitative study of resilience in people with psychiatric disabilities. *Scandinavian Journal of Public Health, 66*, 29–35.

Fukui, S., Starnino, V. R., Mariscal, S., Davidson, L. J., Cook, K. S., Rapp, C. A., & Gowdy, E. A. (2011). Effect of Wellness Recovery Action Plan (WRAP) participation on psychiatric symptoms, sense of hope, and recovery. *Psychiatric Rehabilitation Journal, 34*, 214–222. doi:10.2975/34.3.2011.214.222

Givens, J. L., Katz, I. R., Bellamy, S., Holmes, W. C. (2007). Stigma and the acceptability of depression treatments among African Americans and whites. *Journal of General Internal Medicine, 22*(9), 1292–1297.

Lanouette, N., Folsom, D. P., Sciolla, A., & Jeste, D. (2009). Psychotropic medication non-adherence among United States Latinos: A comprehensive review of the literature. *Psychiatric Services, 60*(2), 157–174.

Larimer, E., Palmer, R., Marlatt, G. A. (1999). Relapse prevention: An overview of Marlatt's cognitive -behavioural model. *Alcohol Research and Health, 23* (2), 151–160.

Lee, S. (1993). Side effects of chronic lithium therapy in Hong Kong Chinese: An ethnopsychiatric perspective. *Culture, Medicine and Psychiatry, 17*(3), 301–320.

Lin, K. M., Poland, R. E., Nuccio, I., Matsuda, K., Hathuc, N., Su, T. P., & Fu, P. (1989). A longitudinal assessment of Haloperidol doses and serum concentrations in Asian and Caucasian schizophrenic patients. *The American Journal of Psychiatry, 146*(10), 1307–1311.

Litrownik, A., Elder, J., Campbell, N., et al. (2000). Evaluation of a tobacco and alcohol use prevention program for hispanic migrant adolescent: promoting the protective factor of parent-child communication. *Preventative Medicine, 31*, 124–133.

Marcos, L. R., & Cancro, R. (1982). Pharmacotherapy of Hispanic depressed patients: Clinical observations. *American Journal of Psychotherapy, 36*(4), 505–512.

Marlatt, G. A., & Gordon, J. R. (1985). Relapse Prevention: Maintenance Strategies in the Treatment of Addictive Behaviours.Eds. New York: Guilford Press.

NHS Confederation/Centre for Mental Health. (2012, June). Supporting recovery in mental health (issue 244). London, UK: NHS Confederation. Retrieved from www.nhsconfed.org/publications (accessed September 19, 2014).

Schaubroeck, J., Lam, S. S. K., Xie, J. L. (2000). Collective versus individual self-efficacy in coping responses to stressors and control: A cross-cultural study. *Journal of Applied Psychology, 85*, 512–525.

Strickland, T. L., Lin, K. M., Fu, P., Anderson, D., & Zheng, Y. (1995). Comparison of lithium ratio between African-American and Caucasian bipolar patients. *Biological Psychiatry, 37*(5), 325–330.

Sue, D. W. & Sue, D. (2003). Counseling the culturally diverse (4th ed.) New York, John Wiley and Sons.

Westermeyer, J. (1989). Somatotherapies. In J. H. Gold (Ed.), *Psychiatric care of migrants: A clinical guide* (pp. 139–168). Washington, DC: American Psychiatric Press.

12

Policy and Training Implications

We have covered the various aspects of adapting cognitive behavioural therapy (CBT) for severely mentally ill people from minority cultures. The book thus far has focused on the individual client and the therapist. It is clear that cultural adaptation of CBT is still in its infancy and for it to be disseminated widely, we need to address three issues. Firstly, we need more research on the efficacy of culturally adapted CBT in different minority cultures and the specific type of adaptations that are effective for various cultures. Secondly, mental health delivery systems should be adjusted to facilitate provision of such therapy, and thirdly, there should be policy decisions at the level of the government to provide adequate resources to train staff to provide culturally competent therapy.

Mental illness is the second leading cause of disability and premature mortality internationally. Becker and Kleinman (2013) noted that in 1990, the global aggregate burden of years lived with disability due to mental illness and behavioural disorder was 22.2% and in 2010, it was 22.7%. In the United States, severe mental illnesses (SMI) collectively account for more than 15% of the overall burden of disease from all causes (Kessler et al., 2005). In the European Union, at least 83 million people (27%) suffer from mental health problems, with 16.7 million in the United Kingdom (Wittchen & Jacobi, 2005). Despite this high degree of prevalence, mental health disorders are not treated as equal to the physical health disorders, evidenced directly by lack of adequate services and indirectly in most health systems through relative neglect of mental health provision. In addition to that, the existing mental health systems often fail to articulate a coherent grand vision or the infrastructure essential to provide quality behavioural care although such visions do exist (www.emotionalwellbeing.southcentral.nhs.uk; Department

Cultural Adaptation of CBT for Serious Mental Illness: A Guide for Training and Practice, First Edition. Shanaya Rathod, David Kingdon, Narsimha Pinninti, Douglas Turkington, and Peter Phiri.
© 2015 John Wiley & Sons, Ltd. Published 2015 by John Wiley & Sons, Ltd.

of Health, 1999; Grazier, Mowbray, & Holter, 2005). For ethnic minorities, access to behavioural health and available treatment options is even more limited (Institute of Medicine of the National Academies, 2002). The main barriers have been discussed in earlier chapters and can be grouped into sociocultural difficulties (health beliefs and mistrust of services), systemic problems (lack of culturally competent interventions), economic issues, and individual barriers like shame and stigma (Ruiz, 2002). This chapter proposes interventions to address the issues at the macro or systems level and at the micro or individual client and family level to (i) increase access to psychosocial treatments such as CBT for individuals with SMI and (ii) reduce the disparities in access to mental health services to ethnic minorities.

Current Issues

Over the course of the last half century in the United States, Europe, and Australasia, the focus of care of severely mentally ill has moved from the state institutions and asylums to community settings through the establishment of community mental health centres (CMHCs) and community mental health teams (CMHTs) that in many countries have been made responsible for providing the services necessary for people with SMI. The population of state hospitals in the United States was at a peak of 339 beds per 100,000 in 1955 and stood at 22 per 100,000 in 2002 (Manderscheid, Atay, & Male, 2002) with continuing decreases since. Similarly in the United Kingdom, there has been a steady reduction of psychiatric beds, from a maximum of 155,000 in 1954 to 27,000 in 2008 with a national plan to reduce further (Tyrer, 2011). Therefore, most of the care for SMI is now provided in the community settings. The CMHCs in the United States were initially funded directly by federal grants, and in the 1970s, responsibility for disbursement of the funds and setting of mental health priorities associated with those funds shifted to the state level. Subsequently, many states diverted these funds to other purposes, and it resulted in many CMHCs being severely underfunded. The number one cost of the CMHCs in the United States and CMHTs in the United Kingdom is their trained personnel, and a lack of funds is reflected in that most teams now do not employ psychologists or other mental health professionals with training in empirically validated psychosocial treatments.

Attempts to control rising health-care costs in Canada, Great Britain, Europe, and the United States strongly influence access to psychosocial treatments although there have been economic arguments made and accepted by the UK government in the past few years for increasing CBT provision for common mental disorders (discussed later). Although cost and efficiency are concerns for all forms of health care, certain features of psychosocial treatments make them vulnerable to cost constraints. These include heavy reliance on human resources, the wide range of people and needs they must serve, and meagre information about cost-effectiveness. Treatment for some severely mentally ill can last for a lifetime, heightening concerns about long-term costs (Clark & Samnaliev, 2005).

Even when studies show the equivalence or superiority of psychosocial interventions, marketing strength favours medications (Clark & Samnaliev, 2005), and effective psychosocial interventions are shown to be highly underutilized in the treatment of illnesses such as schizophrenia (Lehman & Steinwachs, 2003). However, there is an economic case for better interventions like CBT for SMI and care pathways that support recovery (Knapp et al., 2014).

In the United States, the passage of Patient Protection and Affordable Care Act (PPACA), commonly called 'Obamacare' or the Affordable Care Act (ACA), is the most significant expansion of the US health-care system for many years and is bringing about transformative changes in the way health care, especially mental health care, is being delivered (http://www.gpo.gov/fdsys/pkg/PLAW-111publ148/html/PLAW-111publ148.htm). The ACA is expected to bring health insurance to 32 million uninsured Americans. Through the Medicaid expansion, insurance exchanges, and government subsidies, 81% of uninsured African Americans, 60% of uninsured Latinos, and 60% of uninsured Asian-Pacific Islanders will be able to obtain coverage (Doty & Holmgren, 2004). The level of health insurance coverage for all population groups is increasing as a result of the ACA, but disparities in coverage for minority cultural groups remain (O'Hara & Brault, 2013). The need to increase the number of under-represented minority groups in the health-care workforce is addressed by reauthorizing the Centers of Excellence and the Health Career Opportunity Program, which seek to recruit and retain members of racial/ethnic minority groups to the health professions.

In the United Kingdom, the National Institute for Health and Care Excellence (NICE) provides independent, authoritative, and evidence-based guidance on the most cost-effective treatments. Psychosocial treatments are recommended by NICE for most SMI as an adjunct to medication (NICE, 2014). In other countries too, guidelines for SMI, for example, schizophrenia, recommend that CBT be offered and be available for any individual with first-episode psychosis and persistent symptoms despite adequate pharmacotherapy (Dixon et al., 2009). Given that ethnic minorities constitute a sizable portion of people with mental illness, culturally adapted CBT should be available to clients from ethnic minorities. However, formal CBT for SMI is provided by highly trained staff that are not available in CMHCs in the United States or elsewhere, and hence, CBT is not available in most routine clinical care settings (Pinninti, Schmidt, & Snyder, 2013). It is a challenge for both the CMHCs that deliver the mental health services and the organizations that fund them to find more cost-effective ways of providing psychosocial interventions such as culturally adapted CBT for most individuals with SMI.

Task Shifting as an Intervention

One way to address this resource 'crunch' is by use of the methodology of task shifting. Task shifting or 'task sharing' is defined as 'delegating tasks to existing cadres or new cadres with either less training or narrowly tailored training.'

This is a response that is well utilized when there are shortages of human resources in mental health (Kakuma et al., 2011). The approach is to use a variety of existing staff such as case managers (CM), care coordinators (CCOs in the United Kingdom), advanced practice nurses (APNs), and peer counsellors to train them in culturally adapted CBT to significantly increase access and availability of these interventions.

Case management is a substantially funded service at federal and state levels in the United States with equivalents in many mental health-care systems, for example, care coordination in the United Kingdom. It is widely considered the linchpin in the organization and coordination of community services for clients with SMI (Corrigan, Mueser, Bond, Drake, & Solomon, 2008). For most individuals with SMI, the professional they have the most contact with is a CM/care coordinator in the community or counsellor for group therapy in the day programme. Most severely mentally ill do not have an individual therapist, do not see a psychologist, and only see a psychiatrist for a 15–30 min appointment at a frequency of once in 6–12 weeks. Given these staff resources, the way to make CBT interventions available for more people with SMI is utilizing existing staff of CM/care coordinators and counsellors and devising training programmes to help them develop CBT skills. However, it has to be kept in mind that the requirements for case management position is either associate level or bachelor's level with 2–4 years of undergraduate education in any of the social sciences in the United States. CM do not have uniform training, formal certification, or licensing requirements, nor do they need to demonstrate any specific skill set. Hence, there is a wide variation in the knowledge and skill set of CM and is reflected in the perceptions of the clients and family members about case management as well as the outcome of case management services.

A three-step approach to training and skill building to increase workforce in CBT has been proposed before (Beck, 2005; Pinninti, Hollow, Sanghadia, & Thompson, 2006). A similar approach is proposed here for CM and is being developed in the United States in New Jersey and Ohio (by the BeST Practices organization). Using this model, all CM will be taught basic CBT skills and principles of applying it to the different cultural groups they deal with. The curriculum includes an introduction to CBT theory, cultural principles in CBT, basic engagement, and change-oriented skills. The national guidelines for CM practice propose a number of critical tasks for CM that requires a variety of relationship-building and problem-solving skills (Giesler & Hodge, 1998), and basic training in CBT can give them a frame of reference and a methodology to perform the tasks required for effective case management. The CM integrate the CBT interventions into their case management practice. Supervisors of CM receive the next level of training. This is more intensive 6–12-month training along with supervision that leads to certification in CBT. It may also contribute to the formal accreditations offered by the Academy of Cognitive Therapy or, similarly, the European Associations of Cognitive Therapy. They would be the second line of intervention for the cases that are difficult for individual CM to deal with while also training and supervising the CM. However, the more complex cases could be referred to experts in the area of CBT for SMI at least for specific periods to overcome blocks in engagement or therapy. Preliminary studies have shown that bachelor's level staff can be trained in CBT and once they have the skill set, they continue to use CBT interventions with their clients (Pinninti, Fisher, Thompson, & Steer, 2010; Montesano, Sivec, Munetz, Pelton, & Turkington, 2014). In a pilot case study, bachelor's level CM without prior therapy experience worked in tandem with a more experienced therapist in the role of therapy extender to provide CBT interventions for a very-difficult-to-engage client. CM sat in therapy sessions and visited the client weekly to review and help him complete homework assignments including a systematic desensitization plan. Through this arrangement, the frequency of therapy sessions was cut to once a month, thereby extending the ability of the therapist to see more number of people (Pinninti et al., 2013). The research on the use of CM in providing CBT interventions is limited (Turkington et al., 2014) although work is developing in modular approaches using a worry intervention for paranoia (Foster, Startup, Potts, & Freeman, 2010) and low-intensity CBT interventions (Waller et al., 2013). Further research needs to be conducted to see the effectiveness of CM in the provision of CBT interventions in the real-world situations with clients of different ethnic minorities.

Issues in the Training of CM in CBT

Certain issues need to be addressed when the CM are trained in CBT. Some professional bodies consider that therapy is outside the scope of practice for case management and this is based on the lack of uniform training and certification requirements for it. This issue can be addressed if a basic standard curriculum that includes CBT is developed and made a requirement for all CM/care coordinators/key workers. CM/key workers are currently dealing with some of the most challenging people with SMI in community settings without the benefit of formal training, and standardized training tailored to their work is likely to enhance their engagement skills and improve the quality of case management interventions. Training manuals with simple and easy-to-learn engagement strategies have been developed for CM at all levels of experience. Almost a third of individuals who have contact with mental health services disengage due to a variety of reasons including the burden of accessing services and not finding that the services provided are meaningful to their problems and that services are provided by individuals who do not understand their issues (Kreyenbuhl, Nossel, & Dixon, 2009). CM address some of these barriers for engagement by visiting clients in their natural settings, working on instrumental issues such as housing and food stamps that clients find more meaningful, and engaging community resources. Also, CM, by virtue of working in the natural environments of the clients, are able to better understand their strengths, supports and culture, the resources that could be mobilized, and the real-world functional deficits and strengths.

Behavioural and Physical Health Integration

In the United States and the United Kingdom, behavioural health and physical health have been provided by different systems of care (with different funding sources in the United States), different philosophies, organization, and delivery of services. However, the significant co-morbidity of physical and behavioural health problems, the burden on the clients when care is split, and the higher cost of providing split care have made integrated care as a vision and goal for clients. An ideal integrated care model is the provision of medical homes that are one-stop shop for all the medical as well as behavioural health needs of clients. The ACA contains specific provisions to promote the creation of 'medical homes' where comprehensive services are provided in one place for enrollees with chronic conditions (Andrulis & Siddiqui, 2011). The medical homes need outreach services to engage the SMI to help them coordinate their care and address their multifold needs. In future, the CM are likely to become more care managers for both physical and behavioural health needs. There are some pilot studies underway to develop the care manager model in Hispanic community (Cabassa, Druss, Wang, & Lewis-Fernandez, 2011). A similar system is being proposed in the United Kingdom under the umbrella of 'better care funds' that envisages integrated care.

APNs and CBT Interventions

A shortage of psychiatrists in the United States has been the impetus to develop a training programme for nurses with experience in dealing with psychiatric clients to become prescribers of psychotropic medication (APN); similarly, nurse prescribers have been trained in the United Kingdom. These APNs or nurse prescribers in the United Kingdom are providing services in a variety of settings that traditionally had been underserved such as visiting clients in their own homes when they refuse to come for appointments and being part of primary care offices and mental health teams in prisons. In addition, centres that are run by nurses have been providing integrated behavioural and physical health services to clients (McDevitt, Braun, Noyes, Snyder, & Marion, 2005). Community psychiatric nurses trained in CBT have been successfully able to provide therapy as a brief intervention for individuals with schizophrenia and their carers during their visit to the clients with effects enduring after the intervention was completed (Turkington et al., 2006).

There is work underway in the United Kingdom as well to base a CBT for psychosis intervention on a patient-rated outcome measure (PROM) called DIALOG for use by CMHC personnel. Use of DIALOG which elicits client day-to-day concerns alone has been shown to improve quality of life (Priebe et al., 2007); additionally, a solution-focused problem-solving approach is being developed which is supplemented by guided self-help work sheets to address mental health issues such as voices, delusions, and negative symptoms (DIALOG+).

Peer Providers

One of the initiatives to address the stigma of psychiatric illness and instill hope for individuals with mental illnesses is to incorporate peers who have history of mental illness as service providers. The precedent for this is from the treatment of substance abuse (SA) where individuals with prior history of SA go on to become successful SA counsellors. Peers come in with a life experience of dealing with mental illness and have a good working knowledge of the problems and issues with the mental health system, and clients find it much easier to relate to peers and find them to be less threatening than the regular service providers. A number of studies have shown that peers provide mental health counselling services that are comparable to professionals but in a much less expensive way than the traditional services. Peers have been shown to provide effective culturally sensitive engagement and linkage services for individuals with psychosis belonging to African American and Latino communities (Tondora et al., 2010). There have been suggestions that peers can act as wellness coaches and work on life goals (Swarbrick, Murphy, Zechner, Spagnolo, & Gill, 2011). However, there are no studies done to evaluate the effectiveness of training peer counsellors in culturally adapted CBT so that they could work with members of the ethnic minorities. Training in culturally adapted CBT will complement their life experience and knowledge of the mental health system in helping individuals from ethnic minorities.

Interventions to Enhance Community Education and Reduce Stigma

Various ethnic minority communities share one common feature – that of significant stigma associated with mental illness. There are significant negative attitudes towards mental health help-seeking behaviours, and these are more prevalent in people who are less educated and from lower social status, and ethnic minorities are more likely to have these attitudes (Jagdeo, Cox, Stein, & Sareen, 2009). Stigma is thought to be created and maintained due to a complex interplay of social-structural, interpersonal, and psychological factors (Link & Phelan, 2001). It is also viewed as being pervasive, pernicious, and resistant to change, and to be successful, anti-stigma programmes must be comprehensive, multi-pronged, and directed to individual, interpersonal, and systems-level determinants (Stuart, 2008). Three different types of stigma are described as interfering in recovery. They are (i) public stigma, (ii) self-stigma, and (iii) label avoidance (Corrigan & Wassel, 2008). There is good correlation between public stigma and self-stigma, and self-stigma reduces help-seeking behaviours. Effectively addressing and lowering public stigma are likely to lower self-stigma and promote help-seeking behaviour (Evans-Lacko, Brohan, Mojtabai, & Thornicroft, 2012). A variety of strategies are proposed to address the stigma in ethnic minority communities, and the goal is to improve knowledge and attitudes about mental illnesses which should translate into positive behavioural change. The anti-stigma approaches that have been most successful in improving knowledge and attitudes have combined active learning with positive contact with people who have a mental illness (Stuart, 2008), but these improvements have not always translated into positive changes in behaviour. We propose a number of different strategies and approaches to reduce the severity and impact of stigma in ethnic minority communities. These are as follows.

Utilizing community leaders and other ethnic role models

A powerful way to fight stigma associated with any illness is for positive role models who suffer from the illness to talk about their experiences and normalizing the illness. Celebrities have been used effectively to fight stigma (London, Scriven, & Lalani, 2006). Celebrities are routinely used to educate clients and their families and encourage them to seek treatment for a variety of conditions such as HIV infection, epilepsy, and parkinsonism. In addition, the second- and third-generation members of ethnic minorities who are acculturated can play a very active role in reducing the stigma in the community by reaching out to the new immigrants and making it easier for them to accept help for emotional problems. A longer-term strategy is to encourage young people from minority communities to go into behavioural health care to develop the workforce for the future through financial or other incentives. Minority clinicians are under-represented in the workforce, and one study found that in California there were only 29 Latino clinicians for 100,000 clients compared to 173 for 100,000 for the non-Latino counterparts (Organista & Snowden, 2003). The community can also develop or support ethnically specific mental health centres. Similar centres have been developed for Asian, Hispanic, and other ethnic groups (Mirabal-Colon, 2003; Vu, Schwartz, & Austin, 2011).

Ethnic minority-focused support groups

Support groups that are specifically for ethnic minorities can be a tremendous resource for individuals with SMI. They serve a variety of functions including instilling hope, neutralizing stigma, providing emotional support, disseminating information about available resources, and helping individuals navigate the difficult terrain of health-care system. The support groups can be for the clients as well as the family members of those suffering from mental illness. The National Alliance on Mental Illness (NAMI) is the largest advocacy organization for the mentally ill in the United States as well as their families and has chapters in every state and almost every county. They established a multicultural action centre to eliminate the disparities in mental health services for ethnic minorities, to ensure access to culturally competent services for all Americans, and to support individuals with diverse backgrounds who are affected by mental illnesses, and resources for ethnic minorities are available on their website (http://www.nami.org/).

In addition, they promote efforts to involve leaders from different ethnic groups in NAMI initiatives as well as encourage chapters of ethnic subgroups.

In the United Kingdom, the Delivering Race Equality initiative introduced community development workers (CDWs) whose role was to achieve social justice and equality for minority communities by engaging these communities (Bhui, 2009). CDWs tackled discrimination in two main ways: seeking to change community views on mental health issues and service provision and seeking to influence and change service provision. With shrinking resources, sustaining CDWs may be a challenge, and the solution may be for CM/key workers or ethnic centres to adopt the function in an integrated health-care model (Carr, Lhussier, Wilkinson, & Gleadhill, 2008).

Utilizing primary care settings to provide culturally adapted CBT

Many individuals from minority cultural groups are more likely to visit a primary care physician (PCP or general practitioner) to get help for emotional issues as opposed to seeking services from qualified behavioural health providers. In many minority cultures, emotional distress is expressed as more acceptable physical symptoms. Mental health services can be taken to the individuals when they visit PCP by embedding counsellors or nurses trained in culturally adapted CBT in primary care settings where they would provide therapy for clients in the milieu of the medical offices. Many clients who were referred to a psychiatrist by their PCP did not make it to the appointment, and the most frequently mentioned reason was the fear of mental illness stigma, rather than negative expectations about the treatment and its quality (Sartorius et al., 2010). Mental health services provided in PCP offices reduce the likelihood of stigma as well as the logistical burden of finding the time and transportation to visit a different venue (Manoleas, 2008). Currently existing systems such as the federally qualified health centres (FQHCs) or other similar centres such as nurse-managed health centres are the best places to start such service provision. FQHCs are health-care centres established and funded by federal government to address the needs of vulnerable groups of people such as those at risk of homelessness or those from impoverished areas and ethnic minorities, and providing mental health services fits into their mission.

There have recently been funded developments in the United Kingdom to Improving Access to Psychological Treatment (IAPT) which have disseminated CBT for common mental disorders (especially anxiety and depression) using a direct access low-intensity and high-intensity system of provision (www.iapt.nhs.uk). Lord Richard Layard, an eminent economist, made the case to the UK government that increased productivity and reduction in spending on welfare benefits would make this cost-effective (London School of Economics and Political Science, 2006). One of the two original pilot sites was Newham in London which is a very culturally diverse area, and there has been consistent attention to the importance of making the programme accessible and responsive to the needs of the full range of ethnic groups. This programme is now being expanded to SMI – although without new funding. However, training for existing CMHT members and specialist therapists is a major consideration alongside methods of outcome measurement and service redesign to ensure that those who can benefit from CBT receive it. The findings of the culturally adapted CBT project described previously are being fed into this process.

Future Recommendations

There are significant challenges in making culturally adapted CBT accessible for most people who receive care in services. The first one is to address the enormous gaps in research in evaluating the effectiveness of culturally adapted CBT for different cultural groups. Most of the randomized controlled trials for CBT have been conducted in England and Europe, although recently studies have been successfully completed ((Guo et al., 2010) Li & Turkington, submitted) and emerging in China (an early intervention study is currently commencing). However, more research is needed in the United States and elsewhere to demonstrate its effectiveness in real-world situations as well as efficacy with different ethnic groups. The challenges of finding resources to provide psychosocial treatments to SMI in the current environment of dwindling resources are enormous. A number of ways of enhancing the access and availability of CBT are suggested such as using existing staff, incorporating peers in providing therapy, and integrating therapy in the provision of physical health care. Service research is needed to study the efficacy and cost-effectiveness of these implementation suggestions. Although the hurdles, both practical and economic, to be overcome to implement adapted CBT are significant, there is remarkable progress taking place, and it is reasonable to work in the expectation that, over the next few years, we can substantially improve outcomes for people with SMI from a wide range of ethnic groups using culturally adapted CBT.

References

Andrulis, D. P., & Siddiqui, N. J. (2011). Health reform holds both risks and rewards for safety-net providers and racially and ethnically diverse patients. *Health Affairs*, 30(10), 1830–1836. doi:10.1377/hlthaff.2011.0661

Beck, A. T. (2005). The current state of cognitive therapy: A 40-year retrospective. *Archives of General Psychiatry*, 62(9), 953–959.

Becker, A. E., & Kleinman, A. (2013). Mental health and the global agenda. *New England Journal of Medicine*, 369, 66–73. doi:10.1056/NEJMra1110827

Bhui, K. (2009). Editorial enhancing pathways into care & recovery: From specialist services to healthy minds. *International Review of Psychiatry*, 21(5), 425–426. doi:10.1080/09540260903190187

Cabassa, L. J., Druss, B., Wang, Y., & Lewis-Fernandez, R. (2011). Collaborative planning approach to inform the implementation of a healthcare manager intervention for Hispanics with serious mental illness: A study protocol. *Implementation Science*, 6, 80. doi:10.1186/1748-5908-6-80

Carr, S. M., Lhussier, M., Wilkinson, J., & Gleadhill, S. (2008). Empowerment evaluation applied to public health practice. *Critical Public Health*, *18*(2), 161–174. doi:10.1080/09581590701499327

Clark, R. E., & Samnaliev, M. (2005). Psychosocial treatment in the 21st century. *International Journal of Law and Psychiatry*, *28*(5), 532–544.

Corrigan, P. W., Mueser, E. T., Bond, G., Drake, R. E., & Solomon, P. (2008). *Principles and practice of psychiatric rehabilitation: An empirical approach*. New York, NY: Guilford Press.

Corrigan, P., & Wassel, A. (2008). Understanding and influencing the stigma of mental illness. *Journal of Psychosocial Nursing and Mental Health Services*, *46*(1), 42–48. doi:10.3928/02793695-20080101-04

Department of Health (1999) National Service Framework for Mental Health: modern standards and service models. London: HMSO.

Dixon, L. B., Dickerson, F., Bellack, A. S., Bennett, M., Dickinson, D., Goldberg, R., ... Kreyenbuhl, J. (2009). The 2009 schizophrenia PORT psychosocial treatment recommendations and summary statements. *Schizophrenia Bulletin*, *36*(1), 48–70. doi:sbp115 [pii]10.1093/schbul/sbp115[doi]

Doty, M. M., & Holmgren, A. L. (2004). *Unequal access: Insurance instability among low-income workers and minorities* (cited November 2, 2010). Retrieved from http://www.commonwealthfund.org/usr_doc/doty_unequalaccess_ib_729.pdf (accessed September 26, 2014).

Evans-Lacko, S., Brohan, E., Mojtabai, R., & Thornicroft, G. (2012). Association between public views of mental illness and self-stigma among individuals with mental illness in 14 European countries. *Psychological Medicine*, 2012 Aug;42(8):1741–52. doi: 10.1017/S0033291711002558. Epub 2011.

Foster, C., Startup, H., Potts, L., & Freeman, D. (2010). A randomised controlled trial of a worry intervention for individuals with persistent persecutory delusions. *Journal of Behavior Therapy and Experimental Psychiatry*, *41*(1), 45–51.

Giesler, L. J. & M. Hodge (1998). "Case Management in Behavioral Health Care." *International Journal of Mental Health* 27(4): 26–40.

Grazier, K. L., Mowbray, C. T., & Holter, M. C. (2005). Rationing psychosocial treatments in the United States. *International Journal of Law and Psychiatry*, *28*(5), 545–560.

Guo, X., Zhai, J., Liu, Z., Fang, M., Wang, B., Wang, C.,...Zhao, J. (2010). Effect of antipsychotic medication alone vs combined with psychosocial intervention on outcomes of early-stage schizophrenia: A randomized, 1-year study. *Archives in General Psychiatry*, *67*(9), 895–904. doi:67/9/895 [pii], 10.1001/archgenpsychiatry.2010.105 [dio]

Institute of Medicine of the National Academies. (2002). *Unequal treatment: What healthcare providers need to know about racial and ethnic disparities in healthcare*. Washington, DC: Author.

Jagdeo, A., Cox, B. J., Stein, M. B., & Sareen, J. (2009). Negative attitudes toward help seeking for mental illness in 2 population-based surveys from the United States and Canada. *Canadian Journal of Psychiatry*, *54*(11), 757–766.

Kakuma, R., Minas, H., Van Ginneken, N., Dal Poz, M. R., Desiraju, K., Morris, J.E., ... Scheffler, R.M. (2011). Human resources for mental health care: Current situation and strategies for action. *The Lancet*, *378*(9803), 1654–1663. doi:10.1016/S0140-6736(11)61093-3

Kessler, R., Demler, O., Frank, R., Olfson, M., Pincus, H., Walters, E., ... Zaslavsky, A. (2005). Prevalence and treatment of mental disorders, 1990 to 2003. *The New England Journal of Medicine*, *352*(24), 2515–2523.

Knapp, M., Andrew, A., McDaid, D., Lemmi, V., McCrone, P., Park, A., ... Shepherd, G. (2014). *Investing in recovery: Making the business case for effective interventions for people with schizophrenia and psychosis.* London, UK: The London School of Economics and Political Science, and Centre for Mental Health.

Kreyenbuhl, J., Nossel, I. R., & Dixon, L. B. (2009). Disengagement from mental health treatment among individuals with schizophrenia and strategies for facilitating connections to care: A review of the literature. *Schizophrenia Bulletin, 35*(4), 696–703. doi:10.1093/schbul/sbp046

Lehman, A. F., & Steinwachs, D. M. (2003). Evidence-based psychosocial treatment practices in schizophrenia: Lessons from the client outcomes research team (PORT) project. *The Journal of the American Academy of Psychoanalysis and Dynamic Psychiatry, 31*(1), 141–154.

Li, Z., Guo, Z., Wang, N., Xu, Z., Qu, Y., Wang, X., Sun, J., Yan, L., Ng, R., Turkington, D., & Kingdon, D. Cognitive-Behavioural Therapy for Patients with Schizophrenia: A Multicenter Randomised Controlled Trial in Beijing, China. (Under review).

Link, B. G., & Phelan, J. C. (2001). Conceptualizing stigma. *Annual Review of Sociology, 27,* 363–385. doi:10.1146/annurev.soc.27.1.363

London, C., Scriven, A., & Lalani, N. (2006). Sir Winston Churchill: Greatest Briton used as an anti-stigma icon. *Journal of the Royal Society for the Promotion of Health, 126*(4), 163–164.

London School of Economics and Political Science. (2006). *The depression report: A new deal for depression and anxiety disorders: A report by the Centre for Economic Performance's Mental Health Policy Group.* London, UK: Author.

Manderscheid, R. W., Atay, J. E., & Male, A. (2002). *Highlights of organized mental health services in 2000 and major national and state trends.* In *Mental Health United States.* Washington, DC: Center for Mental Health Services.

Manoleas, P. (2008). Integrated primary care and behavioral health services for Latinos: A blueprint and research agenda. *Social Work in Health Care, 47*(4), 438–454. doi:10.1080/00981380802344480 [doi]

McDevitt, J., Braun, S., Noyes, M., Snyder, M., & Marion, L. (2005). Integrated primary and mental health care: Evaluating a nurse-managed center for clients with serious and persistent mental illness. *Nursing Clinics of North America, 40*(4), 779–790, xii. doi:S0029-6465(05)00075-7 [pii], 10.1016/j.cnur.2005.08.004 [doi]

Mirabal-Colon, B. (2003). Developing a center for Hispanic youth violence prevention. *Puerto Rico Health Sciences Journal, 22*(1), 89–91.

Montesano, V. L., Sivec, H. J., Munetz, M. R., Pelton, J. R., & Turkington, D. (2014). Adapting cognitive behavioral therapy for psychosis for case managers: Increasing access to services in a Community Mental Health Agency. *Psychiatric Rehabilitation Journal, 37,* 11–16. doi:10.1037/prj0000037

O'Hara, B., & Brault, M. W. (2013). The disparate impact of the ACA-dependent expansion across population subgroups. *Health Services Research, 48,* 1581–1592. doi:(10.1111),/1475-6773.12067.

Organista, K. C., & Snowden, L. (Eds.). (2003). *Latino mental health in California: Policy recommendations.* Berkeley, CA: University of California, Institute of Governmental Studies.

Pinninti, N. R., Fisher, J., Thompson, K., & Steer, R. (2010). Feasibility and usefulness of training assertive community treatment team in cognitive behavioral therapy. *Community Mental Health Journal, 46*(4), 337–341. doi:10.1007/s10597-009-9271-y [doi]

Pinninti, N. R., Hollow, L. M., Sanghadia, M., & Thompson, K. (2006, September). Training nurses in cognitive behavioral therapy: Enhancing community care of patients with serious mental illness. *Medscape: Topics in Advanced Practice Nursing, 6*(3), 1–9. Retrieved from http://www.medscape.com/viewarticle/544349 (accessed September 26, 2014).

Pinninti, N. R., Schmidt, L. T., & Snyder, R. P. (2013). Case manager as therapy extender for cognitive behavior therapy of serious mental illness: A case report. *Community Mental Health Journal, 50,* 422–426. doi:10.1007/s10597-013-9633-3

Priebe, S., McCabe, R., Bullenkamp, J., Hansson, L., Lauber, C., Martinez-Leal, R., Rössler, W., Salize, H., Svensson, B., Torres-Gonzales, F., van den Brink, R., Wiersma, D., & Wright, D. J. (2007). Structured patient–clinician communication and 1-year outcome in community mental healthcare: Cluster randomised controlled trial. *British Journal of Psychiatry, 191,* 420–426. doi:10.1192/bjp.bp.107.036939

Ruiz, P. (2002). Commentary: Hispanic access to health/mental health services. *Psychiatric Quarterly, 73*(2), 85–91. doi:10.1023/A:1015051809607

Sartorius, N1., Gaebel, W., Cleveland, H. R., Stuart, H., Akiyama, T., Arboleda-Flórez, J., Baumann, A. E., Gureje, O., Jorge, M. R., Kastrup, M., Suzuki, Y., & Tasman, A. (2010). WPA guidance on how to combat stigmatization of psychiatry and psychiatrists. *World Psychiatry, 9*(3), 131–144.

Stuart, H. (2008). Fighting the stigma caused by mental disorders: Past perspectives, present activities, and future directions. *World Psychiatry, 7*(3), 185–188.

Swarbrick, M., Murphy, A. A., Zechner, M., Spagnolo, A. B., & Gill, K. J. (2011). Wellness coaching: A new role for peers. *Psychiatric Rehabilitation Journal, 34*(4), 328–331. doi: 2V239HU973254WKJ [pii], 10.2975/34.4.2011.328.331 [doi]

The National Institute for Health and Care Excellence. (NICE) (2014, February). *Psychosis and schizophrenia in adults: Treatment and management* (Clinical guidelines, CG178). London, UK: Author.

Tondora, J., O'Connell, M., Miller, R., Dinzeo, T., Bellamy, C., Andres-Hyman, R., & Davidson, L. (2010). A clinical trial of peer-based culturally responsive person-centred care for psychosis for African Americans and Latinos. *Clinical Trials, 7*(4), 368–379.

Turkington, D., Kingdon, D., Rathod, S., Hammond, K., Pelton, J., & Mehta, R. (2006). Outcomes of an effectiveness trial of cognitive-behavioural intervention by mental health nurses in schizophrenia. *British Journal of Psychiatry, 189,* 36–40.

Turkington, D., Munetz, M., Pelton, J., Montesano, V., Sivec, H., Nausheen, B., & Kingdon, D. (2014). High-yield cognitive behavioral techniques for psychosis delivered by case managers to their clients with persistent psychotic symptoms: An exploratory trial. *The Journal of Nervous and Mental Disease, 202*(1), 30–34.

Tyrer, P. (2011). Has the closure of psychiatric beds gone too far?. *BMJ, 343,* d7457.

Vu, C. M., Schwartz, S. L., & Austin, M. J. (2011). Asian community mental health services at 35: A pioneering ethnic organization (1973–2008). *Journal of Evidence-based Social Work, 8*(1–2), 124–142.

Waller, H., Garety, P. A., Jolley, S., Fornells-Ambrojo, M., Kuipers, E., Onwumere, J., Woodall, A., Emsley, R., & Craig, T. (2013). Low intensity cognitive behavioural therapy for psychosis: A pilot study. *Journal of Behavior Therapy and Experimental Psychiatry, 44*(1), 98–104.

Wittchen, H. U., & Jacobi, F. (2005) Size and burden of mental disorders in Europe: A critical appraisal of 27 studies. *European Neuropsychopharmacology, 15*(4), 357–376.

Appendix 1
Social Factors: My Immigration Journey

Strengths: My internal strengths, the external help I received, and other factors that helped me deal with process of immigration and its effects.

Pre-immigration	Process of immigration	Post-immigration	Currently
Stressors/traumas	**Stressors/traumas**	**Stressors/traumas**	**Stressors**
Anticipations/ expectations	Thoughts/ observations	Thoughts/ observations	Coping skills
What helped me?	What helped me?	What helped me?	What is helping me?

How do you Complete this Chart?

Steps: Enquire from the client if they are comfortable speaking about their immigration experience and if that might be helpful to them. If the client is ready and willing to talk, then start by asking them the very first time the topic of immigration came up in the house and what they thought. Take them through the process of immigration and get their experiences, thoughts, and feelings at each stage of the immigration process. During this process, check with clients to see if they want to continue with the discussion. As you get information, complete the lower part of the chart.

Cultural Adaptation of CBT for Serious Mental Illness: A Guide for Training and Practice, First Edition. Shanaya Rathod, David Kingdon, Narsimha Pinninti, Douglas Turkington, and Peter Phiri.
© 2015 John Wiley & Sons, Ltd. Published 2015 by John Wiley & Sons, Ltd.

At each of the steps of the immigration process and for each of the traumas that are described, enquire as to what helped them survive the trauma and include that as strengths on the upper part of the chart.

At the end, ask for feedback about how it made them feel. Then give homework assignment to review the document and any thoughts, memories, and observations they get after leaving the session.

Appendix 2
Aida – Longitudinal Formulation

Cultural Adaptation of CBT for Serious Mental Illness: A Guide for Training and Practice,
First Edition. Shanaya Rathod, David Kingdon, Narsimha Pinninti, Douglas Turkington,
and Peter Phiri.
© 2015 John Wiley & Sons, Ltd. Published 2015 by John Wiley & Sons, Ltd.

Predisposing factors	Precipitating factors	Perpetuating factors	Protective factors
Migration to the United Kingdom at 16 Ethnic background – Nigerian Brought up by nun Baptism at 14 (supposed to start serving the Lord)	Drinking/cannabis Abusive relationship Relationship breakdown	Misinterpretation of religious beliefs Voice of God/commands	Lives with aunt Singing Ambitious to be a singer

Current concerns
1. Long periods of fasting
2. Ministering on the bus
3. Isolation
4. Command hallucinations (responding to voice of God)
5. Reading the Bible until messages were received (nature and context)

THOUGHTS
Voice: 'you will serve the Lord'
'Read the word'

FEELINGS
Urge to serve Lord

Reading the Bible
Ministering on the bus
Fasting for a long time

PHYSICAL
Self-neglect impacting on physical health

SOCIAL
Lives with aunt
Loss of friends from Nigeria

UNDERLYING CONCERNS
I am under a voodoo spell
I am being punished

Appendix 3

Setting Goals to Improve Quality of Life

It is important for you to talk with your therapist and decide on life goals that enhance the quality of your life. Below is one way of looking at different aspects of life to help you decide on what is important to you. Review this and **decide on one to three goals** that you want to work on at present (adapted with permission from Cather et al., (2005). A pilot study of functional Cognitive Behavioral Therapy (fCBT) for schizophrenia. *Schizophrenia Research, 74,* 201–209).

Once you have accomplished those goals, you can set next set of goals. These goals are under six categories:

I. Love/relationships
    1. I would like to get better in starting and keeping up conversations with others.
    2. I would like to be more comfortable around other people.
    3. I want to increase the number of friends I have.
    4. I want to be able to socialize more.
    5. I want to be able to mix with people from other ethnic backgrounds.
    6. I would like to find a buddy so that we are supporting each other.
    7. I would like to have a boyfriend/girlfriend.
    8. I would like to avoid frequent arguments with my family.
    9. I would like to have more positive interactions with my child/sibling/ parent.

Cultural Adaptation of CBT for Serious Mental Illness: A Guide for Training and Practice, First Edition. Shanaya Rathod, David Kingdon, Narsimha Pinninti, Douglas Turkington, and Peter Phiri.
© 2015 John Wiley & Sons, Ltd. Published 2015 by John Wiley & Sons, Ltd.

II. Labour/work/education
    10. I would like to know how to prepare my resume.
    11. I would like to be prepared for a job interview (build my interview skills).
    12. I would like learn how to manage my time.
    13. I would like to go back to school but don't know how to get started on it.
    14. I would like to volunteer my time (obtain volunteer work).
    15. I would like to get a part-time job.

III. Leisure and hobbies
    16. I don't know what to do with my free time.
    17. I don't have enough hobbies.
    18. I stay home too much.
    19. I am bored a lot.

IV. Self-care
    20. I want to take better care of myself.
    21. I want to be independent with my medication.
    22. I want to be comfortable with my ethnicity.
    23. I want to feel good about myself.

V. Housing/financial
    24. I want to feel comfortable taking public transportation.
    25. I want to be able to organize my apartment.
    26. I want to move to a different living place.
    27. I would like more control over my finances.

VI. Spiritual
    28. I would like to start attending the church.
    29. I would like to join a prayer group.
    30. I would like to make prayer a part of my routine.

Other _____

Other _____

Other _____

Appendix 4
Voices Diary

Cultural Adaptation of CBT for Serious Mental Illness: A Guide for Training and Practice, First Edition. Shanaya Rathod, David Kingdon, Narsimha Pinninti, Douglas Turkington, and Peter Phiri.

Situation (where were you? What were you doing? Was there anyone with you?)	Were the voices present?	What did the voices say?	How loud were they on a scale of 1–10 (1 being not loud and 10 being very loud)	How did you feel?	What did you do to cope with the distress?	In hindsight, what could you have done differently?

Adapted from Kingdon and Turkington Cognitive Therapy of Schizophrenia. The Guilford Press, New York, London, p201 (2005). Reproduced with permission from the Guilford Press.

Appendix 5
What Do Voices Say?

You are ....
....
.... Rate
strength of Belief on a scale of 0% being not strong -100% being very strong

Evidence for	Evidence against

Conclusion: I ....
....% Belief

Cultural Adaptation of CBT for Serious Mental Illness: A Guide for Training and Practice,
First Edition. Shanaya Rathod, David Kingdon, Narsimha Pinninti, Douglas Turkington,
and Peter Phiri.
© 2015 John Wiley & Sons, Ltd. Published 2015 by John Wiley & Sons, Ltd.

Appendix 6

Working on Coping Strategies: Pleasant Events Schedule

Please identify the activities you can do and spend some time in these activities.

1. Activities at home by yourself
   Cook
   Take a shower
   Listen to music
   Straighten up my room
   Read magazines or newspapers
   Read a few passages from the Bible or other spiritual book
   Repair something that needs fixing
   Take care of my plants
   Play with a pet
   Doodle
   Exercise
   Think about some things to buy: make a list
   Sing around the house
   Draw
   Paint
   Write to a family or friend
   Play a musical instrument
   Sew
   Do a crossword puzzle
   Dance
   Take pictures with cameras
   Write in a diary or letters

(continued)

Cultural Adaptation of CBT for Serious Mental Illness: A Guide for Training and Practice,
First Edition. Shanaya Rathod, David Kingdon, Narsimha Pinninti, Douglas Turkington,
and Peter Phiri.
© 2015 John Wiley & Sons, Ltd. Published 2015 by John Wiley & Sons, Ltd.

Soak in the tub: enjoy the water
Meditate
Pray, visit religious centre

2. Activities outdoors by yourself
Go to a movie
Go for a walk
Laugh
Go to a pet store and look for the pets
Go swimming
Play a sport
Fly a kite
Drive
Garden
Do a jigsaw puzzle
Buy a book
Walk in the woods or on the beach
Go to the beauty parlour/barbershop
Go to a play or concert
Watch cultural programmes on TV like Bollywood

3. Activities with others (indoors)
Talk with family
Play cards
Speak to priest

4. Activities involving others (outdoors)
Take a drive
Practise religion
Go to the beach
Have lunch with a friend
Go on a date
Go camping

Others: Please write

Appendix 7

Preventing a Relapse or Breakdown

You can prevent a breakdown by knowing and recognizing early signs of relapse.

What Are Early Warning Signs?

Early warning signs are small changes in the way you think, feel, or behave that may signal that your symptoms are beginning to worsen. These changes may be so subtle that they do not seem worth noticing.

What Are Common Early Warning Signs?

Sleep/appetite problems:

- Sleeping more or less
- Changes in appetite

Thinking problems:

- Racing thoughts
- Not able to focus

Cultural Adaptation of CBT for Serious Mental Illness: A Guide for Training and Practice, First Edition. Shanaya Rathod, David Kingdon, Narsimha Pinninti, Douglas Turkington, and Peter Phiri.
© 2015 John Wiley & Sons, Ltd. Published 2015 by John Wiley & Sons, Ltd.

Behaviour problems:

- Missing treatment appointments (therapy, day programme, etc.)
- Stopping medication
- Engaging in quirky behaviours or superstitions (e.g. feeling like it is important to wear a particular colour or engage in a particular ritual)
- Suddenly becoming more or less religious than is usual for you
- Not feeling like being around people – withdrawing from family or friends

Feelings and emotions:

- Feeling irritable or 'on edge'
- Feeling like people are watching you or want to harm you
- Feeling like people are against you
- Engaging in unusual activities or behaviours that were similar to those you engaged in when you had more severe symptoms in the past

Other symptoms:

- Hearing voices

Will I Be Able to Recognize and Respond to Early Warning Signs on My Own?

It can often be hard to recognize early warning signs on your own. Most people find it helpful to enlist help from their treatment teams, family, and friends to monitor early warning signs. One way to enlist the help of your support system is to develop a relapse prevention plan.

By filling this out with the help of your treatment team, family, and/or trusted friends, you can minimize your risk for experiencing a relapse.

Some things that I can do on a daily basis to help me to stay well include:

1. _____
2. _____
3. _____
4. _____

Some events or situations that have been relapse triggers for me in the past include:

1. _____
2. _____
3. _____
4. _____

Some early warning signs of relapse that I experienced in the past include:

1. _____
2. _____
3. _____
4. _____

If I experience triggers or early warning signs, some actions that I will take include:

1. _____
2. _____
3. _____
4. _____

Some people that can help me to recognize and respond to triggers and early warning signs include:

Name	Contact info	What they can do to help

Appendix 8
Circle of Support

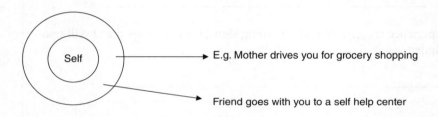

Why Do I Need Support?

All people need support to help them cope with things that they have to face in life. There is a lot of stress in life, and support from people around helps us to deal with these stressors in an effective manner.

What Is a Circle of Support?

A circle of support is a group of people who has agreed to work together on your behalf to help you achieve your life goals.

Cultural Adaptation of CBT for Serious Mental Illness: A Guide for Training and Practice, First Edition. Shanaya Rathod, David Kingdon, Narsimha Pinninti, Douglas Turkington, and Peter Phiri.
© 2015 John Wiley & Sons, Ltd. Published 2015 by John Wiley & Sons, Ltd.

What Does a Circle of Support Do?

The circle can help you develop a vision for the future. They can help you plan steps to reach your desired goal. They can help you identify your strengths and use those strengths to overcome the barriers that get in the way of reaching your goals.

How Can I Develop a Circle?

If you are interested in starting a circle, start by talking to your counsellor or case manager. The two of you can come up with a list of people in your family and friends who can be part of the circle. Then you and your case manager should contact these people to see if they are interested in participating. The next step is to schedule a circle meeting. This can be done as a face-to-face meeting or telephone conference. You will be in charge of who attends the meetings and what will be talked there.

Can I Change My Circle?

It is important for you to know that you are in charge and can change your circle. However, you would want to do it in consultation with your staff member and keeping in mind whether the change will better help you reach your life goals.

Appendix 9
Relapse Prevention Plans

Safiya: Relapse Prevention Plan (Chapter 4)

What have I learnt? What has been useful to me? (Ideas and strategies, facts, new techniques)

- Self-monitoring using symptom diary
- Practising mindfulness exercises on CD
- Using cost and benefit analysis to help me make informed decisions based on facts and not only on how I feel about things
- Playing music and using computer
- Talking about my feelings with someone – to mom and dad
- Relaxing
- Testing beliefs and assumptions to find out whether what is said is so (using evidence for and against what the voices say)
- Engaging in meaningful activities such as walks and art group, hopefully joining gym, and visiting the mosque
- Using hot cross bun to make sense of negative thoughts and the impact they have on my feelings and behaviour and considering alternative views or explanations

How can I build on what I've learnt? (Bringing skills into everyday life, enlisting others help, attending other groups/courses for specific skills – specific action plans)

Cultural Adaptation of CBT for Serious Mental Illness: A Guide for Training and Practice, First Edition. Shanaya Rathod, David Kingdon, Narsimha Pinninti, Douglas Turkington, and Peter Phiri.
© 2015 John Wiley & Sons, Ltd. Published 2015 by John Wiley & Sons, Ltd.

- Planning my day using the activity schedule sheet
- Realizing when symptoms appear and tackling them using the techniques and strategies I have learnt in therapy (for example, test whether what the voices are saying is true or not as I have discovered in therapy when I have looked at the evidence for and against what they have said so far)
- Talking to someone about my feelings and distress and considering alternative ways of coping
- Monitoring my stress levels so that I can reduce them to tolerable levels
- Keep practising my skills and building my confidence
- Keep practising strategies I have learnt so far

What will make it difficult for me to do this? (Things in me, e.g. motivation, hopelessness; environment, e.g. time pressures, lack of support from family)

- Voices coming back (9/10 distressing and loud)
- Lack of confidence
- Lack of sleep
- Demands from others and high levels of stress

How will I overcome these difficulties? (Try to come up with specific strategies)

- Using the notes that I have made during therapy sessions
- Writing down what the voices say to do (voices diary) so that I have time to analyse and test whether this is true and then coming up with alternative views and thinking about the next step
- Talking to others
- Using strategies I have learnt

What might lead to a setback for me? (Future stresses, known areas of vulnerability, life problems)

- Stress related to weight gain
- More independence (less support from family)

If I had a setback, what would I do about it? (Specific skills, cheerleading statements, seek help)

- Enlisting support from mom and dad
- Talking to the psychiatrist
- Using a flash card: Rather than agreeing to or making promises that I cannot keep, I will instead say, **I WILL DO MY BEST**

- Using the techniques that I have learnt in therapy, testing what the voices are saying using evidence for and evidence against (*evidence is something that can stand in the court of law*)
- Considering alternative views to situation
- Practising mindfulness exercises and listening to relaxing music
- Engaging in meaningful activities

Lincoln: Relapse Prevention Plan (Chapter 7)

Staying well planned
The most valuable ideas I've learnt in therapy are:

- Being nice to myself
- Realizing that I can't get my mother to love me
- Knowing that I can change for the better

The most valuable techniques I've learnt in therapy are:

- Physical relaxation/tension relaxing
- Using worksheets to challenge self-criticalness
- Getting up early and being slightly sociable

My most important goals for the next year are:

- Getting into work, either voluntarily or part-time
- Going to the gym on a regular basis
- Being able to go to busy places and tolerating anxiety and paranoia

Events and situations that are likely to be difficult are:

- Feeling awkward and uncomfortable at interviews
- Being rejected by a woman I have just met
- Losing contact with significant family members

The things I can do in those situations are:

- Before the event, doing various relaxation and tension exercises
- Practising interview beforehand (role-play with a friend) and talking about interview afterwards to a friend or family member
- Reminding myself that it can be difficult to get a job and that most people are generally nervous at interviews

In order to maintain my therapeutic gains, I can do the following regularly:

- Continuing with the thought diary
- When setting my mind to something, achieving it, for example, my achievement at the university
- Patting myself on the back more frequently (self-compassion)
- Developing and maintaining a structure to his/her daily activities using a weekly activity schedule sheet

Index